12.50

Cities
Under
Siege

EDITED BY

David Boesel

&

Peter H. Rossi

Basic Books, Inc., Publishers

NEW YORK / LONDON

CITIES
UNDER SIEGE:

An Anatomy of the Ghetto Riots, 1964–1968

This book was prepared under the auspices of, and
with the support of, the Center for Urban Affairs
at the Johns Hopkins University. The editors are
Associates of the Center.

The Authors

RICHARD BERK is Assistant Professor of Sociology at Northwestern University.

ROBERT BLAUNER is Associate Professor of Sociology at the University of California, Berkeley.

DAVID BOESEL is an Associate of the Group for Research on Social Policy and the Center for Urban Affairs at the Johns Hopkins University.

NATHAN CAPLAN is Program Associate at the Institute for Social Research and Lecturer in Psychology at the University of Michigan.

BETTYE K. EIDSON is Assistant Professor of Sociology at the University of Michigan.

JESSE EPSTEIN is a graduate student in the Department of Social Relations at Harvard University.

LOUIS C. GOLDBERG, formerly Assistant Professor of Sociology at McGill University, is completing a book on the Congress of Racial Equality (CORE).

W. EUGENE GROVES is a graduate student in the Department of Social Relations at the Johns Hopkins University.

ANDREW KOPKIND is a journalist and editor of the biweekly newspaper, *Hard Times*.

GARY T. MARX is Lecturer on Sociology, Department of Social Relations, Harvard University, and a faculty member of the M.I.T.-Harvard Joint Center for Urban Studies.

AUGUST MEIER is Professor of History and Senior Research Fellow at the Center for Urban Regionalism at Kent State University.

ANTHONY OBERSCHALL is Associate Professor of Sociology at Yale University.

PETER H. ROSSI is Professor of Social Relations and an Associate of the Center for Urban Affairs at the Johns Hopkins University.

ELLIOTT RUDWICK is Professor of Sociology and Senior Research Fellow at the Center for Urban Regionalism at Kent State University.

DAVID O. SEARS is Associate Professor of Psychology and Political Science at the University of California, Los Angeles.

ALLAN SILVER is Associate Professor of Sociology at Columbia University.

RICHARD C. WADE is Professor of American History at the University of Chicago.

HAROLD R. WILDE is a graduate student in Government at Harvard University and a native of Milwaukee.

Contents

Cities Under Siege

Introduction

The ghetto riots that occurred between 1964 and 1968 sent shock waves deep into American society. The country could absorb, with a certain equanimity, a civil rights movement directed against a reactionary Jim Crow system in the South. There was some comfort, after all, in being able to perceive "race relations" as a southern, rather than a national problem. But when, in ghetto after ghetto, blacks took to the streets, wresting control from the police and property from the ghetto merchants, it became clear that the country was faced not with a regional problem but a national crisis. And it also became clear that a lot more than civil rights was involved: the riots took on the character of revolts against established authority and property relations.

The search for the causes of the ghetto revolts began immediately after the mammoth uprising in Watts, culminating in the Kerner Commission's half-year long scramble for a "theory" of riot causation and trailing off in the inconclusive scholarship of the thirteen-volume report of the Eisenhower Commission on Violence. Each of the inquiries documented what informed observers had long known: that far out of proportion to their numbers, blacks were at the bottom of the American class system; that few of society's major institutions were pressing for a more equal distribution of either opportunities or benefits; and that the level of black indignation had been rising steeply in the decade of the 1960's.

3

Injustice and reactive indignation are among the main causes of the ghetto revolts as the commission reports indicate. Equally important (and largely neglected in those reports) are the changes which had been taking place in the institutional framework which had held blacks under control since the days of Reconstruction. The ghetto revolts were as much an outgrowth of the breakdown of these social/racial controls as they were of the patterns of discrimination and inequality.

It is the purpose of this introduction to draw the reader's attention to the institutional changes which lay behind and contributed to the outbreak of the ghetto revolts in the 1960's. The militant civil rights movement in the South and the riots in the North sprang out of related discontinuities in the patterns of social control. Key to these developments were the breakdown of the post–Civil War accommodation between North and South, the demise of Jim Crow, and the failure of America's liberal welfare policies.

The Breakdown of the North-South Political Accommodation

The compact between North and South that put an end to Reconstruction set the national stance on racial matters for more than half a century. Over a period of time the agreement solidified into political custom; dominant conservative forces in both regions combined to oppose working-class movements and civil rights initiatives. While the "dangerous classes" were presented with a united conservative front, white elites in both regions manipulated lower-class racial and ethnic cleavages to their own advantage.

At the center of this regional accommodation was the coalition in Congress between southern Democrats and northern Republicans. But support also came from the Supreme Court (especially in the *Plessy* vs. *Ferguson* decision) and from the presidency: racism was most glaringly evident in Woodrow Wilson's administration, in part, because of the contrast with his many progressive policies, but it was a standard feature of most other administrations as well. Further, northern philanthropy assumed and supported segregation by giving money to accommodative Negro leaders and institutions, most prominently to Booker T. Washington. Racial and economic conservatism blocked federal intervention in the areas of civil rights and labor organization. States' rights complemented laissez-faire.

With the advent of the New Deal, however, a tentative split between North and South began to develop as urban liberal forces began to exert a decisive influence on national policy. The administration and Congress formulated an array of liberal economic policies, but many of the early programs were received unfavorably by the Supreme Court. In 1938, however, after President Roosevelt's efforts to pack the court, an implicit detente between the two branches of government was reached. In what has come to be known as the "doctrine of the preferred freedoms," Justice Stone suggested that Congress be allowed to decide economic matters without fear of being overruled by the Supreme Court, and that the Court give precedence to the protection of civil liberties and civil rights. The Court's decisions gradually began to reflect this orientation. Consequently, in 1938 the principle of federal intervention in the economy was "ratified," and the first tentative steps toward federal intervention in the racial status quo were being taken.

New Deal economic liberalism, of course, had its origins in mass discontent engendered by the depression. Working pragmatically and with strong popular support, a coalition of labor, intellectuals, and urban Democratic machines succeeded in adjusting federal politics to an integrated national economy. Essentially this meant changing laissez-faire policies and starting to build a welfare state. Blacks became part of the New Deal coalition largely for want of a better alternative, for although civil rights needs were repeatedly sacrificed in order to buy white political support for New Deal programs, the welfare state and industrial unionism provided some benefits that had been lacking in the past.

Economic liberalism, then, did not in and of itself give rise to racial liberalism. Although many of the intellectuals pushed for changes specifically favorable to blacks, there was no agreement among the New Deal coalition elements that major civil rights efforts should be undertaken. Even such elementary matters as anti-lynching and anti–poll tax legislation foundered in the face of staunch southern opposition.

Yet in the two decades after the beginning of the New Deal, racial liberalism did make substantial progress, and although the causes of this development were extremely complex, they were related in part to deep changes taking place in the organization and functioning of the economy. In about the first third of the century the exploitation of lower-class racial and ethnic antagonisms had been functional for a business economy which required massive amounts of cheap, unskilled labor— among other things, it helped to divide the working classes and keep wages down. But after the New Deal this sort of manipulation became increasingly irrelevant. The "recognition" of labor by the New Deal obviated the need for tactics designed to break strikes and hinder working-class organization. The CIO encompassed significant numbers of black workers in such basic industries as steel, rubber, and automobiles. And the growing economic importance of skilled and educated labor, coupled with a highly productive technology, diminished business' stake in keeping wages very low. Moreover, violent racial conflicts, such as the 1943 riot in Detroit which upset wartime production schedules, were perceived as clearly disruptive to the economy. Consequently business and civic elites began to propound a philosophy of racial harmony, most consistently articulated by a growing number of human relations commissions. This approach was consonant with a broader pattern wherein management relied more on positive incentives to secure the cooperation of employees and less on authority and negative sanctions. A philosophy of harmony seemed as appropriate to work relations as to race relations.

World War II also played a major role in the growth of racial liberalism. By creating a tight labor market in industry, it stimulated black migration from the South, which in turn augmented black voting strength and expanded the constituency of civil rights organizations. Increasingly, black leaders were accepted in a civil rights alliance which also included intellectuals, labor unions, church groups, and liberal Jewish organizations. The alliance did address itself to the first order of business—i.e., desegregation in the South. But in the long run it also had some inherent drawbacks from the viewpoint of black interests. Largely supported and led by white liberals, it proved viable as long as civil rights remained the issue and the South remained the focus of common antagonisms. But when, in the mid-sixties, blacks began to insist that their leadership be autonomous and to challenge the structure of power and interest outside the South, many white liberals withdrew their support.

In addition to stimulating an important demographic change, with all the implications that this change entailed, the war also had significant ideological consequences for the racial situation. Blacks who had fought in the name of democracy against racism in its most virulent form became increasingly unwilling to put up with the less catastrophic but still oppressive racism in the service and at home. And blacks were not the only ones upon whom the war had a major ideological impact. American Jews, confronted with the horrifying example of the apocalypse wrought by the Nazis, were galvanized into the most racially liberal of all white groups. The war, more than anything else, caused Jews to take a leading role in the civil rights coalition.

Over a period of years this coalition was able to bring about small but increasingly significant changes in the racial policies of the federal government. After the favorable 1938 Supreme Court decision in the Missouri Law School case, the NAACP began to concentrate on attacking school segregation in the courts. Other civil rights initiatives also began to pay off. The executive branch responded to threats of massive protest by integrating the armed forces in 1948. Congress, the center of conservative resistance, was the slowest to act, but a series of weak civil rights bills began issuing from that body in 1957. As these developments were taking place, southern senators and representatives, who at one time could count on broad support for their racial policies, were becoming increasingly isolated on this issue and more frequently resorted to such procedural tactics as the filibuster to block civil rights legislation.

A clear sign of the growing split between North and South came in 1948 with the Dixiecrat walkout at the Democratic convention. But the split did not reach the crisis point until 1954, when the Supreme Court declared segregated school systems unconstitutional. That decision made it perfectly evident that the old coalition of southern Democrats and northern conservatives could no longer control national policy on racial matters. Southern states reacted by calling for massive resistance. Blacks, on the other hand, saw the opportunity to move against the Jim Crow structure, and in 1955 the activist phase of the civil rights movement began with the Montgomery bus boycott. Deep historical changes had undercut the national racist coalition and caused the breakdown of the North-South compact, thus opening the door to the black revolt in the South.

The Demise of Jim Crow

The undermining of segregationist control over the nation's racial affairs provided the opening for the black revolt. But there had also been substantial changes in the South itself which helped establish the conditions for revolt. At the heart of the matter was the fact that the Jim Crow system, the specific instrument of racial oppression in the South, was becoming archaic.

Jim Crow had been tailored to the needs of the rural and small town

South. It provided precarious southern agriculture with a labor force whose costs were far below those customary for other agricultural workers. It provided cheap domestic service for the well-to-do and for many in the middle class. It provided a status floor below which poor whites, who were not much better off than their black neighbors, could not sink. It enabled whites to retain political control in areas where blacks were in the majority and to ignore potential black voting strength in other areas. Although southern elites decried privately the crudities of lynching and cross burning, their power and position were dependent upon the maintenance of the system; the relatively small middle class also benefited materially; and the ranks of the poor whites, victims of a backward economic system in a generally impoverished region, supplied the mobs with their most vehement members.

Within the social changes occurring in the South, especially after World War II, were currents which progressively undermined Jim Crow. The continuing mechanization of agriculture made more and more black farm laborers and sharecroppers superfluous. The growth of southern industry, supported mainly by northern capital, increased the importance of skilled and technical labor, much of which was imported from the North. Finally, a rising educational level made inroads on racist ideology by confronting southerners with the moral contradictions between the concept of democracy and the concrete existence of oppression.

Although overshadowed by the striking migration to northern urban areas, black movement to southern urban areas was also important. In the southern cities blacks were less vulnerable to intimidation and harassment than in the rural areas and small towns. Their numbers were greater in the cities, they were less dispersed, and the close, personal controls that had prevailed in the countryside were not present. Moreover, the black middle class was growing in numbers and strength, spurred especially by World War II. The sons and daughters of this bourgeoisie, many of them college students, were to be the cutting edge of the liberal Negro revolt in the South.

Another result of the increasing urbanization and industrialization of the South was the emergence of business and Chamber of Commerce moderates whose thinking reflected, albeit in a timid way, the philosophy of racial harmony that was becoming prevalent in the North (indeed, many of the moderates were connected in one way or another with the local branches of national industries). The attraction of an image of racial harmony became considerably more important in the

1950's and 1960's when it was learned that northern corporations planning to locate facilities in the South could be scared off by the threat or fact of racial turmoil. Of course civil rights activists were not slow to turn this anxiety to advantage.

The civil rights movement in the South proceeded out of the contradiction between, on the one hand, the growing industrialization and nationalization of the southern economy and on the other hand its reactionary, segregationist sociopolitical structure. The 1954 Supreme Court decision and its consequences put the segregationists on the defensive, gave the blacks the opening they needed to attack Jim Crow, and enhanced the role of the moderates as peacemakers.

Nowhere was the conflict between a modern economic structure and a reactionary political structure more pronounced than in Birmingham, where an arch-segregationist mayor and police chief came up against the militant action of a black proletariat. And nowhere was the racial contest more massive, bitter, or prolonged. The crisis in Birmingham was the logical culmination of the forces and tendencies that fostered the black revolt in the South.

The Failure of Liberal Welfare Policies

The battle of Birmingham absorbed the attention of the nation, but northern blacks especially watched with intense personal interest. Black consciousness was increasing rapidly, feeding further the unrest that had been growing for years. The American political economy was proving incapable either of incorporating the mass of urban blacks or of providing adequate arrangements for their welfare, containment, and control.

As noted above, earlier in the century the economy had depended on a base of unskilled labor for the performance of essential tasks in semi-mechanized industries. Lately, full mechanization and automation have proceeded so far as to reduce drastically the proportion of the unskilled work force required for industrial production. Yet there is still a need for the unskilled, not at the center of production, but on the edges in the growing service sector. The service sector has become the province of the American underclass, where jobs are menial, hard, often intermittent, and poorly paid. These are the people who work in restaurants, laundries, cafeterias, hospitals, office buildings, and private homes (often cleaning up after others, as lower classes throughout history have had to do). This menial labor force is not central to the economy but is essential to the fullness of American affluence.

Several hundred years of American history have made it nearly inevitable that racial minorities—and especially the blacks—would make up the largest part of the underclass. Race, of course, has been the key factor in determining who would be prepared for underclass work (or rather, unprepared for anything else). And although blacks are significantly represented in industrial unions, most of them are kept outside the protective canopy of unionism, unorganized and subject to manipulation. Lack of education has closed them out of the expanding, technologically sophisticated sectors, and entrenched craft unionism has done the same in the stable or contracting area of the skilled trades. While a sizeable segment of the black population has moved into the middle class, a great many more fill the ranks of the underclass, and the gap between the two seems to be increasing.

The dominant approach to the containment and control of the lower classes has of course changed markedly since the early years of this century. In place of the old emphasis on authority, downward force, and the exploitation of divisions within the working classes, managerial liberalism has stressed the manipulation of incentives to secure cooperation, or at least acquiescence, in arrangements intended to promote social harmony. In the realm of public policy this approach has entailed a heavy reliance on welfare as a means of buying off discontent and securing the consent of the poor to having their lives administered.

Of course to view welfare exclusively as an instrument of social control or an adjunct of fiscal policy (which it also is), would be to disregard the fact that it also reflects progress in the definition of the minimal and tolerable conditions of life in this country. Especially since the New Deal, both Democrats and Republicans have come to subscribe to the thesis that when the system fails the individual or when the individual fails in the system, a set of standby arrangements should prevent utter destitution. There is disagreement about how much standby aid should be given, and over how much of the phenomenon is a systemic or an individual failure. But there is a consensus among most of those with power that decency requires proffering some sort of aid.

At the national level the liberal welfare approach to sustaining and controlling the underclass has been an extension of New Deal policies. At the local level this approach has been geared to geographically confined concentrations of underclass people—typically ghettos—and on

the orderly administration of these areas by city and county governments.

The more controversial of the New Deal depression programs were
phased out with the coming of full employment in World War II; the
WPA lingers on mainly in the memories of older political cartoonists.
But other programs, designed to help the "deserving poor," were either
continued from depression days or initiated after the war. The temporarily unemployed were to be covered by unemployment insurance; low
income workers were to be benefited by subsidies in the form of public
housing; the elderly were to be given Old Age and Survivors payments;
and fatherless children were to be helped by grants under the Aid to
Dependent Children program. Should they be necessary, direct relief
payments to intact poor families were to be a matter for the state and
local governments to work out, with the federal government paying
some of the load.

These programs were intended primarily to supplement the incomes
of people for whom even full employment would not provide a minimum standard of living—the disabled, the aged, the temporarily unemployed, the widowed, and the deserted. A permanent underclass was not
envisioned as a social problem of any magnitude and hence was not
provided for directly. Remarkably, not one of the architects of the Social Security Act, as amended, expected Aid to Dependent Children to
become a major program, let alone a mainstay of social policy.

In an attempt to cope with the growing underclass, the federal government began a piecemeal process of expanding and adapting welfare
programs designed with other ends in view. The result was a series of
haphazard arrangements that were not only inadequate but also, in
many ways, punitive. Thus the ADC program (and its modified successor AFDC) has degraded clients and fostered dependency; the public
housing projects have become huge, grim barracks for the poor; the
public employment agencies have shuffled people from one temporary
job to another; and the manpower-retraining programs have often prepared trainees for nonexistent job vacancies.

But the failure of the liberal welfare approach goes deeper than a
brief account of its origins and adaptations would indicate. In recent
years the war in Vietnam and the ghetto riots have pointed up a central
conflict in our political economy, currently defined as the "priorities
issue"—i.e., spending too much money abroad and on defense and not
enough at home and on general welfare. One result of the present order-

ing of priorities has been to engender a crisis of major proportions for the liberal approach to the sustenance and control of the underclass.

The Keynesian requirement for heavy, controlled governmental spending to support the economy was becoming evident in the later years of the New Deal. Financing the welfare structure, which had been developed on a pragmatic basis to combat the depression, fulfilled a small part of that requirement, but it was primarily the massive military expenditures of World War II that brought a return to prosperity. With the beginning of the cold war a few years later, the establishment of defense as a first priority for the indefinite future made continued prosperity and economic growth increasingly dependent on military spending. (The adverse affects of recent small cutbacks in the Pentagon's budget give some indication of the extent to which the economy is organized for defense.)

In the welfare-warfare state, welfare has been decidedly the weak sister. It has had to beg for money to cope with the underclass while defense has commanded a large portion of the nation's resources. Failing to attract the talents and energies necessary for innovative expansion, welfare has been unable to ward off bureaucratic atrophy. Worse yet, military expenditures have been channeled into the most advanced technological sectors of the economy, stimulating the processes which generate the underclass. The political economy, then, seems to have augmented the ranks of the displaced while it has failed to support existing arrangements for keeping them in line.

National problems have a way of coming home to local roosts. While the existence of an underclass is a problem of the national economy and its institutions, it is local city administrations which have to reckon with the problem in concrete form. The cities' efforts to contain and control the underclass have generally assumed the existence of the ghettos. Since those in the underclass are only marginally related to the economy, many of the traditional class restraints (e.g., the supervision of workers in factories) do not affect them. Instead the limitation of the potentially troublesome black masses to a restricted territory (though not generally as a consequence of public policy) and the exercise of power over that territory have become key principles of social control.

At the same time ghettoization, in bringing masses of black people together, has created among blacks one of the preconditions for the development of group consciousness and common action. The resentments of poor blacks have been echoed in the sentiments of their neighbors and amplified to the point where the ghettos have long since become hostile, self-conscious entities foreign to the dominant society. Welfare and political deals have ceased to be adequate for the containment of urban blacks, and the ghettos have in effect become a quasi-military problem, the police playing the role of an occupying army. That the police are slender reeds upon which to lean is evident in the fact that, like other occupation forces in the midst of hostile populations, they can control only when they are present.

The disruptive energies of the ghettos have confronted local administrations with problems of social control which are beyond their capacity to handle, because they can neither command the necessary resources for a welfare "solution," nor rely on the police to maintain permanent control. The inadequacy of resources, of course, stems from the fact that the largest portion of a citizen's tax dollar goes to the federal government and defense, while local tax revenues have failed to keep pace with the increased demand for services imposed by the growth of the urban underclass.

Local difficulties are compounded by the fact that modern economic processes are organized on regional and national bases while local government is still organized along the lines of counties, towns, municipalities, and the like. The city as presently defined is an archaic political unit in the core of an economically integrated metropolitan area, which in turn is nested in a national economy. Among the effects of this disparity are the almost legendary erosion of the city's tax base and the enfeeblement of many of its governing institutions.

When governments lose their capacity to perform functions that are considered essential, as happens when their organization is drastically out of line with existing social and economic arrangements, they also lose legitimacy and hence the ability to govern. Most cities have not reached this point, but many are approaching it. The numbers of the underclass in the cities continue to grow as those of the middle and upper classes decline. Local institutions fail to respond to the increased pressure for public services. Generation after generation of reform mayors retires, weary and disillusioned. The local underpinnings of welfare liberalism grow weak.

The increasing race pride of the 1950's and the 1960's engendered a groundswell of active discontent among blacks. As they began to demand more than whites with power could conveniently concede, the institutions administering the ghettos were subjected to unprecedented pressures. If their ability to provide resources was strained by the growth of the urban underclass, it was even further taxed by the growth of active demands from the ghettos. These claims were not great (certainly not commensurate with the full needs of blacks); and yet given the current ordering power, they could not easily be met. The bitter fights that ensued over relatively small issues merely reflected the chasm between the interests of ghetto blacks and the capacities of local officials desperately attempting to maintain the status quo. The notion that social harmony could be achieved within the context of present national priorities was dissipating quickly.

The rapid emergence of black pride and the attendant unwillingness to put up with current conditions any longer also cut the ground out from under the old-line Negro leadership class, a key element in the urban control strategy. Their stock-in-trade was the favors of welfare politics, and their position was based on their ability to deliver concessions to the ghettos and order to the authorities. But the price of order was going up, and it was becoming ever more apparent that black quiescence could not be had for any amount that the power structure was likely to pay. Hence the Negro "leaders" increasingly had to plead with the rank and file to stay in line and with the authorities to come through with more concessions. Since neither side proved very obliging, more and more members of this class found themselves out in the cold.

No part of the ghetto population was more vehement in its rejection of the old-line leadership or more contemptuous of the ostensible good will of urban white elites than black youth. Making up a disproportionately large segment of the underclass, they were not only the most race-conscious and aggressive element, but also the least directly affected by standard welfare measures. (The rush to devise programs for ghetto youths in the mid-sixties was a belated response to the inadequacies of earlier efforts.) For young blacks, social control manifested itself less in the form of the welfare worker or the Negro politician than in the form of the policeman.

The surge of black consciousness in the 1960's underlay an increasing number of clashes between ghetto youths and the police. Never very amenable to harassment and arrest, the youths now began to resist actively. As these clashes became more frequent, the potential for larger confrontations grew. While the youths acted as a vanguard in the battles, they would have been detached from the ghetto masses had not the restraining institutions of liberal welfarism been so nearly bankrupt. But with the failure of these institutions and the related decline of local public authority vis-à-vis the ghettos, there was little to prevent a significant portion of the black masses from joining in on the side of the youths. Thus would begin a process of mutual escalation, in which more blacks would call forth more police, which in turn would attract more blacks, and so on. The end result of this process would be a ghetto riot.

It is worth noting that underclass revolts have not been limited to the black ghettos. The big Mexican-American outbreak in East Los Angeles in 1970 followed a series of Puerto Rican riots in New York, Chicago, and elsewhere in the mid-1960's. Like the black ghetto riots, these disorders were expressions of rising social movements defined in terms of national or ethnic identity and given impetus by the black movement.

While the underclass is not the same as Marx's lumpenproletariat (not being completely detached from the dominant economic forces), it does lack the stable class position which he considered essential for coherent political action. Yet it is clear that where the conditions exist for the emergence of strong national or ethnic consciousness, as in the ghettos and barrios, economic marginality is not a decisive obstacle to the development of a forward-looking (as distinct from a nostalgic or reactionary) social movement.

At the same time, the recuperative powers of American liberalism should not be underestimated. If liberal elites manage to reorder priorities—which would involve reforms of New Deal proportions—the situation could probably be stabilized for an indeterminate period. Diminishing the country's role abroad, cutting the military budget, investing heavily in the cities, restructuring the health and welfare systems, and similar measures would no doubt dampen domestic crises. Social control of the underclass should be made easier, at least for the time being. But while the circumstances of the poor and the near-poor might be improved, their economic and political position would be largely unchanged; they would remain a subject population at odds with the society that generated them.

I.
Case
Studies

The Newark case study was drawn from the report of Governor Hughes' riot commission, certainly the best official study of a riot to have been produced in this period. Unlike most of the others, it made specific judgments about people and institutions, went into detail, and did not shun a political interpretation of events for fear of political repercussions.

Newark presented, in the most acute form, the crisis of American cities. As blacks and Puerto Ricans moved in, making up a solid majority of the population, white people and businesses moved out, and with them went tax revenues. The tendency in the city was toward a vast underclass of race-conscious and militant blacks on the one hand, and on the other, the huge but floundering public institutions that tried to administer them—the stark housing projects, the overburdened welfare program, a school system so impoverished that the mayor had to plead for the state to take it over, and a corrupt city government in which the representatives of a diminishing ethnic block held tenaciously to power.

In Newark one sees clearly the development of revolt out of a series of political battles which left blacks with the feeling that routine politics had them running in circles. One important aspect of the situation in Newark which was evident in the Governor's report, but for editorial reasons could not be sufficiently emphasized here, was the bitter hostility between the Newark Police Department and the black community. This mutual antagonism of course exists in all large cities with sizable black populations, but in Newark it was given a special edge by a specific ethnic, as well as racial, conflict: the police force was controlled and manned largely by the Italian community, whose power in the city had crested and was waning in the face of a rising black population.

The Plainfield riot is significant not only because it occurred within Newark's orbit and was touched off in part by events in the larger city, but more importantly because it stands as the clearest example to date of the riot as rebellion. This intensely political riot, manifesting a high degree of collective rationality on the part of the black community, approaches the ideal type, representing what the other riots might have become had they fulfilled their essential tendencies. The effort to disrupt white control over ghetto territory and the concomitant rising against white authority are the key elements in every ghetto riot, but nowhere were they as strongly developed and prominent as in Plainfield. The material for this case study comes largely from the National Advisory Commission on Civil Disorders, and the study itself is a substantially revised version of a paper prepared for the commission by the authors.

The Watts riot in Los Angeles was clearly a black popular insurrection against established public authority, but it was so huge that it never achieved the level of collective rationality evident in Plainfield. Nevertheless, as in Plainfield (and Newark, which it more closely resembles) one sees in Watts the same connection between past grievances and present action, the same struggle against the police for territorial control, the same articulation of demands and meetings with public officials (though less coherent and focused than in Plainfield), and the same efforts to work out a truce (unsuccessful in this case). Moreover, the Watts riot has a special significance in that it is one of those landmark events which affect people's consciousness of the society around them. Watts stands in about the same relation to the northern rebellion as Birmingham did to the southern movement: each was a historic crisis which catalyzed black consciousness and changed white perceptions of blacks as passive and willing to "keep their place."

Milwaukee's riot was less significant in itself than in the way public authorities, and particularly the mayor, reacted to it. The riot, such as it was, reflected a low level of political consciousness; it did not involve a substantial segment of the black community; and only the rudimentary elements of a ghetto riot—black revolt against local white authority and some disruption of white control over the ghetto—were present. The mayor, however, chose to regard it as a Detroit in the making and summoned overwhelming force to put down the rioters. Thus a skirmish which would not have been identified as a riot several years before and which would have been given only cursory attention in a city like Chicago was defined as a major riot in the summer of disorders which prompted the formation of the Kerner Commission.

Even more than in the case of Milwaukee, the definition of the events in Cambridge, Maryland, as a riot was a function of action by public authorities and coverage by the media. A constellation of events which began with a militant speech by black power advocate H. Rap Brown and ended with an enormous fire in the black section of town was perceived and reported in such a way as to create the impression that Brown came to Cambridge to start a riot and succeeded. In fact, the conduct of public authorities was probably the critical factor in the development of events which together gave the appearance of being a ghetto riot. This case study appears as it was originally prepared for, and presented to, the Kerner Commission.

1. THE NEWARK RIOT
New Jersey Governor's Select
Commission on Civil Disorders

The Economic and
Political Framework

Modern technology has drastically altered the face and functions of cities in America today. Improved transportation has made it convenient for the middle classes to migrate to the suburbs. Automation and greater mobility have enabled industry to locate plants outside the city, where larger plots of land are available.

At the same time, industrialization is placing a premium on higher skills and more specialized knowledge. The mechanization of agriculture has uprooted millions of southern Negroes and Spanish-speaking people—mostly from Puerto Rico—who once were able to make their way by farming or by working as unskilled laborers. These people have migrated to the cities, where they thought they would find better homes and jobs.

A recent Rutgers study found that only 17 percent of Newark's Negroes over sixteen years of age were born in Newark. Forty percent have moved to the city since the mid-1950's and a majority of them came from the South. The migrants need a wide range of public services, while they find it difficult, due to inadequate education and skills, to find work. The result is a net outflow of production, human resources, and tax revenues from the city, accompanied by a steep rise in the need for municipal services to the poor.

Some cities still have desirable land and large numbers of middle- and upper-income residents and are able to spread the cost of services. Some cities have remained vigorous as cultural and educational centers, or as centers for trade and finance, office and merchandising operations. However, even these activities can operate in the suburbs, especially as

From *Report for Action,* New Jersey Governor's Select Commission on Civil Disorders, 1968. In editing this material from the report, we have taken unusual liberties in order to adapt it suitably to the format of the book. The chief departure from customary editing procedures has been our changing the sequence of some titled sections to make the material read more smoothly. In addition, the numerous footnotes have been omitted. The report itself is over 200 pages long.

communications and the computer decrease the need for the offices to be within walking distance of one another.

As white middle-class residents moved to the suburbs, unskilled migrants from the South and Puerto Rico came into the city, keeping population figures fairly constant. But the new arrivals, due to lack of skills and to bias, could not compete for many of the available jobs, many of which were filled by the remaining white population—the residuals. This residual group thus gains privileged access to job opportunities in the city. The pattern is especially apparent in the middle echelons of public service. In the process, some mediocre talents are well rewarded. Thus, the decline of the city presents a new opportunity to the older residents. In Newark, only 18 percent of all employed Negro males hold white-collar jobs, whereas 43 percent of employed white males work in this field.

The presence of the new immigrant population has also maintained the city's economy in other areas. For example, in housing, they provide a market for the city's old and deteriorating dwellings. With the aid of the federal government, they even attracted new housing, which has mushroomed into Newark's vast public housing projects.

As these trends continue, the residual population can no longer meet the need for manpower in essential services. This is an incipient problem for the Police Department and has already occurred in medicine. As the decline becomes more apparent, as city services become poorer and as racial tensions mount, the flight of the remaining white middle-class population accelerates, and the city's problems become virtually unmanageable.

What is left is a racial and economic ghetto. A vast portion of Newark can now be called that. The number of black and Spanish-speaking people has steadily increased until they represent more than 60 percent of the city's population. Of the remaining whites, a quarter are in the fifty-five-and-above age bracket, further underscoring the trend toward a completely nonwhite city. Meanwhile, many of the nonwhites are compressed in the tightly packed central core. The area of Newark defined as "core" in the recent Rutgers survey now holds a population that is 90 percent Negro, in contrast to 68 percent in 1960. This same core suffers from an acute unemployment rate, which soars to almost 40 percent among teen-agers. The people in the area who do have jobs frequently earn marginal wages and often do not find full-time jobs.

THE CITY LIMITS

"The residual population" of the city does not refer to a particular ethnic group. The thesis is that members of all ethnic groups in Newark leave the city as soon as they reach the appropriate social-economic level. This apparently is as true of Negroes as of the white groups, and it means that there are very few people in Newark who can be considered affluent.

The people who work in the office buildings on Broad Street are mostly from the suburbs. Both Donald Malafronte, administrative assistant to, and spokesman for, Mayor Addonizio, and Henry W. Connor, executive director of the Greater Newark Chamber of Commerce, see Newark as the core of a city, rather than an actual city. If the city limits were expanded to include all Essex County, the resulting governmental unit would have a much better population balance, with a smaller proportion of those who require a high degree of service and a broader tax base.

Many in Newark believe that at least some of the municipal services should be provided on a countywide basis. The Police Department's deputy chief, John Redden, mentioned his department as one of these. There are now more than twenty municipal police departments in Essex County, which makes for problems in such matters as radio frequencies. A countywide department, even with some elimination of present manpower, would still have about 2,500 men. A force of this size could provide substantial reserves for emergencies, as well as much more efficient police service for the entire county.

THE FISCAL PROBLEM

The city's major source of operating revenue is the real estate tax. Urban renewal, the flight of industry and business to the suburbs, and various other factors have shrunk the tax base. The city has lost millions of dollars in ratables in the last few years.

It has a total of 15,085 acres within its boundaries. Of this, 9,139.94 is tax-exempt. The Port Authority accounts for nearly a third of that amount and pays a million dollars a year for it. Originally the lease, signed in 1947, provided an annual rent of $128,000. In 1962, the city of Newark brought a suit, which it won in 1966. The result was a lump settlement of $6 million, plus an increase to the present amount of rent.

Another suit is pending, in which the city hopes to win a further increase.

The public housing situation further limits the city's tax base. Last year, the city collected only a little more than half a million dollars on the housing authority's property, which has an assessed value of $144,-293,700.

Increasing the frustration is the fact that most occupants of the housing projects are poor people who require much more city service than the average occupant of a tax-assessed dwelling, while they contribute little to the city's treasury.

The 1967 tax rate of $7.76 is nearly confiscatory. This undoubtedly contributes to the decline of Newark. New business construction gets a tax advantage under the Fox–Lance Act, but homeowners, already dissatisfied with life in Newark, are looking at their tax bills and thinking about the benefits of lower-tax communities.

City Finance Director Harry McDowell says the tax rate is driving the middle class out of town, that the limit of bonding capacity has been reached, and so Newark is in deep financial trouble. Mr. McDowell said in a staff interview that there was a direct relationship between the city's financial problem and the riot and that the lack of resources contributed to the crisis.

THE ADDONIZIO ADMINISTRATION'S BEGINNINGS

Mr. Addonizio became mayor of Newark with heavy Negro support. His congressional district had included the Central Ward, which is heavily Negro, and he had been, in the words of Mr. Malafronte, "the Negro's Congressman." Liberals, both black and white, believed he was genuinely interested in Negroes and their problems.

Some of his key appointees disappeared from City Hall early in his administration, among them Paul Busse, his first business administrator, and Samuel M. Convissor, his first administrative assistant. Mr. Busse and Mr. Convissor became disillusioned and resigned. Assemblyman George Richardson, who was named executive secretary to the Insurance Fund Commission, said he was fired for favoring a civilian review board to handle complaints against police.

The City Business Administrator is a key figure in the Newark government, serving as a city manager. It is a difficult job at best. The civil service laws make control of personnel difficult, and some of their provisions, such as cumulative sick leave, are very expensive to the cities.

The employees consider the cumulative sick leave a form of terminal leave to be used before retirement. One long-time Newark civil servant said in a staff interview that he had accumulated 600 days of sick leave, which he would take before he retires. Mr. Busse had the Civil Service Commission work out a total reclassification of Newark's 7,000 city employees. It was intended to cut costs and increase efficiency. The mayor agreed to it, but it was never put into effect.

Mr. Convissor was attracted to the Addonizio campaign because Mr. Addonizio had voiced the conviction that all the physical part of urban renewal was present in the city, but that no one was paying attention to the human aspects. Mr. Convissor was instrumental in forming Newark's antipoverty agency, the United Community Corporation (UCC). He resigned in early 1964. He says of Mayor Addonizio: "The man was a legislator, not an administrator. He didn't know how to take leadership, make decisions."

Assemblyman Richardson testified that Negroes supported Mr. Addonizio for mayor with the idea that he would appoint black people to responsible positions, where they could get the experience needed to take over the city when a Negro mayor was elected. He said, though, that the Negroes found out immediately after the election that the supposed partnership did not really exist. Some of Mayor Addonizio's Negro supporters had hoped that one of their number, Harry Wheeler, a school teacher, would become assistant business administrator, but he was passed over.

As for his own City Hall job, Mr. Richardson said that shortly after he was appointed all decisions were taken away from the office. His theory as to why there are not more Negroes at City Hall is: "Most young, educated, talented Negroes can't be controlled politically. The Mayor is willing to hire them, but they're politically unreliable." The Mayor's answer is: "The Negro politicians won't settle for a piece of the action. They want the whole ball game. Anything we do is opposed."

Mr. Convissor said his efforts to direct renewal and poverty programs in opposition to the plans of Corporation Counsel Norman Schiff or Assistant Business Administrator Dominick J. Miceli elicited this question: "Whose side are you on? Are you with us or against us?" Mr. Convissor added: "They couldn't understand that I was on the side of the community. A series of little pus pockets kept showing up around the city and the noise was quieted, but nothing was really done."

Former Commissioner Salvatore Bontempo had worked in the Addonizio organization in 1963, but withdrew shortly after the election. He said in a staff interview that a committee of businessmen had raised $25,000 for the campaign at one dinner, hoping that the new mayor could save the city from decay. After the election, the businessmen approached Mr. Addonizio about forming a committee to plan a program, he said, and were told: "I'm a politician. I know how to get the votes. I'll make the plans."

MAYOR ADDONIZIO AND
THE NEGRO COMMUNITY

In 1962, there were no Negroes in City Hall positions of any note. The Addonizio administration now points with pride to the number of Negroes appointed to high positions. They include Mrs. Larrie Stalks, Health Director; Grace Malone, Director of the Division of Welfare; Budget Director Wilbur Parker; and Harold Ashby, President of the Board of Education.

Councilman Irvine Turner, through a close and constant 14-year association with the city administration that has helped him to build the power of patronage, has substantial support and influence in the Negro community. Although Mr. Turner has been ill for several years, the commission's survey showed that he is still the most influential Negro in Newark. When Negroes were asked, "Who are some of the Negro leaders who are respected and listened to by Negroes in the Newark area?" Mr. Turner was, by far, the most frequently mentioned. He was named by 18 percent of the Negro respondents. Next came Assemblyman Richardson, with 7 percent, and the Rev. Dr. Martin Luther King, with 5 percent. Councilman-at-large West and Mr. Gibson, the former mayoral candidate, were each named by 4 percent.

Negroes point out, however, that the issue is not simply how many black people are appointed to, or hold, high positions, but whether the administration as a whole is responsive to the black community, and whether Negroes in office are permitted to exercise independent judgment.

These questions are being asked against the background of rising Negro militancy. The black power movement has come to represent a position that goes far beyond mere responsiveness to Negro problems by articulating the need for possession of greater power by Negroes as a requirement for meaningful change.

Advocates of black power feel that only Negroes are in a position to take the lead in setting the priorities and the pace of action designed to promote change in their communities. They feel that much more than economic deprivation is involved. In their view, it is the sense of power-lessness and the feeling of a lack of control over their own and their communities' fate that is the crucial handicap in the quest for Negro equality and for full dignity in society. A still more militant view advo-cates complete black control over black communities.

Meanwhile, Newark's political leadership has a long way to go merely to provide essential services to the disadvantaged communities.

Even whites active in these communities agree. Thus, Monsignor Thomas J. Carey, pastor of Queen of Angels Catholic Church in the Central Ward, says he has found City Hall difficult to deal with. As an example, he noted that in 1964 Hayes Homes had been in existence more than ten years, but that the landscaping and ground lights had not been installed and that there was virtually no police protection for the thousands of residents in the high-rise project. One of the assistants in the parish formed a tenants' league and managed to get 1,000 Hayes tenants to a protest meeting. Mayor Addonizio attended the meeting and produced astonishing results. There was police protection that night, and within a very short time the landscaping and lights were in-stalled.

The priests believe that the mayor was impressed by the size of the meeting and reacted as a politician to a situation that, as a public offi-cial, he should have relieved long before.

Other city services, too, are considered inadequate by ghetto resi-dents. A major source of frustration is housing. The Negro in a public housing project lives with government. The Negro who lives in a sub-standard dwelling can rightly blame the city for its condition. If the City Housing Code were enforced, the building would not be substand-ard.

Even the homeowner can feel housing frustrations. Since urban re-newal and highway projects almost invariably cut through Negro areas, the residents know that their homes have a dubious life expectancy. In addition, there is a frustration that all Newark property owners share, regardless of race: taxes. The owner of an $18,000 home pays nearly $1,400 a year in taxes.

When it comes to welfare, the poor deal with different offices. De-pending on their qualifications, they are supported by either the county or the city. Different interpretations may cause them to be shuttled be-tween the two departments. Red tape may hold up their checks at crucial times. An unemployed father may feel compelled to leave home so his children can qualify for Aid to Dependent Children, which is not paid if the father is living with them.

Negro neighborhoods are dirty because of inadequate street cleaning. A house is gutted by fire and is not torn down. A governmental unit takes over buildings in preparation for urban renewal or highway construction and does not even secure them against trespassers. Cars stand abandoned on the streets for months, but the city does not tow them away, even when complaints are made. They are stripped of usable parts. Sometimes someone sets fire to them, but their hulks still stay at the curb. The abandoned buildings and cars reinforce the feeling of the ghetto dwellers that the city does not care about them. At one point, there was an estimate that the streets contained 1,000 abandoned cars.

A PERVASIVE FEELING OF CORRUPTION

It is said that the city commissions of the 1930's and 1940's left Newark a heritage that has not been shaken off. There is a widespread belief that Newark's government is corrupt.

Knowledgeable and substantial people expressed this belief, off the record. A realtor said business won't move into Newark for three reasons: the racial situation, taxes, and corrupton. A source close to Newark businessmen said he understood from them that "everything at City Hall is for sale." A former state official, a former city official, and an incumbent city official all used the same phrase: "There's a price on everything at City Hall."

In the area of organized crime and police corruption, this belief has been reinforced by four Essex County grand jury presentments in this decade. There was one presentment in 1961, another in 1964, and two in 1965. This commission is concerned that no effective action has been taken to follow up on these presentments.

In April 1965, the grand jury presentment charged political interference with the Police Department and a lack of enforcement of gambling laws in Newark. In addition, the grand jury criticized the appointment of Harry (Tip) Rosen as public relations man for the Police Department at a time when Mr. Rosen still held a part-time job in a firm owned by Gerardo Catena, "who had been widely reputed to be a syndicate leader in New Jersey."

The presentment said:

We have a lack of full confidence in the Newark Police Department's enthusiasm for a crackdown on the underworld. Nowhere has our attention been focused on any policy statement by the Police Department vigorously attacking organized crime.

In December 1965, the grand jury returned another presentment on gambling enforcement. Mr. Spina's public response was to label it "vicious." In a newspaper story on December 1, 1965, he challenged Prosecutor Brendan Byrne to show him the organized gambling in Newark. Within 48 hours, the Prosecutor's Office raided two apartments in Newark and charged 15 people found in them with operating a lottery.

When Deputy Police Chief John Redden was asked about the prevalence of bookmaking and numbers playing in Newark, he told this commission:

Based on my own experience, based on previous Grand Jury investigations, based on the statement—the public statement—of a man such as former Assistant Attorney General Bergin, I would say that it was very prevalent. It is a very large business.

Mr. Redden also cited that presentment as evidence that assignment of police personnel was made for political reasons.

There is a widespread belief in the Negro community that these grand jury presentments were true. Compounding it is the visible evidence in the Negro area of gambling and vice. The feeling was expressed by Assemblyman Richardson in his appearance before the commission:

There are some policemen that are interested in this sort of thing (payoffs, graft). Despite all the dangers of being involved in this all-black community, you couldn't run some of the white officers away from there. In my estimation, that is the reason why (Negro) Captain Williams has not been assigned to one of those Negro precincts, because of obvious pressures from other people that have certain influences in the city.

Negroes criticizing the operation of the Police Department cite, among other things, the 1966 indictment of five members of the auto squad on charges of extorting $9,000 from car thieves. Indictments against one of the five men have since been dropped, but the others are still awaiting trial.

Testimony before the commission, interviews with responsible people in different strata of the city's life, as well as nationally publicized articles (*Life, The New York Times*) leave no doubt that the belief that

Newark is a corrupt city is pervasive. This has implications for the attitudes of citizens toward law and order which this commission cannot ignore.

One of the most consistent complaints of Negroes about the city involves politics in the Police Department. A priest who is familiar with Negro problems says: "The police are the real breakdown in community relations."

When he appointed Mr. Spina as Police Director, the mayor said the appointment was a reward for his political campaign work. Immediately after his appointment, Mr. Spina issued a directive that all personnel assignments would be by order of the director.

When the criticisms of the Police Department were mentioned to Mayor Addonizio during the staff interview, he answered: "If you have a barrel of apples, you're bound to find a bad one in it."

When the riot started, the mayor promoted a Negro, Edward Williams, to captain of police. The administration hoped that promotion of a Negro to that rank would placate the rioters. Mr. Addonizio said in the staff interview: "We had to promote five men to get down to him on the promotion list. It threw our whole table of organization out of whack."

THE CHANGE OF MOOD

Mayor Addonizio's administration has coincided with the civil rights drive in the North, which began about the time he took office in 1962.

The Congress of Racial Equality became active in Newark early in 1963. An article in *The New York Herald Tribune* said that Newark and Brooklyn would be targets for protests against discrimination in the summer of 1963. Police Director Dominick Spina said in testimony before the commission that he first noticed the group in the city when it became active in the Barringer High School demonstration in July of that year. Among those arrested was Robert Curvin, a leader in CORE. The five days of demonstrations ended when Mayor Addonizio formed an organization of civil rights, business, and labor leaders to conduct an apprentice program for the building trades.

There was a new spirit among Newark's Negroes. In 1961, the Clinton Hill Neighborhood Council had given its support to a lawsuit by seven individuals to stop the Clinton Hill Urban Renewal Project because blacks and whites in the area did not want to be moved from their homes. Civil rights groups began to refer to urban renewal as "Negro removal." A suit was filed but did not prevail. Meanwhile, funds for the project were tied up by the litigation.

By the summer of 1964, an organization called Students for a Democratic Society had come into the area and was concentrating on housing. It was led by a young man from Michigan, Thomas Hayden, who described it in testimony before this commission as "a national left-wing student organization." Mr. Hayden brought the SDS to Newark at the invitation of Prof. Stanley Winters of Newark College of Engineering to assist the Clinton Hill Neighborhood Council. The alliance was brief. Mr. Hayden testified that there was a "very unpleasant split" with the neighborhood council. By the end of the summer of 1964, however, the SDS group had organized in Newark, and when the students left town, local people became full-time organizers. The group was renamed the Newark Community Union Project (NCUP).

Mr. Hayden's group concentrated on demonstrations and litigation with landlords. It picketed tenements, issued leaflets charging police brutality or calling for housing demonstrations. The group also demonstrated for traffic lights at various intersections. The traffic light demonstrations were particularly frustrating to Newark officials because they could not install these lights without state approval.

That summer of 1964 was the time when major violence erupted in many eastern cities. There had been violent demonstrations since 1961, but a new phase opened with the riot in Harlem, which was followed quickly by riots in the Bedford–Stuyvesant section of Brooklyn; Rochester, N.Y.; Philadelphia; and—in New Jersey—Paterson, Elizabeth, Jersey City, and Keansburg. There was no rioting in Newark, however.

An incident that many believe might have started a riot in Newark came in 1965. A Negro, Lester Long, Jr., had been arrested on traffic charges and shot dead by policeman Henry Martinez, reportedly while fleeing the police car. The first newspaper report on the morning after the shooting quoted an officer as saying that the policeman had stumbled and fired the fatal bullet accidentally. A later report said he had aimed and fired. The Negro community noted the contradiction and the reaction came quickly. CORE held marches and scheduled Wednesday night meetings in Military Park, inviting civil rights leader James Farmer to one of them. Mr. Spina says the downtown night meetings frightened merchants and caused them to lose business, but CORE refused to call them off.

There was an insistent demand for a civilian board to review complaints against the police. Reacting to the demand, the Patrolmen's

Benevolent Association picketed City Hall. The mayor announced a policy of having complaints against the police forwarded to the Prosecutor's Office for grand jury action or to the Federal Bureau of Investigation for investigation of possible civil rights violations. The public protest subsided.

Nineteen-sixty-six was an election year. Kenneth Gibson, a Negro engineer, entered the mayoral campaign belatedly, but polled nearly 17,000 votes, enough to force Mayor Addonizio into a run-off. NCUP was supporting Earl Harris, a former Essex County Freeholder and one of two Negroes running for South Ward councilman against the incumbent, Lee Bernstein. The Negro candidates battled one another hard enough to divide their bloc in the run-off and Councilman Bernstein was returned to office.

Newark's city elections are nonpartisan. This is a handicap for Negroes who aspire to political leadership, since there are no clubhouses through which they can find their way into the political organization and earn its support. Consequently, they have to form their own organizations—a difficult task for members of a disadvantaged minority.

The mobility of the Negro population also inhibits its political effectiveness. Albert Black, chairman of the Human Rights Commission, said in a staff interview that if 30,000 Negroes were registered in a voting drive, 10,000 of them would be unregistered three years later because they had moved. This reduces their strength at the polls.

Heretofore, the Negro economic level has also entered into the political picture. Newark's whites generally are not far above its Negroes on the economic scale, but there have been fewer Negroes in a position to contribute to a political campaign. A Negro candidate running with only Negro support would have a great deal of trouble in financing his campaign. Mr. Gibson feels, however, that by now he could get financial support from the white business community if he ran again for mayor.

POST-ELECTION ISSUES

In early 1967, there was an outcry from taxpayers who found that their rate was being increased from $5.97 to $7.76. Rubbing salt in the financial wound was the fact that city councilmen had voted pay raises to all employees, including themselves and the mayor. The mayor's increase was $10,000.

A recall movement started promptly, but foundered. This cut across racial lines. There are Negro taxpayers in Newark who felt the increase as deeply as the whites.

At about the same time, militant groups in the Negro community focused their attention on the controversy over the city plan to give a large expanse of land to the New Jersey College of Medicine and Dentistry.

There appeared substantial support for locating the medical school in Newark. It offered both jobs and improved medical care for the community. The objection was to the amount of land demanded by the school and offered by the city. The administration also objected to giving up so much of the city's acreage, but when the school's Board of Trustees decided to move to Madison because there was more land available there, Mayor Addonizio agreed to meet the trustees' demand for 150 acres.

Mr. Malafronte described the administration's strategy:

Here is the way the thing went: We got a copy in advance of the report they were going to make which said, "Newark is a wonderful place. We would love to go there. It has all the wonderful facilities and so forth, but however, we have this recommendation: that there be 150 acres. As much as we would love to come to Newark, we have got to have those 150 acres; therefore, we are barred from Newark. Although we would love you and we would like to come, we have the professionals, which you go to when you are in a hole, and they said 150 acres. Obviously, we wouldn't come to Newark no matter how much we wanted."

We got a copy of the report and said, "We have been undone here." We all sat down with a map and looked around at the area we wanted them to go into, which was Fairmount Urban Renewal Project. It worked out to 20 acres; if we pushed it, 30 acres, which we felt was more than sufficient for a medical school; still do. It was clear we were hung on their 150 acres as a stipulation, but we did have this rather glowing account of all the advantages of Newark.

So we thought we would surprise them in this and we drew a 185-acre area which we considered to be the worst slum area. It included Fairmount and surrounding areas, which was clearly in need of renewal, and we were going to proceed with the renewal in any case for that area.

We asked for a special meeting with them and at the meeting we confronted them with our offer of 185 acres. At that same meeting, they had arranged to release their report and 150 acres, so we were at an impasse. Their report which said Newark is a wonderful place, but we need 150 acres and, therefore, we can't come—they were confronted with Newark's countermove of 185 acres. What excuse do you have? That is when the battle was joined. It became unclear. We, I think, in our hearts always felt they were using the 150 acres to get out of Newark. We felt in the end they would come down to 20 or 30 acres in Fairmount, or in a battle we might have to give up some more acreage. We never felt they would ask for 185. We felt it was a ploy on their part.

Late in 1966, the school agreed to come to Newark on assurance that the city would produce 50 acres within a year and 100 more on the school's call. The city asked where the school wanted its first 50 acres and the request was not for cleared land, but for 50 acres across from cleared land. Mr. Malafronte said:

To us, this was a slap in the face. . . . It was our opinion they were attempting to get out of the situation in which they found themselves, which was an aroused public demand they come to Newark. . . . What they wanted was across the street from cleared land. This to us was insanity and enraging because they knew this was not an urban renewal area. They knew that the urban renewal process is three years and perhaps five.

The school's board of trustees demanded its first delivery from the center of the promised tract rather than in the Fairmount Urban Renewal area. The administration then moved to get the land through condemnation. In March 1967, it obtained legislative authorization for condemnation and the issuance of bonds. Meanwhile, opposition had developed and, to clear the area, it was necessary to declare it blighted. Militant groups had been aroused by the size of the land package, and the blight hearings gave them their opportunity to say so.

The UCC conducted a survey of residents of the proposed site that revealed that:

Seventy-six percent wanted the school to locate in Newark.
Fifty-three percent favored it even if it forced them to move.
In the area to be affected first, forty-five percent favored it even if it forced them to move.
Forty-seven percent wanted to move out of the area anyway.

The UCC also found that its survey was the first news some of the residents had had of the proposed location of the school. The UCC adopted a resolution deploring the methods used to bring the medical school to Newark.

On March 29, 1967, a store on South Orange Avenue was rented by Clinton Bey, who gave his telephone number as that of UCC Area

Board 3. Then a man who called himself Colonel Hassan of the Black
Liberation Army—actually Albert Osborne of Washington, D.C.—
took over the storefront on South Orange Avenue and announced a
rally there against the medical school. The rally was scheduled for
April 28, 1967. Colonel Hassan's presence disturbed the city administration, and the police toured the Negro area displaying copies of his
arrest record (he had been held on charges of writing bad checks) in an
attempt to discourage attendance at the rally. They failed. Among those
attending were Mr. Curvin, Mr. Gibson, Mr. Richardson, Central Ward
Democratic Chairman Eulis Ward, the Rev. Levin West, and black nationalists.

On May 19, there was a complaint that a child had been struck by a
teacher in Oliver Street School. The Black Liberation Army responded
with a demonstration at the school.

On May 22, the blight hearing opened before the City Planning
Board. It was noisy and ended abruptly when Colonel Hassan's lieutenant overturned the stenographic machine and the colonel tore up part of
the tape. Neither man was arrested. The chairman terminated the meeting.

THE PARKER—CALLAGHAN DISPUTE

Meanwhile, it had become known that the secretary of the Board of
Education, Arnold Hess, planned to resign, that Councilman James T.
Callaghan would be appointed to replace him, and that Mr. Hess would
continue as a $25,000-a-year consultant.

On May 23, the National Association for the Advancement of Colored People proposed that City Budget Director Wilbur Parker, the first
Negro to become a Certified Public Accountant in New Jersey, be appointed to the post of the Board of Education. Mr. Callaghan is a
former labor official who never went to college. Besides his council
post, he held a $10,300 a year job as secretary to the Essex County
Purchasing Agent.

The *Newark News* commented editorially that politicians were fond
of saying that Negroes, where qualified, received equal opportunity in
public appointments, but that "in Newark's educational system politics
is paramount to equality of opportunity."

The Board of Education deferred a decision on the appointment and,
on May 29, Fred Means, acting president of the Negro Educators of
Newark, said: "The Negro community is in turmoil over this injustice.

If immediate steps are not taken, Newark might become another Watts."

The Board of Education finally took up the matter at a meeting on June 26. The meeting opened at 5 P.M. There were 70 speakers. It ended at 3:23 A.M. The final decision was that Mr. Hess would stay in his job for another year.

It had been a difficult year for the administration. Mr. Spina testified to the mood that had developed:

As you sit in the office of the Police Director and you see those swirling movements grow surrounding you, you will note that they grew in crescendo. . . . The type of speeches that were made before the Planning Board and the Board of Education tell you, almost predict, that there is going to be blood running in the streets.

The medical school and Parker–Callaghan controversies helped set the stage for the July riot. They served to focus the dissatisfaction of the community. The fact that the hearings had been held back-to-back intensified the high feelings.

Former Commissioner Bontempo maintained that it was bad government for the mayor even to suggest the Callaghan appointment. Mr. Bontempo said that previous mayors had left Board of Education affairs to the board's members and were glad not to have the responsibility.

In this case, with the community already in a mood of dissatisfaction and protest, the mayor made a political move that could be expected to have racial implications. James Threatt, director of the Human Relations Commission, said: "The only issue on which I've seen Negroes get truly excited and concerned was Parker–Callaghan. For the first time, you really had a community."

On Saturday, July 8, the East Orange police were involved in an altercation with a group of Black Muslims at 91 North 14th Street, on the Newark border. The Newark police were called to the city limits to stand by in case they were needed. There was a fight, and the Newark police moved in to help the East Orange police. Mr. Threatt said the Muslims were beaten as they lay on the ground. Each department, he said, "accused the other of doing the beating."

Newark's mood was ugly.

In spite of all the buildup and tension that Mr. Spina could feel in his office, there is no evidence that the administration made any preparations for a riot. Its attitude was that to prepare for a riot might spark one. The riot started on the Wednesday after the incident in East Orange.

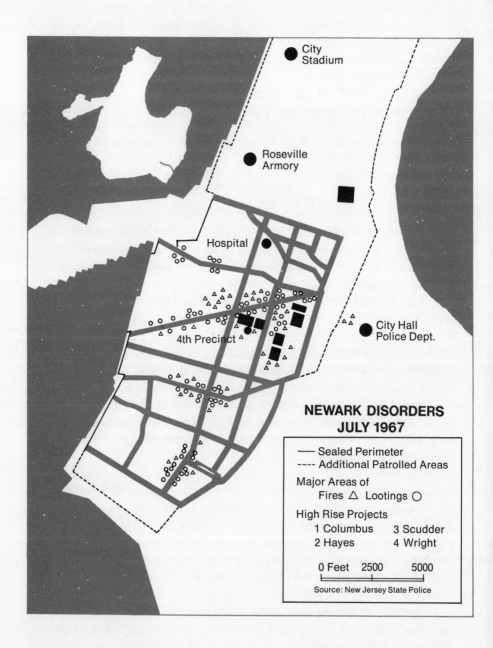

Figure 1-1   The Disorders

PRELUDE

The outbreak of the Newark riots followed the arrest of a Negro cab driver named John W. Smith on Wednesday night, July 12, 1967. But neither the arrest of Mr. Smith nor any other single factor could explain the events that followed. There is no full or logical explanation for mass violence such as Newark experienced last summer. However, there is evidence of deteriorating conditions in the ghetto; of increasing awareness of and frustration with these conditions among its residents; of the emergence of outspoken groups that focused these feelings; and of miscalculations, insensitive or inadequate responses by established authority.

Mayor Hugh J. Addonizio told the commission:

It's not so hard to understand. The material was there in the form of problems in housing, education, and the effects of generations of neglect and bigotry. The atmosphere was right, because of mistakes, because of misunderstandings, and because of the insanity of a few misguided fools who believe riots are a healthy exercise for America.

As the summer of 1967 approached there was a gradual deterioration of relations between the Negro community and City Hall following a series of controversies and incidents that have been described in detail in earlier sections of this report, among them the medical school controversy and the Parker–Callaghan dispute.

Testimony before the commission supplies ample evidence that significant elements in the Negro community felt that, in the controversy over the location of the medical school and in offering the key education job in the Newark school system to Councilman James T. Callaghan rather than to Budget Director Wilbur Parker, the city administration had ignored the interests of the Negro community and the recommendations of many Negro spokesmen. Assemblyman George Richardson testified: "When people lost faith in these legitimate efforts, I think the culmination of the defeats is what brought about the riots we had in the city."

There is no evidence, in the face of these rising tensions, of any significant action by the city administration or other established authorities to moderate or deal with them in a positive manner.

At the same time, the administration did not engage in meaningful discussions with outspoken Negro leaders.

The rising tensions were reflected in the growing hostility between

Negro citizens and the police that had developed over a period of several years.

On July 8, a fight between fifteen Negroes and the East Orange and Newark police on the Newark/East Orange border further heated emotions. Four nights later, when Mr. Smith was dragged by Newark police out of a police car into the Fourth Precinct, with inhabitants of the almost all-Negro Hayes Homes as eyewitnesses, the riot began.

WEDNESDAY NIGHT

The events surrounding Mr. Smith's arrest were the subject of litigation when the commission heard the parties to the incident. Therefore, it was agreed that these witnesses would relate their stories and not be questioned by commission members or staff. The commission heard the testimony of the arresting policemen, Patrolmen John DeSimone and Vito Pontrelli, and of the taxi driver, Mr. Smith. The conflicts in this testimony are glaring and they were not resolved by the commission. Here is the summary of the two patrolmen's account:

Patrolman Pontrelli testified that he and Patrolman DeSimone were on routine patrol duty at dusk on July 12 when Mr. DeSimone observed a Safety Company taxi close in behind the patrol car, which was traveling west on 15th Avenue. Alternatively breaking and accelerating, with its high beam flicking on and off, Patrolman Pontrelli said, the cab tailgated the patrol car for almost a block. Then the cab "shot around us at the intersection of 15th Avenue and South Seventh Street and went approximately one block on the wrong side of the street up to about South Eighth Street and 15th Avenue."

The two policemen pursued the cab to South Ninth Street, where they stopped it. They reported that when the driver was asked for his license and registration certificate, he answered with insults and curses. When Mr. DeSimone told the driver he was going to arrest him, Mr. Smith responded by opening his car door, striking Mr. DeSimone in the chest and then punching him in the face. Mr. Pontrelli came to his colleague's aid and, after a struggle, Mr. Smith was subdued and placed in the patrol car.

After calling another patrol car to tow the taxi, patrol car 42 started for the Fourth Precinct. En route, the two policemen said, the prisoner became violent, fought with Mr. DeSimone, and struck Mr. Pontrelli, who was driving. Consequently, Mr. Pontrelli said:

I put on my red light and siren because I figured if it is going to go on like this I better get down to the precinct fast. They (Mr. Smith and Mr. DeSimone) were fighting almost all the way down from South 10th Street down to the precinct.

At the precinct, the two policemen testified, Mr. Smith refused to leave the car, and when they pulled him out, he refused to walk. Each policeman then took an arm of Mr. Smith and began dragging him across the street. They were met in the middle of the street by a patrolman who took Mr. Smith's feet, and the three carried him to the precinct. Just before entering the building, Patrolman Pontrelli said, Mr. Smith again became violent.

Patrolman Pontrelli said that four or five persons witnessed these events. He heard people shout, "Take the handcuffs off him, stop beating him." The policeman pointed out that Mr. Smith was not handcuffed because "we had all we could do to get him into the radio car at the scene of the arrest."

According to the Police Department arrest sheet, Mr. Smith was booked at 9:30 P.M. and charged with assault and battery, resisting arrest, and the use of loud and offensive language. Later that night he was taken from his cell to Beth Israel Hospital. At 11:30 A.M. the following day, he was presented with traffic citations for driving with a revoked license, following another vehicle too closely, and failure to drive on the right half of the roadway. Later, bail was set at $1,000 on an assault and battery charge and at $250 for driving without a license. At 7 P.M. Thursday, he was paroled in the custody of his lawyer, John Love of Newark.

Mr. Smith offered his testimony:

He had picked up a woman passenger near City Hospital sometime between 9:30 and 11:30 P.M. Wednesday. His encounter with the two patrolmen came after he turned right at the corner of 15th Avenue and Sixth Street. He said a police car was double parked at the corner of South Seventh Street and 15th Avenue. Mr. Smith said he gave a signal and passed, but then was immediately pulled over to the side.

One of the policemen in the car asked for Mr. Smith's license and registration. When the cab driver asked, "What happened?" he was told that he had "popped an intersection" (passing at the intersection going west in the eastbound lane). Mr. Smith said he replied, "I don't see how because you were double parked, and I thought you were working, and I just made a normal pass." Because he felt the policemen were "trying to play games" with him, he added, "Go ahead and do what you want to do."

At that point, according to the taxi driver, the questioning policemen, "evidently . . . incensed, jumped out of the police car and snatched the door open and told me to get out because I was under arrest." The passenger "was insulted" by one of the policemen and told to leave the car. Mr. Smith was placed in the back of the patrol car and another car was called to pick up the cab. When the other car arrived, the first car proceeded to the Fourth Precinct.

On the way to the precinct, Mr. Smith stated, one of the policemen sitting in the front seat turned around and began to punch him. The policeman who was driving told his companion to stop. Mr. Smith quoted him as saying, "No, no, this baby is mine."

As the result of a particularly painful blow in the groin, Mr. Smith said, he was unable to walk out of the car to the police station. He said he was dragged out of the car and down the street until the citizens who were observing protested. "After this outburst from the citizens," he said he was carried into the station.

Once in the station he was taken into a room by the arresting policemen, who, according to Mr. Smith, were joined by seven or eight others, all of whom began kicking and beating him "for a lengthy period of time." He said he was dragged to a cell and the beating was continued. He said that a policeman threw water from a toilet bowl over him, and another—one of the arresting policemen—struck him in the head with a gun butt and in the right side with a blunt instrument.

Finally, Mr. Smith stated, the cell was locked and he was left alone. A little later a group of citizens asked to see him, and, after talking with him about his injuries, requested that he go to the hospital. Doctors at Beth Israel Hospital, according to Mr. Smith, discovered that his ribs were caved in and that he had suffered other internal injuries. After being taped up, he was taken to the stationhouse downtown.

Soon after Mr. Smith was arrested and taken into the Fourth Precinct, rumors began to circulate that he had been beaten to death. There is no evidence indicating where the rumors might have begun, although Patrolman Pontrelli stated he thought they were being spread by "other cab drivers." Because the Hayes project is so densely populated and because Mr. Smith's transfer from the patrol car to the precinct was witnessed by several people, it would not require much for this rumor to begin circulating and to spread widely.

At any rate, the rumor spread rapidly. The police report listed the time of the Smith arrest as 9:30 P.M. According to Inspector Kenneth C. Melchior, who was in charge of the precinct at that time, Mr. Smith could not have been taken into the precinct before 9:50 P.M. Within fifteen minutes several civil rights leaders arrived on the scene. Robert Curvin learned of the Smith incident in a telephone call from a woman who, he said, was living in the Hayes project area. She had called CORE to ask for assistance.

When Mr. Curvin arrived at the precinct, more than thirty-five people had gathered in front of the building, and the crowd was growing rapidly. People were coming out from the Hayes project across the street. Mr. Curvin decided a lawyer should be called, and someone was dispatched to telephone Joe Barry of Newark Legal Services.

When Inspector Melchior arrived, he met Mr. Curvin and two unidentified women who said they represented Area Boards 2 and 3 of the United Community Corporation. Lieutenant Price of the Fourth Precinct gave Inspector Melchior the report of the two policemen who had arrested Mr. Smith.

Inspector Melchior went over the reports and discussed them with the arresting policemen. In the report, it said that Mr. DeSimone's trousers had been torn, but Inspector Melchior testified that he failed to find any evidence of this. He told Patrolman DeSimone to correct the report. Inspector Melchior said the report was signed, although not necessarily typed, by Patrolman DeSimone.

While the inspector was going over the reports, the civil rights leaders and others moved in and out of the precinct house. Mr. Curvin said one of the arresting policemen came out and walked to his car parked in the driveway of the gas station adjacent to the precinct. The crowd moved toward the policeman, as, according to Mr. Curvin, one of the Negro representatives proceeded to ask the patrolman what had happened. The patrolman answered, "He (Mr. Smith) punched me in the mouth," or something to that effect. According to Mr. Curvin, the reaction was ". . . kind of an outburst of disgust and people were saying, 'Oh bull' and 'You are crazy' and stuff like that."

The mood of the crowd outside the precinct was growing increasingly tense. As the word of the Smith incident spread, more people gathered at the windows of the Hayes project and along the sidewalks, facing the precinct. Some began talking of entering the precinct. They were being exhorted by Mrs. Esta Williams, who was described as active in the Hayes Homes Tenants League and highly respected as a community leader. Mr. Curvin quoted her as saying to the crowd, "Don't wait to go

in now. My husband was beaten in that precinct about two years ago.
. . . If we had gone in when they took him in, it never would have happened."

With that, the group started toward the precinct. When they reached
the door, they were met by a number of policemen and were told they
could not all enter. About twelve persons finally went in. This was after
10 P.M., and there were about seventy-five persons outside the precinct.

Having informed himself of the circumstances concerning Mr. Smith,
Inspector Melchior returned to the Negro group in the precinct (Mr.
Curvin and others) to discuss the situation further. He said that Mr.
Curvin did most of the talking. The group said they were there to protest the abuse of Mr. Smith and wanted to see the prisoner.

Inspector Melchior agreed to allow a committee of four to see Mr.
Smith in his cell at about 10:15. Mr. Curvin observed Mr. Smith "lying
on the bench with his eyes closed and his feet up," and appearing to be
in pain. Timothy Still, president of the board of the United Community
Corporation, said he was told that Mr. Smith had been paralyzed.

Thereafter, the group asked Inspector Melchior why the prisoner had
not been allowed to see a doctor. Inspector Melchior said they told him
that Mr. Smith had been "badly injured in the side, that he was in great
agony and pain, and needed immediate hospitalization." The inspector
said the Negro group asked him to go see what was wrong with Mr.
Smith.

Inspector Melchior then dispatched Lieutenant Price to see the prisoner. He returned from the cell block and informed the inspector that
the prisoner was injured in the side and in need of hospitalization.
Inspector Melchior then gave instruction to send the prisoner to the
hospital. Mr. Smith was taken out through the rear door of the precinct,
put into a patrol car, and driven to Beth Israel Hospital. He was accompanied by James Walker, one of the Negro representatives in the precinct and an official in a Newark manpower development program. At
this time, Mr. Still, Don Wendell, acting executive director of the United
Community Corporation, and Oliver Lofton, the director of Newark's
Legal Services Project, arrived.

Inspector Melchior said the crowd outside the precinct, which by
now numbered 250, was told that Mr. Smith was going to City Hospital, when, in fact, he was being taken to Beth Israel. The mistake was
inadvertent, Inspector Melchior said, since he had automatically assumed City Hospital was Mr. Smith's destination.

A number of people followed the patrol car to the hospital because, in Mr. Curvin's words, "frankly no one trusted the police enough to take someone to the hospital even in a situation like that." Mr. Curvin also thought the prisoner's transfer to the hospital might have intensified the suspicion that he had been beaten by the police.

A review of the hospital records indicates that Mr. Smith suffered "hematoma on Laccipital-parietal region skull" and "a fracture of the right ninth rib in the axillary line with slight displacement at the fracture site."

At the time of Mr. Smith's removal, a number of people who said they had witnessed his arrival at the precinct were brought in to speak to Inspector Melchior. According to Mr. Curvin, one woman said:

We don't want to talk about Smith; we want to talk about what we see here happening every day, time and time again. . . . If we are not going to do anything about what we can see from our windows happening in this neighborhood every day, what the hell is it?

As soon as the car carrying Mr. Smith to the hospital had left the area, Inspector Melchior instructed his officers to disperse the crowd so that normal traffic could be restored. Some 10 to 12 policemen were used. They wore regular uniforms and did not carry nightsticks.

Soon after the crowd was partly dispersed, Inspector Melchior went back into the building, where he was greeted by about 25 to 30 persons. He invited the group into a larger room. Three or four policemen accompanied him, but when the group objected to their presence, he asked them to leave.

Meanwhile, a meeting was held off on one side of the room. Among others, it included Messrs. Lofton, Still, Wendell, Curvin, and Walker. They decided to encourage the crowd to go home and to return the next morning for a meeting at City Hall and a demonstration. Mr. Curvin disagreed with this decision, because he sensed that

the crowd wasn't prepared to go home and that there needed to be more concern about doing something with them that was constructive and allow them to express their dissatisfaction with what happened.

Mr. Wendell said that while this meeting was going on "things got very heated outside and Still and Curvin went outside to try and talk to the crowd." Both spoke without bullhorns. Mr. Still recalled that he "urged the people to go home," but was interrupted when fire bombs were thrown at the precinct. According to the Police Department's report on the disorders dated August 21, an unidentified person threw a

Molotov cocktail against the precinct wall between 11:30 P.M. and midnight as the speakers were addressing the crowd. This is the first recorded use of Molotov cocktails in the disorders. Police Director Dominick Spina testified that instructions on how to make Molotov cocktails were described in a leaflet that had been distributed in the community in 1966, but that he could not link the leaflets to any specific organization.

The meeting between Inspector Melchior and the Negro representatives was still in progress when, according to the inspector, a cry came from another part of the building that "the kitchen is on fire." The meeting broke up abruptly and everyone rushed outside.

Inspector Melchior ordered the policemen out of the building under the command of Sergeant Popek, and he also ordered them to determine the extent of damage and to set up a line around the building. Mr. Still said the policemen were wearing helmets and carrying night sticks. When the police encircled the building, according to Inspector Melchior, there was no dialogue between the policemen and the crowd. Mr. Still said there was no physical contact between the policemen and the crowd, but that there was an exchange of "racial epithets."

A fire then broke out in an abandoned car located across the street in the Hayes project. The Fire Department was summoned and three or four policemen were dispatched to the area. After the fire had been put out, policemen and firemen were stoned as they left the area.

After the explosion of the Molotov cocktail, which occurred at about the same time, the Negro representatives asked Inspector Melchior for twenty minutes in which to try to calm the crowd. Mr. Wendell testified:

> Then we asked the inspector, and I am paraphrasing because I am shortening it, to give us an opportunity to talk to the people. He asked us, would we guarantee that we could disperse the crowd? Nobody could guarantee that, and that crowd was in no mood for that. We told him no, we couldn't. We would attempt to channelize this energy, get them down to City Hall, an all-night vigil. That was to get them out of the area.

Inspector Melchior agreed to give them fifteen minutes and gave his bullhorn to Mr. Curvin.

The inspector said he remembered Mr. Curvin as saying something like, "We have got to start a demonstration to show the Police Department that we mean business; that they can't do this type of thing." Inspector Melchior did not listen to the rest of the remarks by Mr. Cur-

vin or Mr. Still, who also addressed the crowd. He returned to the precinct, where he sought to contact Director Spina and Deputy Chief John
Redden.

Negro speakers said they tried to move the crowd out of the area by
having them march to City Hall. Some started to get in line and walk,
with Messrs. Still, Curvin, and Lofton at the head of the column. Mr.
Wendell testified:

We were moving away from the station and people were cheering and
they began to sing "We Shall Not Be Moved." They were in fact moving, and the police could see this out the window. Maybe they were twenty
abreast.

At this point, Mr. Wendell continued:

The police came out, and the crowd said, "Here they come. You can't
trust them. They lied to us." This is when the first stones began to be
thrown.

According to Inspector Melchior, at about 12:15 A.M. "a real barrage
of all types of missiles hit into the street and against the building." Then
twenty to twenty-five policemen charged out the front door of the precinct. Inspector Melchior stated:

I did call out, "Get out there," words to that effect, but I don't think
under these circumstances that anybody would have had to wait for that
order because they were not under direct orders not to leave the building.

Inspector Melchior explained that after he agreed to remove the police for fifteen minutes, he merely told the men to "reenter the building
and remain there until further happenings." He said that when the police came out, it was after the fifteen-minute truce that had been agreed
upon. Mr. Still said, however, that only seven or eight minutes had
elapsed.

As the police came out the second time, the group of marchers broke
up and scattered in all directions. Inspector Melchior said the policemen ignored the older people, who were mainly residents of the Hayes
area, but sought to disperse the younger people. He added:

Groups of young teenagers would keep reforming and would throw missiles sporadically. Almost during the entire course of the rest of the evening
there were missiles being thrown in and toward the buildings or toward any
groups of officers.

At approximately 12:20 A.M. on Thursday, Deputy Chief Redden arrived at the precinct, as did additional patrolmen, bringing the total manpower to about fifty. Mr. Redden divided the men into four squads, putting a superior officer in charge of each. He was about to send them outside when Director Spina entered through the rear door of the precinct and countermanded the order. About fifteen minutes later, Mr. Spina ordered the men outside.

The police, equipped with helmets and nightsticks, patroled the Hayes area in groups. Inspector Melchior said that they were continually harassed by missiles, which "seemed to be thrown by young teenagers who would rapidly form a group, approach, throw two or three objects, and run at the approach of a police officer."

The dispersal of the marchers and of the crowd around the precinct, however, did not end the events of the evening. The next phase was looting.

Mr. Curvin testified that looting began "immediately after the crowd dispersed." Mr. Still reported watching the looting of a liquor store. "Originally only the most aggressive, the boldest of guys would go in," he said, but soon others joined them. He added:

The radio cars were going back and forth and they saw them in there. They saw them in there getting the whisky. They just kept going. They didn't try to stop. As a result of that, all the people saw that the cops didn't care, so they went in, too.

Mr. Still added:

I think if the cops had moved in and did something they may have been stoned but I think this would have been the proper thing to do. A lot of stuff could have been avoided at this point.

Meanwhile, a caravan of perhaps twenty-five taxis traveled from the Fourth Precinct to City Hall. There, they parked and double parked the length of the block. Deputy Chief Redden followed them from the precinct and met with the drivers at City Hall, where he told them it was a bad time to protest since city officials were not present.

As to the police action, Deputy Chief Redden said:

I established heavy motor patrols on Broad Street. I left a couple of plainclothes teams, one north and one south of the City Hall, to report to me what was going on and all the extra policemen I had I sent over to the First Precinct and held in reserve to see what would develop. Fortunately the people drifted off or went to their homes.

Word of the disturbance spread rapidly. Donald Malafronte, administrative assistant to Mayor Addonizio, had just returned from vacation on July 12 when, at 2 A.M. Thursday, he received a telephone call from a newsman who said, "I understand Newark is in flames. What can you tell me about that?" Mr. Malafronte looked out his window and saw nothing amiss, and promised to call the reporter back. He then called Deputy Mayor Paul Reilly, who also was unaware of trouble. About thirty minutes later, however, Mr. Reilly called back with a report of what had happened at the Fourth Precinct.

By 4 A.M. Newark's streets were quiet. The police report showed that damage to the Fourth Precinct was estimated at $2,500 for the destruction of 102 windows, screens, and doors and for miscellaneous damage. Seven men had been arrested for idling and malicious damage, five for looting, one for loud and abusive language, nine for possession of stolen property, and three for breaking and entering—a total of twenty-five arrests.

Following the night's events, Deputy Chief Redden testified, he gave special orders:

About 5 o'clock in the morning I decided that everybody in my command was going on twelve-hour tours of duty. I had been told up at the Fourth Precinct by a police officer that Curvin had promised to be back in front of the Fourth Precinct the next night, that is the night of the 13th, to organize a demonstration. I just felt from the tone of what happened, what had gone on all summer at the meetings of the Board of Education and the Planning Board, the incident at the East Orange line, I was almost certain there was going to be a large-scale disturbance the evening of the 13th.

Mr. Wendell reported talking to Director Spina on the steps of the Fourth Precinct at about the same time. He quoted Mr. Spina as saying:

The situation is normal. Put the windows in early in the morning; get the place cleaned up. Just return it to normal and don't treat it as a situation, because once you begin to look at problems as problems they become problems.

THURSDAY

The city administration attempted to project an image of a return to normal when the new day dawned.

No crowds were moving about; merchants opened for business; windows were being repaired. Mr. Malafronte called the events of Wednesday night "the most serious incident Newark ever had," but of Thursday he said, "Well, of course, it was a tense day, but the tensest people around were the newspapermen and television men." City Hall tried to look upon the previous night's events at the Fourth Precinct as "isolated" incidents and hoped nothing more serious would erupt.

Mr. Curvin disagreed:

To say it was an isolated incident I think was the most tragic mistake that was made following Wednesday night. In fact, one of the reasons that I felt just so terribly frustrated on Thursday afternoon when I went to that meeting was to hear the mayor speak as though it was all over. . . .

Mr. Curvin was referring to one of two meetings that were held in the mayor's office on Thursday afternoon. The first was a previously scheduled meeting of a summer task force selected by James Threatt. The group was to discuss summer jobs for young people. The meeting was "long" and "inconclusive."

At the second meeting, those who met with the mayor were Duke Moore, a board member of the UCC, Mr. Curvin; Earl Harris, a former Republican Freeholder; Harry Wheeler, a Newark teacher; and State Assemblyman George Richardson.

Mr. Malafronte testified that the group made three demands on the mayor:

. . . that the two patrolmen involved in the arrest of cab driver Smith be suspended; that a blue ribbon panel of some sort investigate the Wednesday disorder at the Fourth Precinct outside of the normal investigations procedures; and, third, that a Negro police lieutenant who was fifth on the Civil Service list be promoted to captain as quickly as possible.

According to Mr. Harris, the mayor wanted forty-eight hours to consider these requests.

Mr. Malafronte said the administration accepted these demands: that the policemen were not suspended, but were instead transferred to administrative duties—a normal procedure since 1965 for men against whom complaints had been lodged; that five lieutenants were promoted, including the Negro who ranked fifth on the civil service list; and that the mayor agreed to appoint a panel to conduct an investigation.

Director Spina testified that he met with Mr. Richardson, Mr. Wheeler, and other civil rights leaders Thursday morning in an effort to map a campaign for easing tensions. The police director said the mayor had tried to do the same thing, but "didn't get the kind of people that could reach into the city."

In the late afternoon of Thursday, city officials learned that leaflets were being distributed around the Fourth Precinct. The leaflets said in handblocked letters:

STOP! POLICE BRUTALITY
Come out and join
us at the mass rally

TONIGHT, 7:30 P.M. fourth precinct

City officials believe that the UCC's Area Board 2 had authorized production of the leaflets and, with Newark Community Union Project (NCUP) officials, were responsible for the distribution. The city's first reaction to the leaflet was "shock, fear, and concern."

In response to the leaflets, Mr. Threatt was asked to attend the rally to "monitor it" and to convey to those present the outcome of the meetings in the mayor's office.

At about 4:45 P.M., Director Spina ordered 500 policemen to be available. In addition, provisions were made for emergency recall of off-duty men, for extension of tours of duty, and for detectives to be in uniform during that night.

After coming on duty at 5 P.M., Inspector Melchior attended a briefing by Deputy Chief Redden. Inspector Melchior said:

We were told at that time not to irritate the people; we don't want to inflame them; a minimum of police officers on the scene; they were not to wear helmets and not to carry night sticks. At this time we didn't want to arouse or inflame anybody. The demonstration could be kept peaceful, and not to take any action unless it was absolutely necessary.

At approximately 4:30 P.M., Director Spina said, a television camera crew arrived at 17th and Belmont Avenues, and "immediately this attracted a crowd." Within an hour, he said, there were five more television crews in the area. Mr. Spina estimated that by then a crowd had congregated around the TV cameras. He said of the television reporters: "I blame them a great deal for some of the things that happened."

Subsequently, this crowd dispersed on its own. Inspector Melchior reported that when he approached the Fourth Precinct at 6:45 P.M., there were no crowds and no representatives of the news media, only a group of about ten persons who had formed a picket line in front of the building. The line gradually grew larger. Among those picketing were Jesse Allen, Derek Winans, James Kennedy of Area Board 2, and Melvin Higgins of NCUP and Area Board 3.

By 7:30 P.M., Inspector Melchior estimated, 300 people stood across the street from the precinct, watching the growing picket line. While policemen entered and left the precinct on regular business, there were no police stationed outside the building.

Mr. Threatt arrived between 7 and 7:30 P.M. to announce to the crowd that a Negro police officer was being promoted to captain. Shortly after Mr. Threatt had spoken, at about 8 o'clock a heavy barrage of rocks, stones, bottles, and pieces of wood and metal hit the front of the precinct, breaking several windows. The missiles were not thrown by the picketers, but by the people in the crowd across the street from the precinct, and the picketers fled to escape the barrage. A film shows a woman with a long pole breaking windows in the basement of the precinct.

Inspector Melchior talked to Deputy Chief Redden and received permission to send his men out, equipped with helmets and night sticks. Thus, after the barrage had gone on for about fifteen minutes, sixteen to twenty policemen went out through the back door of the precinct, another twenty-four to thirty through the front entrance. This caused the crowd to flee.

Inspector Melchior testified:

> Again, as the night before, these missiles came from all directions. During the rest of the course of the night, until the action left the Fourth Precinct area, groups of thirty to fifty young teenagers would approach in almost military formation, unleash a barrage of missiles and disperse at the approach of police officers.

Sometime before 9 o'clock, Mayor Addonizio and Mr. Malafronte arrived at police headquarters. At about the same time, Deputy Chief Redden went to the Fourth Precinct, followed shortly by Director Spina.

Mr. Spina and Mr. Redden ordered the policemen who were still outside back into the Fourth Precinct. The precinct then received a radio report that a tavern window had been broken at 17th and Belmont Avenues. A patrol car en route to the site was told to disregard the incident, according to Inspector Melchior, since "sending a car in there unprotected might lead to difficulties."

Between 8:30 and 9 o'clock, the policemen at the precinct were sent out, one squad at a time, and directed to specific areas to disperse the crowds. Reserves were arriving; as more men arrived, they were put under the command of superiors as rapidly as possible and sent out in groups to patrol the area. The police sought to establish a "secure working area" around the precinct. Men were also ordered onto the roofs of buildings to secure these areas and to observe the crowds.

Inspector Melchior said:

As the perimeter of the building began to quiet down and we had the men more established, and the reports were getting worse about Springfield Avenue, I began to send vehicles available with men, four or five in a car, out to the Springfield Avenue area. Gradually, the groups of missile throwers left the vicinity of the Fourth Precinct, and we returned to relative quiet.

Thus, while the Fourth Precinct area had become relatively peaceful by midnight, the disorders spread to other areas.

Looting and vandalism along Springfield Avenue became intense after 9 o'clock. At first, the police pursued a policy of containment, "chasing and keeping the crowds from becoming very large." The first "area of containment" was from Springfield Avenue to High Street and South 10th. It was extended to Central Avenue and Elizabeth and Clinton Avenues.

About midnight, there was a short period of relative quiet. Mayor Addonizio said of this period: "We felt the situation was pretty well in hand." Director Spina said that by 12:30 A.M. on Friday "it appeared to me . . . that perhaps we had won and that the violence was all over."

Shortly after 12:30 A.M. there was a sudden sharp increase of incidents outside the containment area, far out in the South Ward on Elizabeth Avenue, in the East and North Wards. There was also a good deal of activity in the lower West Side. At this time, a Sears, Roebuck store was broken into and twenty-four rifles taken.

Up to the midnight lull, the only word of shooting was an unsubstantiated report that a shot or two had been fired. Immediately after the lull, however, the firing phase began with "sporadic shooting."

The State Police log contains the following entry for the period just after midnight:

Presently, bands of eight to fifteen people traveling on foot and in cars, looting and starting fires. Four policemen injured, four new areas have broken out in the past fifteen minutes. There is still no organization within the Newark Police Department. All available transportation in use. The Fourth Precinct appears to be running its own show. There are no barricades. No requests for State Police assistance from Director Spina.

Both Inspector Melchior and Deputy Chief Redden made tours of affected areas after midnight. The inspector testified that stores on Spruce Street, near the Fourth Precinct, were completely looted. Deputy Chief Redden said he found people had broken into stores and were "in there literally shopping." He found that on Clinton Avenue, from Jelliff Avenue to Osborne Terrace—some seven blocks "there was just no effective control whatsoever. Businesses were being ransacked."

At 2:20 A.M. Friday, Mayor Addonizio called Governor Hughes to request State Police and National Guard assistance.

There were several premature and unofficial calls for aid. At 10:10 P.M. Thursday, Inspector Donnelly of the Newark police called Trenton and requested State Police assistance. He was advised to notify the mayor to contact the governor. Governor Hughes said he had received one or two calls for help from Newark policemen who were "not in authority."

Thus, when Mayor Addonizio's request for assistance to the governor was made early Friday, the State Police and National Guard commands were prepared and ready to implement their plans. At 2:30 A.M. Newark officials announced to their local police over the police radio that help was on the way.

FRIDAY

When Governor Hughes received Mayor Addonizio's call for assistance, he acted immediately. His first call was to Attorney General Arthur J. Sills. State Police records indicate that their forces were activated at 2:39 A.M. on Friday, July 14. The governor personally ordered the National Guard into action at 2:45 A.M. The governor then contacted several members of his staff and prepared to proceed to Newark.

At the very moment when State Police forces were activated, Major Olaff called Newark to discuss plans with Director Spina. He advised Mr. Spina that State and Newark police officials should meet at the Roseville Armory and that the State Police would be responsible for the "troubled area." At State Police headquarters, previously prepared teletype messages were sent out to all troops.

While these orders were going out, Colonel Kelly proceeded to Newark. He arrived at about 3 A.M. and immediately went to City Hall to meet with Mayor Addonizio. Colonel Kelly testified:

I asked him (Mayor Addonizio) what the situation was. He said, "It is all gone, the whole town is gone." I asked him where the problem was. He said, "It is all over." I asked him if he had any idea of the instigators or troublemakers or what we should look for. He didn't know.

Colonel Kelly then went to the Roseville Armory. Within the hour, other officials began to arrive. General Cantwell came in at 4:35 A.M. Governor Hughes testified that he arrived in Newark about 4:30 A.M. and went directly to the armory. Next, Mayor Addonizio and members of his staff arrived, and shortly thereafter Director Spina came to the armory.

The "planning stage" in the armory lasted from 4:30 until 9:15 A.M. Shortly before 5 o'clock, Governor Hughes, Colonel Kelly, Mayor Addonizio, Director Spina, Deputy Chief Redden, and other officials met to determine how the various law enforcement agencies were going to operate. At this meeting, it was agreed, but with some reservation by General Cantwell, that Colonel Kelly would be the commanding officer over both the State Police and the National Guard, and that Mr. Spina would be in charge of the local police. Mr. Sills testified that "almost all police action was left in the hands of Dave Kelly and almost all policy matters gravitated toward the governor." General Cantwell testified that State Police–National Guard actions were a "joint operation" and that Colonel Kelly was not in command of the National Guard. However, the general added, "if it came to a difference of opinion or a showdown, we would comply with the request of the State Police."

Newark officials were critical of command operations and command structure. Director Spina testified that in his view conferences between General Cantwell and Colonel Kelly took too long and delayed decisions. This, he said, "is not good operations." Mayor Addonizio felt that, "during the whole course of this thing I was sort of left out of a lot of things that were going on, and this is my city and I have to stay here after all the people pull out." The governor observed, however, that Mayor Addonizio "almost completely withdrew from any sharing of the direction of this situation."

As joint operations of the three law-enforcement elements got under way, the communications problems between state and local police manifested themselves and limited their effectiveness. The State Police, the National Guard, and the Newark Police Department operated on different frequencies, and neither city nor state units were equipped to send or receive messages on the frequency assigned to the other. In this period, the Newark police liaison officer stationed at the armory, who had a line to Newark Police Headquarters, was the only source of information about the operations of the local police. Routine matters were not reported. Colonel Kelly testified that the State Police did not get information on the movement of Newark police patrols, or on looting incidents known to the Newark police. Nor did the State Police at that time have knowledge of citizens' calls or complaints since Newark residents placed calls for help with the Newark Police or Fire Departments. The Newark police or firemen responded to these calls, and the State Police were relegated to following the Newark patrols or fire trucks. Colonel Kelly testified: "What we would have to do is follow them and just observe or stand outside just to protect them."

Another problem for the State Police was its inability during this early phase of its involvement to obtain a clear definition of the riot perimeter, or even a statement of where activity was heaviest. The Newark police could not supply maps of the city. Eventually, Colonel Kelly found some maps and learned from the Newark police that Springfield Avenue was the major problem area. By "trial and error," the State police mapped out the riot area, and then drew up a patrol sector plan, coordinating with Inspector Daniel Dughi of the Newark Police Department. The plan divided Newark first into six, then into eight, and finally into twelve sectors. Patrols were assigned on the basis of the size of an area, the incidence of gunfire and other relevant factors.

The National Guard also had problems in coordinating with the Newark police. The National Guard Report on the Newark disorders notes that

the execution of plans was delayed by a reluctance of local authority to recognize the full extent of the difficulty until damage had been done over a wide area and the difficulty encountered in getting intelligence quickly from local authorities already heavily committed. Future planning must emphasize the necessity for local authorities providing supporting forces with prompt intelligence.

Between 8 and 9:30 A.M., top officials toured the riot area. The group was headed by the governor and included Mayor Addonizio, General Cantwell, Colonel Kelly, and Director Spina. They observed the police in action and the arrest of forty to fifty persons. At 9 o'clock, the governor ordered the closing of all stores selling weapons.

Acting on the advice of Attorney General Sills, Governor Hughes issued an emergency proclamation under the National Defense Act of

New Jersey. The proclamation was drafted on Friday morning and went into effect at once. It was broadcast over the police and Guard networks at 10:15 A.M. and formally filed with the Secretary of State at 9:34 A.M.

By Friday, the State Police committed almost half its entire force—about 600 men—and the Guard 3,464 men. The Guard reached a total of 5,367 men by Monday.

As looting subsided, weapons fire grew more intense and became a serious problem. Before Friday, only one sniping incident had been reported. However, during Friday reports of sniping began flooding headquarters. Half of the twenty-three deaths from gunshot wounds that occurred throughout the riot period came between midnight Thursday and midnight Friday.

Law enforcement agencies report that the highest number of shooting incidents occurred on Friday. Most of the firing took place on Springfield Avenue, but some incidents occurred in other areas, such as Clinton and Central Avenues; and at the intersections of Sussex Avenue and Jay Street; Oriental and Broadway; and Orange and Norfolk. . . .

On Friday, and possibly as late as Saturday, the communications problem resulting from the use of different radio frequencies by different police elements was relieved. State Police radiomen at a central relay point in the city were able to receive transmissions from Newark police radio system and to relay them over the State Police network. In addition, the Newark police, the State Police and the National Guard stationed operators side by side at the armory. These men relayed communications from one system to the other.

By Friday afternoon, Colonel Kelly felt that most of the looting activity had been brought under control and that the crowds had been contained. It was on that day that most of the arrests during the entire riot period were made—906 out of a total of 1,465, or 63 percent. On Thursday night, only 34 persons were arrested, and after Friday the arrest totals trailed off steadily—to 238 on Saturday, 120 on Sunday, 70 on Monday, and into the 20's or fewer on succeeding days.

The commission heard testimony from witnesses who charged that police used excessive force, without provocation, against members of the Negro community who were innocent of any wrongdoing. Testimony described incidents in which people were fired at, beaten with weapons, kicked or otherwise physically mistreated, and subjected to verbal abuse.

Albert Black, chairman of the Newark Human Rights Commission, testified that on Thursday evening, July 13, he observed policemen at the Fourth Precinct handling prisoners roughly and using obscene language. He testified:

Now Director Spina was at the desk of the precinct and these men were being brought in, many of them handcuffed behind their backs being carried like a sack of meal, and the fifth policeman would be hammering their face and body with a billy stick. This went on time after time. Many times you would see a man being brought into the police station without a mark on his face and when he was taken out, he was brutally beaten up.

Janie Carter testified that on the same day, she was standing on a street corner when some policemen who had been driving up Springfield Avenue got out of their cars. She said:

They didn't say a thing. They just started beating people with the sticks and some had guns and they were shooting in other directions from where I was. So I started to run across the street, but when I looked back, one grabbed Mrs. Jiminez from the back of her head, pushed her down and started beating her, and the others were beating her.

The Reverend Herbert G. Draesel, an Episcopal priest, testified that on Friday evening, July 14, he was standing on a corner when several police cars drove down the street, stopped in front of the Colonnade Bar, and began firing into the bar for no apparent reason. Suddenly, Father Draesel said, the policemen changed their firing from the bar to the group standing on the corner. The witness was not sure whether the police who fired were Newark police or State Police. Two men were wounded in this encounter. Father Draesel testified further that later that evening Building 82 of the Christopher Columbus Homes was sprayed with bullets for about one-half hour.

John A. Thomas, a former teacher and presently a Title I project coordinator in Newark, testified that he was driving in an automobile on Bergen Street. He was stopped at the intersection of Custer Avenue by several state troopers who dragged him out of his car. His car was searched and he was knocked to the ground by the butt of a carbine or rifle, beaten, and subjected to extreme verbal abuse as to his race.

Oliver Bartlett, program director for the James Weldon Johnson Community Center in New York City, testified that on Thursday evening, July 13, while standing on a corner, Newark policemen and state troopers with guns pushed his wife down on the ground. Mr. Bartlett testified:

Everybody there were people who owned homes and had some sort of responsibility to the law. It seemed this didn't work. They kept on pushing and acting like we were dogs. We had no kind of respect. They can't say, "Please move."

Mr. Bartlett testified further that when he took his cousin to the train station, National Guardsmen stopped, searched, and harassed him. White people, Mr. Bartlett testified, were not stopped or searched.

Carol Bartlett, the wife of Oliver Bartlett, corroborated her husband's account of the incident and described in detail how a policeman pushed her in the back with a rifle.

The Reverend Dennis A. Westbrooks, a Newark clergyman, testified that on Friday evening a group of policemen at a blockade assaulted him with clubs, seeking to prevent him from walking home and pushing him in the opposite direction.

The minister also testified that early Saturday morning he was at City Hospital when a group of policemen pushed, shoved, and cursed him for refusing to leave.

The minister testified that the police refused to believe that he was a clergyman and

that leads me to believe all the more that I think it was simply a matter of color, because he wouldn't believe who I was. I told him it made no difference. There wasn't anything I could do.

Although the extent of the excesses cannot be determined by this commission, they have left a legacy of bitterness, disenchantment, and frustration within the Negro community; and they have demonstrated a lack of respect for the rights of Negro citizens, regardless of whether they were involved in unlawful activity.

SATURDAY—SUNDAY

On Saturday, July 15, the riot area was sealed off. The perimeter that had been established by State Police and National Guard forces ringed an area of fourteen square miles, which was completely controlled by the police. Patrols spent most of the day clearing roof tops of debris to prevent it from being showered on passing troopers. During the day, Colonel Kelly said, ". . . our patrols ran into a kind of resistance, a kind of resentment."

Although shooting had diminished after Friday night, six private citizens and Fire Captain Michael Moran were shot and killed on Saturday. Another uniformed officer, Detective Fred Toto, had been shot and killed on Friday.

A group of Negro volunteers received permission from Mayor Addonizio and Governor Hughes to move among the people in an effort to calm the atmosphere. When they arrived, however, they were hampered by the patrols. Governor Hughes told the commission:

It was reported to me that they went out on the streets on Saturday and got into so much trouble and were chased around so much by people who suspected them as participating in the riot that they had to abandon their efforts. . . .

When night fell, Colonel Kelly said, burning, looting, and sniping again erupted. The major problem during the night was gunfire. This shooting was occurring in new areas, west of South Orange Avenue, Colonel Kelly said. Captain Moran was killed while answering an alarm. Saturday night appeared to Colonel Kelly much like the night before.

In the eyes of the Negro community, however, the character of violence Saturday night was changing.

The commission received many allegations from different sources to the effect that police and National Guard forces shot into Negro businesses, and that much damage was wrought. These stores, even including some not owned by Negroes, had been marked with "Soul" signs to spare them from attack or looting by rioters.

The commission heard from a number of witnesses who provided detailed evidence on that night's occurrences. A summary of this sworn testimony follows.

Testimony by Mrs. Enez King / Mrs. Enez King and her husband live behind their dry cleaning shop on Avon Avenue. At 3 or 3:30 A.M. on Sunday, the sound of breaking glass awakened them. From their darkened room, they could see state troopers come into the store, where there was some light. Mrs. King said:

When we heard the glass break, we got up to look out the window. They took the clothes with the butts of their guns, knocked them off the rack and just went around knocking things around. . . . By accident they hit it (the cash register). They opened it. One came over and took the money, and then they looked around and [they] were saying, "There is nothing else left here, let's go."

The Kings then took their daughter up the back stairs to their third-floor apartment and looked out the windows from there. Mrs. King said they then observed the troopers:

They got in the middle of the street Avon Avenue, and they shot back into the store, plus they were shooting up. There was a candy store there and also a lounge across the street from in front of us. They started open firing, shooting up the places that was around.

Mrs. King said the police cars were numbered 530, 535, and 491.

State Police Major Victor E. Galassi testified before the commission that the State Police records show that these cars were in Newark at the time of the riots.

Testimony by Nancy Ferguson / At about 2 or 3 A.M. Sunday, Nancy Ferguson, who owns a furniture and appliance store on Bergen Street, went out to see whence shots were being fired. She saw a police car and a foot patrolman a few blocks away. Then, she said, three policemen, not wearing Newark uniforms, approached and ordered her to return to her store. Mrs. Ferguson testified:

One of them finally said, "Step aside" and I said, "I'm not going anywhere" and they said, "We will kill you." I said, "Well, I am here to die." They walked toward the corner of the store because my door is like a post, and they started shooting. They shot through the windows. The bullets pierced the furniture and went into the walls.

Mrs. Ferguson said that one of the policemen dropped a clip of bullets, which Mrs. Ferguson produced for the commission and a photograph of which was introduced in evidence. It was M-1 ammunition.

Testimony by Alfred Henderson / At midnight Saturday, Alfred Henderson, who owns a photography studio on Clinton Avenue and who also lives at this address, heard shooting. After one or two hours, he said the shooting sounded closer. From a second-floor window he saw a black unmarked car, a State Police car, and two National Guard trucks drive slowly up the street. A man in shirtsleeves in the unmarked car fired a weapon toward his studio on the floor below. The next morning, Mr. Henderson said, he found that the plate glass had been broken. He had written "Soul Brother" on the front of the studio.

Testimony by Bow Woo Wong / Between 1 and 2 o'clock Sunday morning, while watching television in his home above his laundry on South Orange Avenue, Bow Woo Wong heard the sound of a jeep and shots. After waiting 15 or 20 minutes, he said, he went down and saw bullet holes in his window. Later he heard shots again. He looked out and saw a man with a rifle standing near a jeep. In the morning he counted three bullet holes. Somebody—not Mr. Wong—had written "Soul Brother" on the outside of his laundry.

Testimony by Bertha L. Dixon / Mrs. Bertha L. Dixon owns a luncheonette on South Orange Avenue and lives in an apartment above it. She testified about events after midnight Saturday, July 15:

I heard this shot, zing, went through the building and that woke me up. . . . It was in the middle of the night some time. . . . Then I heard the rest of the shots. . . . Some people across the street kept hollering and telling me, "Your burglar alarm went off." . . . There was shots across the window, across the door, all on the inside of the building.

I locked the place up and I walked outside and stood there for a minute. In the meantime, two carloads of state troopers pulled up. They said, "What are you doing out here?" I said, "I came out here to cut my burglar alarm off. You all shot up my place." All of them said to me, "We will shoot you if you don't get back upstairs." One of them spoke that. It was two carloads. I turned and looked and went upstairs.

Eight other witnesses who were not present in or near their business establishments when damage was done late at night also testified. Some were called by people in the neighborhood where the stores were located. Others found the damage when they returned to do business. These witnesses were:

Pedro Felix, owner of a luncheonette on South Orange Avenue
Eddie Hardy, owner of a ladies' wear shop on Clinton Avenue
Herman W. Jackson, owner of a barbershop on South Orange Avenue
Willie J. Odom, owner of a card and gift shop on Bergen Street
Laura Peters, owner of a tailor shop on Bergen Street
Robert H. Pitts, owner of a pet shop on Bergen Street
Elmo J. Sessoms, owner of an appliance service on Springfield Avenue
Courtney A. Weekes, Jr., owner of a cleaning store on Springfield Avenue

Mrs. Ferguson's store is located near Mr. Pitts' pet shop. She testified that she saw Mr. Pitts' store shot up by the same policemen who shot up her store. Joseph E. Hayden, Jr., a resident of Bergen Street, said he observed shooting by uniformed personnel riding in a car with three large numbers on top under his apartment. Mr. Hayden lives above Mrs. Peters' store.

Except for Mr. Jackson and Mr. Sessoms, all these witnesses testified that the shooting into their stores had occurred in the night from Saturday, July 15, to Sunday, July 16. Mr. Jackson said the damage to his store was done between Friday evening, July 15, and Saturday morning, and Mr. Sessoms, who testified that he was not working in his store on Sunday, said he found the damage when he returned on Monday morning, July 17.

Dickinson R. Debevoise, president of the board of trustees of the Newark Legal Services Project, testified that this agency received 250 complaints of alleged abuse and misuse of force by law-enforcement officers, including eighty-four of store shootings. These complaints were received in evidence as a commission exhibit.

Official Responses / The commission was aware that the governor had instructed the State Police and National Guard on Sunday, July 16, to investigate these allegations of destruction of property. The commission then requested these agencies and the Newark police to testify regarding their investigations. The National Guard, the State Police, and the Newark Police Department all indicated a willingness to receive complaints and to process them according to their respective investigative procedures.

Major Galassi, who heads the Criminal Investigation Section of the State Police and who was responsible for investigating allegations of State Police misconduct, explained that the size of the area, the number of policemen involved, the use of unmarked cars, and other factors hampered efforts at investigation. He said: "Great difficulty was encountered in unearthing many of the essential elements of these allegations." In the early stages of the operation, he pointed out, the State Police command attempted to maintain the integrity of the various troops by assigning them to certain sectors of the city, but as the intensity of the disorders increased, it became impossible to keep the various troops separated.

Major Galassi said:

Men, vehicles, and patrols were continually changed and interchanged to meet sporadic emergencies in every section of the riot-torn area. Because of these factors, the accurate identification of specific times, dates, places, individuals, and incidents was either difficult or impossible to ascertain.

The major also testified that, as of the date of his testimony, December 7, thirty-three allegations of abuse of authority by law-enforcement personnel were reported to the State Police. These included twenty-five reports of breaking of windows and damage to property. He said each charge of State Police abuse had been investigated as thoroughly as possible and a report forwarded to the Attorney General and the Superintendent of the State Police. Some charges, he said, did not involve the State Police. He said many complaints did not withstand scrutiny because of conflicts among supporting witnesses.

Major Galassi said that the Attorney General and the State Police Superintendent had decided that each report of an investigation was to be submitted to the prosecutor. The witness added that, as of the date of his testimony, no recommendations had as yet been made as to possible disciplinary action, and that the investigations were continuing.

Major Galassi testified that three days prior to his appearance before the commission—on December 4—the State Police had received a group of complaints from the Newark Legal Services Project, but since these had just come into his office's possession, they did not figure in his testimony.

On behalf of the National Guard, Colonel Charles A. McLean testified that the total of complaints of misconduct against National Guard personnel brought to his attention was six. Colonel McLean, who was assigned to the investigation of such charges, said his inquiry showed involvement of National Guard forces in only one complaint, and in that case the return of fire was in the normal course of duty. He said all information on these matters had been turned over to the Essex County Prosecutor or the Attorney General. He said he knew of no general investigation by the National Guard.

Speaking on the same subject for the Newark Police Department, Inspector Thomas M. Henry testified that five complaints had come to his attention—two from the Newark Legal Services Project and three directly. Inspector Henry said one complaint had little foundation, that two complainants were satisfied with explanations provided by the police, and that two were still pending at the time of his testimony before the commission.

All the agencies have operated on the basis of complaints received.

The commission is also not aware of any general grand jury investigation—county, state, or federal—into these allegations.

FINAL STAGES

With the coming of daybreak on Sunday, tensions seemed to ease in Newark. Colonel Kelly said: "Sunday, it seemed to taper off."

Governor Hughes testified that the efforts at pacification "were renewed early Sunday morning and were successful at that time." From then until midweek, violence steadily diminished.

Food was becoming a major problem, since many people in the Negro community go shopping "only for a day in advance, don't have freezers and forward buying that more prosperous people have, and yet they were afraid to go on the streets because they might be killed or hurt."

Sunday morning, Colonel Kelly and Stanley Van Ness, the Governor's Counsel, toured the riot area, looking for grocery stores that might open. When owners were found to be either unable or unwilling to open, Commissioner Paul N. Ylvisaker arranged for delivery of emergency food supplies.

The food was distributed by the National Guard. It was picked up at a variety of points, including the Jersey City waterfront, and taken to City Hospital. Sniper fire was encountered at both the hospital and distribution points, according to General Cantwell.

Sunday turned into a day of discussions and meetings, both formal and informal. Governor Hughes said: "I had constant meetings with members of the Negro community and people whom I regarded as leaders."

As Sunday night fell, the city was quieter than it had been since Wednesday, when the Smith incident sparked the disorders. During the day, Governor Hughes had announced he would offer executive clemency to any person accused of nonviolent plundering or looting in return for information leading to the arrest and conviction of a sniper. But, the governor said: "This was completely abortive. No one came forward and no information came in."

Sunday night there were a few incidents of sniping, but fewer than on previous nights. There were two fatal injuries Sunday, including the slaying of James Ruttledge, whose body was riddled with bullets and shotgun pellets.

At the Sunday meetings with state and local officials, Negro leaders had begun calling for the withdrawal of the State Police and the National Guard. Police Director Spina explained:

It was the feeling of the Negro leaders that the augmentation of city police by the State Police and the National Guard created and intensified the unrest.

About midnight Sunday, Attorney General Sills and Major Olaff of the State Police discussed the possibility that continuing a roving patrol within the riot area might be stimulating sniper fire. Mr. Sills said it was the feeling at that time that it might be wise to withdraw the troops to checkpoints and to discontinue roving patrols.

At about 12:30 o'clock Monday morning, Governor Hughes held a meeting with United States Attorney David Satz, Commissioner Paul N. Ylvisaker, Colonel Kelly, Tom Hayden, and Robert Curvin.

The group worked through the night. Governor Hughes testified:

About 6:30 that morning, I decided, with Colonel Kelly and with all the other people that were advising me, we should pull out the National Guard and the State Police except for a skeleton crew to help convey food supplies and to do some little emergency service.

The decision to remove the troops was announced about noon Monday, and by midafternoon the state and Guard forces began to leave Newark.

Director Spina said of the withdrawal:

I have a feeling, too, that when we removed the National Guard from the scene there came a feeling amongst the populace that things were going to be all right again.

✍ 2. REBELLION IN PLAINFIELD
David Boesel / Louis C. Goldberg / Gary T. Marx

Chronology of Events, July 1967 *

Wednesday, July 5: A little over a week before the riot in Plainfield, New Jersey, police were called to a housing project to intervene in a black family's dispute. The officer at the scene had a reputation for toughness and was disliked by ghetto blacks. When the woman in the argument, Mrs. Mary Brown, became obstreperous, the police officer handcuffed her and placed her under arrest. On the way out of the building, she fell down a flight of stairs. The police captain in charge of the department said that she had had alcohol on her breath and had stumbled. Project residents said she had been pushed. After Mrs. Brown's release, her husband took pictures of her injuries.

Monday, July 10: A group including Mrs. Brown and an NAACP leader tried to lodge a formal complaint against the arresting officer with the city clerk, but for administrative reasons the complaint was not accepted. Subsequently a dozen or more youths, ranging in age between sixteen and twenty-four, spread word of the incident throughout the ghetto. At some point near the beginning of the riot, the pictures her husband had taken were circulated around the black community as evidence of police brutality. Some of the youths were particularly incensed, and there was talk of evening the score with the police.

Thursday, July 13: Dramatic accounts of the Newark riot began to appear on television. Racial tensions in Plainfield were noticeably heightened.

Friday, July 14: By the morning of the 14th, rumors of impending riot were circulating. One of the two black councilmen, Harvey Judkins, warned Mayor George Hetfield on Friday morning that an outbreak was likely to occur that evening. The young people were tense and angry not

---

* We wish to thank Elizabeth Jameson for preparing an earlier version of the chronology, the basis of the present one.

6 7

only about the latest charges of police brutality, but about a series of grievances which had been articulated over the past several years.

The spark which touched off the disturbance that evening occurred at about 10:00 P.M. at the White Star Diner, a lunchroom hangout frequented by teen-agers of both races. The police officer accused of misconduct in the Brown case was off-duty serving as a private guard there. A fight broke out between two black youths, one of whom, Glasgow Sherman, was knocked to the pavement, his face bloodied. Other youths present demanded that the officer arrest the aggressor and call an ambulance for Sherman, but he refused to intervene. The youths saw his refusal as reflecting a double standard, thinking that, had the combatants been white, the officer would have acted differently. Sherman was finally taken to the hospital in a police car. After treatment, he asked for a ride back to the diner, but the police refused.

Shortly after the youth had been taken to the hospital, fifty or more young blacks left the diner and began to assemble at a nearby housing project to air their grievances. As the session continued, the number of youths grew to between 100 and 150. Black Councilmen Judkins and Everett Lattimer addressed the assemblage, trying to reduce tensions. But anger in the group increased; forty to fifty youths split off and went to the edge of Plainfield's business section where they broke some windows. Before long they were turned back by police.

At about 12:30 A.M., a young black newspaperman, David Hardy, and the two black councilmen met with the group and discussed their grievances. A meeting with the mayor was scheduled for the following afternoon (Saturday) at the Teen Center. Shortly thereafter police were notified that black youths were making firebombs at a filling station. They dispersed the youths and found about a dozen badly constructed Molotov cocktails.

Saturday, July 15: At 1:30 P.M., Mayor Hetfield met at the police station with Councilmen Lattimer and Judkins and with several other officials, including police. The mayor discounted the grievances that were reported and thought the situation well in hand, though word of the Molotov cocktails disturbed him. In case of trouble, it was decided to minimize arrests in the hopes of reducing tensions.

At the Teen Center meeting, which lasted from 7:00 to 9:30 P.M., Mayor Hetfield, Lattimer and Judkins, David Hardy, and other interested parties met with about 50 to 100 black youths. Complaints about the behavior of police in the ghetto and about recreational facilities, including a long-standing demand for a swimming pool, did not seem to make an impression on the mayor. Ten youths stalked out angrily, and the meeting broke up. Immediately thereafter black youths began breaking store windows in the area. Eight fires were set, but none resulted in the destruction of buildings. By 10 o'clock the police had arrived in numbers; all officers were put on alert and help was requested from departments in nearby towns. Officials decided to contain the disturbance rather than to try arresting and dispersing the youths. The disturbance began to wane, and by 3:00 those still out on the streets were scattered by a rainstorm.

Sunday, July 16: Officials considered the situation under control in the morning; most police officers were sent home. The area was flooded with white sightseers, many of them on their way to or from church. There was some verbal abuse of the whites and later on, after 1:30 P.M., some rock throwing. Around 2:00 the mayor took control of the police department and, anticipating a serious outbreak, called for assistance from the State Police and the National Guard. At a meeting of 200–300 black youths on Plainfield Avenue, one young man, Lenny Cathcart, began to emerge as leader. (In his twenties, Cathcart worked in a local chemical plant, was married and the father of seven children. Formerly a Black Muslim, he had left the organization as his militancy turned more in a political direction.) Since the meeting was growing rapidly and there were some small disturbances around the edges of the gathering, a black member of the Plainfield Human Relations Commission, David Sullivan, persuaded the group to move to Green Brook Park. Local police were notified of the action. At the park the meeting proceeded in an orderly fashion; ten representatives had been chosen and a list of grievances to be presented to officials was being drawn up. Then the chief of the Union County Park Police, which had jurisdiction over the park, arrived to tell the group that the meeting could not be held since no permit had been issued. After Cathcart and Sullivan had made futile attempts to negotiate with the police, the meeting broke up. The two hundred or so angry youths left in a caravan of cars and returned to the ghetto. Sullivan and Cathcart met with the mayor at the police station and agreed to try to reconvene the meeting, but their efforts were to no avail. By 4:00 young blacks had overturned several cars; windowbreaking and looting were becoming widespread. Some fires were started, but they did not become extensive. At 5:00 all police were called in and neighboring departments were again asked for aid. By 6:00 the riot was beyond the control of authorities. The State Police arrived to help local police seal off the area.

At around 8:00 P.M., one of the officers stationed on the perimeter, John Gleason, saw two white youths being chased toward him by a black youth, Bobby Williams. Gleason went after Williams as the latter retreated into the ghetto. There was a confrontation between the two, the details of which are not clear, but the results are: Gleason shot Williams but did not kill him, and was then pursued by a mob of furious blacks. Caught by the mob, he was knocked down, beaten, and stomped nearly to death. He died in the hospital at 8:45.

One hour later, as fear of retaliatory action by the police grew, forty-six carbines were stolen from a local manufacturer and passed out in the ghetto. Sniping followed, and a fire station in the ghetto was in effect put under siege. Police maintained their cordon around the armed ghetto, but did not attempt to enter the area except for specific purposes. At 12:30 the National Guard arrived and armored personnel carriers were used to relieve the besieged fire station. The violence continued until after 3:00 A.M.

Monday, July 17: The police continued containment and tried to draw sniper fire. New Jersey State officials began to arrive, among them Paul Ylvisaker, Director of the Department of Community Relations, and State Attorney General Arthur Sills. At 2:00 city and state officials met at the police station with adult representatives of the black community; local police, however, were excluded from the meeting. It was agreed that the contending sides must be kept apart: the police would maintain the perimeter and blacks would police their own area. At 4:00 Ylvisaker and Hardy met with about fifty youths in the Teen Center; ten black representatives were selected for a 7:30 meeting with officials. Present at the City Hall meeting were the mayor, Ylvisaker, Sills, and the ten youth representatives. Among the grievances discussed were the swimming pool, housing and rental practices, and police brutality. At 7:45 a black representative walked in and said that blacks wanted something done before dark. It was decided that an attempt should be made to talk to a crowd of 300–400 Negroes assembled at the housing project. Ylvisaker, Sills, the mayor, and Colonel Kelly—the State Police commander—went to the ghetto. The mayor spoke first, from atop a pickup truck, but the crowd was in no mood to listen to him. They were more receptive, however, to Ylvisaker and Sills, who seemed more sensitive to their demands. The meeting ended inconclusively, and officials returned to City Hall at 8:45. A half hour later Cathcart rushed in to say that violence, including the use of grenades, was imminent unless black prisoners arrested in the riot were released by 10:00. State officials took the lead in the discussions that followed. Colonel Kelly opposed releasing any prisoners; Ylvisaker and Sills were for the idea. While all concerned insist that no "deal" was made, it was decided, on the one hand, that twelve prisoners would be released by midnight as a token of good faith and, on the other, that Cathcart would try to recover the carbines by noon Wednesday. The police, who were not present at this meeting, vehemently opposed the arrangement. At 11:00 there was some sniping; Cathcart denied that rioters were responsible. At midnight David Hardy, Cathcart, one of his lieutenants, and an NAACP official went to tell ghetto residents about the impending release of prisoners. Near the housing project two carloads of police stopped and frisked them. No violence resulted, and the area remained quiet except for sporadic gunfire after 1:30 A.M. At 4:00 A.M. a dozen prisoners were released over the objections of police.

Tuesday, July 18: Later in the morning ghetto residents started cleaning the streets. During the day the Department of Community Relations distributed food and milk from stations set up in the riot area.

Wednesday, July 19: About 10:00 A.M. funeral services were held for officer Gleason; police bitterness about the slaying was evident. The deadline for returning the carbines was extended until 2:00 P.M., but as it looked increasingly probable that the guns would not be returned, Governor Hughes, without obtaining warrants, ordered a mass search for the weapons. Late in the morning, to the dismay of the police, the scheduled search was announced over the local radio. Colonel Kelly prepared to lead the search, involving State Police officers, National Guardsmen, and a few Plainfield policemen. As the operation was about to begin at 2:00, Ylvisaker stopped the twenty-eight-vehicle armored search column and ordered the Plainfield policemen out of the search in the name of the governor, an action which further antagonized the already angry police force. As the searchers went through 143 units in the public housing project they broke into some apartments, disordered and damaged personal effects, and left behind hundreds of angry blacks. When the operation ended at 3:35 P.M., only three guns had been confiscated, none of them carbines. At 4:00 P.M. Plainfield police met and threatened to resign unless Ylvisaker left town immediately; he did so.

Thursday, July 20: A cleanup of the riot area, begun earlier, continued. Debris clogged the sewers, causing damage estimated at $750,000 by the mayor. After 5:00 P.M. the National Guard and State Police left.

Friday, July 21: At 8:00 P.M. the curfew was lifted and the perimeter

patrol removed. Two stolen carbines were found in a cemetery. The
area was quiet.

Analysis of Events

BACKGROUND

Plainfield is a well-to-do suburban community of about 50,000 which
until recently had little difficulty functioning as a small, homogeneous
city. Since its white citizens require a few public services, local government has remained small. Organized in such a way as to reinforce the
informal power of an old-line conservative business elite, its mayoral
and council positions are part-time jobs, its public boards have a high
degree of autonomy, and in general it is characterized by a limitation
and decentralization of public powers. Government in Plainfield is a
sort of caretaker operation, concerned more with keeping taxes low
than with providing services.

The dominant image of Plainfield fostered by public officials and
business leaders is that of a harmonious community untrammeled by the
conflicts of larger cities. In the view of local elites, decisions should be
as non-controversial as possible, following precedent closely in order to
avoid the disruption and antagonism that go with public debate. Articulate grievances should, of course, be minimized, and the acknowledge-
ment of social ills should be avoided: Plainfield's requests for anti-pov-
erty money have been kept low, apparently because poverty is
considered out of character.

The tenacity of this pattern of thinking is evident in those respondents who still maintain after the riot that Plainfield doesn't *really* have
a racial problem and in those who even refuse to recognize the riot as
anything more than a minor disturbance. The prevalence of the "outside
agitator" theory among influential citizens and officials, many of whom
admitted that they had little knowledge of the details of the riot, is another indication of the strength of community-harmony assumptions: for
if all is well in Plainfield, the riot must have been caused by outsiders.

Since institutions and power relations in Plainfield have been shaped
by the demands of white suburbanites and business leaders, the city has
no tradition of ethnic and minority-group politics. It was therefore particularly ill-prepared to accommodate a growing lower-class black population.

Fifteen years ago there were only a handful of black people in the city, but more recently immigration has brought the black population up to about 14,000, or 28 percent of the total. The black middle class lives in the older, more stable East End ghetto. The new migrants and the black lower class live in the West End, an area in which the proportion of blacks has risen from 37 percent in 1960 to somewhere between 80 percent and 90 percent in 1967. Influential whites in Plainfield seem not to have grasped the fact that this new black population has changed the character of the city's social and political relations.

NEGRO POLITICS

Given the structure and workings of government in Plainfield, conventional politics has not been very useful to the city's black people. The government is organized to accommodate conservative interests, and as a practical matter blacks have little access to the decision-making processes. For white business and residential interests there seems to be a good deal of informality in the operations of the community power structure. But for blacks, who do not enjoy this sort of access, there are few formal structures for the expression of grievances. Thus the lower-class blacks, who lack the resources to develop private facilities and services, are also those least able to secure public measures to meet their needs.

There are two black members on the eleven-man common council; a third, like the others, a Democrat, had to resign when his company transferred him; and a white woman—Republican—was selected by the council to fill the vacancy. Her appointment became increasingly unpalatable to her West End "constituents" as her votes began to diverge from those of the two black councilmen. They themselves have not been able to accomplish much, both because of the inherently conservative structure of local government, and because they are rather consistently outvoted on racial issues by the white majority.

Among the groups representing black interests in Plainfield, the NAACP has had some success in such matters as appointments to local public agencies, but its effect on substantive policy issues has been minimal. Mayor Hetfield asserted that he could not be influenced by NAACP political demands and never consulted the local leadership when a political decision was to be made. As the mayor saw it, even the NAACP's filing a conventional legal suit on school integration was "causing unrest." In February 1967 the NAACP, out of a sense of frustration, tacked a list of complaints and demands on the door of City

Hall. Six months later, at the time of the riot, the council had not acted on any of them, nor had city officials even acknowledged the list.

The Human Relations Council has had even less influence than the NAACP. As long as the HRC acted merely as a conciliatory agency, public officials regarded its activities as legitimate and worthwhile. But when the council attempted to investigate charges of police misconduct, the mayor and other public officials objected, charging that the HRC had gone beyond its jurisdiction.

The Community Action Program has likewise been a token effort. The mayor has shown a preference for remedial action by private charitable organizations, and hence has kept CAP funding requests nominal. He has drastically circumscribed the role of the agency in the community.

Not only are black people in Plainfield frustrated because they cannot get their substantive demands fulfilled; they are also generally angry at the local government because they cannot get it to work for them. They are even angrier at the police department because they feel that they cannot stop it from working against them.

POLICE

Blacks assert that there are two standards of justice in Plainfield. Police, they charge, are more responsive and responsible to whites than to themselves. They cite the case of a seven-year-old black boy who was virtually abducted from his home by Plainfield police for interrogation in connection with a case of vandalism. At the police station questioning proved futile because the boy became hysterical. When his father returned home, he looked for the boy and learned from neighbors what had happened. Outraged, he went to the police station with members of the Human Relations Council and the NAACP. By that time the boy had been released. According to a member of the HRC, although all parties agreed on the facts of the case, the police went so far as to tell the group that such complaints could only serve to undercut law enforcement.

Racism unquestionably exists in the department. Until 1966, when the chief ordered the practice abandoned, the word "nigger" was commonly used on the police radio. Black people were also incensed at the fact that one officer flew a Confederate flag from the antenna of his car.

More immediately connected with the riot, of course, were the misconduct charges in the case of Mrs. Brown and the White Star Diner incident. Together, these incidents, involving the same officer, served to crystallize and focus the longstanding antipathy of blacks toward the police. The younger blacks especially were vehement in their opposition to police practices.

Nevertheless, antagonism toward the police was by no means indiscriminate. On the one hand, the black community had generated a list of the "ten most wanted" officers—a list that was commonly known and widely subscribed to before the riot. (The officer in the White Star Diner incident was number two.) On the other, a few of the police officers were so well liked by ghetto residents that an effort was made during the riot not to subject them to physical or verbal abuse. Moreover, the black community's assessment of the police seems to have little to do with the race of the officers. There are five Negro policemen on an eighty-one-man force. Of the five, two are on the "ten most wanted" list. And the best-liked officers are white. These variations, however, should not obscure the fact that on the whole the police are heartily disliked.

As in other cities, there are few mechanisms for the redress of grievances against the police. Plainfield has no civilian review board, and complaints are ordinarily handled within the department itself. According to the police chief, a few cases of alleged physical abuse have been forwarded to the prosecutor, but there have never been any convictions. However, Plainfield does have a police board which oversees the operations of the department and serves as a limited check on its power.

One instance in which police behavior was influenced from outside the department occurred in the case involving the use of the word "nigger" over the police radio. Prompted by black complaints, a white councilman, also chairman of the police board, listened in on the radio and found the complaints justified. He then wrote a memorandum for the signature of the chief ordering that the use of such language be stopped.

THE INGREDIENTS OF REVOLT

Considering the size of the city, Plainfield's riot was one of the most severe in the country. The reasons for this are not to be found in the list of "conditions" usually cited to explain riots. Conditions in the West End are no worse than those in other ghettos, and in some ways they are better.

The West End is not as depressing a place as Newark's Central Ward or Cleveland's Hough district. The dwellings are for the most part single-family homes set a reasonable distance apart. Trees line the streets; heavy traffic is the exception rather than the rule. Blacks in the West End are poor, but not desperately so: the median income in 1966 was $4,561 compared with $7,200 for whites. At the same time blacks received an average of 7.9 years of education, while whites received 11.7.

In the short run, "conditions" are stable. The riots are best understood not as a response to conditions per se, but as part of a dynamic process in which blacks contend with the white power holders.

In looking for the most active force among blacks in Plainfield, one immediately recognizes the youth. In the years prior to the riot the city's black youth had shown themselves to be exceptionally articulate, militant, and sophisticated. Race consciousness among them was pronounced. Though not formally organized, they were becoming an increasingly cohesive force through common action, often against white authority.

Moreover, since the West End was a new ghetto, not having had time to develop an infrastructure of institutions, the youth were in effect moving into a power vacuum. There was no political machine there, and one of the areas "representatives" was a white Republican woman. The NAACP and the Human Relations Council were both middle class and ineffectual; the Community Action Program, which might have channeled dissident energies, was deliberately being kept small.

The black youths were, without realizing it, becoming a genuine political force. It is quite possible that a skillful and flexible city administration could have contained that force, but Plainfield did not have such an administration. Indeed, city officials and white elites in general displayed a remarkable obtuseness on racial matters. The mayor, for example, though not ill-willed, never quite seemed to get the point. The constant reiteration of black demands, with increasing emphasis, did not impress him as stemming from real grievances. Instead, he was inclined to dismiss them as "the same old hash." And the mayor's attitudes were not atypical; they accurately reflected those of the city's conservative white elites.

In the years immediately preceding the riot a series of encounters grew out of the conflict between black race-consciousness and an inflexible white socio-political structure. One focus of the contest was the schools. It required strikes and boycotts to integrate the school system, and then black students found themselves segregated on a different basis in the track system. Assigned mostly to the lower track, they bristled at the indignities of the new form of segregation. Black junior high students boycotted the school cafeteria protesting discriminatory practices. In 1966 they carried on a campaign of intimidation against white students in response to unfair treatment of a black student by a white teacher. Four of the blacks active in the campaign had also been instrumental in setting up the cafeteria boycott.

Another focus of antagonism for young blacks was the recreational system. When the post of Commissioner of Recreation was to be filled, a well-qualified black man was passed over in favor of a white man considered unsympathetic to the demands of black youths. Moreover, a popular and competent black recreation worker, who was trying to develop a badly needed program for youths over 14, was unable to get his contract renewed.

One of the most volatile issues leading up to the riot concerned the demand of black youths for a swimming pool. "If it wasn't the pool," said the recreation commissioner, "they'd be complaining about something else." The issue came to a head in the summer of 1966, when the mayor narrowly averted a riot by promising to build a pool. But the following summer, instead of building a pool the city arranged to bus black youngsters out to the county pool—for a fee and only on weekdays.

Finally, the black youths were strongly opposed to an antiloitering amendment under consideration by the common council—the proposal's assumption being, perhaps, that loitering, like poverty, was out of character with a city of Plainfield's reputation. The youths felt threatened by the proposed act, judging that it was directed against them and that it would give the police even more opportunities for harassment.

THE POLITICAL RIOT: REBELLION

The Plainfield riot in its inception, course of development, and consequences reflects a crisis which is as much political as it is racial. The term "rebellion" is perhaps better for descriptive purposes than "riot" for several reasons. There is a well-documented set of political and racial problems in Plainfield to which the use of violence by young blacks was a definite and connected response. There was a deliberate alternation in the response between the use of violence and steps to negotiate with city authorities. There were social developments within the ghetto from the precipitating incident to the terminal action which gave rise to a loosely structured black leadership and to the establishment, partly by default, of physical control of the ghetto itself by armed youths. And there was the emergence of a high degree of racial-communal solidarity which continued after the riot and which provided the base for the development of new, politically conscious organizations. Among the elements at the beginning of the riot were several familiar ones. The incident precipitating the outbreak took place, as often happens, at a youth hangout. It involved a perception by black youths of unfair treatment by a disliked police officer who was believed to have injured a black woman recently. Also, a group of young blacks said to have been ready for action since the time of that alleged beating on July 5 may have played an important role in precipitating the riot, though detailed information is lacking.

Another factor contributing to the Plainfield outbreak was undoubtedly the "spillover effect" from the concurrent Newark riot. Many blacks in the West End ghetto had moved to Plainfield from Newark and retained ties of kinship with black people in the Central Ward. Tension in the ghetto increased visibly after word of the Newark riot got around—so much so that Councilman Judkins warned the mayor Friday morning that violence was expected. The riot in Newark seems to have provided a kind of psychological "cover" which made violent collective action seem more plausible and justifiable to the youths.

One of the most significant aspects of the Plainfield riot was the rapidity with which grievances were voiced once the violence began, indicating that previous discussion on common issues had already politicized the youth. At the spontaneous meeting Friday night a wide range of grievances was aired, among them the war in Vietnam and Muhammed Ali's (Cassius Clay's) fight with the draft; there was even mention of the fact that Lew Ayres, the movie actor and pacifist, was not imprisoned for his conscientious objection to World War II.

The inclination of the youths to meet and talk, rather than immediately blowing up, is a sign of the unusual degree of collective deliberateness and rationality characteristic of this riot. While there was talk, there was little violence, and vice versa. Whether as a result of leadership or spontaneous reaction, the participants, especially the youths, showed a keen appreciation for the use of speech and violence as political alternatives.

The second meeting, on Saturday afternoon at the Teen Center, ended with the walkout of ten to twelve militants, evidently a rejection of the mayor and/or the promises which he made at the time. When the meeting broke up, the youths took their grievances into the streets.

The third meeting, Sunday afternoon at Greenbrook Park, was the crucial turning point in the sequence of events. By this time the assemblage of black youths had begun to take on the rudiments of organization. Lenny Cathcart, emerging in a leadership role, had helped to transfer a prior meeting from the housing project to the park. Nowhere was the political character of the events more evident than at the park. The meeting began in an orderly fashion, the group of two hundred or so sitting on the grass. Ten spokesmen were selected, and in the best democratic tradition they were about to draw up a petition of grievances when the Union County Park Police broke up the assembly. As their efforts at elementary democracy proved futile, the youths again took to the streets, this time setting off the worst night of violence in the riot.

It was on Sunday night that the outbreak clearly became a rebellion. The theft and distribution of the forty-six carbines was an effort to "arm the ghetto" against threatened attack. The youths were in effect staking out and preparing to defend a piece of territory. An alien official presence, the fire station in the West End, came under a sniper siege which had to be lifted by an armored vehicle. Another fire station and the police department came under sniper fire. After an incursion into the ghetto by police and guardsmen in the early hours of Monday morning, a decision was made to pull back to a perimeter to await reinforcement. At this point the ghetto was effectively beyond the control of public authority, and young black leaders were exercising a loose *de facto* control in the West End.

The standoff continued through the daylight hours of Monday, when there were several meetings between the youth, or their representatives, and authorities. That evening the mayor spoke to the crowd from the back of a pickup truck, but he reported that the mood was drunken and ugly; there was no communication.

Finally, on Monday night Cathcart walked into police headquarters with a number of demands. At the urging of Ylvisaker and Sills, the mayor agreed to a truce involving a four-point program:

1. Twelve riot arrestees were to be released as a token of faith.
2. Cathcart was to make an effort to recover the carbines, whose presence in the ghetto was especially disturbing to the state officials.
3. Guardsmen and police were to stay out of the ghetto for thirty-six hours, remaining on the perimeter.
4. Ghetto residents were to patrol their own area.

This agreement, whether implicit or explicit, resulted in no substantive improvement over the preriot situation of blacks; the arrangement was temporary and linked directly to the standoff which had developed Sunday. But as a truce it was extremely valuable, for it permitted both sides to disengage themselves from a battle which neither wanted. Though the evidence indicates that the police would have welcomed the opportunity to avenge the death of their comrade, they were restrained particularly by the New Jersey State officials with the concurrence of the mayor. While it is only speculation, it seems probable that had there not been outside intervention by the state the mayor would not have been able to withstand pressures to give the police a free hand; and the probable result of that would have been a few dead policemen and many dead black people.

PARTICIPATION

The political character of the Plainfield riot is evident not only in the course of events which took place, but also in the patterns of participation. The nucleus of black leadership in the riot seems to have been a small group of militant young blacks. At the Saturday meeting at the Teen Center, ten to twelve militants walked out. On Sunday in Green Brook Park ten youths were selected as representatives. On Monday evening at the Teen Center ten spokesmen were again selected. We do not know for certain that the ten or so youths were the same in each case, but it is a fair guess that there was substantial overlapping.

Surrounding this core of local militants was a circle of some 200 youths who attended the mass meetings and undoubtedly participated in the violence. It seems that the core, with their leader, could influence the actions of the larger group, but to what extent it is difficult to tell.

This nucleus and the surrounding assemblage of 200 may be regarded as the politically conscious protesters or rebels. They would be young and mostly northern-born or reared. As the riot developed, especially on Sunday night, other elements were drawn into the violence from the "edge" of the action. These would be older people on the average, representing a wider age range, less interested in protest and more interested in loot. They would also be more southern than the rebels.

Northern-born blacks were significantly overrepresented among riot arrestees (see Table 2–1). The northern-born arrestees tended to be younger than their southern-born counterparts (twenty-three years median age as opposed to twenty-eight years), and were concentrated in a

Table 2–1 / **Riot Arrestees by Place of Birth**

	Northern Born	Southern Born
Total black population in West End (%)	27	73
Total black arrestees (%)	55	45
Total arrested for possession of stolen property (%)	42	58
Median age of arrestees (years)	23	28

narrower age span (mainly adolescents and young adults). Of those arrested for possession of stolen property, the majority were born in the South. (Their median age was twenty-seven years.)

Protest violence, then, seems to have been more the province of rebellious northern youths, while attempts to steal consumer goods were more the province of a wider range of people, including more older, southern-born adults. Many of those involved in looting were women. The latter did not make the riot; they joined it. They did not give it definition; they took advantage of it.

REFLECTIONS IN THE AFTERMATH

The actions of the major parties to this violent racial contest—the black youths, state and local officials, the police—must be seen primarily as components of a dynamic political process which was going on before the riot began and continued after it ended. During the riot the forms of the conflict changed, escalating to violence, but the substance and structure of the conflict—the clash between a newly conscious and aggressive black community, on the one hand, and an unyielding and uncomprehending white power structure, on the other—remained the same.

In a violent showdown it would have been no contest, since local authorities could call on state and, if necessary, national forces to put down the rebellion. As it happened, the politics of repression was complex, and it stopped far short of the total exercise of force.

The police, of course, resented being "handcuffed" and not being included in the critical decisions, especially those involving the truce. Above all they were bitter about Ylvisaker's role in the process; their cup spilled over when he ordered them out of the search, and by threat of mass resignation they forced him to leave town. There were some suggestions, though not supported by available evidence, that the police viewed Ylvisaker's intervention in the search as a doublecross because they had come to regard the operation as a payoff for frustrations suffered during the riot. In any event police morale suffered grievously from the handling of the riot and its aftermath, a fact which underlines the more general problem of the position of police in our society: what would have been required to keep police morale high?

The search itself, though it occurred well after the major violence, must be seen as an integral part of the repressive process. State and local officials were, of course, anxious to recover the stolen carbines, but the announcement of the operation over the radio practically eliminated any chance of success along those lines. Yet plans for the search were carried out, complete with a column of armored personnel carriers and two of the three official forces, the National Guard and the State Police. (Had Ylvisaker not intervened "in the name of the governor"— a claim which the governor never substantiated—the police would have participated too, rounding out the picture.) The search focused on the housing project, a center of riot activity, and was abandoned after an hour and a half. In short, the search was to a considerable extent a show of force for the rebellious—something that had not been considered feasible a few days earlier.

The rebellious, for their part, were not easily intimidated, for the riot had engendered a considerable amount of communal solidarity in the West End. A few months later Cathcart observed:

> You see how things are changing? It used to be that one black man couldn't stand to see another black man do something. We were all jealous of one another and each one tried to pull the other down. . . . But since the riots, we're not niggers any more. We're black men, and most of the people in the community have learned this.

At the time this growing solidarity expressed itself in black efforts to patrol the ghetto and in a cleanup campaign which was large enough to cause extensive damage to the sewers. After the riot it was evident in a quick and decisive black campaign to defeat the antiloitering amendment. The day after the search angry blacks packed Common Council chambers to protest the amendment. The council had not intended to take up the issue, and word had it that most of the council members would vote for the amendment when the time came. But the inundation of the meeting by black people only a few days after the riot caused councilmen not only to take up the issue, but to defeat the amendment by a substantial majority.

A self-conscious political movement was clearly developing in the Plainfield ghetto, and the solidarity was primarily racial, cutting across class lines. The militants supported three blacks for city council, including the two black incumbents. There was also a good deal of cooperation between the militants, the two councilmen, the NAACP, and the Human Relations Council.

By the summer of 1968, when Black Panthers from nearby Paterson arrived, at Cathcart's invitation, to help organize Plainfield's black political potential, the assumptions of racial politics in the small New Jersey city were changing rapidly. While many whites were shocked and frightened by the move, some close to the sources of official decisions conceded that the Panthers were reasonable and willing to negotiate, though extremely tough. It seemed that blacks were becoming a rather powerful political bloc at the local level, but it remained at best an open question of whether political solutions at this level would be adequate.

3. THE LOS ANGELES RIOT OF AUGUST 1965
Anthony Oberschall

T H E Watts–Los Angeles [1] riot has not yet received the scholarly attention it deserves. Most newspapers and national magazines reported it at some length since it was an eminently newsworthy event. Four months after the riot, the commission which Governor Brown appointed to make an objective and dispassionate study of the riot handed in the report of its findings.[2] The *McCone Report* was a mere eighty-

From *Social Problems* 15, no. 3 (Winter 1968): pp. 322–341. I wish to thank Mr. Borden Olive for helpful comments and assistance in locating some of the data on which this account is based.

eight pages in length, and in it the actual description of riot events received no more than fifteen pages of space. The report concentrated mainly on cataloguing the social, economic, and psychological conditions which prevailed in the South Los Angeles area prior to the riot and on suggesting changes designed to prevent a future riot. No attempt was made to provide anything but a superficial explanation of the motivation of the rioters and the patterns of their actions.

Popular and Official Views of the Riot and the Evidence

Immediate public reaction was a mixture of shock, fear, and belief that the riots were organized and led by some radical and disaffected groups in league with gangs and hoodlums; that quite possibly a conspiracy was at work; that it was a typical manifestation of irrational crowd behavior, unpredictable and similar to an animal stampede; that the rioters were well armed after they had systematically looted gun stores, hardware stores, and pawn shops; and that the riot consequently was an armed uprising by Negroes against the police, the political authorities, and the white man in general.

This initial climate of opinion was a result of the news coverage and the pronouncements of officials. They focused selective attention upon those events that did in fact fit the above loose conception of what the riot was all about. The irrational aspect of the riot was highlighted in Police Chief Parker's widely quoted phrase describing the rioters as behaving like "monkeys in the zoo." The insurrectionary aspect was stressed by *Time* and by the *Los Angeles Times* coverage, both of which reported extensively on the weapons allegedly used by the rioters and seized from them.[3] The conspiratorial and organized aspects of the riot, after its start, were stressed by Mayor Yorty [4] and other officials such as Police Chief Parker in his testimony on the use of bullhorns during the riot and the "expertly made" Molotov cocktails used by the rioters.[5] Indirect evidence for police belief in riot organization is the August 18 police siege, storming, and subsequent destructive search of a Black Muslim Temple which was "deliberately provoked by false telephone calls to police that Negroes were carrying guns into the building." [6] The police did not question the veracity of the anonymous callers because the information fitted their belief of some formal riot leadership and organization. The reaction of fear by the white population of Los Angeles is illustrated by the run on gun stores, which took place far beyond the residential areas adjoining the curfew area.[7]

While the conspiracy theory was popular with some officials and could be used as a political alibi, the McCone Commission found no evidence for a conspiracy in setting off the Los Angeles riot. The commission wrote that "there is no reliable evidence of outside or preestablished plans for rioting," although it pointed to some evidence of the promotion of the riot by gangs and other groups within the curfew area after the riot had started, such as the "sudden appearance of Molotov cocktails in quantity" and of "inflammatory handbills." [8] The commission did not elaborate a comprehensive theory of its own, yet it nevertheless hinted at another theory that has often been invoked in the explanation of violent collective outbursts, namely the "criminal riff-raff" theory of rioting. According to this view, every large urban ghetto contains a disproportionate number of criminals, delinquents, unemployed, school dropouts, and other social misfits who on the slightest pretext are ready to riot, loot, and exploit an explosive social situation for their private gain and for satisfying their aggressive antisocial instincts.[9] Thus the commission emphasized that many Negroes were caught in a frustrating "spiral of failure," that they had been encouraged "to take the worst extreme and even illegal remedies to right a wide variety of wrongs, real and supposed," that nonetheless only a small minority of Negroes were involved in the disorder, and that a majority of those arrested had prior criminal records.[10]

But as Blauner has pointed out in a perceptive analysis, the report is, in the main, silent about who the participants were and what their motivations were. It did not attempt to explain how in the absence of planning and formal leadership a collective action on the scale and duration of the riot could be sustained in the face of a major show of force by over 1,000 police and eventually 13,000 National Guardsmen.[11] Indeed, if the commission's figure of a maximum of 10,000 Negroes taking to the streets is accepted,[12] this represents about 10 percent of the age cohorts 15 to 44, male and female, of the Negro population living in the South Los Angeles area, which roughly corresponds to the curfew area. Moreover, one should distinguish between several levels or degrees of participation. There are some who participated to the extent of physically fighting the police, of obstructing the firemen, of beating white motorists, and of breaking into stores and setting them on fire, in short, the activists. There are others who helped themselves to the merchandise in the stores already broken into. Still others, far more numerous, simply milled about in the streets, jeered at police, and openly encouraged the activists. Finally there were those who were not involved beyond being curious observers, or just went about the business of survival at a time of disaster. Among active participants in a riot, adolescents and young adult males can be expected to predominate. But if a substantial proportion of the remaining population overtly manifests sympathy and support for the active participants, the riot can only be interpreted as a broad group response to shared grievances, and not as the expression of an unrepresentative, lawless minority.

In examining the arrest statistics from the riot * what strikes one is the extent to which the riot drew participants from all social strata within the predominantly lower-class Negro area in which it took place. The riot cannot be attributed to the lawless and rootless minority which inhabits the ghetto, though, no doubt, these were active in it as well. The riot is best seen as a large-scale collective action, with a wide, representative base in the lower-class Negro communities, which, however much it gained the sympathy of the more economically well-off Negroes, remained a violent lower-class outburst throughout. If there were numerous jobless among the participants and many youths from families with problems, it is precisely because such cases abound in the neighborhoods in which the riot occurred.

Police–Negro Relations

The conspiracy and criminal riff-raff theories of the riot are not supported by the evidence on arrests. The key to a sociological explanation is the state of police–Negro relations before the riot, for it was a major source of Negro frustrations and accounts for the presence of a generalized belief which is a necessary ingredient in producing collective action. The objective factors producing strain among Negroes in the South Los Angeles area, such as a high unemployment rate and stationary (even declining) incomes at a time of increasing prosperity in the rest of Los Angeles and the country at large, have been well documented and noted.[13] The increases in racial tensions due to other than economic factors have also received the attention they deserve. In the November 1964 election, California voters repealed the Rumford Fair Housing Act in a constitutional referendum by a 2:1 margin. Repeal was partic-

* The author's discussion of the arrest statistics has been omitted. Studies of riot participation are discussed in Nathan Caplan's "The New Ghetto Man," pp. 343– 359 of this volume.

ularly high in Southern California and even higher among the white population surrounding the Negro neighborhoods in Los Angeles County. White areas there were in favor of the repeal in the 80 percent to the 90 percent range, whereas Negro precincts voted against it in the 90 percent range. The vote was widely interpreted as a hardening of white public opinion with respect to integrated housing. While most major U.S. cities had come up with acceptable organizational structures within the Poverty Program by the summer of 1965, events took a different turn in Los Angeles:

Advance billing with respect to federal programs had created the false impression that more job opportunities would be available than actually developed. The endless bickering between city, state and federal government officials over the administration of the authorized programs—most particularly the Poverty Program—has disappointed many.[14]

There were no compensating factors in Los Angeles such that Negroes would be conscious of progress in some matters directly affecting them. The civil rights movement has not been very active in Los Angeles, and its crowning achievement, the passage of the Civil Rights Act of 1964, has not had any impact on the city's Negro population since segregation did not exist in Los Angeles, and California has had, for many years, laws against discrimination in employment, political participation, and other activities.

The charge of police malpractice and of police "brutality" is of course not confined to Los Angeles, but has been a problem in most large U.S. cities and a precipitant in the 1964 and later riots in the U.S. The situation in Los Angeles had been the subject of hearings held in Los Angeles in September 1962 by the California Advisory Committee of the U.S. Commission on Civil Rights, headed by Bishop Pike of San Francisco. The purpose of the hearings was to ascertain the state of police–minority group relations after an April 1962 incident involving Los Angeles police officers and Black Muslims became a focal point of organized Negro protest against alleged discriminatory treatment by Los Angeles police.[15] According to the committee,

Most of the Negro and civil rights organization spokesmen who testified believe that there is discriminatory law enforcement in Los Angeles. The types of discrimination most referred to was excessive violence at the time of the arrest, greater surveillance and arrest in areas of minority group concentration, the arrest of Negroes and Mexican–Americans for conduct for which Caucasians are not arrested, discourteous and uncivil police language, conduct and other behavior directed against Negroes and Mexican–Americans, unjustified harassment of Negroes and Mexican–Americans, and an unwillingness and inability to distinguish between law-abiding and potentially law-breaking minority group members. These charges, with one exception, were directed against the Los Angeles Police Department (as opposed to the Sheriff's Department).[16]

Police Chief Parker's testimony stated however that

he did not think that the Police Department had a "bad image among the Negro community, the majority of them," and that "basically I do not believe that there is any difficult problem existing in the relationship between the Los Angeles Police Department and the Negro Community." The Chief did allude however to elements who are trying to inflame the Negro community with false charges of police brutality.[17]

Already in 1962, therefore, the lines of cleavage were sharply drawn. On the one side a generalized belief in police brutality and discriminatory law enforcement was widespread and gaining strength within the Negro community. On the other side there was a denial of these charges by the police and the elected city officials, with the added insinuation that the belief itself was being spread by agitators who were trying to exploit certain racial tensions for their own political ends.[18]

There can be little doubt that the cleavage itself contributed to bring about the very situation both parties were trying to avoid. In the words of John Buggs, Chairman of the Los Angeles County Human Relations Commission, who testified before the committee,

A situation is being created in which the claim by minority group persons of police brutality and the counterclaim by police of minority group resistance to police authority are beginning to be a self-fulfilling prophecy.[19]

In concrete terms, a belief on the part of a Negro about to be arrested that the arrest is going to involve the use of force has the consequence of an attempt to avoid or resist arrest, thus increasing the probability that force will in fact have to be used to implement the arrest; whereas a belief on the part of police that an arrest is going to be resisted might produce a behavior in which force is in fact used. Thus the ground is prepared for the fulfillment of the prophecy.

One of the most controversial issues was and still is the existing procedure for handling citizen complaints against police conduct. The Police Department has an Internal Affairs Division (IAD) which has the responsibility of investigating and evaluating serious charges of misconduct made against police officers by citizens and by other police or public officials. Other charges are investigated by the operating divisions themselves, subject to review through the IAD.

The minority groups contend that the existing machinery for registering complaints and disciplining police is such that the police department is able to and in fact does whitewash police conduct, and by pressures and intimidations even prevents many complaints from being filed in the first place. Consequently, the Negroes demand a civilian police review board, independent of the police department. Chief Parker opposed a civilian police review board on the ground that the wrong kind of people would get on it, and that police discipline and morale would be harmed.[20]

The whole matter of police–Negro relations in Los Angeles is a complicated one. Police brutality refers to more than the excessive use of physical force during an arrest, the manhandling of suspects in the police station and in jail, and other physical acts usually associated with the term "brutality." It means arrests, questionings, and searches of Negroes by police without apparent provocation, the use of abusive and derogatory language in addressing Negroes, such as the word "nigger," and a general attitude toward the minority groups which represents an affront to their sense of dignity.[21] Police brutality in this sense is a reality to be reckoned with in the Negro ghetto, no matter how exaggerated some incidents turn out to be and regardless of whether political or criminal groups try to exploit the issue. The presence of the police in the South Los Angeles area was a constant source of irritation and left behind a legacy of bitterness and hostility. Two years before the riot, a study conducted by the Youth Opportunities Board with 220 people in Watts, Avalon, and Willowbrook on their attitudes toward several agencies operating in the community found that a majority of both adults and children felt that "the behavior of the police aggravated the problems of growing up in the Negro community rather than contributed to their solution," in marked contrast to the respondents' attitudes towards schools, probation officers, and health agencies.[22] It is important to note, however, that the tension-filled relations between police and Negroes have a structural and situational, as well as a personal, origin. The police as the daily visible representative of a white-dominated world bears the full brunt of the accumulated frustrations and hostility of the ghetto. Negro attitudes towards the police are not merely a reaction to police behavior and attitudes, but to their total situation in the society. The role of the police in this situation is as unrewarding as it is dangerous.

One reason for the deterioration of Negro–police relations in Watts can be attributed to Parker's "reforms." Whereas before Parker, policemen patrolled city blocks on foot, thereby getting to know personally the people living in an area, and therefore being able to use selective judgment in making an arrest (i.e., they would be able to tell a professional gambling game from an improvised neighborhood crap game, or know which drunks were troublemakers, which ones cared for by family and friends), Parker took the police off the beat and put them into police cars. In a matter of months police lost the special knowledge and contacts with neighborhoods which alone makes law enforcement bearable, especially in lower-class neighborhoods. When police enforced the law strictly and without exception, it was violating previous practices that had become part of the social structure, and hence caused hostility and resentment. These, in turn, led to resistance to arrests, with local groups helping the victim evade arrest, which in turn led the police to intensify its law-enforcement practices in this "lawless" community. Thus a dangerous spiral of suspicion and antagonism was allowed to develop.

Negro objections to the pro-police bias in the existing system of reviewing citizen complaints against police malpractice are borne out by the record. In 1961, 540 complaints were filed against police officials, 64 percent of these by ordinary citizens. Of 121 citizen complaints alleging the excessive use of force, only 5 were sustained, as opposed to 243 complaints sustained of the remaining 419 complaints (mainly drunkenness on duty, bad debts, etc.).[23] In 1964, of 412 complaints alleging police misconduct received from citizens, 42 complaints were sustained, a higher proportion than in 1961, but still only slightly above 10 percent.[24] These figures strongly suggest that in the overwhelming majority of cases of alleged police misconduct in dealing with citizens, the existing review machinery ruled in favor of the police. Moreover the recommendations of the Pike Commission with respect to a civilian police review board, a police community program, and increase in the proportion of Negro police, have still not been acted upon.[25] Furthermore, neither the Pike nor the McCone Commission has done anything beyond looking at dozens of case histories of police malpractice on file with various civil rights and Negro organizations. Both commissions have felt that any action based on these complaints was outside their jurisdiction.

The Precipitating Incident and
Mobilization for Action

Prior to the start of the riot, therefore, Negroes in South Los Angeles were subjected to considerable strain due to unemployment, low income, police–Negro relations, frustrated hopes about the war on poverty, and similar factors. The normal channels for voicing Negro grievances had been ineffective in bringing about a change in the conditions producing these strains. A widespread belief in police brutality had existed for some time and was coupled with deep hostility against the police. The Frye arrest on the evening of August 11 provided the spark which ignited the accumulated frustrations of the South Los Angeles population. In order to explain how a simple traffic arrest could escalate in a short time into a full-fledged riot of the magnitude and duration of the subsequent events, one has to examine the characteristics of the precipitating incident, the communications processes within the riot-prone population, the ecology of the South Los Angeles area, and the nature of the police effort to control it.

Marquette Frye, a twenty-one-year-old Negro, driving his mother's car, with his brother as a passenger, was stopped by a California Highway Patrolman after he failed to stop at a red light, about 7 P.M., near, but not in, Watts. Marquette Frye had been drinking and was unable to produce a driver's license. The officer, soon joined by two more, was getting ready to arrest him. The evening this occurred was the hottest one so far of the summer; a lot of people were simply hanging about on the sidewalks outside their homes. A small crowd quickly gathered to observe the arrest. Everything went without incident until Frye's mother, living nearby, arrived on the scene. What happened after that is still not clear since the police, the Fryes, and witnesses have sworn to contradictory testimony.[26] Apparently, while at first Mrs. Frye turned against her son to discipline him, eventually the three Fryes, with encouragement from the onlookers, turned upon the policemen and had to be forcefully subdued and arrested. Meanwhile the highway patrolmen had radioed for reinforcements, and Los Angeles police officers arrived for help. By 7:25 P.M. the patrol car, with the Fryes under arrest and a tow truck pulling the Frye car, left the scene.[27] As the patrolmen were about to leave, a woman in the menacing crowd spat on one of them, and an officer went into the hostile crowd to arrest her. She was wearing a shirt outside her skirt. The rumor immediately spread that the police were beating and arresting a "pregnant" woman—which she was not—just as the crowd had earlier "seen" the policemen use excessive force to subdue the Fryes. By the time the last police car left the arrest location, it was stoned by the crowd and the riot had begun.[28]

Regardless of what actually happened, the events surrounding the arrest fitted in with preconceptions and the generalized belief about police brutality. In a confusing context such as an arrest in the evening with lots of people milling about and a high noise level, it is plausible that, apart from a few Negroes who actually eyewitnessed most of the arrest-events, many others pieced out an incomplete perceptual record of these events according to their preconceptions and predispositions.[29] It is particularly important to note the belief and the rumors about the police beating of a pregnant woman, for such action is one of the clearest violations of a basic norm of human conduct and arouses everywhere condemnation and revulsion. Person-to-person communication in a neighborhood on a hot night, with many individuals hanging around in the streets or in their houses but with windows open, can spread a message rapidly over a large area, and subsequent movement of people reinforced by the sound of police sirens further revealed where the focal point of the action was.[30] It seems plausible then that the original "witnesses" to the Frye arrest interpreted what they perceived as an act of police brutality, which fitted in with a long prior history of similar behavior that was expected from the police. Later arrivals had no particular reason to question this interpretation of the precipitating event and, sharing the beliefs and emotions of those already present, reacted to it similarly.

The original incident was widely reported in the news media, and in all probability a majority of the entire Los Angeles population knew the next day that a riot had taken place in a particular location in Watts during the previous evening and night. This piece of information in turn acted as a significant clue for the collection of crowds in the vicinity of the original arrest location the following day in the absence of any explicit coordination. Anybody, whether merely curious or wishing to settle an old score with the police, had but the same piece of information to go on, namely the location of the incident of the night before, and knew that everybody else, too, had the same clue to act upon. Hence the original location acted as a magnet and as the focal point for the collection of similarly disposed crowds on Thursday evening and Friday morning before the riot eventually spread throughout the South Los Angeles area.

During the entire riot a common thread was the aggression against the police. Yet from the start the riot was more than just a police riot. The Los Angeles riot did not exhibit the character of the classic race riot in which crowds of one race systematically seek out and assault isolated individuals and smaller groups of another race. Nevertheless the first two nights witnessed many incidents which fit the classic pattern as unsuspecting (and later curious) white motorists driving through the riot area were pelted with bricks and bottles, pulled out of their cars and beaten up, and news reporters and TV crews were assaulted. It is difficult to document how the subsequent major pattern of breaking into stores, looting, and burning them down became established. The fickleness of hostile crowds as they move from one object to another has been well established in other instances of rioting and collective behavior. People with frustrations and grievances other than the specific grievance against the police witness and join in the riot. The situation becomes defined as one in which a broad class of race-related grievances can be translated into direct aggressive behavior, and targets other than the one involved in the precipitating incident become the objects of aggression.[31] The pattern of store breaking and arson was not totally devoid of some leadership, apparently provided by gangs, though it is impossible to establish the magnitude of this factor.

One of my informants stated that the big-time professional criminals, in anticipation of a police dragnet, took the first opportunity after the riot started to get out of the riot area and even out of Los Angeles. Many petty thieves and other small-time professional crooks came individually or in small groups into the riot area to seize this opportunity of breaking into stores while the police were busy with the rioters. These groups were not, however, interested in leading the riot crowds to loot and destroy the white-owned stores, since that would have interfered with the efficiency of their operations. Another informant who has been close to some of the gangs in the South Los Angeles area reported, however, that gang members, in an effort to prove their claims upon leadership in a certain territory and in competition with each other, were vying for leadership over the crowds during the riot, and this meant among other things actively participating in the skirmishes against the police, breaking into the stores, and setting them on fire.

The success of the store breakers, arsonists, and looters in eluding the police can in part be put down to the role of the mass media during the riot week. The Los Angeles riot was the first one in which rioters were able to watch their actions on television. The concentration and movements of the police in the area were well reported on the air, better than that of the rioters themselves. By listening to the continuous radio and TV coverage, it was possible to deduce that the police were moving toward or away from a particular neighborhood. Those who were active in raiding stores could choose when and where to strike, and still have ample time for retreat. The entire curfew area is a very extended one. It was not possible to seal off several blocks and trap rioters, as could be done in cities where apartment houses are built side to side. People could move from street to street through gardens, driveways, and alleys.

The magnitude of the riot measured in terms of its duration, the area affected, and the casualties and injuries sustained, can in part be accounted for by the measures taken to bring it under control. Officials at all levels underestimated the riot at the start. Deputy Police Chief Murdock stated on Thursday morning that "Wednesday was just a night to throw rocks at policemen." [32] Friday at dawn the police department felt that they had the situation under control, and Mayor Yorty flew to San Francisco later in the morning to keep a speaking engagement before the Commonwealth Club under the impression that the riot had mostly spent itself.[33] Police Chief Parker requested formally on Friday at 10:50 A.M. that National Guardsmen be brought into South Los Angeles, yet because of the conflicting reports he received about the seriousness of the situation, Lt. Governor Anderson, who was acting in the absence of Governor Brown vacationing in Greece, did not sign the papers until 5 P.M. on Friday. While some guardsmen were deployed in the riot area by Friday night, it was not until after three nights of rioting had taken place that the 8 P.M. curfew was imposed on Saturday and the National Guard fully deployed.[34]

The police were of course outnumbered and undermanned, given the size of the riot area and the number of riot participants. Its efforts to disperse rock-throwing crowds proved singularly ineffective. Motorcycle officers who penetrated through the thick of the crowd in an effort to disperse it and arrest the rock throwers were vulnerable to physical assault. The crowds afforded a convenient shield for hit-and-run tactics.[35] Much of the police effort on the first two nights of the rioting consisted of protecting itself, motorists, firemen, and news reporters from physical assault. Realizing that it often acted as a stimulant and focal point for the rioting, the police periodically withdrew from physical proximity to the rioters. In retrospect it would appear that the proposal of John Buggs of the Los Angeles County Human Relations Commission and of Reverend Brooking on Thursday afternoon to Deputy Police Chief Murdock to withdraw white, uniformed police, and let community leaders control the crowds with the help of Negro officers in civilian clothes, which was turned down, might have been a more effective way of limiting the riot.[36] As it turned out, the partial show of force happened to be a demonstration of vulnerability and weakness, and acted more as an incitement than a deterrent to the riot.

Riot Behavior and Motivation

No one would deny the extensive property damage perpetrated by the rioters in looting and burning the stores, the physical assault upon police, white motorists, firemen, and others. One can, however, question whether this behavior is essentially an irrational stampede and orgy of destruction, and hence void of collective social significance and personal meaning. Nothing is gained by defining riot behavior as irrational *a priori*. There is considerable evidence that the rioters observed certain *bounds,* that they directed their aggression at *specific targets,* and that they selected *appropriate means* for the ends they intended to obtain.

The fact that no deaths resulted from the direct action of the rioters is evidence that they observed certain bounds and limits. The first two nights when white motorists were dragged out of their cars and beaten, and when newsmen were severely roughed up, none were beaten to death or killed, as might easily have happened since the police were unable to offer protection at the time. Furthermore, the sniper fire directed at police and firemen did not result in any fatalities either, despite reports that it was widespread and lasted throughout the riot week and the fact that police and firemen were easy targets. It seems that sniping was aimed toward obstructing law enforcement and fire fighting and not toward killing officials.

The riot crowds gave evidence of being able to pick specific targets for their aggression. Negro business establishments, many of them carrying signs such as "Blood Brother" or "Soul Brother," were for the most part spared. Private houses, post offices, churches, schools, libraries, and other public buildings in the riot area were not broken into and burned down, vandalized, or otherwise purposely damaged. Some white-owned stores also were spared. While the McCone Commission states that "our study of the patterns of burning and looting does not indicate any significant correlation between alleged consumer exploitation and the destruction [of stores]" [37] insufficient evidence is cited to back up this conclusion which would require a careful and controlled study of all stores and their practices in the riot area. Some informed observers have disagreed with the commission's conclusions on this point. Moreover, the Los Angeles police, the main target of preriot hostility, was also the main target of riot aggression. Only ten National Guardsmen out of a maximum of 13,900 were reported injured, as compared to ninety Los Angeles policemen out of a combined total of 1,653 police at the time of maximum deployment.[38] The evidence, meager as it is, supports the view that there was a systematic relationship between the specific targets of aggression and the sources of the rioters' grievances.

The destructive and violent behavior of the rioters was confined to specific kinds of events within the riot situation. Eyewitnesses reported that rioters and looters in cars were observing traffic laws in the riot area—stopping for red lights, stopping for pedestrians at crosswalks—even when carrying away stolen goods. Firemen were obstructed in putting out fires set to business establishments, yet one incident is reported where "people beseeched firemen to save a house which had caught fire when embers skipped to it from a torched commercial building," [39] and during which firemen were not hindered in any way from carrying out their job. These and similar incidents testify to the ability of riot participants to choose appropriate means for their ends. While riot behavior cannot be called "rational" in the everyday common meaning of that term, it did contain normative and rational elements and was much more situationally determined than the popular view would have it.

Looting is furthermore quite common in disaster situations other than riots and need not be interpreted as expressions of specifically racial hostility. Its attraction to people lacking the consumer goods others take for granted needs no complex explanation beyond the simple desire to obtain them when the opportunity to do so involves a low risk of apprehension by the police. Such action is facilitated by low commitment to the norms of private property expressed in the propensity of "the poor to seek a degree of elementary social justice at the expense of the rich," [40] the fact that others were doing the same thing, and the fact that the stores sacked in this case belonged to "Whitey." These observations can be illustrated by an eyewitness account of one such incident:

One booty-laden youth said defiantly: "That don't look like stealing to me. That's just picking up what you need and going." Gesturing at a fashionable hilltop area where many well-to-do Negroes live, he said: "Them living up in View Park don't need it. But we down here, we do need it." [41]

Looting was a predominantly neighborhood activity, often uncoordinated, and carried out by small groups. Between 50 and 65 percent of the minors were arrested less than a mile from their home, and a little over 63 percent were arrested in the company of others, mainly for "burglary," that is they were apprehended in or near stores broken into.[42] The casual process through which individuals would get involved in looting, and the group and neighborhood aspects of it, are illustrated in the following statement of an arrested minor to a probation officer:

[Minor] states that he was at home when his brother came home and said there was a riot going on in the streets. Minor states that he went out on the streets to watch and met a friend who said that people were going into a store on Broadway and "taking stuff out." Minor states that he and the companion went to observe and after arriving there and seeing everyone taking stuff from the store, he decided that he would take something also. The only reason Minor offers for his behavior is that "everybody else was taking stuff; so I decided to take some too." [43]

While the actions of some looters were described in some accounts as that of a savage mob bent on plunder and fighting each other for the spoils, other descriptions and material, such as a photograph showing two women and one man rolling a fully loaded shopping cart past firemen, suggest a much more relaxed and calm mood.

Looting as well as other riot activity were essentially group activities during which participants and onlookers experienced a sense of solidarity, pride, and exhilaration. They were bound together by shared emotions, symbols, and experiences which a black man inevitably acquires in white America and which makes him address another one as "Brother." [44] They were also bound together by the common enemy, "Whitey," and struck out against Whitey's representatives in the flesh, the police, the firemen, the merchants, the news reporters, and the motorists, and they felt good about striking out. Bystanders were swept along in this tide of we-feeling. One such Negro who was attracted out of curiosity into the riot area on Thursday night and immediately afterwards recorded his impressions and feelings into a tape recorder, described what he experienced in the following words:

> A brick came out of nowhere and smashed through the window of a hot dog stand across the street. Someone yelled: "That's Whitey's, tear it down." A number of people from both sides of the street converged on the stand and began breaking all the windows. Several men climbed into this stand and began passing out Cokes and other beverages to the people outside. . . . As they passed a small gas station, several people wanted to set it afire. One of the people standing nearby the station told them: "Let it stand. Blood owns it." A liquor store and a grocery store were the next targets. . . . Next to the liquor store was a meat market. These windows were also smashed and people in cars drove up and began loading meat into the trunks of their cars. Two young boys . . . came running out of the store . . . carrying a side of beef. The crowd roared its approval and greeted the boys with laughter and cheers. Several men came walking towards me laden down with liquor. One of them paused in front of me and asked: "What do you drink, brother?" He and the other stopped right here on the street to have a drink. My reply was: "Whiskey." They opened a bottle of whiskey and handed it to me. I drank a large swallow and handed it back. Twice around and the bottle was empty. We laughed and they continued down the street. . . . A cry went up the street: "One-Oh-Three. Hit the Third!" It referred to 103rd Street, the business center of Watts (a mile to the east and the north). The people piled into cars and headed for 103rd Street. Others followed on foot. As I was getting back into my car to drive to "One-Oh-Three," several men jumped into my car and said: "Let's make it, baby." [45]

The narrator adds at the end of his impressions: "I did not feel like an outsider at any time during the night. While my involvement was passive and some of the sights I witnessed appalling and saddening, I felt a strong bond with these people."

The rioters did not form an amorphous mass, a collection of individuals acting out private frustrations and hostility. Rioting was a group activity in the course of which strangers were bound together by common sentiments, activities, and goals, and supported each other in the manner typical of primary groups. The riot was a collective celebration in the manner of a carnival, during which about forty liquor stores were broken into and much liquor consumed. It was also a collective contest similar to that between two high school or college athletic teams, with the supporters cheering and egging on the contestants. One could settle old scores with the police, show them who really controlled the territory, humiliate them, and teach them a lesson. Just as a rioting youth was quoted by two Negro newsmen as saying: "This is what the police wanted—always messin' with niggers. We'll show them. I'm ready to die if I have to." [46] Police Chief Parker mistakenly boasted, "We are on top and they are on the bottom." [47] Both sides in this tragic and deadly contest had a high emotional stake in the outcome. While the riot was put down eventually, many Negroes saw it as a victory for their side and derived a sense of pride and accomplishment from this public demonstration of their collective power.

In assaulting the police and breaking into business establishments, some rioters were not only responding to the long-standing frustrations and humiliations suffered at the hands of the police and the exploitative practices of merchants, but were reacting along racial lines which can only be understood in the wider social context of the Negro in the U.S. Rioters were pelting motorists and firemen with rocks while shouting: "This is for Bogalusa! This is for Selma!" The riot situation became defined in global, dichotomous, we–they terms, where we and they stood for the two races and the long history of conflict associated with them. In such a situation, when one status (racial membership) becomes predominant and one's other statuses and role obligations irrelevant, mediation becomes impossible because one cannot remain sitting on a fence. When Negro Assemblyman Mervyn Dymally tried to calm some rioters a boy asked him: "Who you with?" Dymally answered: "I'm with you, man," to which the boy retorted: "Then here's a rock, baby, throw it!" [48] Those who bridge the dichotomy by siding with the opponent are perceived as traitors, and will be singled out for special abuse as was the case with a Negro National Guardsman who was called a "white nigger" by the crowd. [49]

Conclusion

These considerations about the actions and motivations of the rioters enable one to come closer to a characterization of the Watts riot. Was it a police riot, a race riot, an insurrection, a revolt, a rebellion, a nationalist uprising, or a revolution? A lot depends upon how these terms are defined, and they are often used loosely and interchangeably. There is no point in engaging in a definitional exercise with which many will take issue. It can, however, be pointed out that in all the above manifestations of collective behavior, common grievances, sentiments, emotions, and we-feeling bind the actors together, common targets become the object of aggression, and violent physical means are used by the participants. These cannot therefore be used to distinguish a riot from a revolt or a rebellion. One must examine what collective goals and demands are voiced by the actors. If their actions are directed at overthrowing the constituted authorities, if political demands are voiced such as the resignation of certain leaders and officials, if an attempt is made to achieve physical control in an area or territory by forcing out the existing authorities and substituting for them other authorities, then one is dealing with a revolt, rebellion, insurrection, or uprising. If, on the other hand, the main purpose of the action is to inflict damage and/or injury upon certain groups or a category of persons, such as police, merchants, or or whites in general, then one is dealing with a riot.[50] The Los Angeles events therefore constituted a riot rather than anything else.

The riot was remarkable for the lack of any leadership and organized effort to express collective demands of the rioters and the Negro population in South Los Angeles. However many persons in that area may have wished to see the resignation of Police Chief Parker, or the establishment of a Civilian Police Review Board, no banners proclaiming these demands were raised.[51] No attempts were made to address the crowds to spell out collective aims. No spokesmen emerged from the ranks of the rioters to make a statement to the authorities or the press.[52] No effort was made to hold an area after the police were forced out of it and to coordinate action designed to prevent its comeback. No barricades were thrown up. Single individuals sniped at police and firemen from different locations and on numerous occasions, but there was no attempt to create a more organized form of armed resistance. While the precipitating incident touched off a police riot, which soon thereafter widened into a riot during which the targets of aggression became other whites besides police, subsequent days and nights produced a repetition of the same sort of behavior over an ever-wider area and involving greater numbers of participants, but did not produce a change toward a more insurrectionary or revolutionary pattern of action.

It is the magnitude of the Los Angeles riot, both in duration, participation, amount of damage and casualties, and the forces needed to control it, which led many to characterize it as more than just a riot. But aside from magnitude, the Los Angeles riot was structurally and behaviorally similar to the Negro riots in other cities during the summers of 1964, 1965, and 1966. The collective significance of these events, however, is that the civil rights gains made by the Negro movement in the last few years, which have benefited the southern Negro and middle-class Negroes, have not altered the situation of the lower-class urban Negroes outside of the South and have not removed the fundamental sources of grievances of a large proportion of the Negro population in the United States.

NOTES

1. While the riot engulfed a far wider area of South Los Angeles than the Watts district, it has come to be known as the Los Angeles or the Watts riot, and I use both these terms interchangeably. The question of whether the events that took place are best characterized as a "riot" or something else will be dealt with below.

2. Governor's Commission on the Los Angeles Riots, *Violence in the City—An End or a Beginning,* December 2, 1965, popularly known as the *McCone Report* after the commission chairman's name.

3. *Time,* 20 August 1965, p. 16: "After looting pawn shops, hardware and war supply stores for weapons, the Negroes brandished thousands of rifles, shotguns, pistols, and machetes." See also the *Los Angeles Times,* 17 and 18 August 1965.

4. *Los Angeles Times,* 15 August 1965.

5. *Ibid.,* 20 September 1965.

6. *Ibid.,* 16 September 1965.

7. While the immediate reaction about what the riot was all about is to my mind distorted, the news media, statements by many officials, especially Negroes, as well as the later *McCone Report,* did reveal at least a moderate amount of sophistication and acceptance of ideas current in social science when it came to a description of the broader social and economic conditions that made the riot possible and even likely.

8. *McCone Report,* pp. 22–23.

9. On how both the conspiracy and criminal riff-raff explanations have been traditionally invoked by contemporaries to explain riots and rebellions in the eighteenth and nineteenth centuries see George Rudé, *The Crowd in History* (New York: Wiley, 1964), esp. chap. 14.

10. *McCone Report,* pp. 1, 4–6, 24.

11. Robert Blauner, "Whitewash over Watts," *Transaction* 3 (March–April 1966). Blauner himself concluded from published statements of Negro leaders and the reports of his informants that the McCone Commission had underestimated the widespread support for and participation in the riot, and explicitly rejects the view that the riot was primarily a rising of the lawless.

12. *McCone Report,* p. 1: "perhaps as many as 10,000 Negroes took to the streets in marauding bands."

13. See "Special Census Survey of the South and East Los Angeles areas: November 1965," *Current Population Report,* Technical Studies, Series P-23, 17 (March 23, 1967). This survey contains up-to-date figures and allows a comparison to be made between the separate districts making up the South Los Angeles area. Other pertinent information is contained in the *McCone Report.*

14. *McCone Report,* p. 40.

15. U.S. Commission on Civil Rights, California Advisory Committee, *Police Minority Group Relations in Los Angeles and the San Francisco Bay Area* (hereafter referred to as the *Pike Report*), August 1963, p. 1.

16. *Pike Report,* p. 9.

17. *Ibid.,* p. 8.

18. Mayor Yorty's campaign flyer (*Mayor Yorty Reports*) distributed in March 1966 at the start of the 1966 Democratic gubernatorial primary contest linked the Communist Party and other left-wing organizations with the antipolice campaign. *The Los Angeles Times,* 18 August 1965, part I, p. 3, quotes Yorty as saying that "for

some time now there has existed a world-wide campaign to stigmatize all police as brutal. . . . The cry of 'police brutality' has been shouted in cities all over the world by the Communists, dupes, and demagogues irrespective of the facts. Such a campaign has been pushed here in Los Angeles."

19. *Pike Report*, p. 8.

20. *Pike Report*, pp. 14–15.

21. On these points, see Ray Murphy and Howard Elinson, eds., *Problems and Prospects of the Negro Movement* (Belmont, Cal.: Wadsworth Co., 1966), p. 232; Robert Blauner, "Whitewash over Watts," *Trans-action* 3 (March–April 1966): 8; and Jerry Cohen and William S. Murphy, *Burn, Baby, Burn* (New York: Dutton, 1966), p. 210.

22. Blauner, *op. cit.,* p. 6.

23. *Pike Report*, p. 12.

24. *McCone Report*, p. 32.

25. In 1962 the Los Angeles police department had apparently about 150 Negro police officers out of a total force of 4,700. The reason given by police officials for the low proportion of Negroes on the force was their inability to meet eligibility standards and the scarcity of applicants (*Pike Report*, p. 34).

26. The most plausible reconstruction of the incident is presented in great detail in chaps. 2–4 of Jerry Cohen and William S. Murphy in *Burn, Baby, Burn.*

27. *McCone Report*, p. 11.

28. *Ibid.,* p. 12.

29. Evidence for these psychological processes can be found in Bernard Berelson and Gary Steiner, *Human Behavior* (New York: Harcourt, Brace and World, 1964), pp. 101, 115.

30. The fact that August 11 was one of the hottest days in the entire summer has been regarded by some as the precipitating factor. Actually it was important insofar as more people than usual do hang around on the streets near their homes in the slums on hot nights, so that an incident immediately attracts a larger number of spectators than usual and news of events travels faster and uninterruptedly by word of mouth. To the extent that people tend to be more irritable and "on edge" at the end of a day with high levels of heat, smog, and humidity, these factors in themselves were also contributory causes after the precipitating incident had occurred.

31. On these processes, see Neil Smelser, *Theory of Collective Behavior* (New York: Free Press, 1962), pp. 258–260.

32. Cohen and Murphy, *op. cit.,* p. 74.

33. Cohen and Murphy, *op. cit.,* pp. 121, 126.

34. *McCone Report*, pp. 17–19.

35. Cohen and Murphy, *op. cit.,* pp. 69–70.

36. Cohen and Murphy, *op. cit.,* p. 88.

37. *McCone Report*, p. 62.

38. *Ibid.,* p. 20.

39. Cohen and Murphy, *op. cit.,* p. 157.

40. See Rudé, *op. cit.,* p. 244, and *passim* for historical instances of this.

41. *Time,* 20 August 1965, p. 17.

42. *RPS*, pp. 16, 18. Comparable data on adults arrested are not available.

43. *RPS*, p. 19.

44. A Negro student recalls driving his run-down automobile during the riot outside of the curfew area, and stopping at a red light next to a late-model car driven by a middle-aged, prosperous-looking Negro. The other driver, a total stranger and probably mistaking the student for one of the active rioters, smiled broadly and told him before driving off: "Where are you going to strike next, Brother?"

45. Quoted in Cohen and Murphy, *op. cit.,* pp. 111–112.

46. *Time,* 20 August 1965, p. 17.

47. *Time,* 27 August, 1965, p. 11.

48. Cohen and Murphy, *op. cit.,* p. 119.

49. *Ibid.,* p. 195.

50. "A riot is an outbreak of temporary but violent mass disorder. It may be directed at a particular individual as well as against public authorities. But it involves no intention to overthrow the government itself. In this respect riot stops short of insurrection or rebellion, although it may often be only a preliminary to the latter" is the definition of Smellie in the *Encyclopedia of the Social Sciences.*

51. Although some handbills from an unidentified source denouncing Parker were passed out during the riot.

52. Negro leaders and influentials did of course speak out during the riot on television and through other means. They expressed Negro demands such as Assemblyman Dymally's call for Parker's removal. But the leaders were reiterating views that they had long held and publicly voiced. They were not asked by the rioters to be spokesmen for riot goals or terms of negotiation with the authorities.

✍ 4. MILWAUKEE'S NATIONAL MEDIA RIOT
Harold R. Wilde

O N Sunday, July 30, 1967, Milwaukee, a city known for its peaceful small-town atmosphere, its provincialism, and its Germanic heritage of honest government and good beer, suddenly erupted into violence. At about nine at night crowds of Negro youths gathered following some church dances in the city's Negro "core." All at once boys and young men began breaking store windows, throwing bottles at passing cars, and jeering at police who rushed into the area. Apparently with nothing but vandalism in mind, they set dozens of small fires, almost all of them in vacant buildings. They broke into stores, but seldom stopped to loot them. It was not at all clear whether or in what sense the outbreak was "racial," for the youths knocked out windows in the Urban League headquarters, the Black Muslim Temple, and twelve storefront Negro churches.

Police Chief Harold Brier at first assured Mayor Henry W. Maier that his men could handle the disturbance. At 2 A.M., when he got word that several of his men had been shot by a "sniper," he changed his mind; on the chief's advice the mayor at once declared a state of emergency and asked the governor to send in the National Guard. By this

Reprinted with the permission of The Macmillan Company from *Urban Government,* ed. Edward Banfield. Copyright © by the Free Press, a Division of The Macmillan Company, 1969. This essay, written in April 1968, is the author's abridgement of a longer and more documented study of the 1967 riot in Milwaukee.

time it had begun to rain and the rampage by youths was over. The
guard arrived, however, 4,800 strong, and the next day the mayor put
the whole city under a strict curfew. The suburbs followed his lead and
for twenty-four hours not a store, factory, or office was open anywhere
in the metropolitan area. For three days there were isolated incidents
—a few fires, some looting, and some sniping—on the third day
(Wednesday) the police shot and killed an eighteen-year-old college student who was alleged to be looting. After that the incidents soon
ceased. The mayor tapered the curfew off over a period of a week and
nine days after its arrival the guard was withdrawn.

Superficially, it looked as if Milwaukee was "another Detroit." That,
certainly, was the theory of the mayor, who behaved as if he expected
the whole metropolitan area to go up in flames; of the newspapers, the
headlines of which screamed "RIOT"; and of Father James Groppi, the
militant civil rights leader, who announced "this is not a riot—it's a revolt." As it turned out the facts did not really justify such language.
Fewer than 300 persons participated in the disorders Sunday night, the
police chief reported, and it was then that the action was heaviest. In
the course of nine days 1,740 persons were arrested, but most of them
were charged with nothing worse than violation of the curfew. Three
people were killed and a dozen injured, but two of the deaths were
caused by the police (the looter was one; the other was an old woman
hit in her room by a stray bullet) and the third death (that of a policeman) and most of the serious injuries (also of policemen) were inflicted
by one man, probably deranged, who fired a blast from his house with a
shotgun. One hundred and twenty-nine fires were set, the fire chief said,
but the total damage from the fires was estimated at only $116,262. The
main money cost of the riot was in extra pay for police and firemen
and, especially, in lost retail sales and lowered factory production and
employment. These costs resulted from the protracted curfew rather
than from the riot itself.

It is hard to doubt that the mayor did the right thing in promptly
calling out the guard. It was his duty to protect the city from violence,
whether that of teen-agers or others. (Former Mayor Frank Zeidler, a
vigorous critic of the mayor, said that he too would have called out the
guard.) What *is* surprising, however, is that the mayor, the newspapers,
Father Groppi, and everyone else of importance in the city perceived
the affair not as a youth rampage or even a riot but as a RIOT. Milwaukee seemed to mistake itself for Detroit, Newark, or Watts. In fact,
its Negro district was small (Negroes constituted about 12 percent of

the city's population) and conservative (about 40 percent of the families owned their own homes). Anyone who knew anything about the "core" knew that the people who lived there—even the few militants among them—were more likely to sing "We Shall Overcome" along with the Reverend Martin Luther King, Jr., than to burn the city down. But the mayor and indeed the city as a whole talked and acted as if this was a real possibility. This general misperception of the situation requires explanation.

If one asks why everyone in Milwaukee from the mayor to the man on the street perceived a youth rampage as a RIOT the obvious answer is that real riots in other cities had dominated the news for many weeks causing Milwaukee to wonder if what had happened in the other cities might not happen there, too. (Indeed, the very day Milwaukee's riot broke out the *Journal* carried a front-page article comparing conditions in Detroit, where there had just been a riot, to those in Milwaukee.) If one pushes the question farther back, asking why the city was so suggestible, the answer is to be found in changes of a fundamental sort that have been going on for some time. A decade or so ago Milwaukeeans were, so to speak, face to face with local reality; at that time they would have seen a rampage of youths as just that, not as a riot and still less as a RIOT. Now they see the city and its life not directly but through a glass darkly—the glass being a television tube and the images that it projects being supplied by a few people whose perceptions, insofar as they are of reality at all, are of the reality of the largest cities, above all, New York. In short, Milwaukee's political system has in recent years become oriented to the national media and has come to take its cues from them rather than from the facts of life in the city. The city's perception of the rampage as a RIOT is an example of this general phenomenon.

The change in the city's political style first became apparent with the election of Mayor Maier. In 1960 he became the city's first "national media mayor"—the first mayor, that is, to see the city in terms of concepts supplied by the national media, to communicate with it via the national media, and to employ the rhetoric of the national media. His thirty-six predecessors had all been locals; for two generations Milwaukee had been governed by homespun German Socialists who seemed hardly to know that the rest of the country existed. In those days, a mayor's staff reflected the city's ethnic and neighborhood composition; they had to be locals because their job was to deal with the locals who constituted the interest groups and the electorate. In the old days a mayor knew every block of the city, and he depended on face-to-face relations to solve problems and win elections. City Hall was where the buck stopped; there was no use looking to Washington for a way out or an excuse. The result, of course, was conservative government. Projects were not launched unless it was clear that the local people wanted them —wanted them enough to pay for them.

Maier brought a new style to City Hall. He had a master's degree from the University of Wisconsin, and he not only read books but wrote them (his *Challenge to the Cities* was published by Random House in 1966). To his predecessors the city was a patchwork of neighborhoods and interest groups that knew what they wanted—namely, honest and economical administration. To him it was three-quarters of a million people beset by the nationally advertised complex of problems known to the media as "the urban crisis" and accordingly requiring the services of experts like himself. As he explained in his book (subtitled *An Approach to a Theory of Urban Leadership*):

A key figure in the new world of urbanism is the mayor or chief executive of the large city. He occupies the only position that can provide overall leadership to cope with the demands of the modern urban policy. But his position is not a simple one. He faces multiple pressures and problems as complex as our society. His life is complicated by the fact that he must be one part institutional leader, one part political leader, one part educator, one part scapegoat, and some other part for whatever purpose his community wishes to use him. Of his various roles, however, that of institutional leader stands out as basic and crucial.

Mayor Maier was in close touch with the national centers of opinion and action in urban affairs. He had been a member of the President's Committee on Youth Employment, chairman of the advisory committee of the United States Conference of Mayors, and president of the National League of Cities, and when his book appeared the Under Secretary of HUD took him to the White House to present a copy to President Johnson. Because of all this national reputation and professionalism, Milwaukee stood somewhat in awe of its mayor. The press, the civic leaders, and even the aldermen were all oriented—more at least than their predecessors had been—to the national media and therefore took such signs of national repute very seriously.

The mayor's style was apparent in the way he handled the riot. He began preparing for it fifteen months before it occurred by working out elaborate contingency plans. Among other things, he installed a "hot line" to the governor's office, worked out the legal and other preliminaries to imposing a curfew, and established a procedure for calling out the National Guard on very short notice. These contingency plans were a source of great pride to him and his associates, and during the second day of the riot he released them to the press to show how well the city government had prepared for what happened. A week before the riot, planning had gone forward feverishly. The mayor had canceled plans to go East to a convention, ostensibly because he wanted to work on a "tax crusade" project, but actually because he expected a riot at any time. The police and fire departments went on the alert and the hospitals made ready extra emergency facilities. While he waited for the riot to occur, he drafted a long statement for use after it was over. The statement said, among other things, that the American metropolis could have no future until the walls separating the central city from the suburbs were torn down and it called on Congress to help tear them down. Both the tone and the substance of the statement were what one would expect of a national expert on urban affairs rather than of a mayor addressing his fellow citizens in an emergency,

This time of concern should be a time of commitment to the fight for the central city . . . a time for the long-overdue massive infusion of federal and state funds needed to translate that concern into action which will treat and cure the hard core economic and social ills which blight not only the life of the central city but also the fabric of American society.

Although the mayor used portions of his statement in a message addressed to the city the morning after the rampage, it was written mainly for use as an advertisement in the *New York Times,* where it appeared on August 3. Asked why it was placed in the *Times,* the mayor's principal assistant answered, "It's a toss-up between the *Times* and the *Washington Post.* Congress is what you have to affect."

During the actual riot the mayor did not forget that his most important constituents were in Washington. A journalist complained that "while it was difficult for local reporters to gain access to the mayor's office, Maier made himself readily available to reporters from the national television networks and from out-of-town newspapers." Negro leaders also found him inaccessible. During the riot he was too busy to talk to them. But he had not paid much attention to them in the months before either. For well over a year he had not made a visit of any length to the black "core." Nor had he established close ties with any of the recognized Negro leaders in the city. Almost all the plans that he had made were for handling the riot, not for averting it. Opportunities to conciliate Negro opinion did not seem to interest him. Civil rights militants had long been demanding an open housing ordinance; such an ordinance would have had very little practical effect (few Negroes were in a position to buy or rent housing outside of the "core" anyway), but it would have been symbolically important to them; despite this, the mayor insisted that the city not have open occupancy unless the suburbs also had it, and on that principle he stood righteous and immovable against the mounting anger of the Negroes.

From the mayor's standpoint it may have been less important to avert a riot than to handle one well if it occurred. The national audience that he most wanted to reach would be impressed by a city administration that had done a first-rate job of planning to cope with a riot; in the nature of the case this audience would not even be aware of a city administration that succeeded in preventing a riot from occurring. It was a fact too, of course, that a riot would dramatize the need for new revenue sources and programs to deal with fundamental problems. In the mayor's view, one such problem was lack of metropolitan organization. By placating the militants with an open occupancy ordinance the mayor might perhaps reduce the probability of a riot somewhat, but if he did this he would fail in his responsibility to educate the public to see the necessity for metropolitan solutions to metropolitan problems. Since he considered his "basic and crucial" role to be that of "institutional leader" the mayor may well have deemed the education responsibility most important.

Whatever his motivations, the mayor hastened to use the riot to propagandize for measures that he, along with most national opinion leaders, had long favored. He sent off a long (ten–twelve page, single-spaced) letter to the President of the United States offering his thoughts on the problems of the cities and telling what he thought the federal government should do about them. A week after declaring the emergency over he met with a group of Negro clergymen of his selection (the militants were not invited) and put before them a 39-point program. Thirty of his 39 points, it turned out, were ones that could be implemented only by the county, state, and federal governments. Some had remarkably little to do with the matters that had been engaging Milwaukee's attention. One, for example, called for a federal program to abate air and water pollution!

The mayor's list contrasted sharply with another list that had been put forward by a coalition of militant and other leaders. This list said nothing of county, state, and federal governments; it called for actions that the city government itself could take: put a Negro on the fire and police commissions, suspend without pay policemen involved in fatal shootings, appoint a Negro to command the police of the Fifth District, pass an open occupancy ordinance, and so on. The mayor brushed these demands aside peremptorily; he had no time for people who wanted to play the old-fashioned game of locally oriented politics, bargaining about specifics. In his view, the important thing was to mold public and, ultimately, congressional opinion with regard to the largest issues of federal, state, and local government relations. It happened, of course, that this enlarged view was also good politics for him, since anything that the city government might do would entail hazards of one kind or another. The mayor, however, was probably mainly concerned to exhibit a style of urban leadership that would win respect in Washington, New York, and the other far-away places from which (as he saw it) solutions to Milwaukee's problems would ultimately have to come. To people brought up in the earlier locally oriented style of politics, however, his emphasis on county, state, and federal matters looked like a plain and simple case of buck-passing. As one activist Negro minister told the press,

I don't believe the mayor addressed himself to the problem. He is passing the buck to the county, the suburbs, the state. Though, of course, these people have a responsibility in the matter, it is very obvious that the mayor is shirking his own responsibility. He is not using the influence and authority that he does in fact have.

Whether one calls it "institutional leadership," "buck-passing," or something else, there is no doubt that the mayor's strategy produced the results. A few months after the riot the state provided an extra $3 million in school aid to the city's "core." At about the same time the state established a Department of Local Affairs which was to distribute more than another $1 million in the core. The federal government, of course, contributed heavily, the Labor Department allocating $2.4 million to attack "hard core" unemployment and the Office of Economic Opportunity announcing that it would make a large grant. In April 1968 the mayor was reelected with an unprecedented 90 percent of the vote, although he had rested on his laurels as a metropolitan statesman without campaigning at all.

Mayor Maier's theory of urban leadership has been thoroughly vindicated in Milwaukee. Those who before the riot were only groping for a national media strategy have learned from the mayor's example and are becoming adept at his style of leadership. Father Groppi, the militant civil rights leader, for example, has led daily demonstration-marches and has organized boycotts that have attracted national attention. Negro teen-agers are, of course, looking forward to putting Milwaukee on the map again and to the television coverage that they may expect. Even conservative Negroes are solemnly telling whites that "there's another one coming, and it's going to be a REAL RIOT." In the future, obviously, there will be at least two sides playing the RIOT game. It is safe to say that Milwaukee will never settle back to the old style of politics which involved discussion and bargaining about concrete local issues. From now on matters will be decided by confrontations of sides, all getting their cues from Washington, New York, Los Angeles and all addressing the others via the national media. In this new style of politics there will probably be less room for facts, reason, or compromise and none at all for behind-the-scenes negotiation. Milwaukee, it seems, has ceased to be the city of good beer and honest government and has become "Any Big City, U.S.A."

✄ 5. CRISIS IN CAMBRIDGE
David Boesel / Louis C. Goldberg
with a chronology by Jesse Epstein

Chronology of Events, July 1967

What has come to be known as the "Cambridge riot" was in fact a low-level civil disturbance. For a few hours on the night of Monday, July 24, and an hour on the night of Wednesday, July 26, there were small-scale disorders by Negro crowds, but nothing of the magnitude anticipated by local authorities or reported in the press. Here is a chronology of the events:

July 21: The Maryland State Police learned that Rap Brown would speak in Cambridge on July 24. The Cambridge police were contacted and an official told the State Police, "This looks bad to me, and I think we had better prepare for it." [1] The Cambridge police had already ordered all guns and ammunition in stores removed and locked up. Preparations were made by the State Police and a meeting with the National

Guard, State Police, and Cambridge police was held prior to July 24.

July 24, morning: While at the Easton Barracks of the National Guard, a state policeman suggested the Cambridge company be called for a "routine" training session. He was told that July 24 happened to be a regularly scheduled training night.

4:00 P.M.: The State Police dispatched twenty-eight men and three K–9 teams to the state road barn near Cambridge. Twenty additional men remained on standby in Easton.

7:00 P.M.: The State Police visited the police chief of Cambridge in his office. "They engaged the chief in a conversation over a rifle in the office, which the lieutenant identified as a 45–70 caliber. The chief confirmed this and displayed ammunition which he stated had been bought the same day." [2]

Approximately 7:45 P.M.: Officials of the National Guard, State Police, and city police gathered at the office of the chief of police.

9:00 P.M.: Rap Brown began his speech late. It was scheduled for 8:00 P.M. The police chief stationed his Negro officers (five in all) in the crowd. They were to report periodically on the speech and the crowd's behavior.

10:00 P.M.: A newscaster returned to police headquarters with a tape of Brown's speech. All present listened to the tape.

10:05 P.M.: After his speech, Brown, followed by twenty-five to thirty people, walked toward Race Street, the Negro–white dividing line. Without prior warning, a deputy sheriff stationed on Race Street discharged a shotgun twice. Brown was slightly wounded by one of the pellets. The group retreated, gathering back on Pine Street where it grew to about 100. The chief was informed of this and remained in his office.

Approximately 10:10 P.M.: A compact car carrying four white teenagers made a run along Pine Street, either shooting or throwing firecrackers from the windows.

Approximately 10:25 P.M.: The compact made a second run along Pine Street. Some of the crowd on Pine Street returned to their homes for safety or to get arms. Members of the crowd asked the Negro patrolmen to stop the car. The police replied that nothing could be done because the car's occupants were white.

Approximately 11:00 P.M.: A small fire at a store was extinguished by an officer.

Approximately 12:00 midnight: There had been a considerable lull since the small fire; as a result, law enforcement officials unanimously agreed to release the National Guard.

Approximately 12:30 A.M.: The compact car made its third and final run along Pine Street. The car was stopped at a State Police barricade. No weapons were found and the occupants were released after questioning. Their car had been hit by two shots.

Approximately 12:45 A.M.: A crowd of 100 youths poured gasoline onto the street and lit it.

Approximately 12:45–1:15 A.M.: An officer was shot at Pine and Douglas away from the area of most activity. He was hit by shotgun pellets which were fired when he responded to a report that windows in a laundry had been broken (three windows broken, no looting). Prior to the shot, the youths, according to the wounded officer, were acting as if they fully expected and were very afraid that the police car would open fire on them.

When the police chief received the report of the shooting, he became highly agitated. After asking that every man be mobilized, he left. The police then received a report that the wounded officer's condition was not serious. Several additional squads of State Police were called into town from the barracks. General Gelston of the National Guard issued orders for the recall of the men who had been dismissed earlier. The police chief in the meantime had returned to the station, saying there were about 125 people on Pine Street and that he still wanted to go down there to clear the streets. The captain of the State Police unit asked advice from the attorney general, who had arrived in town and was listening to the tape of Brown's speech in the mayor's office. The State Police captain was advised that any action should be delayed, if possible, until General Gelston had arrived, whereby a meeting of minds might take place.

Approximately 1:45 A.M.: A meeting was held in General Gelston's office in which two State Police captains, Attorney General Burch, the police chief, the mayor, and the state's attorney were present. The State Police captain who had been on the scene continually inquired of the attorney general of the advisability and legality of asking the course of action desired by the police chief. It was finally decided that the State Police tactic would be to seal off the Negro ward rather than to move into it. This standard tactic, to isolate and contain a racially tense area, had been used effectively in the past. At the time this debate was going on about what action should be taken, there were no fires in the Negro section, and there were no riotous bands moving at will within the area. The police chief expressed anger at the failure to adopt the tactic of cleaning out the area, which he had proposed, and left the meeting.

Very shortly thereafter, however, word was received that the governor wanted the State Police and the National Guard to move into the Second Ward. But before his tactics were implemented, word was received that 1,000 people were now out on Pine Street.

2:00–2:15 A.M.: The cause of the large crowd was a fire at the Pine Street School. The fire spread, finally enveloping two blocks. A crowd of black people gathered to watch the blaze. The crowd was not violent; many wanted to help put out the fire. White linemen, working in the neighborhood, were not molested.

Many firemen, however, reported fear of going into the Negro ward to fight the fire. The chief of police supported them. The Maryland State Police offered protection for the firemen and sent two squads of men to an intersection one block from the fire for the purpose of escorting the fire equipment into the ward.

2:45–3:25 A.M.: It was not until 2:45 A.M. that the fire gong summoning other volunteer firemen to the firehouse went off. When the alarm went off, the Cambridge fire apparatus was finally pulled out of the firehouse, but did not proceed immediately to the rendezvous point with the State Police. It remained parked on a side street. The president of the city council, a Negro, tried to get the fire equipment dispatched to the scene of the fire. At 3:25 A.M. he also called the command post, since the fire equipment had still not arrived. In the meantime, the fire was rapidly spreading. The fire trucks were finally moved from their parked position, but not to the scene of the fire. They were pulled instead into alleyways for the purpose of protecting the main business district. At this point, both the mayor and Attorney General Francis Burch were vigorously urging the firemen to move in. It was not until approximately 3:30 A.M. that Attorney General Burch, answering a challenge from the firemen, boarded a truck and moved out with them toward the scene of the fire. The fire was not extinguished until daybreak. While the blaze was being fought, there was a rumor that several Negroes were planning to stage a march on City Hall, but the march did not materialize.

8:00 A.M., *Tuesday, July 25 until 9:00* P.M., *Wednesday:* All quiet.

Approximately 9:00 P.M., *Wednesday:* Negroes held a rally at Main and Pine Streets; during the rally a National Guard jeep passed by. An empty beer can was thrown at it.

Approximately 10:00 P.M.: Negro youths went on a minor rampage. An overturned telephone booth formed a barricade; a Negro policeman's car and a white car were pelted with rocks and bottles; tops were knocked off parking meters; and there was attempted arson against several buildings.

Approximately 11:00 P.M.: After a warning, the crowd on Pine Street was dispersed by the National Guard using tear gas. The speaker at the rally was arrested.

This ends the series of events termed the Cambridge "riot." If we accept widespread mass violence as one of the definitive characteristics of a riot, the term seems inappropriate to the events in Cambridge.

Interpretation of Events

Cambridge, Maryland, is a small Eastern Shore town of about 14,000 people, 65 percent of them white, 35 percent Negro. Its economy is based largely on the gathering and processing of seafood and on truck farming, though its industrial facilities are beginning to diversify. The town used to be dominated by a single, large cannery, but the industry went into decline around 1938, and shortly after World War II the remnants were sold to a Chicago firm. The local economy declined along with the industry, and throughout the late 1940's and the 1950's unemployment and economic stagnation were chronic. In 1962 the Department of Labor put the surrounding Dorchester County on its first list of depressed areas. But by that time Cambridge had begun to attract a number of new small industries. Unemployment decreased from 13.8 percent in 1961 to 8.5 percent in 1963 to an estimated 3 or 4 percent today.

As a result both of its 1962 depressed area status and the bitter civil rights struggle that took place there in 1963, Cambridge has received a good deal of aid from the federal government. Since 1963 about $4.7 million in federal funds has gone into the town, in addition to sizable MDTA and ARA expenditures borne jointly by the state and federal governments. The Cambridge area has a poverty program which has received $594,036 since 1965, but it seems significant that few Cambridge Negroes interviewed were aware of the program.

BACKGROUND AND INSTITUTIONS

Though located on Maryland's eastern shore, Cambridge is more like a deep southern than a middle-Atlantic town in its racial attitudes. Almost all facilities were segregated until the massive Negro demonstrations of 1963 forced token integration. Today there seems to be a grudging acceptance by whites of Negro gains, but old attitudes prevail. The assistant chief of police is quoted in an interview as saying, "When you tell a darkie something, you've got to mean it." Another interview with white junior high school students brought forth such comments as, "If the Good Lord had wanted the races to live together, He wouldn't have put them on different continents," and "The best solution to the Negro problem would be to ship all Negroes back to Africa."

The managers of the recently arrived industries constitute a new stratum of white society in Cambridge, more moderate in its racial attitudes than the old-line white elite, more concerned with community harmony and business as usual than with segregation of the races. While many Negroes refer to the new managers as part of the white power structure, the fact that they have not significantly moderated the racial stance of city officials seems to indicate that as a group they are not prime movers in Cambridge politics. They seem to be relatively uninvolved in the town's racial turmoil, entering politics only when the immediate interests of their companies are at stake.

The center of power in Cambridge seems to be a small group of influential white citizens, most of them long-time residents of the town. Reports about the number of people in this group vary. It is thought to include a prominent attorney, the editor of the local newspaper, a downtown merchant, an insurance man and landlord, and one of the new managers.

The local fire department, a volunteer organization, is a considerable force in city politics; it has consistently opposed Negro demands. Being a voluntary organization, it maintains itself through the ties among its members and the various social service benefits it can provide. Politically, it functions as the Cambridge equivalent of "Tammany Hall," and it affects the content of public policy issues. The fire department actively campaigned for the defeat of the local public accommodations law in 1963. The present mayor, a segregationist, was a former member of the volunteer fire department. The department also ran a segregated swimming pool which was a source of community tension for a period. No Negroes belong to the department, and they are not wanted as members. During a crisis period in 1963–1964 when the firemen refused to fight fires in the Negro area, the former mayor had to threaten replacing them with a paid fire department before the volunteers would fulfill their responsibility.

Politically, Negroes have little representation, and the men presently running the city government were elected without Negro support. The present mayor received only 3 votes out of 1,700 in the predominantly Negro Second Ward. There is one Negro councilman, a seventy-four-year-old man who is also president of the city council and has been on the council for over fifteen years. He has tried to cooperate closely with whites, working for gradual change within the context of community harmony as the path for Negro progress. Many whites apparently respect him, and he reportedly had a considerable following among older Negroes. But the gains he has been able to achieve for this community have been minimal, and he exercises little power. A petty illustration of his lack of power is the fact that the small park bearing his name is run down and uncared for. A more fundamental indicator of his importance was his inability, during the recent crisis, to persuade the fire department to go into the Negro business district and keep it from burning down.

The grievances and demands of Cambridge Negroes were fairly specific and well defined in the months before the events of July 24–26. The interview data show substantial agreement among Negroes on the need for change in the following areas.

1. Housing / Following the 1963–1964 period, some new low-cost housing for Negroes was built. The quality of the new housing is very good, but Negro informants complain that there is not enough of it, while dilapidated housing which was supposed to be replaced is still in use. Commission investigators found that some Negro families were living in converted chicken coops. Negroes believe that the city administration is dragging its feet in putting up more public housing. There is also a good deal of frustration over the failure to enforce the local housing code. One of the accomplishments of the militant period was the passage of a modern housing code which, if enforced, would compel white landlords to improve considerably the many ramshackle buildings in which Negroes live. Enforcement of the code, however, has been minimal at best.

2. Police and Administration of Justice / There was strong resentment at what were felt to be discriminatory practices in the police and administration of justice. Of particular concern was the limited authority of Negro police. An unwritten rule of the department is that the Negro police can only arrest Negroes for law infractions and that they must call the main station for permission to arrest whites. The lack of complaint channels is also a problem. Few complaints are ever lodged against the police by Negroes because there is a general belief that it would just be a waste of time.

3. Employment Training and Poverty Programs / Negroes feel that existing government programs have failed to reach the people who most need them, that many job-training programs are irrelevant—people trained for specific jobs finding that they cannot gain employment after completing the program—and that there is a lack of training in such areas as building and construction. That latter area is recognized as a lucrative source of employment and high wages, and Negroes at present are almost totally excluded. Although the employment situation in Cambridge, according to businessmen, is "tight," Negroes complain about the low access to higher-paying, status jobs. Businessmen, on the other hand, complain about the lack of reliability in their Negro workers.

4. Education / In 1964 the Dorchester County School Board began a "freedom of choice" program of school selection by students. The program has resulted in 21 percent of the Negro students being enrolled in desegregated schools. But Negroes argue that white students are allowed to travel across town to predominantly white schools, while Negroes are confined to the schools within their community. There is one all-Negro high school in the county and one all-Negro elementary school. A major source of controversy in the community had been the continued use of the black elementary school which a local policeman said he had attended nearly a half-century before. The school was widely considered a firetrap, yet the school superintendent refused to transfer its Negro students to other schools because of the possibility of overcrowding. The Negro community suspected that the school superintendent did not want to be put in the position of having to integrate classes at the lowest levels. The program of school integration had, from the perspective of the militants, been going very slowly. Many Negro teachers were also dissatisfied with their position in the school system, over twenty of them resigning at the end of the spring 1967 semester.

5. General Attitudes of Authorities toward Negroes / Finally, the attitudes of public authorities toward Negroes continued to be a source of considerable bitterness. Negroes believed that city officials considered talking with the militants a waste of time—a belief supported by interview data. Negroes thought the police chief was totally unwilling and unable to talk with Negro representatives on a man-to-man basis. And they felt that the school superintendent was similarly intransigent in receiving requests and suggestions from Negroes, no matter how reasonable and logical they might be.

THE LEGACY OF 1963: COMMUNITY POLARIZATION

In order to understand the response of the Negro community and local white authorities to H. Rap Brown's visit and to ensuing events, it is necessary to refer to the confrontation between the races that occurred in 1963. At that time Gloria Richardson was leading a militant Negro movement which was stubbornly resisted by white authorities. Violent attacks by white citizens led Negroes to arm themselves for self-defense and to respond violently. The town was finally placed under martial law, the National Guard enforcing an uneasy peace.

Subsequently, Richardson left town, and the Negro movement, deprived of her leadership, dissolved. Local organizations such as the NAACP and the Nonviolent Action Committee became relatively inactive. Civil rights organizations in Baltimore which had aided the Cambridge movement were carrying on activities elsewhere between 1964 and 1967. On the surface, at least, all was quiet relative to the previous period of militant protest, street marches, and intense confrontation between Negro demonstrators and white authorities.

The white authorities, for their part, viewed the sharp decline in overt militancy after Richardson's departure and the withdrawal of the National Guard as a confirmation of their interpretation of events. They saw the disturbances in 1963–1964 as primarily the work of outsiders, the national press, hidden subversive groups, and General Gelston of the state National Guard. They believed that Gloria Richardson was a local malcontent motivated by personal ambition and jealousy; that Gelston staged demonstrations so that he could get publicity and recognition; that Negroes had no legitimate grievances; that Cambridge did not have a serious racial problem.

The prolonged period of conflict between the races during 1963–1964 produced a polarization of forces in the town. When the former mayor, a moderate on racial issues, retired, he was replaced by a segregationist candidate who drew almost no support from the Negro community. The mood in the Negro community in the meantime had undergone a considerable change. Prior to the protest period, there was some reason for local officials to think Cambridge Negroes were happy because "they never asked for anything." The protests, if nothing else, had developed the feeling among Cambridge Negroes that they did have the right to expect benefits from the government and to make demands upon it.

The protests also made public officials and white citizens understandably sensitive about the town's reputation. There is considerable antipathy toward the national press for its treatment of the 1963 struggle and an inclination to think that the local newspaper presented the only accurate and reasonable account of those events. A number of the interviews with prominent local officials suggest a state-of-siege mentality which may account in part for their response to Rap Brown's visit.

As can be seen, community peace in Cambridge rested on a very tenuous basis during 1964–1967. The tensions generated by a high grievance level among Negroes, on the one hand, and an unwillingness by whites to grant Negroes genuine political access, on the other, made the maintance of surface harmony a precarious balance—one that could easily be upset. What was lacking to upset it was new leadership and organization to replace the 1963 protest structure, which had since dissolved.

A NEW PHASE OF CONFLICT

With Negro organizational efforts in June 1967 the racial situation in Cambridge began to move toward a second and higher phase of conflict. The precipitating incident was a fight between a Negro youth and a white youth, in which the latter's brother set loose a dog on the Negro boy. The angry father of the Negro youth went to the state's attorney of Dorchester County to protest and met rebuff. The state's attorney's failure to act on this matter of symbolic importance quickly generated intense anger in the Negro community. Matters were not helped when the white youth, found guilty in court, was given a suspended fine at the same time that a Negro youth was held on $25,000 bond for setting false fire alarms.

There were signs in subsequent weeks that Cambridge was heading toward another crisis period. Two or three attempts had been made during June and July to burn down the ramshackle Pine Street Elementary School. The school had been a source of great bitterness in the Negro community. Negroes considered it a firetrap, as did many whites, and there was some agreement among blacks that it ought to be destroyed. For Negroes the school had become a symbol of an intransigent school system and of a city administration that had been persistently unresponsive to their interests.

Another event which helped set the stage for developments on the night of July 24 was a fire which burned down the Negro Elks Lodge, a center for social activities. Negroes suspected that the fire had been set by a white arsonist (although an official at the club says he believes it was done by a disgruntled member). When the volunteer fire department trucks arrived, stones were thrown at the equipment. (This event provided some basis in reality for the fears of white firemen about going into the Negro area on the evening of July 24.)

Along with unorganized expressions of discontent, there were significant developments in the area of Negro leadership and competition between emerging "moderate" and "militant" elements. Gloria Richardson returned to Cambridge to provide support for the local NAACP just a few days before H. Rap Brown arrived. The Ministerial Alliance attempted to take the initiative in representing the moderate elements in the community. At the same time, several quiescent militant groups were drawn together to form the Black Action Federation. One of their first acts was to appear at a July 2 rally held by the States Rights party, a meeting subsequently broken up by the police, to demand equal time. This incident put them in the public eye, and to attract new followers and reactivate the militance of Cambridge Negroes, the federation invited H. Rap Brown to speak at a meeting. Rumors of his impending arrival began circulating two weeks before he was to appear.

But more than Negro militance, that invitation reactivated the fears, anxieties, and hostility of white people in Cambridge. The mutual alienation of the Negro and white communities led to remors and misconceptions that affected both sides but were particularly exaggerated among local authorities. Brown's presence, or the anticipation of it, served to bring out old antagonisms and predispositions to action—especially on the part of the Cambridge officials.

When the mayor, police chief, and others heard of Brown's plans to come to Cambridge, they anticipated a dramatic escalation of the type of collective action led by Gloria Richardson in 1963–1964. As Richardson had organized and directed marches, so they expected Brown to organize and direct a riot. As they saw it, there was a plan to trap police and firemen in the ghetto, thus opening the downtown business district to attack. They had, in fact, met several times before Brown's arrival to set a course of action appropriate to the tactics they expected him to employ. Since an attack on the downtown business district was anticipated, for example, police were stationed at Race Street ready for action. The police were prepared to assume that any large group of Negroes walking toward the business section had arson on their minds and that force would be necessary to turn them back.

This view of impending events and the anticipatory countermeasures were no doubt reinforced by an awareness of recent violence in other cities and claims that outbreaks were the work of outside agitators.

A RECURRENT PATTERN OF CONFLICTS

The events of July 24–26 were in a way a partial reenactment of the 1963 experience—a Negro rally organized by militants; a near-violent white reaction (the two shotgun blasts by the deputy, the carful of white nightriders); a violent, though limited, counterreaction by Negroes (firing at the nightriders, the shooting of the officer, the window breaking and attempted arson at the laundry, the arson at the school); retributive violence by local white authorities (allowing the school fire to become a major conflagration); and at this point the entry of the National Guard. There was no evidence of a Negro plan of action, little Negro violence, and, with one exception, no violence by white citizens. But local authorities and Cambridge Negroes respectively acted *as though* there would be.

Three specific factors provided the immediate context which confirmed the belief of authorities that the disorders were solely the product of outside agitation: (1) The content of Brown's speech and the excitement it generated or was seen to generate; (2) the communication of information about Brown's speech (and the crowd response) by the Negro police who were the informants for white authorities; and (3) Brown's walking toward the white business district followed by twenty-five to thirty Negro youths.

Brown's speech was unequivocally militant and revolutionary. About half the speech was taken up in denouncing the "White Devil," the other half in exhorting Negroes to defend themselves, take control of their communities, and be prepared to use violence against the white oppressor. Race war was portrayed as the basic character of Negro–white relations.

Within this ideological context, specific references to Cambridge were made:

1. Cambridge needs a riot.
2. Negroes should have burned down the local elementary school.
3. Whites burned the Elks' home so that black people couldn't enjoy themselves.

4. Get rid of your "five nigger cops."
5. Tear up the town, if the man doesn't come around.

The relation between Brown's remarks and the events that followed the speech is far from clear, however. Even the seemingly obvious connection between the speech and the fire at the Pine Street School becomes more tenuous upon examination. As noted, the school had for some time been an object of considerable Negro resentment, and several attempts to burn it down had already been made. The youth who was first accused of setting the fire was said to have confessed, giving as a reason for his action that people had been saying the school ought to be burned. But when asked for copies of confession, the police chief and the state's attorney explained that it hadn't been a written confession. And very recently the Cambridge newspaper has been carrying an ad by the state's attorney offering a substantial reward for information leading to the arrest of the person who set the fire.

Although generating considerable excitement among his listeners, there is little evidence that Brown's speech stirred the crowd to action. Indeed, the interviews indicate that the response to his exhortations was not universally favorable, some Negroes present taking exception to his strident militancy. And immediately after the speech the crowd began to disperse.

Members of the Black Action Federation say that Brown then went upstairs to their office to discuss the talk and to exchange addresses. Later, according to this account, Brown agreed to escort a Negro girl who had been intimidated by the presence of the police, and in the process of walking her home attracted an entourage of twenty-five to thirty young Negroes. A Negro officer on the scene, on the other hand, says that Brown did not go upstairs after the speech, but immediately began to march toward the white business district, followed by the Negro youths. This message, together with an alarming assessment of the potential for Negro violence, was passed on to white authorities waiting at the police station.

Given the interests of both informants, it is difficult to tell which version is accurate. There is evidence, however, that the crowd was dispersing after the speech. Further, the fact that twenty-five minutes passed between the end of Brown's speech and the time he was shot leaves open the possibility that he might have gone up to the office and weakens the contention that he immediately led a march downtown. And finally, the fact that so little Negro violence actually occurred that night weakens the Negro officer's assessment of that potential, although its failure to materialize might be attributed to the response of white authorities. In any case, police at the scene interpreted Brown's walk or march as confirmation of their expectations, and a deputy sheriff fired two blasts from a shotgun as warning. A pellet from the second blast hit Brown in the forehead, and the little crowd retreated back down the street. Thus began the chain of disorderly events that were to mark the rest of the evening.

At this point responses conditioned by the events of 1963 came more fully into play. After a carful of white youths had made one or two passes through the Negro section, shooting guns or setting off firecrackers, a rumor began to circulate that there was about to be an attack on the area by large numbers of whites. Negroes immediately armed themselves and prepared to defend their territory. In 1963 this response to white nightriding had become so well developed that armed Negroes would go to assigned stations, arranged along the streets in such a way as to prevent their shooting at each other.

The police chief's reaction to events as he perceived them also harks back to 1963. In the present event, when he got word that a white officer had been shot, according to the Maryland State Police Report, he

rushed into his office, and grabbing the rifle (that he had shown a state police lieutenant earlier that day) and two boxes of ammunition, he shouted, "They have shot one of my officers. We're going to get every son-of-a-bitch down there. I'm getting goddamned tired of fooling around.

The ex-mayor (mayor at the time of the 1963 disturbances) noted that the police chief was a man who was subject to emotional stress and tended to become erratic at such moments. He said that during the 1963 demonstrations he and the state's attorney had had to "sit on" the chief to prevent him from acting irrationally. For example, the ex-mayor observed, at one point while the protest marches were going on, the police chief had wanted to stop buses full of demonstrators coming into Cambridge and shoot them.

The volunteer firemen's refusal to put out the blaze that started at the Pine Street School also recalls the events of 1963, when the mayor had to threaten to replace them with a paid fire department to get them to go into the Negro section. This time a different mayor made no such threat. There is reason to believe that the firemen were afraid to go into the Negro section this time, but that can only be part of the story. Even after two squads of State Police were marshaled on the perimeter ready to escort them into the area, the firemen waited more than an hour before moving their equipment less than half a block into the Negro neighborhood adjoining the scene of the fire.

Brown's speech, the "march," the shooting of an officer, and the fire at Pine Street School all tended to confirm the preconceived notions of local authorities, but beyond this, the authorities often acted in such a way as to bring about results which would further reinforce their preconceptions. Thus, the deputy's shooting of Brown initiated a disturbance where there had been none before.

Similarly the shooting of the white police officer when examined in context appears as much a reaction to the immediate police conduct as it does an outgrowth of Brown's speech. Brown had already been wounded, and the wounded officer observed that the conspicuous display of weapons by the police was intimidating to Negro youths on the street. When he received a call to investigate a broken window in a laundry, he and several other officers drove to the scene, police rifles sticking out the windows of the car. As they went down the street, he noted that Negro youths, seeing the car, hit the ground like a series of tin soldiers. A moment later he was hit by a shotgun blast, though not seriously wounded. Like the shooting of Brown, this act is best seen as an overreaction to the events of the day. The deputy fired into the ground to stop what appeared to be an aggressive and hostile crowd; the shot directed toward the police might have been based on the belief that they were about to open fire. Both acts were based on a judgment that a real danger existed which fit the expectations of armed conflict. If the police car had approached the laundry in a less-threatening manner it is possible that the shot may not have been fired.

Other official actions also tended to reinforce official preconceptions. For example, the refusal of the police chief and firemen to respond to the blaze in the Negro section in effect created an enormous fire which could then be perceived as the heart of the "riot" and in fact was so reported in many news accounts.

Four factors seem to have been involved in this refusal. The first was vengeance. The leader of the Black Action Federation says that the police chief told him, "You goddam niggers started this fire, now you goddam niggers watch it burn." The State Police reported overhearing the remark, "They started the fire—let them put it out," but the report does not indicate the source of the remark. The second factor was an inability in the event to distinguish between different members of the Negro community. The black population as a whole was seen as responsible for the fire. The third was a perception of the crowd at the fire as violent and a consequent unwillingness to risk the "dangers" of entering the area to put it out. The fourth was the fear that committing firemen to the Negro section might divert them from fires to be set downtown in accordance with the "riot plan" thought to have been put into effect.

The net result, from the point of view of local authorities, was *a fire* started by a violent crowd of Negroes, whose violence provided a rationale for inaction by the police chief and the fire department.

Now it is worth noting that there was no crowd at all at the beginning of the fire, so it could hardly have been the product of a violent mob of Negroes. Things had become quiet enough by midnight to justify sending the National Guard contingent home.

Further, when a crowd did assemble to watch the fire, it was entirely peaceful. One observer noted that the majority of the youths in the crowd were the offspring of the town's "good Negroes." Not only were repeated pleas for help made to the chief and firemen, but there were repeated offers to help from members of the crowd. Negroes borrowed a hose from one of the trucks on the perimeter, but it would not fit the hydrant. (This was reported to the police chief as theft of the hose.) When fire trucks finally did come in, Negro youths came with them to help water down the rubble. And the two (or four) white linemen who were at work clipping wires were not bothered at all.

Even the fire might have seemed only minor destruction had the police chief had his way. He was at odds with the commanding officer of the Maryland State Police contingent about whether the latter would go into the crowd Monday night to help the chief disperse it. At this point, about 1:00 A.M., the Cambridge police officer had just been shot, and the chief had rushed into the office to get his rifle and ammunition. (Earlier that evening the chief had discussed the rifle with two State Police officers and had told them that he had bought the ammunition the same day.) He demanded that every man be mobilized to help clear the streets, left for a moment, and returned to reiterate his demand. The State Police captain in charge of the contingent refused to comply, saying that his orders were to secure the perimeter. He was afraid of dire consequences should the chief carry out his intentions, and said as much to both the mayor and the state attorney general at the time. Neither the State Police nor the local police went into the Negro section at the time, and there was almost no further violence that night. But had the chief gone into the area with the backing of the State Police, he might very well have precipitated the riot he expected.

RESTRAINTS ON VIOLENCE

The interesting question about the July 24 disturbance is not why there was some racial violence, but why there was not more of it. It could be suggested that some were afraid to act because of the potential for violence in white arms, but the fact that others showed a readiness to pick up guns and fire at the carful of white youths argues in the other direction.

A more satisfactory though partial explanation lies in the fact that the Negro population of Cambridge has been quite stable in recent years. The absence of large population shifts among Cambridge Negroes suggests that the social disruptions attendant on migration do not exist to any pronounced degree there. We may, therefore, expect to find a more stable family structure and more social control internal to the Negro area than would be the case, say, in a ghetto which has experienced a large in-migration within the last fifteen years. A related factor is the size of the town and of the Negro section in particular. Negroes in Cambridge live in a tight-knit community; most of them know each other personally, and many of them are related to each other. These community bonds tend to reduce their potential for the explosive sort of violence characteristic of big-city riots. A third factor, perhaps, is that, unlike most large northern cities, there are few white-owned businesses in the Negro area, and thus few immediate targets to attack. However, the most important factor in the restraint of violence on both sides was undoubtedly the role of the State Police and National Guard. Many Cambridge Negroes were ready to pick up guns at a moment's notice, were in fact armed on the streets the first night, and had in the past demonstrated their willingness to use arms. The police chief, for his part, was ready to use violence against the Negro crowd. The State Police captain's restraint at the time the police chief came into the office to get his rifle was probably the most crucial of official decisions in preventing widespread violence. His decision was later confirmed at the less volatile meeting attended by the National Guard commander and other authorities. By the time the National Guard troops did finally move into the Negro section, the situation on both sides had become calmer. The continued presence of the National Guard, which enjoyed a good deal of confidence in the Negro community as a result of its role in the 1963 disturbances, contributed further to the maintenance of order, once established. Without the presence of the State Police and the National Guard as neutral intermediaries in the first twelve hours, the culmination of events on July 24 could have been disastrous.

THE RESPONSE OF THE PRESS

Despite the fact that a riot did not occur, newspaper accounts of the disturbance tended to propagate the notion that Brown incited a riot in Cambridge. A careful reading of available clippings indicates that newspapers in reporting the specific instances of violence were pretty close to the mark. But nevertheless, the overall impression one gets is of widespread violence following immediately upon Brown's speech. This impression is created in a number of ways. First, in headlining and generalizing about the event, terms such as "riot," "widespread violence," and "a night of gunfire and arson" create a backdrop to the details which make them seem specific instances of a general conflagration. Second, the space given to statements by local officials assured that their interpretation of events would predominate. Significantly, in none of the articles available was there an interview with members of the Black Action Federation, the group which invited Brown and whose members were present when the incidents started. Third, there was a pronounced tendency to emphasize the connection between Brown's speech and the generalized violence that was presumed to have occurred after it. About two weeks later, for example, in referring back to the event, an influential east coast newspaper remarked as a matter of course on "the July 24 violence that followed a speech in Cambridge by Black Power leader H. Rap Brown." No explicit causal connection is made, but the constant repetition of "Brown—riot in Cambridge" in the press cannot help create the impression that he started a riot. And when certain parts of Brown's speech are quoted—e.g., "that school should have been burned down a long time ago"—there remains little doubt in the reader's mind as to what happened.

It may be emotionally satisfying to think that Brown came to Cambridge and that therefore a riot followed; it may be simpler for the public to grasp. But the facts are more complex and quite different.

Brown's role seems to have been this: to have induced in city officials a sense of an impending riot, which then became the basis of their subsequent actions and interpretation of events. To the extent that Brown encouraged anybody to engage in precipitous or disorderly acts, the city officials are clearly the ones he influenced most. Indeed, the riot existed for the most part in the minds of city officials, and to the extent that Negro disorder occurred, it can best be interpreted as a response to their actions. Brown was more a catalyst of white fears than of Negro antagonisms, the disturbance more a product of white expectations than of Negro initiative.

COMMUNITY TENSION AND THE ABSENCE OF LEADERSHIP

In the aftermath of the disorder, however, neither the fears nor antagonisms, whether real or imagined, show any signs of diminishing. The basic sources of tension continue to exist. One immediate problem, certainly, is the continued intransigence, or state-of-siege mentality, of key public officials. It is difficult to expect an improvement in the racial situation in Cambridge without a change of officials presently responsible for formulating policy. Men not wedded to segregationist doctrine, men considerably more open-minded and flexible in their approach to Cambridge's racial problem, would seem to be required. And one business leader mentioned that it was certain that Cambridge would have "new leadership" after the next election.

A more basic problem is the continuing social alienation between whites and Negroes. Little energy, if any, is forthcoming from within the local white community for restructuring the general pattern of race relations in Cambridge. There are very few individuals or groups among the whites of Cambridge that publicly support the Negro cause. The churches, with the exception of the Catholic Church, have not taken a leadership role toward actively counteracting prevalent racial attitudes. Most ministers either reflect, or acquiesce in, the predominant social sentiments of their parishioners. Those who speak in support of Negro grievances have faced the severe penalty of social ostracism.

Local businessmen have shown a lack of interest in the race problem, or at least an unwillingness to take a leadership role in improving the situation. This in part seems to be accounted for by the wage and industry situation in Cambridge. New industry was attracted to the town by the low wage scale and the promise of a tax-free period. There is a fear that unionization of Cambridge's unorganized workers would considerably raise the wage scale. And there is some indication that businessmen see the present race situation, which divides white and black workers, as a positive factor in preventing the development of a strong union movement in Cambridge.

And within the Negro community leadership and organization continue to be fragmented. Although articulating essentially the same programs, the community leadership remains split between "militant" and "moderate" factions, who have considerable difficulty in cooperating with each other. According to informants, personal disputes and rivalries continue to prevent the development of a unified leadership coalition with which to confront the problems of the community. At the same time, due to the already extensive history of structured conflict, the Cambridge Negro community remains highly conducive to militant action in the future—with violent confrontation looming as a distinct possibility.

NOTES

1. Maryland State Police Report.
2. State Police Report.

II

The Riots and Public Authority

The riots signaled the failure of containment by liberal means. Previous racial-political contests escalated into violence, and the underlying issue of power came to the surface as police and blacks struggled for control of the ghetto streets. The rudimentary public-political character of the riots was evident in the fact that they usually started in places that were heavily populated and in some sense "belonged" to blacks—main avenues in the ghettos and large public housing projects, for example. Moreover, the big supermarkets and chain drugstores, most heavily frequented in normal times, were most likely to be taken over during the riots as the common property of blacks. Under the definitions which emerged in the ghettos during the riots the New Left slogan applied without exaggeration: "The streets (and the stores) belong to the people."

The response of public authorities to the riots was characterized by a good deal of confusion and disorder. For the police and other control forces the absence of tactical precedents, the problems of coordination, the political and jurisdictional tangles, and sometimes the sheer massiveness of a riot all had a disorganizing and disruptive effect. In the larger riots the courts were often overwhelmed by a flood of arrestees; records and identities were lost in the confusion; judges were presented with hundreds of cases based on the scantiest evidence; lawyers, friends, and relatives searched the courts and jails for people who may have been arrested. In the aftermath of the riots, commissions were hurriedly set up and given a short time in which to produce reports that were supposed to be accurate, enlightening, and above all politically acceptable.

Underlying the confusion, however, was an implicitly recognized common cause: to put down the revolts. With due allowance for the benign sentiments of liberal officials, the fact remains that where immediate decisions were required, the overriding aim of authorities was to reestablish an ordering of power that was inherently oppressive to blacks. Whatever the means employed and whatever the rhetoric, the end was summed up in Chief Parker's powerfully simple phrase—to see to it that "we're on top and they're on the bottom."

It is worth emphasizing that the common cause of public authorities could give rise to diverse tactics, ranging from persuasion and negotiation (on secondary issues) to outright force. It is also worth emphasizing that putting down the riots was not necessarily the same as reasserting the rule of law; often the law was simply ignored as authorities reimposed order. Nor were organizational discipline and established procedures a necessary part of the repression, for police and even judges in some cases "rioted" effectively against blacks.

Usually the conflict between police and ghetto rioters (a subject discussed by Louis Goldberg and Gary Marx) did not constitute a state of war; it was more a violent contest for social and territorial control. In most cases both sides recognized certain limits on violence: police would use their clubs rather than shooting blacks (in *most* cases), and rioters would hurl taunts and bricks at police, but rarely try to kill them. Much of the contest took place on a symbolic level, each side trying to demonstrate its power. When black crowds filled ghetto streets, isolated policemen stationed in front of stores often stood by and watched as looters hurried out with their arms full. Since they recognized that they were on foreign soil and that the rules of the game had changed, they were effectively neutralized by the blacks' demonstration of power. On the other hand, a massive show of force by police often squelched incipient riots without violence.

In the smaller riots, where the resources of public authorities were not stretched to the limit, there was some room for maneuver in the situation. Alternate courses of action were open to them, and the possibilities for resolutions on the political level were considerable. But in the largest riots, when local public authorities had their backs against the wall, official violence was often seen as the only alternative. Local au-

thorities ordinarily did not accede to negotiations or other symbolic set-
tlements (such as withdrawing police from the ghettos) when they were
in a position of weakness, because they could always count on reinforcements from higher levels of government.

In these giant riots the situation approached a state of war at the
point where the rioters, having disorganized the police and broken their
control, began to lose the initiative in the face of official reinforcements.
Under these circumstances there emerged among the police a set of
collective norms which, as Gary Marx points out, defined all blacks as
the enemy and condoned assaults on the black community *as such*. Just
as the black community had supported the rioters, so the police now
supported members of the force in antiblack retaliatory riots. The crucial difference in the normative support on either side was that the
black community generally stopped short of deadly violence while the
police in these cases did not. The result was a very one-sided "war"—
something more akin to a massacre.

As the articles from the two university law reviews illustrate, the
courts in the largest riots often functioned without apologies as part of
the repressive machinery. Judges worked hand in hand with police and
prosecutors to get black people off the streets and into jails. Just as the
police showed a tendency to arrest, beat, and sometimes kill indiscriminately, so the judges were sometimes inclined either to mass-process
prisoners, or taking them one by one, to view them as representatives of
the rioting ghetto. In these massive upheavals, it is quite appropriate to
view the riot sequence in collective and institutional terms as follows:
the black community having rioted, it was then arrested, brought briefly
before the judge, and jailed.

There were significant exceptions to these patterns in the largest
riots. An individual exception, noted in the *Michigan Law Review*
study, was Judge George Crockett of Detroit, a black man, who insisted
that the cases brought before him be considered individually and on
their merits. A year later Judge Crockett aroused the fury of many
whites in Detroit by releasing some 147 men, women, and children arrested at a meeting of the Republic of New Africa inside a church after
a black guard outside apparently killed one policeman and wounded another.

A broader exception to this pattern of repression was the conduct of
public authorities in Washington, D.C. Because Washington is controlled by the federal government, federal as well as local officials were
involved in every stage of policy-making vis-à-vis the riot, from preriot

planning through the adjudication of cases in the courts. The influence of a powerful liberal administration was pervasive: old-style civil libertarians from the Justice Department worked with crisis-management liberals from the Defense Department and elsewhere; a federally appointed Director of Public Safety, also liberal, was in charge of the police; capable judges presided over the federal courts, which have jurisdiction over Washington. To these factors, which contributed to official restraint in putting down the riot, was another of equal importance —the availability of enormous numbers of federal troops. Despite the size of the riot, public authorities apparently never felt the impulse to utter Mayor Addonizio's despairing words, "It is all gone, the whole town is gone."

The riot commissions, the subject of the third part of this section, were more than official afterthoughts on the riots; they were part of the political dynamics which included the riots. Their main function was to explain these crises to the public in terms consistent with dominant political assumptions. They also served to buy time by giving the appearance of motion where the political and other costs of more positive policies were considered too high. And in some cases they served as arenas for the various interested parties—black militants and moderates, police, political leaders, academics, and the like.

Although the riot commissions were ordinarily set up as instruments of executive policy, some possessed a sufficient degree of independence and represented a sufficient diversity of political forces to issue reports somewhat out of line with expectations on high. One can assume that the report of the McCone Commission did not greatly disturb Governor Brown, but President Johnson greeted the report of the National Advisory Commission with an obvious, disgruntled silence. Even so, the Kerner Commission was only slightly less myopic than the McCone Commission; for the most part it detailed what everyone already knew and ignored the most important (and most volatile) questions. Robert Blauner and Andrew Kopkind examine these two commissions from a radical perspective, and Allan Silver, in a more broadly historical piece, discusses the political uses of social science in interpreting riots.

Revolt and Repression

6. GHETTO RIOTS AND OTHERS: THE FACES OF CIVIL DISORDER IN 1967
Louis C. Goldberg

Introduction

Civil disorders in American cities in 1967 were not all of the same kind. The term "riot" has been too loosely applied to denote disturbances, often quite varied, which occurred last summer and in the previous three years. It has been used to refer to anything from a group of excited teen-agers breaking windows after a dance to a general social upheaval. All were civil disturbances; but only a few warranted the label "riot."

It is misleading also to think of the civil disturbances simply as "Negro riots." To do so suggests that the immediate responsibility for the course of the disturbances and the extent of the damage lie solely with the Negro participants. It is necessary, of course, to underscore the reality of violent and aggressive mass actions involving looting, burning, and defiance of local authority within Negro areas, and the initiative of Negro rioters in events. But the threats to civil order and innocent life and property did not come only from the Negro side. In some cities, the behavior of various official control agents—police, National Guardsmen, and the courts—in fact constituted official lawlessness: abuses of power in the name of law and order. For the largest disorders especially, the concept of a "tandem riot"—a riot by Negroes against public authorities, followed by a riot of control agents against Negroes—is appropriate.

From the *Journal of Peace Research 5*, no. 2 (1968); pp. 116–131 with deletions recently made by the author. This paper is based primarily on data published in *The Report of the National Advisory Commission on Civil Disorders* (New York: Bantam Books, 1968). The ideas for this particular analysis were formulated while I worked as a member of the social science research group of the commission.

In other cities, "Negro riots" were more imagined than real. For such disorders, we must distinguish between *actual* collective violence by Negroes and the *perception* of a riot by white authorities. There is much evidence that in several cities white anticipation of Negro violence led to heavy-handed uses of official force that provoked violence which might not have otherwise occurred.

The news media, for their part, sometimes contributed to building expectations of community violence by overdramatizing disturbances and helping to create an emotional climate in which even minor incidents were seen as major riots.

Prominent Features of Disorders: Classifying the Riots

A sample of twenty-three disturbances which occurred last summer shows clearly that the particular combination of circumstances in each city was to some extent unique. But at the same time certain characteristics of different disturbances were so similar that we may *group the disorders, particularly the largest ones, on the basis of their most prominent features.*

GENERAL UPHEAVALS

Over a period of time a disturbance may develop into an upheaval which draws in thousands or tens of thousands of participants from a Negro ghetto, exhausts the resources of local police, severely taxes the capacities of city institutions, and involves an extraordinarily wide range of lawless activities on the part of both Negroes and control authorities. After the disorder has ended, an area often looks as if it has been through a state of civil warfare. Such was the case in Detroit and Newark, 1967, and in Los Angeles, 1965. These disorders were so massive, events so much beyond the control of either civil authorities or Negro community leadership, the points of street confrontation between police and Negroes so numerous and widespread, that it is difficult to characterize the whole complex of actions over the course of a disturbance in simple terms.

In all three cases, however, a similar pattern of development stands out: the violence in each went through two distinct phases. *In the first, widespread and aggressive action by ghetto Negroes overwhelmed local police forces, leaving them virtually powerless to enforce order in the streets. In the second, reinforced control authorities engaged in harsh retaliatory actions to reassert dominance.*

Phase 1: Negro Rebellion. In this phase collective violence was initiated by Negroes. In Detroit and Newark, as well as in Watts, aggressive action by Negroes escalated spontaneously from an initial confrontation with police into a highly generalized rebellion against white authority and white-owned property in the ghetto. In the face of an expanding rebellion, local police lacked the resources to act with the even-handed decisiveness necessary to bring the violence under control; their efforts inflamed rather than quieted Negro participants.

As the ability of police to enforce control of the streets diminished, more and more segments of the Negro community—older people, women, children—joined the young men who had been in the forefront. At the peak of this phase there was a euphoric realization among Negro rioters that they had nullified police control over their territory. Overwhelmed, the police floundered helpless and frustrated.

Phase 2: Control Force Retaliation. Under the strain of widespread rioting, police order had begun to dissolve; many officers became subject to the same principles of crowd behavior that motivated Negro rioters. Deep-rooted racial prejudices surfaced. The desire to vent hostility, to reestablish dominance, and to avenge police honor became compelling motives. Rumors and racist attitudes fed into each other as determinants of police behavior with the breakdown of routine arrest procedure, police communication systems, and police leadership control of the men on the street.

Once reinforcements arrived in the form of State Police and National Guard units, the second phase of disorder was inaugurated. With police discipline severely weakened, many lawless acts initiated by lower-echelon police officers coincided with the reassertion of police dominance over Negro rioters. Many National Guardsmen, ill-disciplined and afraid, showed little restraint in using weapons in areas in which they were strangers. This period was characterized by a marked tendency among control authorities to treat all Negroes categorically as enemies. The presence of massive official force, or its withdrawal, or the exhaustion of Negro rioters and control authorities alike, would finally bring the violence to an end.

Patterns of Escalation

Detroit: Phase I. These two phases of disorder in Los Angeles, Detroit, and Newark—in part the product of a high level of community polarization prior to the upheaval—directly emerged as a result of re-ciprocating hostile actions by police and Negro activists.

In Detroit, the first phase had five escalation points, each occurring within twelve hours from the start of the disturbance.[1] The initial event was a police raid on a blind pig [2] that mobilized a crowd. The second escalation point occurred shortly after the police left the scene; looting began as an agitator, emerging from the crowd, which had grown angry, broke the first window. This was followed by several hours in which the police, returning to the area undermanned, made no visible effort to stop the looting going on under their eyes. Police inaction encouraged a massive expansion in community participation. Then, a sudden and in-effective crackdown—a sweep of the streets by a tough elite riot squad armed with bayonets—outraged the community while simultaneously demonstrating police impotence as the dispersal tactic failed. Shortly thereafter, firebombing, with Negro youths at the forefront, greatly ac-celerated. The riot had become totally out of control.

Newark: Phase I. The steps in the development of the Newark rebellion—which preceded and gave impetus to the one in Detroit—differed somewhat from the first phase of the Detroit upheaval but par-alleled it in basic process. As in Detroit, a police incident initiated the chain of events. Here the first step was the arrest and beating of a Negro cab driver, which initially mobilized a large and angry crowd of Negroes in front of the police station. While the police in Detroit were permissive in the face of the initial stage of looting, those in Newark were both indecisive and punitive toward an increasingly hostile and ag-gressive crowd that literally began to lay siege to the police station. A cycle occurred in which the bombardment of the station with bricks, bottles, and Molotov cocktails by some members of the crowd would be followed by a rush of the police toward the crowd, a backoff of the crowd, a police withdrawal to the station, and a reassembly of the crowd to begin the process again. Each time this occurred the crowd's contempt for the police and its own sense of power grew.

As the police sweep in Detroit was followed by firebombing, so in Newark a period of minor looting followed a police charge which nulli-fied efforts by civil rights leaders to organize a march away from the station. Police action subsequently alienated a major source of grape-vine information in the ghetto. Twenty-five cabdrivers who had trans-ported some people down to city hall to conduct a nonviolent protest and picket became extremely indignant to find their doubleparked cars being ticketed and towed away.

The difference between Newark and Detroit at this point, however, was that the possibility existed to save the situation through a political agreement between the Italian city administration and Negro militant leaders. Such a solution did not materialize.

Then on the second evening, escalation began again. Events moved almost directly into a period in which rioting was out of control, completing the process that was truncated the evening before. The stopping of a picket line in front of the police station to announce a concession considered trivial by the crowd catalyzed Negro youth into stone throwing at the station. The police in turn charged the crowd. Discipline cracked. Even Negro newspaper reporters, and in one instance a Negro policeman, were beaten by white policemen caught up in an antiblack frenzy. While police in Detroit were permissive toward looters in the first stage, those in Newark had already lost control on the second evening when the looting started in earnest. The absence of police in many areas and the widespread looting in turn produced pressures for participation that proved irresistible for many ordinarily law-abiding people.

Detroit: Phase II. With the introduction of State Police and National Guard and removal of constraints on use of weapons, the character of the riots began to change.

In Detroit the removal of restraint on the use of weapons by control authorities caused violence to escalate on both sides. For the control forces frequent gunfire, and some firing of weapons by some Negroes, led to pervasive rumors of massive Negro sniping activity. Fear combined with motives for revenge led many troopers to see themselves as embattled soldiers in a war situation against an enemy people, and they acted accordingly. Lack of command discipline in the general confusion led to situations in which Guardsmen became lost, made mistakes, or violated standing orders (e.g., even after federal troops arrived and the commanding general instructed guardsmen to unload their weapons, 90 percent of the guardsmen did not).

A similar situation occurred for the police. With the top leadership of the police department having lost control over lower-echelon officers by midweek, the latter being fatigued from overwork and the arrest procedure system having fallen apart, many policemen engaged in vengeful action. It was not until regular army troops arrived, official violence brought under control, and all parties reduced to a state of exhaustion that the disorders finally ceased.

Newark: Phase II. In Newark, the statements of the governor telling Negroes they were forced to choose between "the jungle" and "law and order" became interpreted by some policemen as a license for summary justice. Police retaliation was further spurred by the killing of one officer: acts of ritual revenge were even carried out in his name. As in Detroit, rumors of snipers, lack of coordination between police and guard forces, and motives of retaliation produced massive onslaughts of gunfire directed at Negro-occupied or -owned buildings. With a growing retaliatory mood among Negro youth, violence did not end until the governor ordered the Guard units withdrawn from the Negro areas.

RIOTS AS POLITICAL CONFRONTATIONS

Newark and Detroit are extreme examples of massive disorder in the summer of 1967. A few disturbances showed many of the characteristics of these general upheavals but developed over time in a distinctly political direction. As in the general upheaval, the level of disorder in the streets was quite large. *But in these disorders explicit political confrontation* [3] *between Negro leadership and civil authorities was at least as important a feature of the riot as violent street confrontation between Negro masses and the police.* This was true in such cities as Cincinnati and Plainfield.

On the first night of disorder in Plainfield, for example, a local Negro politician tried to steer the youth toward a meeting with the mayor to talk about their grievances. The meeting was held, but was unsatisfactory, the youth leadership representatives walking out twice, a minor riot occurring after the second walkout. On the next day, a meeting they were having in a park to formulate grievances and reduce them to writing was broken up by the police. Shortly thereafter violence rapidly escalated as a policeman was killed by a mob after he shot a youth, and the youths, fearing retaliation from the police, stole forty-six carbines from a gun factory. Later, one of their representatives—a young man who has since become an important political figure in the community —attempted to use the possession of the guns as a bargaining tool, offering to exchange them in return for a sign of good faith from the authorities. An agreement was reached and Negro-initiated violence ceased, although the guns were not in fact returned. During a two-day period when police were kept out of the area of disturbance, the youths in effect took responsibility for keeping order. In the aftermath, the activities of the youth militants have involved the use of pressure-group tactics in council meetings, their first victory being the defeat of an anti-loitering amendment.

Unlike the general upheaval, events in Plainfield, although violent, were not entirely out of the control of community leaders. In Detroit, where there may have been tens or hundreds of bands of rioters at work, any kind of coherence or control over events was impossible. In Newark, the possibility for a political solution was quickly foreclosed by the severe political polarization between the mayor and the middle-class Negro militants, and the lack of control of the latter over the young. But in Plainfield, the existence of a leadership group among the youth who were rioting, and their willingness to negotiate, made possible a political compromise of sorts.

Indeed, a politicized focus and coherence to events occurred wherever rioters were sufficiently organized to select their own leadership for negotiation, or where there were leaders within the general community who would act and be accepted as spokesmen. In such cases, militancy around the conference table would match, and often substitute for, militancy in the streets.

THE RIOT AS EXPRESSIVE RAMPAGE

While many of the larger disorders had pronounced instrumental and political components, there is also a type in which a quality of expressive rampaging on the part of the Negro participants was predominant. All the ghetto riots involved the spontaneous gathering of an angry crowd in the first phase. But in this third type, the behavior of rioters gained little focus or direction over time. The clearest image is a wandering street mob, angry, drunken, milling about, lacking leadership or direction, engaged in breaking windows, or random acts of vandalism.

The riot in Dayton in 1966, which preceded two smaller disturbances during the summer of 1967, was of this type. From the start those engaged in the disturbance were a bar crowd of petty hustlers and drunks, marginal elements in the community. Efforts by the mayor to reach a political solution to the riot by negotiating with a militant civil rights leader on the scene was ineffective, because the rioting crowd was organized around drinking and chaotic emotional expression. Efforts to organize the crowd into a meeting to express grievances and negotiate failed totally. The disorder was finally suppressed by heavy arrests once local police were buttressed with National Guard forces.

THE RIOT AS FULFILLMENT OF ANTICIPATIONS

While the largest disorders generally began with an aggressive ghetto riot followed by a tough police response, there is another category of disturbance in which the flow of events proceeded in the opposite direction. *The first acts of collective aggression came not from Negroes but from control forces—subsequent Negro responses tending to be defensive, protective, or retaliatory.* In such cities as Cambridge, Maryland; Jersey City and Elizabeth, New Jersey, anticipations of Negro lawlessness, rather than actual lawlessness itself, led to periods of disturbance.

These were initiated by precipitous riot control tactics or shows of force by white authorities. Compared with cities that did have massive ghetto rioting, such disturbances remained fairly minor, although their actual proportions were often greatly exaggerated at the time they occurred.

In Cambridge, Maryland, the presence and speech of H. Rap Brown had a great effect in stimulating local authorities to acts of disorder against the Negro community. His mere presence evoked images in the minds of white leadership that there was an organized conspiracy afoot to lead Cambridge's Negroes in a rampaging pillage of the town's white business district. His inflammatory speech, although failing to galvanize Negro youth to start breaking things up, did produce a wave of hysteria in the Negro police officers who heard it. These reported that a riot was underway—thus confirming the worst fears of local white officials. At one point, after an injury to an officer, the local police chief wanted to go shooting into the area, and only restraints by state authorities prevented bloodshed. Later on, the white volunteer fire department refused to go into the Negro area to put out a small fire that finally spread into a blaze consuming a block of Negro businesses. This nonaction stemmed in part from a fear of a preplanned plot to trap fire department equipment in the Negro area, thus leaving the downtown area to be burned and plundered.

In a few disorders, white anticipatory action overlapped with an expressive rampage by Negro youth. In Milwaukee, the first evening of disorder began with window breaking and looting by youths on a hell-raising spree after a dance. But the authorities had been waiting for some time in anticipation for a try at containing a riot. The response of officials was to call for the mobilization of 4,800 Guardsmen, 200 State Police, and 800 policemen.

In a few cities *joint expectations* held by *both* Negroes and whites that a "riot was coming" had something of a self-fulfilling character. However, in the absence of truly intense community polarization, the disturbances possessed a staged or simulated quality. The participants seemed to be going through the motions of a riot more than carrying out serious conflict. Lacking was the quality of vengeance and retribution which pervades so much of the behavior on all sides during a riot out of control.

Staged conflict in this sense occurred in New Brunswick, where youths put on a riot in the main street. An effective political response by the lady mayor brought a quick end to the disorder. The second night of rioting in Tucson was staged in another sense. Following queries by a newspaper reporter as to where and when they were going to riot that evening, youths put on a minor riot for the benefit of the press.

THE RIOTS THAT DIDN'T HAPPEN: "MINI-RIOTS" AND OTHERS

In most of the events in which anticipations of violence played an important role, the level of disorder on the Negro side was so minimal as to suggest calling these disturbances "Negro riots that didn't happen." There were also some low-level disturbances—"mini-riots" is an apt term—that reflected in germinal or aborted form dimensions more fully developed in the largest disorders.

The Atlanta disturbance showed many characteristics in common with certain northern disorders. As in Newark and Detroit, a crowd formed in a community gathering place in a high-density area. The scene in this instance was a neighborhood shopping center where police-related incidents had occurred the two previous nights. Stokely Carmichael, present to urge the crowd to take to the streets, found an audience willing to take matters into its own hands. But (1) the police immediately moved in with major force and were extremely effective; (2) the mayor quickly responded to the political aspect of the event by beginning visible construction the next day on long-delayed projects demanded by area residents; and (3) a newly formed Negro Youth Corps helped keep the rest of the summer cool.

In a northern city like Dayton, there was a significant potential in its two 1967 disturbances for a major Negro riot. The first disturbance followed a meeting protesting the cut of a grassroots poverty program. H. Rap Brown was the featured out-of-town visitor at the meeting. He excited youth who were already looking for an excuse to riot.

The second followed a bitter meeting protesting the release of a vice squad officer after a controversial killing of a middle-class Negro professional. An initially decisive police response and the cooling effect of the Dayton White Hats in both cases rapidly attenuated the escalation potential in the disturbance.

Finally, in the category of riots which did not occur is the traditional race riot which has often marked American history. The potential nevertheless was there. In Cincinnati, New Haven, Newark, and Cambridge, whites were attracted to the scene, ready to take up the banner against Negroes and to defend white property. In such cities, effective police practice prevented white outsiders from coming into Negro areas, thus aborting the race riot process. In Cambridge, where there has been a continuing danger of racial confrontation for several years, the state National Guard acted in its customary role as a buffer against violence.

Processes in Developing Disorders

URBAN UPHEAVALS AND SATELLITE RIOTS: THE PROPAGATION OF VIOLENCE

As a nationwide phenomenon, the propagation of violence across the land follows the close link between major ghetto upheavals, or reports thereof, and satellite disorders in which authority overreaction occurs. The former has clearly acted as a trigger to the latter. In the wake of a disturbance the size of Newark or Detroit, rumors of small incidents in a local area become magnified as the beginning of a riot. On the white side, a climate of anxiety is produced by stories of planned violence and fears of outside agitators and conspirators.

After the Detroit upheaval, eight other Michigan cities reported disorders. After the Newark riot, fourteen cities in the surrounding area had some sort of disturbance. *In at least two-thirds of fifteen cities studied in which disorders occurred shortly after major riots, the immediate precipitant of disorder seems to have been a police action prompted by ghetto violence elsewhere.*

The Propagation of Disorder in the New Jersey Chain / To illustrate the propagation effect, let us examine some of the cities in the chain of disturbances that occurred in New Jersey in the aftermath of the Newark riot. In Englewood, police outnumbered participants three to one. In Jersey City, 400 armed police occupied the Negro area several days before the disorder occurred. In most cases, relations became strained as the appearance of armed police patrols increased the likelihood of confrontation with Negro residents. The most frequent citizen demands were for police withdrawal and/or a less visible show of arms. In six of the seven New Jersey satellite cities, removal of police from the ghetto signaled an end to violence. Rumors of violence often become self-fulfilling prophecies when credited and responded to with a visible show of force and fear.

Errors in judgment produced by a climate of fear in the white community were typified in many New Jersey cities. One prominent example was officials reacting to rumors that Stokely Carmichael was bringing carloads of Negro militants into the community, although Carmichael was in London at the time. Planning for disorder by New Jersey police departments, even before the Newark upheaval occurred, showed similar elements of irrationality in the face of uncertainty.

On June 5, 1967, the police chiefs of at least seventy-five New Jersey communities met in Jersey City. They discussed rumors of planned violence by various militant groups who reportedly intended to kill Jersey City police officers in their homes and foment disorder in other New Jersey communities. Jersey City, Newark, and Elizabeth were said to have "Triple A" ratings for violence over the summer. Plans to coordinate control efforts were established, and the chiefs were informed of the procedures for calling in the State Police and National Guard.

Thus, a month and a half before Newark erupted, there were rumors of planned violence, and counterplans were designed. Riot control training was held in a number of communities. In one instance, Negro residents became alarmed when tear gas used in a practice exercise drifted into the Negro section of town. Whether the rumors of planned violence were solid or merely a product of the preconceptions of city officials is difficult to say. But these rumors existing prior to the Newark riot were confirmed in the minds of officials in other New Jersey cities when Newark erupted, subsequently becoming the basis for riot control responses.

Another force in the proliferation of disturbances in the vicinity of the big-city riots is the network of kinship and friendship relations between Negroes in major cities and outlying areas. For some it was literally true that "the brothers" in Newark or Detroit were "getting some of the action." Many people in Grand Rapids, for example, have relatives in Detroit. Reports that some of these relatives were killed in the

Detroit riot increased tension and the potential for violence in that city.

The intensity of the flow of personal information from the Newark and Detroit ghettos to outlying areas at the peaks of the riots is indicated by the high number of out-of-town phone calls from the areas of greatest disturbance. These equaled top loads for a Mother's Day weekend, one of the periods in the year when telephone lines across the country become overloaded.

THE MEDIA AND THE PROPAGATION OF DISORDER

The majority of people in outlying areas and across the country do not, of course, learn about a riot through immediate personal information. TV can bring people hundreds or thousands of miles distant directly to the scene of a major disorder. *The effect can often be that of the crowd acting at long distance*. This was a typical feature of the nonviolent demonstrations of the civil rights movement at its peak. TV pictures of mob violence in the South would spark spontaneous sympathy demonstrations all across the North. And, in many instances, local civil rights movements would indigenously evolve from there.

In the case of the recent disorders, the "crowd at long distance" generated the impression that there was in fact a conspiracy some place for New Jersey to go up all at once. Actually, outbreaks of civil violence were quite spontaneous and unplanned, information from the media lowering the threshold for disorder all across an area.

One definite effect of the media seems to be the determination in time and place that latent tensions will surface into disorder. The potential for major riots in Plainfield and Detroit led by militant Negro youth had been there for some time. It was the Newark riot that dramatically changed the mood in Detroit and helped galvanize Negro youths to aggressive action in Plainfield. They might have blown anyway, if not at that time, then perhaps at a later date. On the other hand, these cities went through crisis periods before in which a major disorder could have exploded, but did not. Perhaps if Newark had not occurred or if information about it had been totally suppressed, other cities might have weathered the storm—at least temporarily. Progress through institutional channels might have kept one step ahead of the chaos breathing on its heels.

OUTSIDE AGITATORS AND THE SPREAD
OF DISORDER

A discussion of the mass media effects in propagating disorder naturally leads into an examination of the actual influence over events of such nationally known, headline-making Negro radical leaders as Stokely Carmichael and H. Rap Brown. Their role in spreading disorder is by no means simple.

A cursory overview of the points where the distribution of disorder around the country crosses the distribution of appearances of Stokely Carmichael or H. Rap Brown would indicate that most disturbances occurred without their presence to help things along. Of the twenty-three disturbances in our sample, in only six were either Carmichael or Brown around the scene at the time. And in only three of these were their appearance and rhetoric immediately linked with the immediate precipitants of disorder. In the other cities they arrived at the scene after action was already underway. In Cincinnati, for example, Brown's major role was presenting a list of some twenty demands from a nationalist group to a representative from the Human Relations Commission on the fourth day of the disturbance.

Thus the number of specific situations with which the presence of a national firebrand could be associated with disorder were very few. *And considering the large number of communities where Brown and Carmichael appeared which did not have riots, their "riot batting average," if indeed their purpose was to provoke a disorder on the spot, was extremely low.* Nevertheless, Carmichael and Brown do have influence over some events, which stems from the particular way they lead people. Their leadership is symbolic rather than organizational. They cannot command others to riot—at least at this time—by coming in from out of town and passing down orders from the top. But as a symbolic focus for hopes and fears they can generate the emotional predisposition which might encourage disorder.

In this respect, a good deal depends on the mood of their audience when they arrive on the scene. In Atlanta, Carmichael's speech to a crowd suggesting that they force the police to work until they "drop in their tracks" brought a tumultuous response. In Dayton the youth were "looking for an excuse to riot" before Brown arrived. However, in Jersey City, Negro youth quickly fled a meeting at which Brown was speaking when a rumor spread that the police were coming. Brown reportedly left town muttering "the people here aren't ready."

White authorities, as the Cambridge and New Jersey cases illustrate, have often been emotional followers of the leadership of Brown and Carmichael, in the sense that fears of the influence or presence of the latter generated precipitous actions.

It should be stressed too that the influence process between audience and agitators is a two-way street. In Detroit it was an unknown local man who took upon himself the role of the agitator. But in so doing, he was responding as well to the mood of the crowd and a situation which commanded agitation. And while Brown and Carmichael have a utilitarian interest in seeing violence directed against white society's control of Negroes until equality is produced, most of the evidence indicates that crowds use them as much as they use crowds.

Like headliners and public men everywhere, they become tools of community groups in developing motivation and commitment in followers, creating resources, and getting actions going. Thus far, they have been the focal point for a great deal of emotional energies on the part of both Negroes and whites. It is easier, for example, for whites to see riots as caused by H. Rap Brown and Stokely Carmichael, with whom they are familiar, than by the conditions of local Negro communities, with which they are not. Negroes, for their part—especially the young—experience great jubilation in hearing a speaker "tell it like it is" and frighten whites in the process.

Whatever their role at a specific local disorder, however, the major source of influence of leaders like Brown and Carmichael over events is that the media provides them with a national audience. Brown and Carmichael have argued that violence is necessary—violence is occurring around the country—both are reported side by side on TV and in the press. Such a recurrent linking of spokesmen for disorder and actual violence produces cause-and-effect associations difficult to dispel. Brown and Carmichael become seen as having the extraordinary and dangerous power to spellbind Negroes into rioting.

While such a conclusion greatly exaggerates their power, we must not underestimate the real importance of their posturing as revolutionaries in the creation of an emotional climate around the country which is conducive to violence. But here too they are not alone. The news media, the political authorities, the reports of the occurrence of actual riots are also central elements in creating a riot climate.

It would, perhaps, be more appropriate to consider the development of a major ghetto riot, and the appearance of symbolic leaders arguing that violence is legitimate, as but different reflections of the processes of polarization going on throughout the society. It is the role of spokesmen for rebellion created by the fact that ghetto rebellions are occurring which is significant, and not Brown or Carmichael specifically. Previously that role was singularly filled by Malcolm X: now new men are moving to fill the gap, rushing to keep up with events more than they are guiding them.

The real source of Brown and Carmichael's influence thus far has been the failure of the white community to make their role irrelevant. Lacking recognition from the white community in other respects, without a place in society for themselves, young Negroes learn quickly that whites are afraid of Brown and Carmichael. *When whites fear your power to cause riots they take you seriously: that is the lesson of events. In this respect whites load the dice. The role of the militant demagogue and activist is rewarded again and again.*

INITIAL CONDITIONS IN THE SPREAD OF DISORDER

Loading the dice occurs within disturbances. At any phase, the events that have gone before shape the events that follow. This begins before actual violence erupts. If aspirations have been raised but community issues and conflicts continually find ghetto Negroes on the losing end, if a high degree of community polarization has developed, if racial solidarity and militancy within the ghetto have been growing, if there is a large pool of aggressive and ambitious youth available for confrontation, it may be as difficult to contain a disturbance in its first phase as to contain an atomic chain reaction once the critical point has been reached.

This was the case in Detroit where events happened extremely fast, telescoping in a matter of hours community involvement processes that took three days to develop in Watts. In other cities where a truly explosive potential did not exist, it was very likely that a disorder would have died out of its own accord through normal processes of communal restraint without formal authority controls (e.g., mothers scolding sons for rampaging, the youth not being serious about rioting, etc.).

Initial features of a disorder—where it was located, the time of day, who was involved, the weather, etc.—also were important in determining the direction an incipient disturbance was to move. Rain stopped some incipient riots. Whether the people who initially became riotous were marginal elements of the Negro community or whether they were stable residents was an important consideration. Disorders that pulled in ambitious, achievement-oriented people were more violent.[4] Disorders that began near housing developments, shopping centers, or other places where ordinary people in the community gathered always had an extremely dangerous potential.

GRIEVANCES IN THE RIOT PROCESS

Like the question concerning the role of Negro leadership in events, the question of the role of grievances, or the grievance process in disorders, is complicated. A popular model of riot causes sees a high level of grievances producing community tensions, which in turn produce riots. This theory is popularly held by people with programs or ideas they would like to sell that would ameliorate tensions by reducing grievances.

But there were cities in which the grievance level, in an absolute sense, was very high during the summer of 1967 which did not experience aggressive Negro riots. There were others in which the grievance level was much lower which did have aggressive ghetto rioting.

The importance of grievances in an event seems to be determined less by the *level of grievance* than the *kind* of grievance involved. People do not riot *for* better schools, but they will riot *against* the police and government as outside oppressors. Concerns for territory, domination, and hatred of double standards (social injustice) run like a common thread through most of the largest disorders.

Item: In Plainfield, the double-standard issue of a policeman failing to make an arrest that Negro youth thought he should have was the immediate precipitant.

Item: In Cincinnati, the issue of double standards in the courts generated a sense of rage as a Negro was sentenced for murder and a white man for manslaughter within the same month. The first act of direct action was the stopping of delivery trucks by youths objecting to whites getting most of the jobs in Negro areas.

Item: In Detroit, the failure of a white newspaper to carry news of a Negro Vietnam veteran's murder at the hands of a white mob created bitterness as the local Negro newspaper reported the incident, including the miscarriage of the murdered man's pregnant wife, in full detail. A few weeks later, and a short distance from where the murdered man lived, a police raid on an after-hours club where a party for some Negro servicemen was in progress found an agitator telling an angry crowd that the police wouldn't do this in a white area.

Item: In Los Angeles in 1965, plaintive appeals of a Negro youth that he was not going to let the police take him to jail aroused a tug-of-war between local community residents and white police which was the first incident in the Los Angeles riot.

Item: In Newark, a massive urban renewal project which would displace thousands of Negroes became the source of a bitter political struggle between the Italian political leadership and Negro militants, and was considered an important cause of the riot. Later, the belief of neighborhood residents that the police had not only beaten a taxicab driver but had beaten him before they got him to the police station catalyzed a mood of rebellion and community solidarity.

Grievances of one Negro group against another can also be considered as having a role in precipitating and shaping several disorders.

Item: Leadership competition between the Negro militants opposed to the mayor of Newark and the group of conservative Negro leaders who supported him in part prevented an effective counterriot response to the developing Newark crisis.

Item: In Cincinnati, the first outbreak of violence followed a speech by a Negro conservative at a protest rally in which he supported an antiloitering law and angered Negro youths.

Item: In Dayton's June 1967 disturbance, an intense controversy between militants and conservatives over the funding of an antipoverty program found a militant leader threatening a riot which shortly occurred.

Item: In Cambridge, white fear began to mount as two newly forming Negro groups, one conservative, one militant, began to compete for the leadership role left vacant since Gloria Richardson had left town.

Item: In Grand Rapids, entrenched vice elements in the Negro community who were being threatened by the rising influence of poverty workers in the community attempted to use the disorder to buttress their declining position.

Item: In Detroit, a developing indigenous community organization leadership of a very militant character was threatening established middle-class leaders who were well incorporated into the Detroit political system. The latter were willing to go along with a policy of extreme repression the first day of the disturbance. Since the riot they have been outraged at the willingness of city leadership to meet directly with lower-class representatives, and have fought increases in power for the militant groups.

Finally, the *grievance process*—the effectiveness of the response of authorities to Negro grievances—can be a crucial source of grievance itself. The substantive grievances (police practices, neighborhood services, schools, housing, etc.) serve as indicators for measuring exactly how much and in what manner white authorities care about Negroes. They become tests of commitment.

In this respect, liberal or moderate cities are far more vulnerable to incidence of disorders than racially conservative ones. Examination of the twenty-three disorders in our sample indicates that those cities characterized by a general liberalizing, more humanitarian trend in elite attitudes—i.e., public recognition of the legitimacy of Negro complaints —are more likely to have the largest and most violent disorders. This is not surprising. Prolonged aggressive action by Negroes in racially conservative cities is less likely because whites promise little, and what they do promise is immediate and extreme use of violent force to quell any disturbance at the outset, regardless of the merits of Negro complaints. In these cities, Negroes are continually reminded of "their place," and if some do not accept this definition they may be persuaded to refrain from violent protest anyhow.

The tokenistic pattern of race relations in more moderate or racially liberalizing cities encourages Negro demands for equality and lifts the fear of extreme force (policemen increasingly attack the civil libertarian and community-relations emphasis of liberal government on the grounds that "law enforcement is being handcuffed"), yet generally fails to bring about substantial changes in the conditions of ghetto life. Individual members of the group have greater mobility and opportunity than ever before, but many still lag behind, their increased desires for advancement unfulfilled. The dilemma of liberalizing governments is that lifting the more overt forms of repression and making promises of equality encourage a more rapid rate of change in the psychology of Negroes than anything else. In such circumstances, where old dominance relations are being undermined or are uncertain, grievances can be expected to escalate as Negroes test out white commitments in more and more areas. Growing black consciousness and sense of community increase the desire for action against obstacles that cramp ghetto Negroes in daily life, at the same time that white reaction to Negro "pushiness" invokes a sense of betrayal.

This seems extremely crucial for developing a mood of rebellion. Prior to the disorder there, Newark would have been considered a city undergoing racial liberalization. A Negro–Italian political coalition had put the mayor into office, and there had been many promises to the Negro community. Compared with other northern cities, the level of political access of Negroes in Newark might have been considered fairly high. But a split had developed in the coalition with the Italian political leadership, and Negro community elites engaged in bitter, emotionally charged disputes over police practices, a plan to tear down Negro-occupied areas to construct a medical complex, appointments to the board of education, and other issues. The Negroes saw broken promises and an attempt by the Italians to establish their political hegemony at Negro expense. By the second evening of disorder in Newark, people were far beyond the stage where they would be willing to accept a token concession at the price of mitigating the righteous vengeance which had been so long in developing. Once that mood was there, a sudden concession itself triggered disorder as Negroes, so to speak, threw the concession of a Negro police captain back into the faces of the authorities with the attitude "keep it, you can't buy us that cheaply *now*."

THE COMPETITIVE PROCESS IN DEVELOPING DISORDERS

Negotiations at such points fail because many people want combat more than peace. During a disorder itself, a competitive sense among Negro youths may become a powerful impetus to keeping the violence going. In Newark, some youths did not want to stop the riot because the score in deaths stood "25–2" with the police and Guardsmen leading.

The Game of Riot—Emasculating the Police / Within various groups on the street, people were quite conscious of the heroism and daring exhibited by young men. For Negro youth, challenging the police with taunts and dares involved a dangerous and dramatic competition. Their goal was to disrupt police order, to make the police "lose their cool," to produce situations in which police worked until they "dropped in their tracks." Much of the behavior of the youth during a riot can be accounted for by this motivation: *they are interested not in killing policemen, but in humiliating them.* As Negroes have been rendered powerless for so long, as the police have continually disrupted the activities of the ghetto, the disorder becomes the grand opportunity to turn the tables.

In this respect, the riots also serve the functions of ritual ceremonies in which manhood is demonstrated. Many acts of confrontation (e.g., laying bear the chest and taunting police to shoot), which have a great intensity and seriousness about them are also dramatic posturing—open and public proof to both oneself and the police that things have changed. The test has dangers, but afterwards one can never go back to what he was before.

This form of street confrontation with the police, it should be noted, is not new. If we include the southern nonviolent movement, it has been going on for six years. In the South during 1962–1965 militant civil rights activists, many of whom were of northern background, became experts in the technique of disorganizing southern police through nonviolent demonstrations.

Negro youth in the North are now the aggressors. Instead of nonviolent demonstrations, breaking white property, setting fires, and racial taunting have become major aspects of the techniques of breaking up the police.

Much Negro youth crime has always had this quality of testing by street games with authorities. Confronting police and courts in efforts to construct a self-definition in which one does have some kind of place in society—if only a criminal one—does have a functional basis. Those who have served time return to their old associations with a new status as someone who is really tough and knows the ropes.

What is distinctive now is that this same process feeds into community confrontation. Traditional street testing behavior by Negro youth is channeling into the disruption of city institutions. The massiveness of the disruption in a riot stems from the fact that a great number of youth are getting their badges of manhood all at once. Previously this occurred through the orderly and recurrent process of one-by-one confrontation which white institutions easily handled in the past.

Cross-city Competition / Evidence in our data indicates that cross-city competition among youth—"who holds the record, now?"—becomes a salient force once control by police is lost. Cities that have already had major upheavals acquire symbolic value and become standards for comparison in other disturbances. For some participants there is a quite explicit desire to outdo New York, or Watts, etc. A Negro girl in Newark asked a reporter "Was the Harlem riot worse than this?" and assured that it was not, she cried, "That's good, that's great!"

Distinctive features of several major disturbances during the summer of 1967 can in part be attributed to the excitement generated among young Negroes that they were either doing something in a riot that had not been done before, or that they were doing it better than ever. Negro youths in Newark were quite proud that they were the first ever to lay siege to a police station. As the governor passed by in a National Guard tank, there were heated street-side discussions on "How do you get into a tank with a Molotov cocktail?"

There is no reason to preclude the possibility of disruptive acts more consequential than any that have yet occurred. The first tank to be firebombed, the first power station to be blown up, are but logical extensions of the present pattern of disorder. "We're number one!" after all is an old American tradition.

NOTES

1. This brief analytical summary is not designed to capture the richness and concrete details of the events. The reader is encouraged to refer to the excellent narrative of the Detroit, Newark, and other disorders provided in *The Report of the National Advisory Commission on Civil Disorders*, pp. 35–108.

2. A "blind pig" is a slang term for private social clubs that serve as after-hours drinking and gambling spots.

3. The use of the term "political" here is not meant to imply (1) conspiracy, (2) prior organization to achieve specific political objectives through the use of violence (e.g., intimidating election opponents or forcing a city administration to grant a specific concession), or (3) a precipitant which was markedly "political." Nor is calling some disturbances "political riots" meant to imply that the general upheavals in Newark and Detroit lacked a powerful political component. A high level of political grievance on the part of Negroes, and the lack of significant responses by civil authorities, contributed greatly to events in Newark and Detroit. But it would not do justice to the many nonpolitical aspects of generalized chaos in those cities to refer to their disorders as simply political riots. However, in cities like Plainfield and Cincinnati, the actions of Negro participants became directly focused at civil authorities. In turn, the responses of civil authorities to demands—particularly the demand for recognition—dramatically affected the level of aggressive action by Negro rioters.

4. As in other areas of community life, the quality of a riot is affected by the level of energy and competency people bring with them. Those who participate in riots (see pp. 174–178 in the *Report of the National Advisory Commission on Civil Disorders*), as compared with those who do not, tend to be younger, better educated, more politically aware, more achievement-oriented, more acculturated to the values of an industrialized urban society, and more dissatisfied with their place within it. Across cities, there is some evidence that the quality and character of Negro mass actions (political focus, degree of organization, volatility) are affected by differences in the level of unincorporated youthful talent.

7. CIVIL DISORDER AND THE AGENTS OF SOCIAL CONTROL
Gary T. Marx

O N E of the justifications for social research is that it goes beyond our common sense views of the world. Merton suggests that an important task of social research is to point out the latent or unintended consequences of human action.[1] Thus, however corrupt early twentieth-

From *Journal of Social Issues* 26, no. 1 (1970): 19–57. An earlier version of this paper was presented at the 1968 American Sociological Association meetings. I am grateful to the M.I.T.-Harvard Joint Center for Urban Studies for support and to the National Advisory Commission on Civil Disorders.

century political machines were, they were important in the assimilation of Irish and other immigrants. Prostitution, whatever its moral implications, may make an important contribution to family stability. However, there are more interesting cases where unintended consequences are the direct opposite of intended ends. Thus we have learned that propaganda designed to reduce prejudice may actually reenforce it, that youth institutions may create juvenile delinquents who are later made into knowledgeable criminals by the prison system, that mental hospitals may encourage mental illness, that welfare institutions may create dependency, that schools may impede learning, and that doctors sometimes injure or even kill patients.

In the same fashion a review of police behavior in civil disorders of a racial nature through the summer of 1967 suggests a number of instances where the behavior of some social control agents seemed as much to create disorder as to control it. After a consideration of police behavior in earlier racial disturbances, the present essay examines some of the forms and contexts in which control behavior has had these unintended consequences. As Park and Blumer and later students have noted, collective behavior has an emergent character to it. It involves elements that can't very well be predicted by a static consideration of the predisturbance variables. Civil disorder involves a social process of action and counter-action. It is here that a consideration of police behavior is relevant.

Police Behavior in Historical Perspective [2]

In reading about police behavior in earlier twentieth-century interracial violence I found several recurring themes: (1) the police were sympathetic to (white) rioters and sometimes joined the riot themselves; (2) police often failed actively to enforce the law; and (3) when police did try to maintain law and order this often was not done in a neutral and impartial manner.

Police as Rioters / Racial disorders are more likely during periods of social change, as the increased indignation of the oppressed confronts the threat to the status quo felt by the dominant group.[3] Police represent the dominant group whose power is threatened, and they tend to be recruited from those parts of the population most likely to hold negative stereotypes and to be in direct competition with blacks. It is thus not surprising that in the past police involvement in racial violence was sometimes on the side of the (white) mob rather than against it. This involvement has varied from statements of support to active participation in violence directed against Negroes.

The August 1900 New York race riot, one of the first of the twentieth century, was precipitated by a Negro's killing a plainclothes policeman after the latter grabbed his woman and accused her of being a prostitute. The subsequent riot was led in part by the predominantly Irish police. In what was called a "Nigger Chase" policemen and other whites dragged blacks off streetcars and severely beat them on the street and in hotels and saloons. At the time, a white observer felt that the ambition of the police seemed to be to "club the life out of" any Negro they could find. The *New York Tribune* printed a cartoon of a massive Tammany tiger in a police uniform swinging a club. In the background was huddled a bloodied Negro.[4]

The 1906 Atlanta riot growing out of the move to disenfranchise blacks saw police arresting Negroes who had armed for self-defense and an officer shooting into a crowd of Negroes. The head of a seminary where blacks sought asylum was beaten by a police official.[5]

Some of the worst instances of official rioting may be seen in the relatively well-documented East St. Louis riot of 1917, which was triggered by the killing of two policemen. In an act called "a particularly cowardly exhibition of savagery" by a congressional investigating committee, police shot into a crowd of Negroes huddled together not offering any resistance. Some of the soldiers led groups of men and boys in attacks upon Negroes.[6] Police relayed false reports of black reprisal attacks on the outskirts of the city, in order, according to the *Post-Dispatch,* "to scatter the soldiers so that they would not interfere with the massacre."[7] Police also confiscated the cameras of newsmen because they had incriminating evidence. Guardsmen followed the cues of the police department. Some gave their weapons to the mob. Following the shooting of two blacks by "khaki-uniformed" men, rioters, according to a press account, "slapped their thighs and said the Illinois National Guard was all right."[8] After indicating a number of instances of official complicity, the congressional investigating committee stated, "Instead of being guardians of the peace they [the police] became part of the mob . . . adding to the terrifying scenes of rapine and slaughter."[9]

The Chicago Commission on Race Relations, while noting the unusual circumstances of the 1919 riot, felt that ". . . certain cases of discrimination, abuse, brutality, indifference, and neglect" on the part of police were "deserving of examination." The "certain cases" included things such as a policeman approaching a Negro who lay wounded from mob attack, with the words, "Where's your gun, you black—of a—? You damn niggers are raising hell," whereupon the officer then reportedly knocked the Negro unconscious and robbed him; and the case of a Negro who, after asking police for protection, was searched and clubbed by them and shot when he attempted to run away.[10]

In the 1919 Knoxville, Tennessee, disorders troops "shot up" the black section of town following an unsubstantiated rumor that Negroes had killed several whites. According to John Hope Franklin, a Negro newspaper declared, "The indignities which colored women suffered at the hands of these soldiers would make the devil blush."[11]

In Tulsa, Oklahoma, May 31, 1921, after fighting broke out between whites and Negroes over the latter's effort to stop a lynching, local police invaded the Negro area and did much damage.

The 1943 Detroit riot was preceded by interracial violence at the Sojourner Truth Homes where police openly sided with whites and joined in fighting Negroes trying to move into public housing. During the 1943 riot, claims were made to the effect that ". . . rather than protecting stores and preventing looting, the police drove through the troubled areas, occasionally stopping their vehicles, jumping out, and shooting whoever might be in a store. Police would then tell Negro bystanders to 'run and not look back.' On several occasions persons running were shot in the back."[12] It was claimed that police forced Negroes to detour onto Woodward Avenue, a street where violence against blacks was very intense.

A study of the 1943 Detroit riot reports the case of a black man shot as he fled a streetcar attacked by the mob. The man ran to a policeman and shouted, "Help me, I'm shot!" He later stated, "The officers took me to the middle of the street where they held me. I begged them not to let the rioters attack me. While they held me by both arms, nine or ten men walked out of the crowd and struck me hard blows. Men kept coming up to me and beating me, and the policemen did nothing to prevent it." This is followed a few pages later by the report of a white who stated, "A gang of Negroes suddenly seemed to assemble from nowhere at all. They dragged me from the car and were roughing me up when three policemen appeared and rescued me."[13]

Passive Police / More common than police rioting was police passivity. In a useful article on conditions conducive to racial disorders

Dahlke stresses the relevance of weak agents of external control, police who either cannot or will not make aggressive efforts to uphold law and order.[14] As with lynch violence, such a situation characterized many earlier racial disorders. Even when they wanted to take action, police were usually understaffed and lacked the appropriate means to quell the disorders. Technical incapacity mixed with a nonaggressive control ideology and sympathy for the rioters often produced inaction.

The 1904 Statesboro, Georgia, riot started when a mob entered the courtroom and overpowered the militia, whose rifles were not loaded "in tender consideration for the feelings of the mob." Two Negro prisoners were burned alive and a "wholesale terrorism" began. The leaders of the mob were not punished.[15]

The congressional investigating committee studying the East St. Louis riot reports:

> The testimony of every witness who was free to tell the truth agreed on condemnation of the police for failure to even half-way do their duty. They fled the scene where arson and murder were in full swing. They deserted the station house and could not be found when calls for help came from every quarter of the city. The organization broke down completely and so great was the indifference of the few policemen who remained on duty that the conclusion is inevitable that they shared the lust of the mob for Negro blood, and encouraged the rioters by their conduct. . . .[16]

Rudwick notes, "At least six or seven guardsmen stood around like 'passive spectators' during the hanging at Fourth and Broadway, and ignored pleas to save the victim's life. A few blocks away at Collinsville and Broadway a bloodied Negro sought the protection of eight guardsmen. Their mute answer was to turn bayonets on him, forcing the victim back into the arms of five assailants." [17] There are reports of lawmen "laughingly held captive" while the mob attacked blacks.

Organization on the part of both the police and militia seemed to break down as they scattered throughout the city without officers. Fraternization with the mob was common and not conducive to efforts at restraint. Many soldiers openly stated that they "didn't like niggers and would not disturb a white man for killing them." It was reportedly a common expression among them to ask, "Have you got your nigger yet?" [18] The day after the riot, as an ambulance came to remove part of the burned torso of a Negro victim that a soldier was exhibiting to throngs of people with the words, "There's one nigger who will never do any more harm," a crowd of militia men "saluted . . . with shouts of merriment." [19]

In Longview, Texas, in July 1919, police did not intervene when a group of whites with iron rods and gun butts beat a black man suspected of writing an article in the *Chicago Defender* on lynching. Nor did they try to stop the mob from burning a number of blacks' stores and homes. [20]

Local authorities and police lacked the resources to control a riotous mob bent on lynching in Omaha in 1919. Some policemen surrendered their clubs and guns peacefully when the mob demanded them.

The 1919 Chicago riot was triggered by the drowning of a black swimmer who drifted across the "line" separating the "white" water from the "black" water. A white policeman refused to arrest the white thought (by Negroes) to be responsible for the death and then proceeded to arrest a Negro on a white man's complaint. Police were accused of leaving the scene of rioting on "questionable excuses." The chief of police and the mayor refused to ask for troops, although the former acknowledged that his force was insufficient. [21] Outside pressure finally compelled the mayor to ask the governor for aid.

The following report on the 1919 Washington, D.C., riot clearly indicates something of the social process involved in the development of a collective definition conducive to violence on the part of both blacks and whites. Blacks come to arm themselves for self-defense and out of indignation, while whites interpret police behavior as granting them permission to use violence against blacks.

Failure of police to check the rioters promptly, and in certain cases an attitude on their part of seeming indifference, filled the mob with contempt of authority and set the stage for the demonstration the following night.

In the early hours of Monday morning the attacks on Negroes were carried into sections where the black population is heavy. The whole Negro element of Washington suddenly became aware of a war on their race. . . . By Monday night the colored population held themselves to be without police protection. The mob elements among the blacks armed for war, while many of the better element of their race armed in obedience to the first law of nature. [22]

W. E. B. Du Bois charged that the Washington police intervened to stop the violence only when whites began to get the worst of it. [23]

In Detroit in 1943 the NAACP took the position that "there is overwhelming evidence that the riot could have been stopped in Detroit at its inception Sunday night had the police wanted to stop it." [24]

Beyond police passivity in the face of attacks on Negroes, officials were criticized for delays in calling out higher levels of force and for the hesitancy to use force against whites. According to some sources the disturbance stopped only when troops appeared and a shoot-to-kill order was given wide publicity. [25]

The "inactivity" involved in the failure to call out higher levels of force is very different from that involved in failure of control agents to act once they are on the scene. Although at a more abstract level the consequences may be much the same.

In the Cicero disturbance of 1951, the mob roughed up a black man attempting to move into an apartment, attacked the apartment, burned his furniture, and was "completely out of control." These activities were not prevented or hampered by the local police who were present. In fact, the local chief of police earlier had told the black that he needed a permit to move in and threatened to arrest him if he tried to move in. The disturbance stopped only after the decision of the governor of Illinois to send out National Guard troops. [26]

Police Partiality / In spite of well-documented instances of police involvement in rioting and failure to take decisive action, to hold an image of general police inaction or complicity is incorrect. In most cities efforts were made toward the control of violence. However, when police did try to maintain law and order, this was frequently not in a neutral and impartial manner. Given white control of police and a tradition of differential law enforcement, such partiality is not surprising. Partiality was often involved in the precipitating incident as well as in the police arresting Negroes beaten by the mob, or those armed for self-defense, on charges of rioting. The pattern of stopping Negro attacks on whites was much more common than the reverse.

During the 1900 New York riot, local police courts were filled to capacity—but only with Negroes. A magistrate criticized the police and asked to see "some of the white persons who participated in the riot." His request was fulfilled when a white teen-ager was brought in for trying to trip a policeman. [27]

In East St. Louis, "after a number of (white) rioters had been taken to jail by the soldiers under Colonel Clayton, the police deliberately turned hundreds of them loose without bond, failing to secure their names or to make any effort to identify them." [28]

A report on the 1919 Washington, D.C., riot notes:

Although the aggressors were white mobbists led by white men in the uniform of the United States [armed forces], ten Negroes were arrested for every white man arrested.[29]

In a 1919 Phillips County, Arkansas, disturbance, according to the Negro view (later supported by affidavits of whites present at the time), whites fired from autos and then burned a church where a black tenant farmers' union was meeting. This spurred a week of violence. A few whites and many Negroes were killed. According to Waskow, "hundreds of Negroes . . . were charged with murder or arrested as 'material witnesses' or for 'investigation.' "[30] No whites were arrested at all except for one who was believed to be on the Negroes' side. Even the U.S. Army seemed less neutral here than in other disturbances. According to the *Arkansas Gazette,* the troops were anxious to get into battle with blacks in order to prevent a supposed plan to kill whites (a plan "discovered" by telling tortured Negroes what to confess to).

During the 1919 Chicago riot, twice as many Negroes as whites appeared as defendants although twice as many Negroes were injured. The state attorney of Cook County stated:

There is no doubt that a great many police officers were grossly unfair in making arrests. They shut their eyes to offenses committed by white men while they were very vigorous in getting all the colored men they could get.[31]

In a telling example, Walter White reports:

In one case a colored man who was fair enough to appear white was arrested for carrying concealed weapons, together with five white men and a number of colored men. All were taken to a police station; the light colored man and the five whites being put into one cell and the other colored men in another. In a few minutes the light colored man and the five whites were released and their ammunition given back to them with the remark, "You'll probably need this before the night is over." [32]

A criminologist expressed the belief that the police showed greater readiness to arrest blacks than whites because the officers felt they were "taking fewer chances if they 'soaked' a colored man." [33]

After soldiers and sailors beat Mexican–Americans in the 1943 Los Angeles zoot suit riot, police who had been onlookers would move in and arrest the Mexicans for vagrancy or rioting. Military authorities were reportedly lax in not canceling leaves.[34]

In writing about the 1943 Detroit riot, Supreme Court Justice Thurgood Marshall suggests:

The trouble reached riot proportions because the police once again enforced the law with an unequal hand. They used "persuasion" rather than firm action with white rioters, while against Negroes they used the ultimate in force: night sticks, revolvers, riot guns, submachine guns, and deer guns.[35]

Differential law enforcement can also frequently be seen in the different sentences received by white and black arrestees and, at another level, in the failure to punish control officials in those cases where force was misused. Grand juries and official investigating commissions have tended to label police killing of Negroes "justifiable homicide."

Variation in Control Behavior / In this effort to characterize control behavior in collective interracial violence prior to the 1960's, I do not mean to suggest that these themes of police rioting, inaction, and partiality were always present, nor when they were present that they applied to all actions of all policemen. Among striking examples where such a characterization does not apply are the 1919 Charleston riot between Negroes and white sailors and the 1935 and 1943 Harlem riots.

Even where control behavior was the worst, heroic action on the part of some officials could be noted, as can cases of the police failing to interfere or arrest Negroes who had beaten whites. Nor should it be forgotten that often, as the mayor of Detroit said in 1943, "The police had a tough job. A lot of them have been beaten and stoned and shot." And beyond being unprepared for their task and usually undermanned, they were the recipients of various insults about their lineage, manhood, and the nature of their maternal relationships. Under such conditions some observers might choose to emphasize their degree of restraint.

Significant variation in control behavior can often be found to be dependent on things such as region of the country, type of disturbance, nature of the issues, unit of control, and time period.

Other factors being equal, conscientious impartial action to maintain law and order has been more likely when the rioting whites were not local citizens, where the disturbance was an insurrection against the local government as well as a black pogrom, where a strike or labor issue was involved, where the precipitating incident did not involve a Negro killing a police officer, and where only blacks rioted.

While conscientious impartial action is related to effectiveness, it is not synonymous with it. Among factors that seem related to effective control are prior training, experience and planning, strong leadership from command officers and local government, the maintenance of organization and discipline within the control organization, the rapid mobilization of large numbers of personnel, and the use of Negro as well as white agents of control.

Control behavior has tended to be better the higher the level of control agency (state police, militia, and U.S. Army) and the later one gets into the twentieth century (1900, 1919, 1943). In many cities disturbances came to an end with the appearance of outside forces, and except for the state militia in East St. Louis, relatively few criticisms of unprofessional behavior or ineffectiveness were directed against them. This is related to the fact that the army and state units often came in fresh at the end of a riot cycle. As outsiders they were uninvolved in local issues and perceived as being neutral. Their larger numbers, superior training, and military organizational structure better suited them for coping with such disorders.

However, in considering the dynamics of the riot, rather than an abstract score card of police behavior, the effect of well-publicized instances of policy brutality, inaction, or partiality was often sufficient to escalate greatly the level of riot activity. Such misbehavior to Negroes became symbolic of past injustice and part of a generalized belief justifying self-defense and retaliatory violence, while whites interpreted it as giving them license to attack blacks.

Control Efforts in the 1960's

In spite of the variation and qualifications noted above, in accounts of earlier disturbances the themes of police rioting, inactivity, and partiality could often be noted. Perhaps they were particularly apparent because they contrast rather markedly with police behavior in recent disturbances. We have come a long way since the 1863 New York Draft riot in which the president of the police board, when asked about taking law-breakers into custody, is said to have replied, "Prisoners? Don't take any. Kill! Kill! Kill! Put down the mob."

Police today have been much quicker to take action, and this action has generally been more restrained than previously. The law has been enforced much more impartially. Particularly in the North there are few, if any, reports of police failing to stop interracial assaults or of police firing into unarmed, noncombative crowds. Considering the absolute number, size, intensity, and duration of recent disorders, there has probably been much less police rioting and brutality and relatively less injury inflicted upon Negroes by the police than in the past; this is all the more salient since police have been provoked to a much greater extent than earlier and have had many more opportunities to use legal force against blacks than they did in previous riots.

Where police rioting has been present, as in Watts, Newark, and Detroit, it has tended to be primarily in the later stages of the disorder as police are unable to control the situation and as they become subject to the same collective behavior phenomena as blacks (the breakdown of social organization, rumor, panic, innovative efforts to handle strain, etc.).

This contrasts with earlier disorders where police rioting was present from the beginning of the disturbance. That police behavior has shown considerable improvement, of course, should give no cause for rejoicing, since numerous well-documented instances of undue and indiscriminate use of force, often deadly, can be cited.

In trying to account for changes in police behavior during riots, changes in the police and in the type of disorder must be considered. Police now are more professionalized and have better resources. Perhaps equally important, the maintenance of law and order now involves suppressing blacks rather than whites.

Just as the nineteenth-century emergence of a bureaucratic police force greatly reduced the fear of riots, today mobile units and modern communications have made it easier for the police to take rapid action. In some cases the availability of nonlethal weapons may have inhibited the use of deadly force.

Beyond such technical factors is modern society's decreased tolerance for internal disorder and the ethos of the contemporary police department. The complexity and interdependence of contemporary society may have increased its vulnerability to civil disorder; at any event its tolerance for internal violence has certainly been decreasing since 1900. American traditions averse to governmental interference in private violence have tended to disappear.

Just as blacks have the misfortune of being poor when most other groups aren't, they have the misfortune of being a lower-class, urban, migrant group at a time when tolerance for the violence characteristically associated with such groups is less than ever. The state has increasingly come to monopolize the means of violence. To a degree that can't be very precisely measured, earlier police behavior transcended racism and must be seen in the context of police ambivalence about the control of private violence.

Citizenship rights in theory, and to an ever greater extent in practice, have been extended to all people, even the ethnically stigmatized lower classes. While this stress on the inclusion of the lower class, at least as far as blacks are concerned, can no longer be used to explain the presumed decline of violence in American society, it is still useful in accounting for the restraint shown by authorities once violence breaks out. Police departments increasingly have come to stress universalistic criteria of law enforcement, as well as effective neutrality and limits on the use of force.

Yet to interpret these changes only in light of abstractions such as professionalization would be naïve. The police today, while in many ways different from the police in 1917, are also dealing with a very different kind of racial violence. Rather than whites attacking Negroes under a white supremacist ideology also held by police, we find Negroes attacking stores and police under an ideology clearly not held by the latter. Since the reimposition of law and order today coincides with the repression of Negroes rather than whites, it is not surprising that the police have been more ready to take action.

Given the above factors one might be led to believe that police would have been much more successful in quelling recent disorders than in the past. Yet to suggest that police behavior in recent riots represents an improvement over earlier periods is not to argue that it has always been effective or humane. While the old adage told me by a veteran police official that in the past "the riot didn't start until the police arrived" may seem less true today, this is certainly not to say that the riot now stops when the police do arrive. It is ironic that although police are technically better prepared to control disorders and have a greater will to do so, they often have been unsuccessful. Two important factors here are the general nature of police–black community relations and the actual behavior of police during the disturbance.

POLICE–COMMUNITY RELATIONS

In its riot analysis (inspired by what it felt were failings in the reports of the New Jersey and National Riot Commissions) the New Jersey State Patrolmen's Benevolent Association finds a "growing disrespect for law and order" to be "one of the root causes" of recent civil disorders.[36] While much in this document could be disputed by social scientists, there is an element of truth here, although the adjective "white" might have been added to "law and order." As blacks have gained in power and self-confidence through civil rights activity, and have become more politicized, the legitimacy granted police has declined. This is especially true for many of those blacks most prone to participate in the disorders. For many of this group, police are seen as just a group of white men, meaner than most, who are further responsible for the historical and current sins of their racial group. From the point of view of one youth in Watts, "The policeman used to be a man with a badge; now he's just a thug with a gun."

To be sure, this view is held by only a minority of the black community, but it is held disproportionately by the most riot-prone group. For the general Negro community, complaints of police brutality are matched by the demand for greater police protection and indignation over the behavior of Negro lawbreakers.

The New Jersey Governor's Select Commission on Civil Disorder notes that "there was virtually a complete breakdown in the relations between police and the Negro community prior to the disorders. . . . Distrust, resentment and bitterness were at a high level on both sides."[37]

Indeed, for some blacks, police come to be seen as an occupation army. As the various (largely unanalyzed) organizational ties between the police and the Department of Defense become stronger, the view of the police as a counterinsurgency force takes on added significance. In reviewing police preparations for future riots, a journalist notes, "One would think the police were readying for war. Or waging it."[38]

Useful parallels can be drawn to the way police were often seen in other ethnically mixed societies (such as India and Pakistan in 1948 or Cyprus and Israel, more recently) during tense periods. Police are viewed not as neutral representatives of the state upholding a legal system but as armed representatives of their ethnic communities. At this point, whatever obedience police can command emerges primarily out of gun barrels and not out of respect for them or the law and order they are enforcing. Even here the symbolic hatred that police may inspire can inhibit the effectiveness of threats of force. In such situations using ethnically alien police to stop an ethnically inspired riot may be equivalent to attempting to put out a fire with gasoline.

In such a context control agents may not be successful even when they "refrain from entering the issues and controversies that move the crowd, remain impartial, unyielding, and fixed on the principle of maintaining law and order" (one of "an effective set of principles for troops to control a rioting mob" suggested by Smelser).[39] This is precisely because even in being neutral the police are in one sense not being neutral. By the mere act of maintaining white (or the status quo) law and order the police have in fact entered "the issues and controversies" and on a side likely to aggravate potential rioters. As Joseph Lohman, a former police scholar and official, has noted, "The police function to support and enforce the interests of the dominant political, social, and economic interests of the town." [40]

Yet beyond these general factors that seem conducive to police ineffectiveness, a number of more concrete aspects of police behavior in the actual disturbance situation must be considered.

POLICE BEHAVIOR IN RECENT DISTURBANCES

As noted, earlier police inaction in riots has generally given way recently to action. Yet many disorders have escalated, not as in the past because of what police failed to do, but precisely because of what they have done.

I have found it useful to organize police behavior that was ineffective or seemed to create rather than control disorder into the following three categories: (1) inappropriate control strategies, (2) lack of coordination among and within various control units, (3) the breakdown of police organization. The remainder of the paper is concerned primarily with police behavior up to the end of the summer of 1967.

Inappropriate Control Strategies

Crowd Dispersal. Here I want to consider ideas held by some control officials about disorderly crowds and the kind of police action that has flowed from such views. In the spirit of Gustav Le Bon it is sometimes assumed that crowds are uniformly like-minded, anarchic, irrational, and hell-bent on destruction. From this it may follow that all people on the street are seen as actual or potential rioters, that crowds must always be broken up, that a riot will not terminate unless it is put down, and that only a technical approach involving the use of massive force is adequate.

In all too many cases police have not gone beyond a nineteenth-century riot manual which stated that "crushing power, exercised relentlessly and without hesitation is really the merciful, as it is the necessary, course to be pursued." [41]

Police were often responsible for the formation of the initial crowd by responding to fairly routine incidents with a large number of squad cars with loud sirens and flashing lights. In some cities, applying the traditional strategy of dispersing the crowd had unanticipated consequences and served to escalate and spread the disorders. The control problem then shifted to guerrilla-like hit-and-run activities.

While the gathering of a crowd at the beginning of a riot itself may be conducive to a lessening of inhibitions, the anger it feels may be heightened and released by precipitous police action. Here it may be useful to examine a series of precipitating or initiating events.

In New Haven in 1967, for example, after some initial minor violence the crowd's mood was still tentative. A small crowd walked down the street toward police lines. As the perimeter was reached, police fired three canisters of tear gas. The crowd then ran back, breaking windows and starting to riot seriously.

According to a report on the 1964 Harlem riot, following the efforts of New York City's tactical patrol force to clear an intersection by swinging their clubs and yelling "Charge!" as they plowed into the crowd and broke it into smaller segments, "Hell broke loose in Harlem." [42] The angry crowd members then began pulling fire alarms, starting fires, and beating whites.

In Englewood, New Jersey, in 1967 police efforts to force Negro bystanders into houses, whether or not they were the right houses, angered and sparked violence on the part of young men. In Rockford, Illinois, the first instances of rock and bottle throwing were inspired by police efforts to clear a late-night crowd off the streets.

A peaceful rally protesting school practices in Philadelphia in 1967 was violently broken up by the civil disobedience squad using riot plan number three. This elicited a violent response from the Negro youth. The superintendent and the president of the school board subsequently blamed the police for starting a riot.

Failure to Negotiate. The treatment of disorders as strictly technical problems of law and order to be solved only by force has meant that negotiations and the use of counterrioters were often ruled out. Such iron-clad rules popular in many police circles completely obscure the variation in types of disorder. Where the disturbance seems apolitical, unfocused, primarily expressive, and not related to current issues or demands, and where there is no minimal organization among rioters and no one willing to take counterriot roles, from the perspective of control authorities there would seem to be no alternative to the graduated use of force. However, where the disturbance develops out of a very focused context involving specific issues (the demand for finding promised jobs, a particular instance of police brutality, discrimination by a business firm, disagreement over school policies, etc.), where grievances are clearly articulated and demands are present, where there seems to be some organization among rioters, and where actual or would-be spokesmen and potential counterrioters come forth, disturbances have been stopped or dampened by entering into dialogues, considering grievances, and using counterrioters. To resort only to force in such a situation is more likely to inflame the situation and increase the likelihood of future disorders.

The refusal to negotiate and use strategies other than a white show of force played an important role in the development of the Watts riot. The director of the Los Angeles Human Relations Commission had worked out a plan to send in 400 black plainclothes officers and several hundred antipoverty workers to make inconspicuous arrests and spread "positive" rumors ("the riot is over") and to withdraw white officers to the perimeter. Young gang leaders promised to use their influence to stop the riot and were led to believe that these conditions would be met.

The deputy chief of police rejected this proposal, stating among other things that he was not going to be told how to deploy his troops. He added that "Negro police officers are not as competent as Caucasian officers and the only reason for sending them in would be because they have black skins and are invisible at night." To the director of the Human Relations Commission he said, "I don't want to hear anything you have got to say, you're part of the problem. *We know how to run a riot* and we are going to handle it our way." In response to the promises of gang leaders to stop the riot, he stated, "We are not going to have hoodlums telling us how to run the police department." And, "We are in the business of trying to quell a riot and we haven't got time to engage in any sociological experiments." [43] Following this refusal a full-scale riot ensued.

All Blacks as Rioters. Just as it is sometimes erroneously assumed that all men at a gay bar are gay or all women standing on certain street corners at a particular time are prostitutes, so to the police any black person out on the streets during a period of civil disorders may be considered a rioter. In some cities, orders to clear an area and the panicky use of force (along with beliefs about the efficacy of getting tough) have resulted in its indiscriminate application to anyone with a black face, including innocent bystanders, government officials, policemen in civilian clothes, ministers, and Negro youth trying to stop the disorders. In noting police inability to differentiate rioters from spectators, an observer of the 1964 Harlem disturbance notes, "The result was injuries to spectators and, in many cases, conversion of spectators into players." [44]

The failure of police to distinguish between black rioters and passersby sometimes negated efforts by black citizens to quiet the situation. Failure to use counterrioters effectively may have prolonged a number of disturbances. In Cincinnati, despite an agreement between the mayor and black leaders that the latter would be given badges and allowed to go into the riot area to help calm things, police refused to recognize the badges and arrested some of the blacks on charges of loitering. A somewhat similar situation existed in Milwaukee. In Newark the mayor and governor gave permission to Negro volunteers to go among the people in efforts to calm the situation. Their activities were inhibited by enforcement personnel. According to the governor, they ". . . were chased around so much by people who suspected them as participating in the riot that they had to abandon their efforts." [45]

Beyond the general confusion in the disorders and a racially inspired (if not racist) inability to differentiate among blacks on the streets, this police response was related to a view of the disorders as a technical problem to be met only by a show of force and a feeling that police competence and jurisdiction were being infringed upon. That counterrioters were often black activists, and in some cases gang youth, may have accentuated this feeling.

Official Anticipation. Thus far, the disorders considered have involved the pattern of riotous or at least disorderly Negro behavior followed and sometimes encouraged by the official response. However, there were other instances where the dynamics of the disturbance worked in the opposite direction. Here authorities (with poor intelligence reports) precipitated confrontation by anticipating violence where none was imminent and by overreacting to minor incidents that happened to occur during a major riot elsewhere.

Planning in anticipation of riots sometimes helped to create a state-of-siege mentality, increase susceptibility to rumors, and lay the basis for self-fulfilling prophecies. This is particularly true where police have a get-tough, act-quickly philosophy. Following the Newark riot, fourteen cities in the surrounding area had some type of disorders, and after Detroit, eight additional Michigan cities reported disorders. An important factor (in addition to psychological contagion) in the spread of violence from major urban centers to outlying communities was the expectation of a riot and subsequent overreaction on the part of white authorities.[46]

"Control" of Sniping. It is clear now that much of the "sniping" reported in riot situations actually came from police and Guardsmen, sometimes unwittingly firing at each other, and also from small explosions in fires, snapping power lines, fire crackers, and so on. Mass firing by police and Guardsmen at buildings, sometimes using their private weapons, without an adequate system of accounting for ammunition spent, and not under the command of a superior officer, created much havoc, killed and wounded many innocent people, and helped escalate the violence. Such firing no doubt drew counterfire from angry Negroes who were bent on retaliation or who viewed their counterfire as self-defense. Thus police action sometimes created the very sniper fire it was supposedly trying to stop. The fact that changes in policy from not shooting to shooting looters during the Detroit riot were not announced may have increased the death toll.

The Levels of Force. In the use of force to quell a disturbance the police have traditionally faced a dilemma. To underreact out of concern with heightening tensions, because of technical incapacity, or because the seriousness of the situation is not appreciated, may permit disorders to spread rapidly as new norms conducive to disorderly behavior emerge and as people see that they can break rules without fear of punishment. On the other hand, to use too much force too soon may create incidents and escalate the disorders as bystanders become involved and the already involved become ever more indignant. In cities such as Watts, Newark, and Detroit, police departments moved from a pattern of underreaction to overreaction, in each case inadvertently contributing to the disorders. The example of Milwaukee shows that an early display of overwhelming force can stop disorders, though the closing of airports, the presence of 4,800 National Guardsmen, 800 policemen, and 200 State Police to control about 150 youths who broke windows and looted after a dance seems rather out of proportion.

There is a curious confusion in the image of man held by proponents of the get-tough policy. On the one hand, they assume that the potentially riotous individual is cold and calculating and carefully weighs the consequences of his actions and hence will be frightened by the potentially strong sanctions. On the other hand, they also usually hold an image of rioters as completely wild and irrational people caught up in an "insensate rage."

The tensions which generate riots are not likely to be reduced by a tough-talking mayor or police chief. Such rhetoric would seem to have little deterrent value and may help further to polarize the atmosphere, create fear of genocide in blacks, and foster plans for self-defense (which are then likely to be taken by police as proof of the need to be even tougher). However, after the beginning of a disorder an immediate show of massive, nonlethal force has often served to quell disorders.

Lack of Coordination among Control Units / In the face of major, unanticipated disorders involving a wide area and large numbers of people engaged in hit-and-run guerrilla-like tactics, local decentralized, autonomous police, organized primarily to fight crime, control traffic, and keep the peace, were usually ineffective. The control of such disturbances required training and activity that were almost opposite in nature to those needed for normal police operation.[47] The largest riots necessitated calling in other control units differing in training, organizational structure, ethos, and familiarity with the local area. Not surprisingly, difficulties often emerged as a result.

While the inability to admit failure, bureaucratic entanglements, petty rivalries, and political considerations delayed the calling out of higher levels of force, the lack of prior planning and an unclear chain of command all meant further delays once other control agents finally did arrive on the scene.

Local, state, and National Guard units did not merge easily. Guard units, accustomed to acting in patrols, were fragmented, and Guardsmen were isolated from commanding officers, while police usually organized as one- or two-man autonomous patrol units were to become disciplined members of military units relying on commands from superiors and not on their own discretion. While officers from different units were together, they were often responding to separate orders. In Newark the three enforcement agencies were issued separate orders on weapons use.

Technical as well as social communications problems contributed to ineffective coordination of control activities and clearly furthered the disorders. Regular radio frequencies were heavily overtaxed, and local police, State Police, and the National Guard operated on different frequencies. Though this had been a problem two years earlier in Watts, little had changed by the time of Detroit and Newark. In the beginning stages of the latter, State Police were unable to get a clear definition of riot perimeters or of areas where activity was heaviest. They could not obtain information about the movement of local police patrols or citizens' calls and were obliged to follow local police and fire trucks responding to calls.[48] Inability to communicate was a factor in police and guardsmen firing at each other and in the belief in widespread sniping.

Poor communication within departments also had serious consequences. One reason the Los Angeles Police Department failed to employ sufficient manpower when needed was the reluctance of subordinate commanders to expose themselves to ridicule and downgrading by possible overreaction. While the Los Angeles police possessed some of the most skilled investigators in the world, trained to deal with master criminals, they could not get a true picture of what was happening in the early stages of Watts. Early on the third day of the riot, field forces knew the situation was out of control, but the downtown command post was still optimistic. This is the classic problem of information flow in a bureaucracy. This highly professional department was unable to admit that a handful of what it considered hoodlums could create a major disturbance that it couldn't control.[49]

In other cases, as in Los Angeles, Boston, and New York, agreements reached by mayor's special representatives, human relations officials, and police-community relations officers who had rapport with rioters were not honored by other policemen, creating great indignation and a sense of betrayal.

In Los Angeles, the police-community relations inspector was reportedly not called into the inner circle of police advisors. The chief of police was unaware that his department had been represented at an important community meeting held during the riot.

A potentially ugly incident might have emerged in Detroit on May 21, 1968, when mounted police outside a building tried to drive supporters of the Poor People's March back into a building, while police on the inside were trying to drive them out.

In Rockford, Illinois, in 1967, as people poured out of bars that were closing, police tried to drive them off the street that other police had already barricaded.

In Birmingham in 1963 police circled several thousand blacks, on one side swinging clubs and on the other side turning water hoses on them, catching bystanders as well as protesters. Though this was no doubt all too well coordinated.

Breakdown of Police Organization: One Riot or Two? / An additional source of police ineffectiveness and abuse stems from the breakdown of organization within enforcement agencies.

In most discussions of recent riots undue emphasis has been given to the behavior of rioters. The normal concepts used to analyze collective behavior have been applied to them—emotional contagion, the spread of rumors, panic and the expression of frustration, the lessening of inhibitions and innovative efforts to handle certain kinds of strain. Yet in several major disturbances, this perspective might equally be applied to the police. Police, lacking training and experience and often uncertain of what they were to do, sometimes became fatigued (frequently working 12-hour or more shifts with insufficient rest periods and nourishment) and were thrown off balance by the size of the disturbance and by being drawn frantically from one area to another (in some cases for false alarms seemingly coordinated with attacks and looting). As large numbers of people taunt, defy, insult, and attack them and as they see their fellows injured and in some cases killed, patience thins and anger rises. Rumors about atrocities committed against them may spread.

Police under these circumstances sometimes come to take violent black rhetoric and threats (which are partly related to expressive oral traditions, ritual posturing, and political in-fighting) too literally, as is suggested by the lack of police killed by snipers, by reports that some snipers misfired on purpose, and by the lack of attacks on known racists.

The belief may spread that they are in a war and that all black people are their enemy. Traditional misconceptions about riotous crowds may contribute to an exaggeration of the dangers confronting them. As police control of the "turf" is effectively challenged and rioters gain control of the streets by default, the word may spread (as in Watts, Newark, and Detroit) that rioters have "beat the police." Losing face, humiliated by their temporary defeat, their professional pride undermined, police sometimes have a strong desire for revenge.

In a context such as the above, superior officers may lose the power to control their men. The chain of command and communication between and within enforcement agencies, often unclear to begin with, may completely break down. The most dangerous part of the disturbance is now at hand as the environment changes from a riot to a war. Some police behavior seems as much or more inspired by the desire for vengeance, retaliation, and "teaching the bastards a lesson" as by the desire to restore law and order.

The words of Lee and Humphrey, written shortly after the 1943 Detroit riot, are clearly relevant twenty-six years later. "War is to the army much what civilian outbreaks are to the police. Both offer socially acceptable outlets for the residuum of aggressiveness characteristic of each." [50]

On the third day of the 1967 Detroit riot, an officer was overheard telling a young black on a newly stolen bicycle, "The worm is turning." And turn it did as the police took off their badges, taped over squad car numbers (this, of course, greatly reduced the number of complaints filed), and began indiscriminately and excessively using force against rioters, bystanders, and in some cases each other. The death and injury toll climbed rapidly. Some of the firing stopped only when control officials ran out of ammunition. At this time the Algiers Motel killings and "games" occurred. One of the police officers involved in this incident stated, ". . . there was a lot of rough-housing, you know, everything just went loose (following the killing of a police officer on the third day of the riot). The police officers weren't taking anything from anyone." [51] This was something of an understatement.

According to one high police official in secret testimony, by the fourth day of the riot "the police were out of control." There are some reports of police keeping looted goods taken from prisoners and robbing them, and of doing damage to "soul brother" stores spared by the rioters. Claims of brutality filed included charges of the sexual abuse of women and the carving of initials on prisoners.

The chairman of the Newark Human Rights Commission reported that ". . . men were being brought in, many of them handcuffed behind their backs, being carried like a sack of meal, and the fifth policeman would be hammering their face and body with a billy stick. This went on time after time. Many times you would see a man being brought into the police station without a mark on his face and when he was taken out, he was brutally beaten." [52] Although it has been said in jest, there is an element of truth in the claim that Newark was a classical race riot except that the Italians wore blue uniforms.

Police may come to see rioters and suspected rioters, like those convicted of crimes, as having forfeited their civil rights. In Watts an officer responded to a black pedestrian who complained about being stopped on his way home from work: "Don't yell at me. You lost your rights a couple of days ago." [53]

There often seemed to be a tendency for police behavior to become progressively worse as the disorders wore on. In Watts, Newark, and Detroit this was partly related to the entrance of higher-level control units into the disturbance (qualifying the more general pattern noted earlier). The arrival of Guardsmen, restoring predominant force to public authorities, may be seen by the police as offering a chance to reverse earlier humiliation and gain revenge for injury and death suffered by the police. At the same time, inexperienced Guardsmen, isolated from the authority of their commanding officers, may become subject to the same collective behavior phenomena as police and blacks, further adding to disorder-creating activities.

The head of the Detroit police, a former reporter, was hesitant to call out the Guard, noting, "I've been on too many stories where the Guard was called up. They're always shooting their own people"; and "Those poor kids were scared pissless; and they scared me." Calling them out, however, was necessary to gain federal troops.[54]

What is especially tragic is that the symbols of police legitimacy became the cloak under which much indiscriminate force was exercised upon the Negro community, though it is a mistake to attribute such behavior only to the desire for revenge or a hatred of Negroes. Part of it would seem to be equivalent to the behavior of front-line soldiers in their first combat experience who kill many of their own men. That the breakdown of police organization transcends racism may also be seen in their response to protests such as those at Columbia University, Chicago, and various antiwar demonstrations.

It is important to recognize that not only was police behavior in the latter stages of several major riots excessively brutal and probably ineffective, but also that such acts were not idiosyncratic or random but were woven into a social fabric of rumor, panic, frustration, fatigue, fear, racism, lack of training, inexperience, and the breakdown of police organization. While such a situation created widespread fear in the Negro community and may inhibit some rioters, it can lead to (and partly results from) escalation in the level of black violence as the same social processes go on.

There is an interaction process and gradual reciprocal increase in the severity of action taken on both sides. The fact that police abuses were most pronounced in Newark and Detroit, where disturbances were the most serious, does not necessarily lend itself to a one-sided causal interpretation. Here we see the emergent character of the disorders.

The breakdown of police organization and misuse of force did not happen to anywhere near the same extent in all cities that had disturbances. An important question for analysis is why in Watts, Newark, and Detroit, but not in Cincinnati or Boston? The conditions under which such police behavior appears are not well understood. Yet it would seem to be related to things such as training, the extent to which the police disagree with or are threatened and offended by the issues raised by protestors, the extent of the injuries and provocation faced by the police, the size and stage of the riot, the clarity of the orders stressing restraint, the tightness of the command structure, whether high-level officers are on the scene, whether it is made clear to the police that they will be punished for misbehavior, and whether the police expect disturbance participants to be sufficiently punished by the legal system. That there was a breakdown of police organization in two of the most "professional" (according to the standards of the International Association of Chiefs of Police) departments in the United States, Los Angeles and Chicago, suggests that this issue goes beyond what is usually understood as police professionalism. In fact, it may even be that less "professional" police departments such as Boston's have greater flexibility and a less zealous approach to potential threats to "law and order," which permits them to show greater restraint and makes them more effective during tense periods.

QUIS CUSTODIET IPSOS CUSTODES?

A crucial question raised by some of this material is "Who controls the agents of social control?" One of the central intellectual problems for social analysts is the basis of social order. If one resolves the question of social order by relying on shared values and the internalization of standards, then this is not seen as an issue. Yet even those who answer the question of social order by stressing the importance of external force usually ignore the problem. In several of the major disturbances after a period of time the answer to the question of "Who guards the guards?" seemed to be, "No one."

One of the manifestly unfair aspects of social organization is that those with official power are usually also those (or are intimately tied to those) who possess the power to legitimately sanction the misuse of this power.

One means by which the police traditionally have been controlled is through the courts by the exclusionary rule, whereby illegal means used in gaining evidence or making arrests are grounds for the dismissal of a case. However, this rule only has an effect when convictions are sought (a factor often beyond the control of the police). One element in the misuse of official force is the view held by some policemen that they can (and indeed must) "hold court in the street" given the presumed leniency and complexity of the legal system. It would seem that police are more likely to use violence when convictions against demonstrators are unlikely or those arrested will face only minor charges.

Individuals can also bring costly and time-consuming civil damage suits against the police, although those most likely to need redress may be least likely to have the resources necessary for a long court struggle, and establishing proof is difficult. Police have also been controlled through more direct political means. Yet the use of "good government" civil service reforms and the decline of the urban political machine have made this less likely.

The means of control favored by the police is self-regulation, in a fashion analogous to specialized professions such as medicine or law. It is argued that police work is highly technical and only those who practice it are competent to judge it. Though there is much evidence to suggest that, like the rest of us, the police can resist anything but temptation. Internal review mechanisms have been inadequate to say the least. In many departments there is a strong norm of secrecy surrounding police misbehavior; even when known, infractions often go unpunished. Knowledge that police are unlikely to be subjected to postriot sanctioning may lessen restraints on their use of violence.

The consequences, costs, and benefits of various means of regulating the police have not been carefully studied. Yet it is clear from some of the data considered in this paper and more recent events such as the Chicago Democratic Convention, the People's Park in Berkeley, and attacks on groups such as the Black Panthers that in some cases the control of the police is not much affected by the courts, various other checks and balances, internalized norms of fair play, or internal police organization. The question of control and responsiveness of the police is certainly among the most pressing of domestic issues.

It has been suggested that the worst crimes have been committed in the name of obedience rather than rebellion. In the Gordon Riots of 1780 demonstrators destroyed property and freed prisoners, but apparently did not kill anyone, while authorities killed several hundred rioters and hung an additional twenty-five. In the Rebellion Riots of the

French Revolution, though several hundred rioters were killed, they killed no one.[55] Up to the end of the summer of 1967, this pattern had clearly been repeated as police, not rioters, were responsible for most of the more than one hundred deaths that have occurred. Similarly, in a related context the more than one hundred civil rights murders of recent years have been matched by almost no murders of racist whites, although since 1968 this pattern may be changing.

It is increasingly clear that the police today are unduly scapegoated and stereotyped, as well as being underpaid, undertrained, and overworked. They have to face directly the consequences of the larger society's failure to change. The basic solutions to America's racial crisis lie in the direction of redistributing power and income, eliminating discrimination and exploitation, and fostering an appreciation of social diversity. But one important factor in fulfilling the Kerner Commission's plea to "end the destruction and the violence, not only in the streets of the ghetto but in the lives of the people" is surely more enlightened police behavior.

NOTES

1. R. Merton, *Social Theory and Social Structure* (New York: Free Press, 1968).

2. Some of the following discussion is based on reports of groups with vested interests other than, or in addition to, the dispassionate pursuit of truth. The highly charged emotional nature of civil disorder and the fact that it may cover wide areas make research difficult. Traditional norms of police secrecy may require undue reliance on the reports of others, who are interested in overstating police misbehavior. The usual methodological strictures about this kind of historical data apply. At the same time the very unusualness of the events leads to their receiving greater attention, making analysis somewhat easier. Social control behavior is further difficult to describe because in any one disturbance it may change markedly over time and may vary depending on the control unit in question.

3. H. Blumer, "Race Prejudice as a Sense of Group Position," *Pacific Sociological Review* 1 (1958): 3–7; T. Shibutani and K. H. Kwan, *Ethnic Stratification* (New York: Macmillan, 1965).

4. G. Osofsky, "Race Riot, 1900: A Study of Ethnic Violence," *Journal of Negro Education* 32 (1963): 16–24.

5. J. H. Franklin, *From Slavery to Freedom* (New York: Knopf, 1965), p. 433.

6. E. Rudwick, *Race Riot at East St. Louis, July 2, 1919* (Cleveland: World, 1966).

7. *Ibid.*, p. 87.

8. *Ibid.*, p. 48.

9. A. Grimshaw, "Actions of Police and the Military in American Race Riots," *Phylon* 24, no. 3 (1963): 271–289.

10. Chicago Commission on Race Relations, *The Negro in Chicago* (Chicago: University of Chicago Press, 1923), pp. 35, 38–39.

11. Franklin, *op. cit.,* p. 475.

12. Grimshaw, *op. cit.,* p. 277.

13. A. M. Lee and N. O. Humphrey, *Race Riot* (New York: Dryden, 1943), pp. 3, 30; R. Shogan and T. Craig, *The Detroit Race Riot* (Philadelphia: Chilton, 1964).

14. A. Dahlke, "Race and Minority Riots—A Study in the Typology of Violence," *Social Forces* 30 (1952): 419–425.

15. Franklin, *op. cit.,* p. 433.

16. Cited in Grimshaw, *op. cit.*

17. Rudwick, *op. cit.,* p. 76.

18. Grimshaw, *op. cit.,* p. 281.

19. Rudwick, *op. cit.,* p. 67.

20. A. I. Waskow, *From Race Riot to Sit-in: 1919 and the 1960's* (Garden City, N.Y.: Doubleday, 1966), p. 17.

21. Chicago Commission, *op. cit.,* pp. 39, 40.

22. Anonymous article in *The Outlook* (1919) as quoted in Grimshaw, *op. cit.,* p. 277.

23. Waskow, *op. cit.,* p. 34.

24. Lee and Humphrey, *op. cit.,* p. 73.

25. Grimshaw, *op. cit.,* p. 283.

26. W. Grenley, "Social Control in Cicero," *British Journal of Sociology* 3 (1952): 322–388.

27. Osofsky, *op. cit.*

28. Grimshaw, *op. cit.,* p. 274.

29. H. J. Seligmann, "Race War," *New Republic* 20 (1919): 50.

30. Waskow, *op. cit.,* pp. 121–142.

31. Chicago Commission, *op. cit.*

32. W. F. White, "Chicago and Its Eight Reasons," *Crisis* 18, no. 6 (1919).

33. Chicago Commission, *op. cit.,* p. 35.

34. *Time,* 21 June 1943.

35. T. Marshall, "The Gestapo in Detroit," *Crisis* 50 (1943): 232–234.

36. New Jersey State Patrolmen's Benevolent Association, *A Challenge to Conscience* (Maplewood, N.Y., May 1968).

37. Governor's Select Commission on Civil Disorders (New Jersey), *Report for Action* (1968), p. 143.

38. G. Wills, *The Second Civil War* (New York: New American Library, 1968).

39. N. Smelser, *Theory of Collective Behavior* (New York: Free Press, 1962), p. 267.

40. A. Neiderhoffer, *Behind the Shield* (New York: Doubleday, 1967), p. 13.

41. General E. L. Molineux, *Riots in Cities and Their Suppression* (Boston: Headquarters First Brigade, 1884) as cited in D. Garson, "The Politics of Collective Violence" (Ph.D. diss., Harvard University, 1969).

42. F. C. Shapiro and J. W. Sullivan, *Race Riots* (New York: Crowell, 1964).

43. *Proceedings of the Governor's Commission on the Los Angeles Riots,* vol. 11 (Los Angeles, 1965), pp. 59, 61, 63, 65; J. Buggs, "Report from Los Angeles," *The Journal of Intergroup Relations* (Autumn 1966).

44. Shapiro and Sullivan, *op. cit.,* p. 57.

45. Governor's Select Commission, *op. cit.,* p. 120.

46. The author's discussion of the official anticipation of disorder in New Jersey cities covers much the same material found in Louis Goldberg's section on the propagation of disorder (pp. 146–147) and is not included here. Both authors studied the subject at the National Advisory Commission on Civil Disorders. (Eds.)

47. C. C. Turner, "Planning and Training for Civil Disorder," *The Police Chief* 34 (1968):22–28.

48. Governor's Select Commission, *op. cit.*

49. On Watts, see R. Conot, *Rivers of Blood, Years of Darkness* (New York: Bantam, 1967); and J. Cohen and W. Murphy, *Burn, Baby, Burn* (New York: Avon, 1967).

50. Lee and Humphrey, *op. cit.*, p. 114.

51. J. Hersey, *The Algiers Motel Incident* (New York: Bantam, 1968), p. 134.

52. Governor's Select Commission, *op. cit.*, p. 118.

53. Cohen and Murphy, *op. cit.*, p. 195.

54. As quoted in Wills, *op. cit.*, pp. 43, 44.

55. C. Couch, "Collective Behavior: An Examination of Stereotypes," *Social Problems* 15 (1968):310–321.

The Courts

⚔ 8. THE ADMINISTRATION OF JUSTICE IN THE WAKE OF THE DETROIT CIVIL DISORDER OF JULY 1967
Michigan Law Review

Introduction

The Supreme Court of the United States and the Court of Appeals will take care of themselves. Look after the courts of the poor, who stand most in need of justice. The security of the Republic will be found in the treatment of the poor and ignorant; in indifference to their misery and helplessness lies disaster.[1]

The belief is pervasive among ghetto residents that lower courts in our urban communities dispense "assembly-line" justice; that . . . the poor and uneducated are denied equal justice with the affluent. . . . Too often the courts have operated to aggravate rather than relieve the tensions that ignite and fire disorders.[2]

Early Sunday morning, July 23, 1967, the Detroit Police Department raided a "blind pig" at the corner of Twelfth Street and Clairmont Street. An unexpectedly large number of patrons were present at the after-hours drinking establishment, and it took the police over an hour to remove them all from the scene. The weather was warm and humid—despite the time, many people were still on the streets. A crowd of about two hundred gathered while the police were occupied with the individuals arrested in the raid. The last of the arrestees were removed shortly after 5:00 A.M. At that moment an empty bottle broke the rear window of a police car, and an empty litter can was thrown through the window of a nearby store.

From the *Michigan Law Review* 66, no. 7 (May 1968): pp. 1544–1559. This chapter is a section of a longer article in the *Law Review*. Most of the footnotes have been deleted. For a full account of the subject the reader should refer to the original article.

By 6:00 A.M. there were thousands of people on Twelfth Street. Widespread looting began as windows were broken over a wide area. Civil disorder had come to Detroit. It was to continue until Friday, July 28, 1967. In the interim, thousands of State Police, Michigan National Guardsmen, and federal troops were called in to contain reported disorder activity within the city. Over seven thousand people were arrested during this five-day period.

The mass arrests imposed a tremendous burden on the legal establishment of Detroit; fair and speedy processing of the arrestees was required. The *Michigan Law Review* sent two observers into Detroit on August 1 to measure the response of the legal establishment. The observers spent countless hours in Detroit Recorder's Court. Interviewing of defense attorneys, prosecutors, judges, defendants, and others who were concerned with the proceedings continued until March 1968. Others who studied the administration of criminal justice following the disorder volunteered pertinent information throughout the year. This study is the result of these efforts.

Since the focus of this study is the legal establishment's *response* to the burdens imposed by the disorder, the early stages in the processing of the arrestees were of primary importance. The further away in time any legal stage was from the disorder itself, the less effect the disorder had on the proceedings. Accordingly, the most intensive effort was directed at study of the arraignment-on-the-warrant proceedings which took place during the week of the disorder. The preliminary examinations began on August 1 and continued for four to five weeks. The earliest preliminary examinations highlighted the greatest number of disorder-related problems. As the sheer volume of examinations decreased, so did the legal difficulties.

Arraignment on the Warrant

PURPOSE AND NORMAL OPERATION

Under normal circumstances, people arrested in Detroit are brought to one of thirteen police precincts for booking, finger-printing, and interrogation. Each case is then assigned to a detective who investigates the charges and confers with the prosecutor to determine whether a warrant should be issued. If a warrant is authorized, the prisoner's file is sent to the warrant clerk's office in the Recorder's Court where a complaint and an affidavit are prepared. The prisoner is then brought before the court for the arraignment on the warrant.

The primary functions of the arraignment on the warrant are to inform the defendant of the charge against him, to advise him of his constitutional rights, to set bail, and to ascertain whether the defendant wishes a preliminary examination and, if so, to set a date for it. The merits of the case are not considered, and any evidence received is directed toward the setting of bail. Moreover, there are no defenses which must be asserted at this stage, no pleas are required, and, except for the arresting officer, no prosecution witnesses are present. The defendant may, if he so desires and can afford it, be represented by retained counsel at the arraignment on the warrant. The court, however, will not appoint counsel for the indigent, having adopted the view that there are no rights of the defendant which can be jeopardized or need to be protected by counsel at this stage.

With regard to the amount of bail to be set, there are statutory guidelines in Michigan which require consideration by the judge of the seriousness of the offense charged, the previous criminal record of the defendant, and the probability of his appearance at trial. Therefore, in setting bail the judges normally consult the prisoner's file, which contains his past record, the police writeup, the complaint, and any other relevant material that may have been accumulated by the police department. In addition, they will usually question the defendant with regard to such information as his employment, marital, and residence status. Bail is then set and the defendant is either remanded to custody (if he cannot post bail) or released (if he can post bail, or if he is placed on personal recognizance).

ARRAIGNMENT ON THE WARRANT
DURING THE DISORDER—
AN OVERVIEW

Lining up a group of fifteen or twenty unrepresented prisoners before the bench, the judge said, "You're accused of entering without breaking, your bond is $10,000, your examination is set for August 1." Calling the next group, he continued, "You heard what I said to them, the same applies to you." This incident, witnessed by at least two observers, illustrates what might be termed the salient features of the arraignment on the warrant during the disorder: high bail, absence of counsel, failure to consider individual circumstances, failure to inform defendants of their constitutional rights, and an emphasis on expediency. Although each of these things did not necessarily occur at every arraignment or in every courtroom, each was present all too often. Secondary factors contributing to and exacerbating the elements listed included a shortage of judicial manpower coupled with a desire by the court to go-it-alone, a logistics problem in keeping track of and identifying prisoners, and an atmosphere pervaded by mass confusion, fear, and panic.

By far the most pervasive aspect of the arraignment on the warrant, and for that matter of all judicial proceedings in the Recorder's Court involved in the processing of cases during the disorder, was a major breakdown in the adversarial process. The court made a basic policy decision to aid the executive branch in every possible way to break the back of the disorder and restore order to the community. This decision was in some cases made explicit by public statements of the judges; in others, it was implicit, manifested by the conduct of the court.

High Bail / Although complete statistics were not immediately available, it was readily apparent that the judicial policy during the early stages of the disorder was to set extremely high bail. An unofficial sampling of court files covering the first two or three days of the disorder reveals that bonds ranged from $200,000 (for a sniper) to personal recognizance (for a curfew-violating female), but the most popular figures were $10,000 and $25,000. Thus, one judge set 161 bonds out of 175 at $10,000, another set 121 at $25,000 and 42 at $10,000 out of a total of 171, and a third set 81 at $10,000 and 39 at $5,000 out of a total of 130. Interviews with 1,014 prisoners who were arrested during the disorder and incarcerated at Jackson State Prison disclosed that at least 50 percent of them were being held subject to bonds in excess of $10,000 and at least 70 percent on bonds of over $5,000.

The initial decision on the bond policy seems to have been made by Wayne County Prosecutor William Cahalan some time during the first Sunday of the disorder. He publicly stated that his office would ask for bonds of $10,000 and up on all persons arrested "so that even though they had not been adjudged guilty, we would eliminate the danger of returning some of those who had caused the riot to the street during the time of stress."

Recorder's Court judges were almost unanimous in their adoption of the prosecutor's suggestion. According to Cyrus Vance, Special Assistant to the Secretary of Defense:

[T]he judge who was on duty Sunday night and the additional judges who came on during the night followed [the prosecutor's] recommendation to the letter. . . . By Monday morning, twelve of the thirteen judges in the Recorder's Court had begun to uniformly follow the recommendation of the prosecutor and set extremely high bail on each of the prisoners arrested.

The dissenting judge was George W. Crockett, Jr., who, on Wednesday, July 26, wrote a letter to his fellow judges on the Recorder's Court informing them of his "disagreement with [the] suggested 'high bond policy' " and of his view that

each of us has the sole responsibility of fixing bonds in cases assigned to us. I intend to exercise that responsibility as well as accept the responsibility for my action. . . . In my judgment [ten and twenty-five thousand dollar] bonds are not only excessive, they are prohibitive.

On the Monday morning following the start of the disorder, executive Judge Brennan called a meeting of the bench. It was at this meeting that the bond policy was formally agreed on by the twelve judges other than Crockett. Their rationale, like Cahalan's, was that high bonds would help control the disorder by keeping those apprehended from returning to the streets. Brennan was quoted in the *Detroit News* as saying, "We will, in matters of this kind, allocate an extraordinary bond. We must keep these people off the streets. We will keep them off." In the same article, Judge Robert J. Colombo declared, "What we're trying to do here is keep them off the streets. And apparently we're being successful at that. If we let them back on, you know what would happen. . . . In a way we're doing what the police didn't do." "Doing what the police didn't do" is not the typical analysis of the bail-setting function of an independent judiciary.

Although there was no explicit change in policy, on Wednesday, July 26, individual judges did begin to depart from the uniformly high bails, and some defendants were released. By this time the community had begun to return to normal, and the jails in the city and throughout the state were filled beyond capacity. Therefore, "at the urging of a number of persons including federal officials, [the prosecutor's office] began to think in terms of releasing prisoners on personal bond or on reasonable bond."

It is significant that once again it was the prosecutor's office that initiated a judicial policy. According to Cahalan, his office engineered the major part of the release program by undertaking an examination of all the prisoners' files in regard to prior criminal records. If the defendant had no prior convictions, he was recommended for personal recognizance; otherwise, no further investigation was made and the original bond was maintained. Since the court invariably approved the prosecutor's recommendations, this program resulted in the release of 3,000 prisoners on personal recognizance in a period of a few days. An additional 650 were also released on personal bond after a review of their files by the judges themselves. The arraignments on the warrant were completed by August 1, at which time the preliminary examinations began. At this later stage those people still in custody who had not been charged with serious offenses such as sniping or arson were either released on personal bond or their bonds were lowered to what they probably would have been under normal circumstances.

It was noted earlier that a Recorder's Court judge ordinarily has the prisoner's file before him when he sets bond. Because of a clerical log jam, those files were unavailable during the disorder. Although the Clerk's Office of the Recorder's Court operated around the clock, the attempt to process within one week the equivalent of one-half of the entire caseload for all of 1966 proved understandably impossible for an office unprepared for such an emergency. In addition, the Records Bureau of the Detroit Police Department bogged down and was unable to supply necessary records at the pace they were demanded. Finally, the task was complicated even further by the fact that many prisoners gave incorrect names or had the same name as other prisoners.

Many of the judges, including Judge Brennan, asserted that this absence of records was an additional factor necessitating the high bonds. They took the position that since they were unable to tell which of those appearing before them required custody to ensure their appearance at trial, prohibitively high bails had to be set until a judgment could be made on the basis of prior record. Whether this approach was consistent with the presumption of innocence will be examined later. At this point it is enough to note that Judge Crockett was unimpressed with the argument that the serious clerical problem necessitated high bonds, and that in light of the announced policy of "trying to . . . keep them off the streets," it is questionable whether the absence of records actually did account for the high bails.

Representation by Counsel / Since Recorder's Court does not consider it necessary to appoint counsel at the arraignment on the warrant, the existence of the disorder did not alter the situation in regard to the representation of indigent defendants at this stage. As usual, there was no representation. The disorder did, however, have an effect on the representation of those who had retained counsel. In most instances the efforts of those retained attorneys who were present at this stage were greatly impaired by the mass confusion in the community, the courtroom, and the jails. As one attorney put it:

There was no real effort to comply with the elementary right of a defendant to see his lawyer. You couldn't find your client at all except by blind luck. When I did find somebody, I couldn't get to him as there was no procedure by which a lawyer could interfere with the administrative procedures of the police. It was futile to try anything.

Also, the organized bar, which later responded so well to the need for counsel at the preliminary examinations, made no effort to intervene during the arraignments on the warrant. According to Judge John Emery, a municipal judge of Birmingham, Michigan, the bar was wholly inactive during the disorder period, which is when the arraignments were being conducted. Similarly, Professor Frank Sengstock of the University of Detroit Law School observed that "the legal profession in Detroit did not check the court of justice throughout most of the week in which the riot occurred. In fact, the profession was paralyzed."

Although the organized bar as such did not come forward to assist defendants during the early stages of the disorder, several individuals did. On Monday of the week of the disorder Emery suggested to the judges that they consider providing representation for indigents, and volunteered his own services, and those of a few other attorneys, for this purpose. Most of the judges, however, were opposed to the idea. They thought that providing counsel at the arraignments was unnecessary and would only impair the process of appointing counsel at later stages in the proceedings; initially, only three judges permitted attorneys to be present in their courtrooms to "assist" those who requested it, and even they did not formally assign counsel to any one case.

When the volunteer attorneys were present, they attempted to induce overall reductions in the amounts of bail and to increase judicial sensitivity to individual circumstances and hardship cases. In some cases involving pregnant women, although not in all, this resulted in a release on personal bond. But their efforts on the whole were described by Emery as "perfunctory and ineffectual." "We were running around, frustrated, helpless, not able to accomplish much of anything."

Failure to Consider Cases Individually / Apparently it was commonplace during the disorder for a group of suspects to be "rounded up" and arrested at the same place (often a store which had already been broken into or burned), charged with the same offense (typically, entering without breaking but with intent to commit larceny), brought to a police station for booking, and taken to the court to be arraigned— still as a group—before one judge. Moreover, most of the judges continued the pattern of group treatment by addressing the defendants collectively, rather than as individuals, and by setting identical bails for all. Obviously the adoption of these procedures precluded any consideration of individual circumstances or of the probability that any particular defendant would return for trial on the appointed day. Bail was set for offenses, not for people.

Again, the notable exception was Judge Crockett, who attempted to individualize the bail procedure and adhere to the statutory guidelines. He took advantage of the offers of help from attorneys and members of the Neighborhood Legal Service (NLS) Bail Bond Project, using them to aid in the gathering of the information necessary to set an appropriate amount of bail. According to Dennis James, head of the Bail Bond Project, defendants were interviewed privately, the information was presented to the judge, the advice of the interviewer was requested, and bond was then set. And a stern and clear warning was given on the consequences of lying to the court.

The chief reasons given by the other judges for not employing Judge Crockett's procedure were the lack of time, the conviction that the defendants could not be believed, and the fear that dangerous individuals would be freed to engage in further destruction. However, Judge Crockett's experience indicates that in fact it took very little extra time to arraign defendants his way, and that in the long run it actually saved his court a great deal of time by eliminating the necessity of reviewing every bond at a later date. Moreover, he felt there was very little misrepresentation by defendants, and that questionable bail risks and dangerous persons could be weeded out by the volunteers or the court. In addition to the warning to the defendant about lying, telephones were available to the volunteers to aid in verifying information when that was possible and necessary. Finally, Crockett did not think that the absence of any official report of the defendant's prior record precluded individualizing the bond procedure, or that setting bonds at an amount within the financial reach of the defendant jeopardized the safety of the community.

It should be noted that there were a few judges, besides Crockett, who made some attempt to individualize the bond procedure. According to James, Judge Davenport followed Crockett's lead on the second day of arraignments and began to utilize the services of NLS, and to provide a phone for verification purposes; but he also continued to set bonds which were higher than those of Judge Crockett. Two other judges had defendants interviewed and received advice from volunteers in the courtroom—only, apparently, to ignore completely the information and continue to set $10,000 and $25,000 bails across the board.

Failure to Inform Defendants of Their Constitutional Rights / Many of the people who witnessed the arraignments on the warrant during the early part of the disorder have expressed the view that Recorder's Court judges failed to explain adequately to defendants the offenses with which they were charged and to inform them of their constitutional rights. According to Professor Sengstock,

> The right to counsel was not adequately explained to the accused. His right to have an attorney appointed, if he could not retain one, was not ex- plored. He was not advised what a preliminary examination was. . . . The nature of his offense was not explained to the accused and often he was not informed of his right to a jury trial. The assembly-line technique adopted by the court left those uneducated in the process as bewildered after their ar- raignments as before.

Similarly, Judge Emery has maintained that "people just were not ad- vised of their constitutional rights at the arraignment on the warrant— they were shuffled through the line."

Recorder's Court judges reject these assertions. Judges Brennan and Gillis, for example, claim that in their courtrooms each defendant was advised of the charges against him, his right to counsel, and his right to remain silent.

The discrepancy between these two accounts is probably due to a dif- ference of opinion in regard to what constitutes an "adequate" explana- tion of a defendant's rights. Those who criticize the court's performance may feel that it performs unsatisfactorily even under normal circum- stances, since ordinarily the accused is not informed that he has a right to have counsel "appointed," or that he can exercise this right "immedi- ately." On the other hand, if less than the usual amount of time was de- voted to this aspect of the arraignment as a result of the pressure on the court to process suspects quickly, the disorder may also have exacer- bated any deficiencies which normally inhere in the court's warning procedure.

Expediency / Many of the previously mentioned features of the ar- raignment on the warrant can also be explained by the Recorder's Court's preoccupation with expediency. Indeed, expediency seemed to be the prevailing philosophy during this stage of the proceedings. Thus, the high bail policy was a means of removing those allegedly engaged in the disorder from the streets with a minimum of legal complications, and the failure to provide counsel or to accept the offers of assistance from various volunteers reflected a desire to dispense with interruptions on behalf of defendants which would slow the work of the court. The group arraignments, too, indicated a predisposition to proceed as quickly as possible. And even the alleged failure to provide adequate warnings of constitutional rights may be attributed in part to an attempt to dispose of cases rapidly.

The reasons for this judicial commitment to expediency are readily apparent. According to Recorder's Court statistics a total of 7,231 persons were arrested on charges related to the disorder. This means that nearly one-half of the *entire* caseload for 1966 was thrust upon the court within one week in 1967. By the night of July 23, the first day of the disorder, 255 people had already been arrested; that number climbed to 3,740 by July 27, when the worst of the disturbance ended and the rate of arrests per day began to decline. To cope with this onslaught of prisoners the court remained open around the clock. The judges divided the day into 4 six-hour shifts, each of which had one judge handling misdemeanors and the rest handling felony arraignments. This left only three judges at any given time to handle felony arraignments, and forced each to arraign approximately eighty prisoners per shift, or an average of one prisoner every four and one-half minutes, in order to keep up with the pace of arrests.

Despite these enormous burdens, it is questionable whether the expedient measures employed by the court were in fact necessary. During the week of the disorder, the Circuit Court of Wayne County had suspended its operations, leaving twenty-six judges with no official duties. On July 25 the services of these judges and the facilities of the Circuit Court were offered to the Recorder's Court to aid in the arraignments. Moreover, a number of municipal judges from nearby communities also offered their services. Although accepting these offers would have resulted in at least tripling the judicial manpower available to process the disorder defendants, they were rejected by the Recorder's Court. The reasons given were that the Circuit Court judges would be unfamiliar with the procedures of the Recorder's Court, which has jurisdiction over all criminal cases within the corporate limits of Detroit, that in any event the problem was not judicial manpower but a clerical impasse, and that an attempt was made to use clerks from the Circuit Court but they could not be taught the necessary clerical procedures in time to be of any assistance.

These reasons are self-defeating. If there was in fact no problem with judicial manpower (there are reports that some judges were often waiting for people to arraign), then whatever justification did exist for employing the "assembly-line techniques" disappears. If, on the other hand, the concern was that a more deliberate approach would put the court behind schedule, even though it was at the time caught up, then the extra manpower should have been welcome, especially since the claim that it would have been difficult to inform judges from another court how to perform what in essence is a simple procedure lacks conviction. Finally, if it is urged that the lack of records was the key factor compelling the procedures used and that expediency was merely a by-product, the experience of Judge Crockett would be evidence to the contrary.

The explanation one is left with is that the expedient procedures were actually the result of a policy decision by a majority of the court to forgo their judicial function and act instead as an arm of the executive and administrative branches in an effort to help quell the disorder.

NOTES

1. Address by Charles E. Hughes, N.Y. State Bar Ass'n, 42nd Annual Meeting in *1919 Proceedings of N.Y. State Bar Ass'n* 224: 240–41.
2. *Report of the National Advisory Commission on Civil Disorders* (New York: Bantam Books, 1968) p. 337.

✎ 9. CRIMINAL JUSTICE *IN EXTREMIS:* ADMINISTRATION OF JUSTICE DURING THE APRIL 1968 CHICAGO DISORDER
University of Chicago Law Review

In its examination of bail bond proceedings during the 1968 Chicago riot, the Law Review *finds among other things that bail amounts were*

From the *University of Chicago Law Review* 36, no. 3 (Spring 1969): 511–527 and 610–613. This chapter combines two segments of a longer study in the *Law Review*. The footnotes have been deleted.

*not as high as they had been in Detroit and other cities in the 1967 dis-
orders, nor as high as in previous Chicago disorders. Nevertheless, the
bail was high enough to detain a great many arrestees, and bondsetting
was used as an effective instrument of preventive detention. As one
judge put it, "The idea was clearly to get as many people off the streets
as possible." (Editors)*

T H E data suggest that individual circumstances were seldom
taken into account in setting bond. Active participation of defense
counsel in the bond hearing, including the recommendation of an appropriate bond amount, may have had some effect in lowering bond determinations. But defense counsel rarely participated effectively in bond
court proceedings. The ineffectiveness of defense counsel, the pressure
toward using bail for preventive detention, the failure to utilize preset
bail schedules or to operate a sufficient number of bond courts to prevent long delays and crowded dockets, the lack of relevant information
about defendants in many cases, and, in general, the demand for judicial
economy all contributed to the court's tendency to make nonindivid-
ualized bail determinations in the vast majority of cases.

Illinois statutes do not prescribe specific inquiries which must be
made of the defendant in determining bail. Section 110–2, authorizing
recognizance bonds, refers to an inquiry into "all the circumstances";
section 110–5 provides that the amount of cash bail shall be "not oppressive," and "considerate of the financial ability" and "the past criminal acts and conduct of the defendant." Despite these provisions, the
bond hearings seldom included inquiry into the defendant's personal
circumstances to determine the likelihood of his subsequent appearance
in court. Although magistrates and judicial officers have asserted that
relevant information was generally solicited, an analysis of 202 adult
bond hearing transcripts does not support their claim. In only 52 percent of those cases were questions put to the defendant to elicit information regarding his employment status. In only 26 percent were inquiries made regarding the length of defendant's residence in Chicago.
Fifty-three percent of the defendants were asked questions regarding
their marital or family status, but only 26 percent were asked concerning their financial ability. And in only 32 percent of the cases was inquiry made of the defendant concerning his prior criminal record.

Virtually none of this information was available to the magistrate
from other sources, including police records. Prior criminal history
sheets, normally referred to for purposes of bond setting, were unavaila-

ble. Public defenders, especially early in the riot, were not permitted to interview defendants in the bullpen prior to the hearing in order to obtain information. Volunteer lawyers were rarely successful in obtaining relevant information concerning the defendants which could be introduced at the hearing, and no standardized means of verifying privately obtained information was instituted. In addition, overcrowded temporary detention facilities annexed to the bond courts resulted in many defendants being processed through bond hearings in groups of up to four arrestees.

The summary character of most bond hearings is best reflected in the transcripts. The following excerpts are representative:

THE DEFENDANT: I'd like to have a break because I got burned out Saturday because I have no clothes and nothing but what I gots on and my kids the same thing and nowhere to stay. All I got is one lousy five dollars.

THE COURT: Well, look, these are difficult times for a lot of people, and a lot of people are getting themselves into trouble. All I know is the charge that has been filed against you and based on the charge I can't make that less than $5,000. I wish I could.

* * *

THE CLERK: [Announcing the case]
THE STATE'S ATTORNEY: State curfew, your honor.
THE COURT: What were you doing on the corner?
DEFENDANT: Going home.
THE COURT: From where?
DEFENDANT: From a friend's house.
THE COURT: Thousand-dollar bond, April 18th.

* * *

THE CLERK: [Announcing the case]
THE COURT: What were you doing on 63rd and Ellis?
DEFENDANT: I was there with a friend of mine at the ——— Company.
THE COURT: These are riotous conditions going on, get off the street. 11:00 o'clock at night.
DEFENDANT: It wasn't 11:00 o'clock.
THE COURT: Bond, thousand dollars, branch 47, April 18th.

* * *

THE CLERK: [Calling the defendant]
THE STATE'S ATTORNEY: [He] is charged with resisting arrest and ob-

structing a police officer who was attempting to effect an arrest. We suggest the 16th of April and a $1,000 bond.

THE COURT: So ordered, 4/16/68, $1,000 bond, Branch 47.

* * *

THE STATE'S ATTORNEY: In the matter of the bond, since the defendant is not pleading guilty, the State recommends a bond of $5,000. Court date of April 18th.

PRIVATE ATTORNEY: I would like to ask the Court to reconsider his bond on three grounds. [Presenting employment, residence, and family information].

THE STATE'S ATTORNEY: . . . The State remains steadfast that the bond be retained at $5,000 until the time of trial.

THE COURT: . . . The charge [burglary] is an extremely serious charge. In the absence of unimpeachable evidence of the facts stated the Court is not inclined to lower the bond.

PRIVATE ATTORNEY: Your Honor, may I point out that the purpose of bond is to insure presence. They have families and are employed in the city and are residents in the community. That should be an important factor in consideration of setting bond.

THE COURT: The Court denies the request of counsel for the defendants.

* * *

THE CLERK: [Calling defendant]

THE COURT: [Reading the charge] How do you plead?

DEFENDANT: Not guilty.

THE COURT: State's Attorney.

THE STATE'S ATTORNEY: Is it a theft charge, your Honor?

THE COURT: Theft charge.

THE STATE'S ATTORNEY: The Court is asking the State for a bond?

THE COURT: The Court is asking the State for a recommendation.

THE STATE'S ATTORNEY: We recommend a bond of $1,000, on a charge of theft.

THE COURT: This is burglary.

THE STATE'S ATTORNEY: $5,000, your Honor.

THE COURT: The Court accepts the State's recommendation and sets bond at $5,000. Plea of not guilty. Order of Court.

PRIVATE ATTORNEY: Your Honor, the defendant states he has no record. He has been working for ——— Wash for the past eight months.

THE COURT: You say the defendant has no record. Where do you get your information, just from his statement?

PUBLIC DEFENDER: Yes, sir, that is all.

THE COURT: The bond will remain at $5,000.

* * *

THE CLERK: [Calling defendant]

THE COURT: You have been charged by ———— that on or about the 6th of April, 1968, at 2310 West Roosevelt, you committed the offense of disorderly conduct in violation of Chapter 28, Section 26–1(a)(1). Let the record show that a plea of not guilty has been entered in arraignment. Bond will be set at $1,000.

It is important to emphasize that relevant individual inquiry for the purposes of setting bond was made in many cases. But even in these cases there is no indication that the information was taken into account. The magistrate often set bonds at the amount recommended by the state's attorney in these cases, as excerpts from bond hearing transcripts show:

THE COURT: [Calling defendant]

THE STATE'S ATTORNEY: I recommend $5,000 bond on the charges of burglary and disorderly, your Honor.

PUBLIC DEFENDER: I request a lower bond. This man does work, and I don't know what his record is.

THE COURT: How long have you lived in Chicago?

DEFENDANT: I have been here about, I'd say nine years or more.

THE COURT: Married?

DEFENDANT: Yes.

THE COURT: Do you have any kids?

DEFENDANT: About five.

THE COURT: The kids and wife live with you?

DEFENDANT: Yes.

THE COURT: Does your wife work?

DEFENDANT: She don't work.

THE COURT: Have you been employed?

DEFENDANT: Employed?

THE COURT: Are you working?

DEFENDANT: Oh yes. I am working.

THE COURT: Where are you working?

DEFENDANT: Work for ———— Auto Wash, where they wash cars.

THE COURT: How long have you worked there?

DEFENDANT: Four or five years or more.

THE COURT: Five-thousand-dollar bond.

* * *

THE CLERK: [Calling defendant]

THE COURT: How long have you lived in Chicago?

DEFENDANT: Eleven years.

THE COURT: Are you married?

DEFENDANT: Yes.

THE COURT: Any children?

DEFENDANT: Four.

THE COURT: What time of the day was this?

DEFENDANT: I guess it was about two in the morning.

THE COURT: Do you work for yourself?

DEFENDANT: Yes—not exactly, but I am with another guy. We do decorating.

THE COURT: What is the recommendation?

THE STATE'S ATTORNEY: My information indicates a 3:30 A.M. time, and the charge is burglary. Recommend $5,000 bond.

THE COURT: Five-thousand-dollar bond.

* * *

THE CLERK: [Calling defendant]

THE STATE'S ATTORNEY: Your Honor, Mr. ———— is also charged with burglary. . . .

PUBLIC DEFENDER: Tell the Judge. You have a job?

DEFENDANT: Yes.

PUBLIC DEFENDER: How long have you been working?

DEFENDANT: Two years.

PUBLIC DEFENDER: Are you married?

DEFENDANT: Yes, I am.

PUBLIC DEFENDER: Do you have any children?

DEFENDANT: Yes, one. Your Honor, as far as I am concerned, I got a good job. I just got my job. I am making good money. My wife, she is sick. She got cramps from taking these birth-control pills, and she can't work. I don't want to be put in jail because I haven't got any money—I don't want to lose my home and job or nothing.

PUBLIC DEFENDER: We request $1,000 bond.

THE CLERK: What time was the arrest?

THE STATE'S ATTORNEY: Twenty-five after twelve this morning, inside the premises, where obviously he did not belong.

DEFENDANT: No, I wasn't. Sir, I want—

PUBLIC DEFENDER: Is he going to show up for trial? Let's show the fact that he is trying to keep the job.

DEFENDANT: I don't want to lose my job and my home. I will lose everything if I don't go to work.

THE COURT: Is your wife working?

DEFENDANT: No, she can't work. She is under the doctor.

THE STATE'S ATTORNEY: I suggest if he is so concerned about his wife and home, he would have been there.

THE COURT: Five-thousand-dollar bond.

*   *   *

THE CLERK: [Calling defendant, arrested for burglary]

PUBLIC DEFENDER: The defendant states he is working.

DEFENDANT: I was just getting off from work.

PUBLIC DEFENDER: How long have you been working there?

DEFENDANT: For the last three years, sir. . . .

PUBLIC DEFENDER: Do you have a family?

DEFENDANT: Sure, a wife and three kids. I have two jobs. . . .

THE COURT: What were you doing in this building?

DEFENDANT: I was not in the building, Judge. . . .

THE STATE'S ATTORNEY: The State recommends bond for $5,000, court date of April 18th.

THE COURT: Bond, $5,000.

*   *   *

PUBLIC DEFENDER: How old are you, Donald?

DEFENDANT: Eighteen.

PUBLIC DEFENDER: Where do you live?

DEFENDANT: [Answering]

PUBLIC DEFENDER: Who do you live with?

DEFENDANT: My mother and father.

PUBLIC DEFENDER: How long have you lived at that address?

DEFENDANT: Eight years.

PUBLIC DEFENDER: Do you work or do you go to school?

DEFENDANT: I go to school.

PUBLIC DEFENDER: What school?

DEFENDANT: ——— High School.

PUBLIC DEFENDER: What year are you in?

DEFENDANT: I am a senior.

THE STATE'S ATTORNEY: We recommend a $1,500 bond, Judge.

PUBLIC DEFENDER: How much money can you raise for bond?

DEFENDANT: I don't know, $75 or $100.

PUBLIC DEFENDER: Your Honor, we would ask the bond be set at $500.

THE COURT: The bond will be set at $1,500 for appearance in Branch 47 on April 18th, $150 cash we will release you.

* * *

THE CLERK: [Calling defendant, arrested for violation of curfew]

PUBLIC DEFENDER: Are you married or single?

DEFENDANT: I am married.

PUBLIC DEFENDER: And how many children do you have?

DEFENDANT: I have three children.

PUBLIC DEFENDER: Where do you work?

DEFENDANT: I work for the Post Office and also a barber part-time. . . .

PUBLIC DEFENDER: And where do you live?

DEFENDANT: [Answering]

PUBLIC DEFENDER: How long have you lived at that address?

DEFENDANT: I lived there about ten years.

PUBLIC DEFENDER: And how long have you worked for the Post Office?

DEFENDANT: Five years.

THE COURT: Your bond will be $500 for an appearance.

PUBLIC DEFENDER: Your Honor, could you make that an individual bond? This is simply another curfew situation. No other aggravation.

THE COURT: He lives at ————. He was arrested at ————, where we had an awful lot of trouble. That's all.

* * *

THE STATE'S ATTORNEY: [Recommends $5,000 bond on a burglary defendant]

THE COURT: What is the story here?

PUBLIC DEFENDER: Judge, he's been employed at the ———— Company for a year and a half, he has been a resident of Chicago for ten years. . . .

DEFENDANT: I have to go to work tomorrow, I have kids to support.

PUBLIC DEFENDER: How many children do you have to support, Dave?

DEFENDANT: Two.

THE COURT: Twenty-five-hundred-dollar bond. . . .

DEFENDANT: Your Honor, can you drop the bond? I can't raise that much today.

THE COURT: What bond could you make?

DEFENDANT: I can raise a hundred dollars.

THE STATE'S ATTORNEY: I resist that.

THE COURT: I dropped it to twenty-five hundred dollars.

DEFENDANT: I can't raise that.

THE COURT: I can't help you, sir, if you can't raise it. I set the bond, I didn't get you in trouble, you understand that. That will be the order.

DETENTION FACILITIES

During the first days of the riot, no procedure was instituted to enable defendants to post bail immediately after their bail hearings. Even curfew defendants released on their own recognizance were detained overnight at the City House of Correction, the County Jail, or temporary detention facilities. Almost all defendants spent some time in jail; those unable to make bail were often detained for long periods.

Although the State's Attorney's Riot Control Unit had considered the use of other detention facilities in mass arrest situations—including the State Penitentiary at Joliet—only the City House of Correction and the County Jail were used during the April riot. At the height of the riot, a number of convicted misdemeanants who had served over half their sentences were pardoned to make room for riot arrestees in the House of Correction. Conditions at the House of Correction were somewhat better during the riot than at the County Jail, but were not beyond criticism.

The County Jail, a maximum security institution for detention of both convicted prisoners and those awaiting trial, was designed to hold 1,302 males. On March 31, its inmate population was 1,881, 44 percent above its capacity. During the riot, an additional 800 prisoners were sent to the County Jail, because facilities at the House of Correction were inadequate. Riot arrestees were segregated from other inmates at the jail, both to avoid placing them with indicted felons and convicted misdemeanants and because many were not processed prior to assignment to a cell. The jail tiers, which are designed to accommodate 39 men and normally house 70, held as many as 200 prisoners during the riot.

The jail, under an administration which had been in office for only three weeks, had no emergency plan for the processing of large numbers of prisoners. Some 400 prisoners arrived during an eighteen-hour period, as compared with normal daily admissions of 50 to 60. The normal jail staff was not augmented during the riot, although some staff members did work overtime to process riot arrestees. The result was chaotic; records, and even prisoners, were lost. Some arrestees were under seventeen years of age and, once admitted, were unable to secure release without a court order. According to the testimony of the warden, "lots of them [prisoners] were lost"; "everything broke down."

As prisoners entered the jail, there were insufficient temporary detention facilities. The jail bullpen, which normally accommodates 50 men awaiting medical processing, often held over 200. Only two doctors were available to conduct medical examinations. Many prisoners were not permitted to shower before final processing. Cells which normally house two prisoners held as many as five prisoners. According to the chief guard, there were shortages of mattresses, bedding, and blankets. Many prisoners slept on bare floors in the dayrooms of the tiers. Toilet facilities were inadequate. The daily diet of many prisoners consisted of two bologna sandwiches. And, because the County Jail and the House of Correction could not accommodate the large number of arrestees, many prisoners were held in the Criminal Court lockup "for a long time under extremely crowded conditions with no food."

Many prisoners were admitted to the jail with improper or incomplete mittimus papers and this impeded processing and identification. Upon admission, prisoners were given identification cards and photographs were taken. However, by the time photographs were developed, a number of prisoners had apparently traded their identification cards for cigarettes. A limited use of aliases further complicated identification. The problem was aggravated by what several observers referred to as lackadaisical attitude on the part of jail employees.

Under Illinois law, an arrestee has the right to communicate with an attorney or a member of his family "by making a reasonable number of telephone calls or in any other reasonable manner." If he is transferred to a new place of custody, his right to communicate is renewed. The County Jail, however, is not equipped with telephones for the use of prisoners. Defendants who were unable to make telephone calls prior to incarceration had to rely on the services of volunteers or helpful jail personnel. And often prisoners were not assigned to a detention facility until their arrival, which prevented them from notifying an attorney or their families of their location. Record-keeping breakdowns made it impossible for relatives to locate prisoners for hours and even days. Despite long lines of inquiring friends and relatives, the records window at the County Jail was closed at night without explanation. There was no coordination between the records department and the bond clerks or between the jail and House of Correction lists.

Volunteers, including lawyers, were able to track down some prisoners and relay information to friends and relatives. They also acted as court clerks, expanding incomplete records to obtain information needed to post bond for a prisoner. Persons who arrived to post bond sometimes waited as long as two days after payment of bail before prisoners were released.

The Kerner Commission's recommendation that "during any detention period, defense counsel must be able to interview prisoners individually at the detention centers" went unheeded during the week after Dr. King's assassination. Public defenders and volunteer lawyers were often turned away from the jail.

The impact of bail policies on riot arrestees, their relatives, and their friends cannot be fully appreciated without recognition of the hardship of detention under these conditions. Defendants whom we interviewed described their detention in vivid and bitter terms:

We were in the cell, no mattresses, no bed, no anything, five in a cell, no nothing. You know we get to know each other so good that we took turns sleeping. . . . You would have to, you know, take turns sleeping or else you just didn't sleep.

*   *   *

We got one sandwich a day, and if we got smart we didn't get that. . . . The guards would come in there, and if you so much as asked a little question, they'd just spray mace on you. That stuff you just can't breathe.

*   *   *

After I got in jail I didn't trust anyone even if they came and said they were a lawyer and wanted to help. We just couldn't trust them.

*   *   *

Like living in a slum building. Everywhere it was dirty, nasty, smelled like piss and looked like piss. It's enough to make you sick.

*   *   *

They should have at least put me in a clean cell or something. I mean I don't think that you should have put all of us in one room like a bunch of animals with everyone laying on top of one another and everyone needin' a bath and stinkin' in there. And see how they was sweatin'. And ya have to get in the bathroom and go to the window before you could get any air, and at least about twelve guys in the little ole bathroom trying to get to the window. . . . That's the way they treated us, I mean, just like a bunch of animals.

* * *

Well, to me they were like a cowpen where you put cows in, where you put this cow and this cow in this pen, and this cow and this cow in this pen. Only in this case there were a whole lot of cows in this pen, and a whole lot of cows in this pen. It was like on a farm, and the way you would treat animals, . . . I mean, you treat dogs better.

* * *

Like a chain gang. It was overcrowded, you didn't have a place to sleep, you had to sleep in shifts, you had to wash up in shifts, you cleaned yourself in the best way you could.

Conclusion

Civil disorders pose a special threat to any criminal justice system. They bring a massive influx of cases into already overtaxed courts. In the absence of preparation, as the Kerner Commission warned, the result may be recurring breakdowns in the administration of justice. This study has indicated that Chicago had a virtually complete plan— predicated in part on the earlier experiences of Chicago and other cities and on Kerner Commission recommendations—for handling mass arrest cases.

The contingency plan put into effect in April 1968 emphasized the goal of economy in judicial administration and the role of the state's attorney and public defender in safeguarding the achievement of that goal. The state's attorney relied heavily on misdemeanor rather than felony charges; he also relied on curfew, disorderly conduct, and burglary charges, rather than mob action and looting, which would have involved more difficult evidentiary burdens. Form complaints were used. Preliminary hearings were avoided in most felony cases, and automatic continuances were granted in virtually all misdemeanor cases. Bail was generally set at uniform amounts based on the state's attorney's recommendations and the nature of the offense charged. Defense lawyers were not allowed to participate in the postarrest screening process and were unable to interview prisoners individually in precourt detention facilities. Volunteer attorneys, law students, and interviewers were not deployed effectively. Bond reduction hearings were delayed for many defendants until well after the riot had ended. By representing virtually all riot arrestees at the bail hearing regardless of indigency, and most riot defendants at later stages, and by failing to request early bond reduction hearings, the public defender contributed to judicial efficiency.

The goal of judicial economy, however, is significant not so much as a bureaucratic–administrative ideal but as a potential means of assuring due process. When the Kerner Commission lamented recurring breakdowns in judicial administration during civil disorders it hoped to provide an impetus for protecting defendants' rights. Indeed, contingency planning for civil disorders is important primarily because it affords a means of avoiding abuses of due process. But in Chicago, judicial efficiency was perceived mostly in terms of system goals other than due process. Insofar as the goal of efficient administration resulted in the availability of facilities and personnel to process arrestees, it worked toward both administrative ends and due process. But more often the administrative goal impeded attainment of due process, as is evidenced, for example, by uniform bond amounts, avoidance of preliminary hearings, delay of bond reduction hearings, and the role of the public defender. In short, the Chicago plan achieved efficient administration but without achieving the end of due process which judicial economy was presumably intended to serve.

Moreover, the Cook County criminal system apparently sacrificed measures of efficiency when necessary to the attainment of other goals. Some Kerner Commission recommendations which would have expedited judicial processing were rejected. No use was made of a summons in lieu of arrest, or preset bail schedules which the Illinois statutes provided and which the commission endorsed.

That fact as well as deliberate and inefficient police processing of riot arrestees, and the absence of facilities which would have permitted immediate posting of cash bail, suggest that some inefficiencies were tolerated and perhaps designed in order to achieve other goals, such as pretrial detention. This study has highlighted the importance of each discretionary determination by police, prosecutor, public defender, and magistrate resulting in temporary detention of riot arrestees. Predictable breakdowns in the handling of riot arrestees at detention facilities did not result in the abandonment of the policy of pretrial detention. Indeed, rather than abandon that policy some previously convicted prisoners were released.

The use of pretrial detention is significant not only as a reflection of the desire to avoid inefficiencies of formal adjudication at trial but also because it achieves other goals of the criminal system. Pretrial detention is thought to be an effective form of punishment and a measure of general deterrence. It is also conducive to attaining high conviction rates which constitute a public record of effective punishment of rioters. Its use perhaps reflects the inadequacy of formal criminal processes in achieving the deterrent purposes of the criminal law. In effect, pretrial detention accelerates the impact of criminal sanctions through informal and discretionary processes. Formal adjudication, findings of guilt, and sentencing are, for many, a mere formality. The hurried judgments and unarticulated policies of police and National Guard officers become critical, result in the unjustified inconvenience for many of multiple court appearances, and are, in practice, not subject to review.

The use of pretrial detention for deterrent purposes during riots is particularly suspect in light of the fact that, at least in Chicago, it was not the initial rioters or looters who were arrested but what one Cook County official called the "mopes and gawkers" who took advantage of the breakdown in law enforcement. More important, the tendency to rely on informal pretrial criminal sanctions raises serious doubts about the prevailing rule that there is no constitutional or statutory right to a preliminary hearing, in the absence of a showing of actual prejudice at the formal disposition of a defendant's case. It may not be accidental that the locus of informal criminal sanctions is at early stages of criminal prosecution where a defendant's rights and ability to take himself out of the criminal process are most tenuous.

Riot contingency planning is an inadequate response to civil disturbances, then, not only because it offers little assurance of due process, but also because it fails sufficiently to recognize that there are goals of the criminal system during civil disorders which are in tension with the requirements of both efficiency and due process. Furthermore, for most urban criminal systems, contingency plans would require the adoption under extraordinary circumstances of policies and procedures presently unattained under ordinary conditions.

Perhaps the most distressing implication of the study is that the quality of justice dispensed during civil disorders is in many respects only a reflection of the reality of criminal administration under normal conditions. Riots and the ensuing responses of criminal systems are highly visible and politically volatile phenomena. It is not the administration of criminal justice, but society's concern about the criminal justice system which is altered most radically during civil disorders. The over-

whelmingly urgent task is to sustain from day to day the critical attention focused on our cities and lower criminal courts in the aftermath of
civil disorders. Only basic social and judicial reforms will ultimately secure fair and effective administration of criminal justice in urban
America.

The Commissions

✔ 10. WHITEWASH OVER WATTS
Robert Blauner

O N August 24, 1965, just one week after public order had been restored in the South Central area of Los Angeles known as Watts, Governor Pat Brown of California announced the appointment of an eight-man commission of leading citizens. In his charge to the group (which came to be known as the McCone Commission, after its chairman, John A. McCone, former head of the CIA), Brown asked it to "prepare an accurate chronology and description of the riots"; to "probe deeply the immediate and underlying causes of the riots"; and finally to "develop recommendations for action designed to prevent a recurrence of these tragic disorders."

For what appears to have been political considerations connected with possible repercussions of the Watts affair on the 1966 gubernatorial campaign, the commission was given December 1, 1965, as the deadline for the completion of its report. Thus only 100 days were available for a "deep and probing" analysis of the most destructive incidence of racial violence in American history.

In an atmosphere of speedup that made work on an automobile assembly line appear leisurely by comparison, the commission held a series of sixty formal hearings before which eighty sworn witnesses, including city and police officials, leaders and citizens of the white and Negro communities, eventually appeared. It also selected a full-time staff of thirty, primarily lawyers and legal-oriented investigators, to carry out the day-to-day work of assembling data and preparing to write the report. The staff called upon the services of twenty-six consultants (chiefly university professors in the social sciences) for advice and the subcontracting or research; interviewed ninety persons from the 4,000 arrested; and opened an office in the riot area to receive testimony from Negro citizens. After a total expenditure of $250,000, Commissioner

From *Trans-action* 3, no. 3 (March–April 1966): 3–9. Copyright © by *Trans-action Magazine,* New Brunswick, New Jersey.

McCone presented the report to Governor Brown in the fanfare of television cameras on December 6.

In view of the conditions under which it was hurried into existence, it should be no surprise that *Violence in the City—An End or a Beginning?* is a slim volume with only eighty-six pages of blown-up type. But the report of the McCone Commission is not only brief, it is sketchy and superficial. Its tone and style are disturbing. There is much glib writing and the approach as well as the format is slick in the manner of our illustrated news weeklies before their recent upgrading. The depth analysis of this fateful outbreak can be read by an average reader in less than an hour—allowing ample time for contemplating the many photographs, both color and black-and-white.

A comparison with the careful and considered report of the Illinois' Governor's Commission which analyzed the 1919 Chicago race riots in a 672-page book (*The Negro in Chicago*) that required three years of planning, research, and writing to produce may well be unfair. But with the considerable budget and the academic sophistication available today, more was to be expected than the public relations statement presently in our hands.

It is not only the size and style of the McCone document that are disturbing. Its content is disappointing both in its omissions and in underlying political and philosophical perspectives. There is almost nothing in the report that is new or that gives consideration to the unique conditions of Los Angeles life and politics. As Los Angeles councilman Bill Mills commented, most of the material in the report documents conditions in the Negro ghetto that have been common knowledge to sociologists and the informed public for a generation.

More appalling are the report's deeper failures. With a narrow legalistic perspective that approached the riots in terms of the sanctity of law and order, the commissioners were unable (or unwilling) to read any social or political meaning into the August terror. There was no attempt to view the outbreak from the point of view of the Negro poor. The commissioners also play a dangerous game with the thorny problem of responsibility. The Negro community as a whole is absolved from responsibility for the rioting while local and national leaders (civil rights moderates and extremists alike) are taken to task for inflaming mass discontent and undermining attachments to law and authority. (In his two-page dissenting comment appended to the main report, the Reverend James E. Jones, a Negro commissioner, criticizes the report for attempting "to put a lid on protest.")

In a crude attempt at "horse-trading" in the responsibility market, the positions of the Los Angeles police department and city administrators are consistently protected. In discounting the relevance of police provocation and city policies to the revolt without presenting any facts or evidence, the commission not only protects powerful interests; it abdicates its mandate to seek out facts and establish as best as it could the objective reality. My most general and serious criticism of the report is this violation of its responsibility to seek truth and its frequent hiding behind opinion and hearsay.

Causes of the Watts "Revolt"

Lurking behind the Watts violence are three basic problems, according to the McCone Commission:

1. The widespread unemployment and "idleness" in the Negro ghetto
2. The cultural and educational backwardness of black children that prevents the schools from preparing them for the labor market and integrating them into society
3. The troubled state of police–community relations in the Negro neighborhoods

EMPLOYMENT

The chapter on employment is forthright in its emphasis on jobs as a central problem and correct in its understanding that male dignity and family responsibility can hardly be expected when men are unable to find steady work. For example: "The most serious immediate problem that faces the Negro in our community is employment—securing and holding a job that provides him an opportunity for livelihood, a chance to earn the means to support himself and his family, a dignity, and a reason to feel that he is a member of our community in a true and a very real sense." The commission calls upon federal, state, and city government to create jobs for the Negro and Mexican–American poor. Corporations and labor unions are asked to end discrimination once and for all and to police their progress by keeping careful records on minority employment. Because the commissioners are convinced that the majority of jobless Los Angeles Negroes are presently unemployable, they call for an expanded and better-coordinated program of job training; they wisely recommend that control of this effort be placed inside the Negro community.

These proposals on employment are worthwhile and necessary, but they encourage a deceptive complacency. The report does not probe sufficiently into the depth and seriousness of the problem. There is no consideration of the impact of population trends and technological developments on the availability of jobs, especially for the unskilled, and no willingness to face the escalating employment needs in the rapid expansion of Los Angeles' Negro population. The report is irresponsible because its style and tone convey the impression that its relatively mild and moderate recommendations provide real solutions.

EDUCATION

The treatment of education is the one section of the McCone report that is based on a careful and first-hand study. Kenneth A. Martyn, professor of education at Los Angeles State College, investigated five areas within the Los Angeles City Unified School District as a commission consultant. Student achievement was compared for four "disadvantaged areas" (of which two were primarily Negro and close to the riot centers) and one "advantaged" area (predominantly white upper-middle class). Average student reading performances in the fifth, eighth, and eleventh grades reveal a consistent backwardness in the lower-class Negro and Mexican districts. The gap is most dramatic at the eighth grade, since by the eleventh many of the poorest "achievers" are already drop-outs. The average student in the white middle-class area is in the 79th percentile in reading vocabulary based on national norms; the average students in "Negro" Watts and Avalon are in the 13th and 14th percentiles; the averages in the primarily Mexican areas of Boyle Heights and East Los Angeles are 16 and 17.

Martyn investigated the possibility of discrimination in educational facilities. Some inequalities were found, but hardly enough to explain the systematic backwardness of minority students. The commission thus locates the problem of Negro school performance in what today is fashionably called "a culturally impoverished environment." Parents have little education and their own background does not foster an orientation toward achievement and learning. Crowded housing conditions are not favorable for disciplined study. And the precariousness of employment and the lack of models of achievement may further dull incentive. In order to break this pattern and "raise the scholastic achievement of the average Negro child up to or perhaps above the present average achievement level in the city," the commission calls for an intensive infusion of educational resources into the Negro community focusing on three programs: preschool learning on the model of "Headstart"; the reduction of class size; and the improvement of academic and behavioral counseling.

The McCone report accepts the conventional position that it is the "vicious circular" connection between education and employment that is the crux of the dilemma of the Negro poor. And it places its main bet on education and the future, rather than creating jobs to solve the problems of the present. If the achievement levels of present and future generations of Negro children can be sufficiently raised, they will be motivated to remain in the school system and assimilate the skills and training that will begin reversing this cyclical process. Unfortunately, the middle-class ethos which underlies the commission's emphasis on future-orientation and achievement is irrelevant to the needs and outlook of the lower-class adult group whose problems of work and training are likely to intensify.

But even with a crash program in education, can the average poor Negro youth be motivated toward achievement and excellence when the condition of his people and community places him in a position of alienation and powerlessness vis-à-vis the larger society? What is missing in the report's analysis is a total picture of the Watts community as consistently deprived and disadvantaged in relation to Los Angeles as a whole. Fragmented hints of this picture abound in the report, particularly in the excellent discussion of the woefully inadequate transportation system, but the fragments are never pieced together. If they were, municipal officials would then have to bear some responsibility for permitting this systematic deprivation to persist. By singling out education as the strategic sphere for ameliorative efforts, the commission aims its biggest guns on the target area in which the city's hands are relatively "clean" and in which it is relatively easy to suggest that the cultural backgrounds and individual performances of *Negroes themselves* account for a good part of the problem.

THE POLICE ISSUE

If we don't get no good out of this, it will happen again. By good I mean an end to police harassment, and we need jobs. I got eight kids, and I've only worked 10 days this year. I ain't ever been a crook, but if they don't do something, I'm gonna have to *take* something. I don't know how they expect us to live. (Young man in "a striped shirt" quoted by Louise Meriwether, "What the People of Watts Say," *Frontier*, October 1965.)

When a deprived segment of the population breaks out in a violent attack on society and its representatives, the *underlying* causes refer to those long-term elements in its situation that have produced its alienation and despair. *Immediate* causes refer to those more short-run irritants and grievances that have intensified feelings of anger and hatred and focused them on specific targets. The immediate grievances and conditions that spark illegal violence must have the effect of weakening the oppressed group's normal disposition to accept, at least overtly, the authority structure and legal norms of the society—otherwise mass violence could not erupt. The young Watts Negro quoted above seems to be saying that from his standpoint "jobs" are the underlying cause, "police harassment" the immediate issue. The governor's commission disagrees with his analysis and has its own explanation for the ghetto's sudden loss of attachment to the legal order.

It answers its own question, "Why Los Angeles?" in a way that almost totally relieves the city and county of implication. The rapid migration of southern Negroes to the city's ghetto serves as their starting point, for these Negroes are unrealistic in expecting that California living will solve all their life-problems. In the context of this "crisis of expectations" Negro frustration and despair were fanned by three "aggravating events in the twelve months prior to the riots":

1. Publicity given to the glowing promise of the federal poverty program was paralleled by reports of controversy and bickering over the mechanism to handle the program here in Los Angeles, and when the projects did arrive, they did not live up to the expectation.
2. Throughout the nation, unpunished violence and disobedience to law were widely reported, and almost daily there were exhortations, here and elsewhere, to take the most extreme and even illegal remedies to right a wide variety of wrongs, *real and supposed*.
3. In addition, many Negroes here felt and *were encouraged to feel* that they had been affronted by the passage of Proposition 14—an initiative measure passed by two-thirds of the voters in November 1964 which repealed the Rumford Fair Housing Act and unless modified by the voters or invalidated by the courts will bar any attempt by state or local governments to enact similar laws. (Italics mine.)

The argument is clear. Aside from some blunderings over the antipoverty war, it was Negro leadership that undermined the commitment of law-abiding black citizens to authority and legal methods of redressing their grievances. What is important is the assumption that the Negro poor's attachment to law and political authority was not weakened by its own experience with police and other official representatives of society, but was instead subverted by an extremist and opportunist leadership. Such an analysis gives the commission a free field to discount the role of the Los Angeles police and their presence in the ghetto as immediate precipitants of the violence. In short, the commission has "bought" the line of Chief of Police William Parker who has consistently argued that the riot was a revolt of the criminal and lawless element, prodded on by a Negro leadership which inflamed the Los Angeles black community with the "bugaboo" of "police brutality."

The report devotes a chapter to law enforcement and police-community relations. It takes note of the severe criticism of the police department by many Negro witnesses and frankly admits "the deep and longstanding schism between a substantial portion of the Negro community and the police department." Considering the virtual unanimity in the Negro community concerning police practices as the foremost immediate cause of the outbreak, why did not the commission seriously investigate the role of law enforcement in the ghetto? The commission acknowledges that Negro *feelings* of oppressive police action were significant conditions of the rioting. However, it violates its responsibility to truth and impartiality by refusing to examine the factual basis of Negro opinion while stating the beliefs and hearsay of white officers in an aura of established truth:

The police have explained to us the extent to which the conduct of some Negroes when apprehended has required the use of force in making arrests. Example after example has been recited of arrestees, both men and women, becoming violent, struggling to resist arrest and thus requiring removal by physical force. Other actions, each provocative to the police and each requiring more than normal action by the police in order to make an arrest or to perform other duties, have been described to us.

Precisely the same line is taken with respect to Chief Parker. The commission duly notes that the outspoken chief is a focal point of criticism and is distrusted by most Negroes. They feel he hates them. Yet the report conveniently omits all rational and objective evidence for such Negro "belief" based on a whole series of public statements made long before the riots. The inference is that Negro belief rests on misinterpretation of fact and paranoid reactions.

However, not only embittered Negro attitudes, but *facts* exist about the police presence in the ghetto—if the commission would have only looked for them. There was a Youth Opportunities Board study available to the commission based on intensive interviews with 220 people in the Watts, Willowbrook, and Avalon districts undertaken only two years before the outbreak in this very area. The sample included 70 delinquent and nondelinquent children, 26 parents, and 124 high administrators and lesser personnel of the major agencies in the community (schools, welfare and probation, recreation and youth groups). Attitudes toward the critical agencies of the community were probed, and it was found that of all the "serving institutions" of the larger society greatest hostility was directed toward the police department. A majority of adults as well as children felt that *the behavior of police aggravated the problems of growing up in the Negro community rather than contributed to their solution;* this was in direct contrast to their attitudes toward the schools, the parks, the health services, and the probation officers.

The real issue has perhaps been muddied by the outcry against "police brutality," the term that Negroes use to sum up their felt sense of grievance against law-enforcement agents. The police liberalization policy of recent years may well have reduced the number of cases of "classic" brutality—beatings, cruel methods of questioning, etc. What the Negro community is presently complaining about when it cries "police brutality" is the more subtle attack on personal dignity that manifests itself in unexplainable questionings and searches, in hostile and insolent attitudes toward groups of young Negroes on the street or in cars, and in the use of disrepectful and sometimes racist language—in short, what the Watts man quoted above called "police harassment." There is no evidence that this assault on individual self-esteem and dignity has ceased.

Another facet of police brutality is the use of excessive force to control criminal and illegal behavior. Characteristically the commission passed on its opportunity (and obligation) to assess the use of force by the various law-enforcement agencies that put down the August violence, despite its considerable attention to their logistical and coordination problems and the concern of Negroes and liberal groups like the ACLU with what appeared to be unnecessary shootings of looters, including young children.

The police chapter is primarily devoted to the adequacy of procedures presently available for processing complaints against officer misconduct and to recommendations for improving both them and the general relation between law enforcement and the Negro community. Yet, the demand of Negro leaders and white liberals for an independent civilian review board is described as "clamor"; the proposal is rejected because this device would "endanger the effectiveness of law enforcement." Experience with its use in two cities "has not demonstrated" its "advantages," but characteristically no evidence is given and the cities are not even named. Instead the report advocates the strengthening of the authority of the present Board of Police Commissioners, the civilian heads of the department, and establishment of the new position of Inspector General under the authority of the chief of police. The latter "would be responsible for making investigations and recommendations on all citizen complaints." In addition, the police should improve its community relations programs in the ghetto areas and strive to attract more Negroes and Mexicans to careers in law enforcement.

The commissioners are aware that "police brutality" has been an issue in all the northern Negro riots in recent years and that each began with a police incident. But instead of asking why poor Negroes come to believe that law and authority are not *their* law and their authority, they go on to sermonize:

Our society is held together by respect for law. A group of officers who represent a tiny fraction of one percent of the population is the thin thread that enforces observance of law by those few who would do otherwise. If police authority is destroyed, if their effectiveness is impaired, and if their determination to use the authority vested in them to preserve a law-abiding community is frustrated, all of society will suffer because groups would feel free to disobey the law and inevitably their number would increase. Chaos might easily result.

Character of the Watts Outbreak

There is very little explicit consideration of the character and meaning of the outburst in the McCone report, in spite of its great concern with causes. The commission missed an important point of departure by not viewing the Watts violence as a problematic phenomenon, the essence of which needed to be determined through a careful weighing of evidence and through social and political analysis. For this reason the report's implicit assumptions must be inferred because they are introduced in passing and never clearly spelled out.

The analytical perspective is overwhelmingly *riot control* rather than collective or crowd behavior. The attempt of responsible Negro leaders to cool off the mobs is discussed, but the major emphasis is on the tactics used by the various law-enforcement agencies. After a fairly thorough discussion of the arrest which set off the events, the Negroes who participated in violence are almost excluded from the story. The very language of the commission suggests that it has prejudged "the meaning of Watts," even though the debate that has been going on in Negro circles as to the appropriate term of reference suggests that determining the character of these events is a real and difficult question.

On page one of the report, the outbreak is called a "spasm" and "an insensate rage of destruction." Later it is called "an explosion—a *formless, quite senseless,* all but hopeless violent protest" (italics mine). Only in its discussion of the business targets which were looted and burned does the commission attempt to locate a meaning or pattern in what the rioters did, and here it concludes—unlike most informed observers—that there was no "significant correlation between alleged consumer exploitation and the destruction."

The legalistic perspective of the commission and its staff seems to have blocked its sensitivity to the sociological meaning of the riots. When viewed simply as an uprising of the criminal element against law and order (aggravated of course by the more social, economic, and political causes of frustration already discussed), the commissioners need not look seriously at its human meaning nor need they understand what messages may have been communicated by the rocks, gunfire, and Molotov cocktails. Let us not romanticize the Watts violence. I don't claim that everyone involved and everything done had rational motives. But it is a more humble and scientific attitude to leave the question open and to examine the limited evidence that is available. For the assumption of meaninglessness, the emptying out of content and communication from any set of human actions—*even nonrational violence*—reduces the dignity of the actors involved. In the present context it is a subtle insult to Los Angeles' Negroes. The report ostensibly avoids such an insulting stance by minimizing Negro participation and exculpating the bulk of the community from responsibility for the antisocial outbreak—except of course its leaders who aggravated the underlying tension:

In the ugliest interval which lasted from Thursday through Saturday, perhaps as many as 10,000 Negroes took to the streets in marauding bands. . . . The entire Negro population of Los Angeles County, about two-thirds of whom live in this area (that of the riots), numbers more than 650,000. Observers estimate that only about two percent were involved in the disorder. Nevertheless, this violent fraction, however minor, has given the face of community relations in Los Angeles a sinister cast.

No evidence is presented for the 2 percent estimate, nor for the total of 10,000 participants on which it is based. We are not told how the commission defines being "involved in the disorder." A number of distortions are apparently obvious, however. Even if 10,000 were upper limit, this figure would indicate much more than 2 percent participation. For the Negro curfew area of some 500,000 residents contains many neighborhoods of comfortable middle-class people who were far from the riot center; they should be eliminated from a calculation of the extent of participation in an outbreak of the Negro poor and dispossessed. Second, the total population figures include women, children, and the aged. A more appropriate (and still difficult) question would be the extent of participation of young and mature Negro males in the low-income districts that were the centers of the action.

The Spirit of Revolt

Unfortunately, I cannot answer this question precisely, but in view of the commission's unscientific methodology and dubious deductions there is no reason to accept their view of the participation issue. Consider on this matter Bayard Rustin, who visited Watts with Martin Luther King a few days after the outbreak:

> I could not count heads but reports I have received and my experience with the people leads me to believe that a large percentage of the people living in the Watts area participated. But most of them did not themselves loot and burn, but they were on the streets at one time or other.[1]

As Rustin suggests, the question is not simply how many engaged in lawless acts. Essential to the meaning of the revolt is the attitude of the "nonparticipants" toward those who erupted in hate and violence. In the most popular revolutions it is only a small minority that storms the Bastille or dumps tea in Boston Harbor. Only through considering the viewpoints of the "silent mass" is it possible to know whether the Watts riots represented an action of a large segment of Los Angeles Negro poor rather than a cutting loose of a small "violent fraction." Had the McCone Commission done its job, it would have conducted a systematic survey of community opinion to determine the distribution of sentiment in Negro Los Angeles.

My informants reported widespread support within the ghetto for the violent outbreak. Moral approval (as well as active participation) was stronger among youth and among the poor and working class. Old people and middle-class Negroes were more likely to feel ambivalent and hold back. But there seems to have been at least some participation from all segments of the black community. In the countless interviews and feature stories that appeared in the press and on television, Watts Negroes were more likely to explain and justify the riots rather than to condemn them—certainly the mass media would have little interest in censoring accounts of Negro disapproval. In a statewide public opinion survey conducted in November only 16 percent of the Negroes interviewed attributed the riots to "lack of respect for law and order" in contrast to 36 percent of the whites; "outside agitators" were seen as a most important cause by a scant 7 percent of the Negroes compared to 28 percent of the whites. Seventy-nine percent of the Negro respondents fixed upon "widespread unemployment" and "bad living conditions" as prime causes, compared with only 37 percent of the whites. And months after the rioting a poll conducted by ABC television found that the proportion of Watts residents who felt that the summer's events had helped the Negroes' cause was twice as much as those who felt it had hurt them.

If the Los Angeles revolt was not simply a "spasm" of lawlessness reflecting the violent inclinations of a minor criminal group, but represented instead the mood and spirit of the low-income Negro community —then we must look more closely at what the crowds were attempting to communicate in their assault upon society.

As the governor's report correctly notes, the uprising was not organized in advance. Yet it was neither formless nor meaningless. The Negro crowds were expressing more than the blind rage and the anti-white hate epitomized in the "Burn, baby, burn" slogan. They seem to have been announcing an unwillingness to continue to accept indignity and frustration without fighting back. They were particularly communicating their hatred of policemen, firemen, and other representatives of white society who operate in the Negro community "like an army of occupation." They were asserting a claim to territoriality, an unorganized and rather inchoate attempt to gain control over their community, their "turf." Most of the actions of the rioters appear to have been informed by the desire to clear out an alien presence, white men, rather than to kill them. (People have remarked how few whites were shot considering the degree of sniping and the marksmanship evidenced in accurate hits on automobile lights and other targets.) It was primarily an attack on property, particularly white-owned businesses, and not persons. Why not listen to what people in the crowds were saying as did Charles Hillinger of the *Los Angeles Times* on the night of August 13:

1. "White devils, what are you doing in here?"
2. "It's too late, white man. You had your chance. Now it's our turn."
3. "You created this monster and it's going to consume you. White man, you got a tiger by the tail. You can't hold it. You can't let it go."
4. "White man, you started all this the day you brought the first slave to this country."
5. "That's the hate that hate produced, white man. This ain't hurting us now. We have nothing to lose. Negroes don't own the building. You never did a decent thing in your life for us, white man."

A "Native" Uprising

Any appraisal of the Watts uprising must be tentative. All the facts are not yet known, and it always takes time to assimilate the full significance of historic and traumatic events. I suggest, however, that it was not primarily a rising of the lawless, despite the high participation of the *lumpenproletariat* and the clearcut attack on law and authority. Neither was it a "conventional race riot" for the Los Angeles terror arose from the initiative of the Negro community and did not fit the simple pattern of whites and blacks engaging in purely racial aggression. And it was not a Los Angeles version of a mass civil rights protest. Its organization was too loose. More important, the guiding impulse was not integration with American society but an attempt to stake out a sphere of control by moving against that society.

Instead my interpretation turns on two points. On the *collective* level the revolt seems to represent the crystallization of community identity through a nationalistic outburst against a society felt as dominating and oppressive. The spirit of the Watts rioters appears similar to that of anticolonial crowds demonstrating against foreign masters, though in America of course the objective situation and potential power relations are very different. On the *individual* level, participation would seem to have had a special appeal for those young Negroes whose aspirations to be men of dignity are systematically negated by the unavailability of work and the humiliations experienced in contacts with whites. For these young men (and reports indicate that males between the ages of 14 and 30 predominated in the streets), violence permitted expressing their manhood in the American way of fighting back and "getting even" —rather than the passive withdrawal which has been a more characteristic response of the Negro poor.

The gulf between Watts and affluent Los Angeles is disturbingly similar to the cleavage between the lives and interests of "natives" and their colonial masters. The poor Negro's alienation from the institutions and values of the larger society was made clear during the revolt. The sacredness of private property, that unconsciously accepted bulwark of our social arrangements, was rejected; Negroes who looted, apparently without guilt, generally remarked that they were taking things that "really belong" to them anyway. The society's bases of legitimacy and its loci of authority were attacked.

Thus Watts was not simply a racial uprising. Negro police and "responsible" moderate leaders were also the objects of the crowd's anger. Black businessmen who were seen as close to the Negro community were spared damage. From the standpoint of the poor, there was thus an implicit division of the Negro middle class into those two segments that are found in the colonial situation: a "national bourgeoisie" on the side of liberation and a "native" middle class that serves as agents for the dominant power arrangements.

Sartre has argued that colonialism reduced the manhood of the people it subjected in violating the integrity of indigenous ways of life and in creating the social status of "natives." The condition of slavery in the U.S. and the subsequent history of economic exploitation and second-class citizenship have constituted a similar attack on the manhood of Negro males. The chief contemporary manifestation of this crisis, according to the controversial "Moynihan report," is the precarious position of the man in the lower-class Negro family. The active dominance of the Negro woman and the male's relative passivity and instability are in part a residue of this historical process of manhood reduction; it is of course intimately reinforced by the unavailability of employment and the crisis of authority this brings about in the family. Unable to validate a sense of manly worth in terms of the larger cultural standards of economic responsibility, the lower-class youth orients himself toward the all-male street society whose manhood centers around other values and styles—hip, cool, and soul.

A new generation of Negro militants have created in the civil rights movement a vehicle for the affirmation of their manhood in the political struggle against its systematic negation. But the nonviolent movement which grew up in the South (with its more religiously oriented population, cohesive communities, and clear-cut segregation problems) is not well adapted to the social condition and psychological temper of the northern Negro. Unless new possibilities for the expression of initiative, assertiveness, and control are opened, we can expect that violent revolt will become increasingly frequent.

The Watts revolt was also a groping toward community identity. South Central Los Angeles has been a vast Negro ghetto with very amorphous neighborhood and district boundaries, with a glaring lack of leadership and organization. Most of the major civil rights groups were nonexistent in the ghetto; the gap between official Negro spokesmen and the poor was even greater than is typical. The word "Watts" itself as a locational reference for the ambiguously defined district around 103rd and Central had become a stigmatized term among Negroes as well as whites and was rarely used by residents. During the August uprising a reversal in all these tendencies became apparent. The mass action strengthened feeble communal loyalties. The term "Watts" appeared painted on walls and windows as an expression of pride and identity. Youth gangs representing the adjacent neighborhoods of Watts, Willowbrook, and Compton ceased their long-standing wars and united to provide a core of organization during the rioting and the subsequent rehabilitation work. Many middle-class blacks saw that their interests could not be severed from those of the ghetto's poor, particularly when their streets and residences were placed within the curfew boundaries drawn by the militia—thus dramatizing the fact of common fate. And since August, a proliferation of community organizing, political action, and civil rights groups has risen up in the Watts area. All these processes —intensified communal bonds, ethnic identity, the hesitant return of the middle class, and a new sense of pride in place—are graphically summed up in the experience of Stan Saunders, a Watts boy who had moved out of the ghetto to All-American football honors at Whittier College and two years abroad as a Rhodes scholar. His return to Watts two weeks before the revolt may be prototypical:

At the height of the violence, he found himself joyously speaking the nitty-gritty Negro argot he hadn't used since junior high school, and despite the horrors of the night, this morning he felt a strange pride in Watts. As a riot, he told me, "It was a masterful performance. I sense a change there now, a buzz, and it tickles. For the first time people in Watts feel a pride in being black. I remember, when I first went to Whittier, I worried that if I didn't make it there, if I was rejected, I wouldn't have a place to go back to. Now I can say 'I'm from Watts.' " [2]

The McCone Commission missed the meaning of the Watts revolt due to the limitations inherent in its perspective. The surface radicalism of its language (in calling for "a new and, we believe, revolutionary attitude toward the problems of the city") cannot belie its basic status-quo orientation. The report advocates "costly and extreme recommendations," and while many of their excellent proposals are indeed costly, they are by no means extreme.

Truly effective proposals would hurt those established institutions and interests that gain from the deprivation of Watts and similar communities—the commission does not fish in troubled waters. Possibly because they do not want Negroes to control their ethnic neighborhoods, they do not see the relation between community powerlessness and the generalized frustration and alienation which alarm them.

In their approach to the integration of the alienated Negro poor into American society, the commission is guided by values and assumptions of the white middle-class ethos which are of dubious relevance to the majority of lower-class blacks. Their chief hope for the future is the instillation of achievement motivation in the ghetto poor so that they might embark upon the educational and occupational careers that exemplify the American success story. I am not against middle-class values —but in the immediate critical period ahead "middle-classification" will be effective only with a minority of today's poor.

What is needed—in addition to jobs—is an experimental program for finding innovations that might link the values and social patterns of the Negro lower class with the social and productive needs of the greater society, thus reversing the trend toward alienation. Before the meaningful recommendations can be made that are in line with the enormity of the problem, the sociological and cultural character of the Negro low-income community must be understood. The legalistically oriented commission—with its primary commitments to control, law and order, a white-dominated status quo, and a middle-class ethic—has not been able to do this.

NOTES

1. *New America,* September 17, 1965.
2. *Life,* August 27, 1965.

11. WHITE ON BLACK: THE RIOT COMMISSION AND THE RHETORIC OF REFORM *
Andrew Kopkind

''**A S** America gets worse and worse,'' Murray Kempton once wrote, "its reports get better and better." No report of a commission investigating America's recent crises has found so warm a public welcome as the Kerner Commission's study of the season of civil disorders in the summer of 1967. In its official and private editions, the "Riot Commission" Report has sold more than two million copies. Countless critiques and analyses have greeted it in the press, and it has turned to grist for thesis-mills in the nation's graduate schools and colleges. The careers of several commissioners, staff officials, and consultants have been considerably enhanced by their association with the report (and only a few reputations have suffered). All in all, the report has become a basic document in the platform of American liberals for social reform, a catalogue of problems and a program of solutions.

But by and large, those who were cheered by the report's solemn platitudes or impressed by its torrent of statistics missed its essential political functions and its crucial social consequences. It presented—and legitimized—a specific view of the riots and a particular understanding of America that now constitutes the standard approach to the treatment of social ills. The commission was able to do that job because of the way it was set up, staffed, manipulated, and terminated; because of the promises and rewards it offered those who worked for it; because of its punishments for criticism and dissension; and because of its calculated presentation to the public through press and mass media.

Reportage and analysis of the commission's work have largely failed, and for the same reasons: reporters and analysts became deeply implicated in the "success" of the report. Although there was an unusual

* A condensed version of this study appeared in the biweekly newspaper *Hard Times*, edited by Andrew Kopkind and James Ridgeway, no. 44, September 15–22, 1969, pp. 1–4. Copyright ©1969, The New Weekly Project, Inc.

amount of reportable conflicts during the commission's seven months of operation, reporters never got past the vague rumors of friction between liberal and conservative forces, or the whispered hints of White House interference. Tom Wicker, who was then the Washington Bureau Chief for the *New York Times,* was given favored access to the commissioners and staff, and was chosen to write the introduction to the report for the Bantam Books edition; but both he and his newspaper either failed to report, or misreported, the most important political aspects. For instance, the firing of 120 staff members in late 1967 was never explained; the substantial hostility of black staffers toward the commission's own "institutional" racism was never mentioned; the "underground" commission document, "The Harvest of American Racism," was never examined; the White House veto on employment of staff and consultants active in antiwar work was never disclosed; the tacit agreement to "forget" the war in Vietnam throughout the commission's investigations and its report was overlooked; and the secret plan of Commissioner Charles ("Tex") Thornton to torpedo the report just before launching is still an untold story.

In similar ways, the political analysts who pored over the long document never got past its liberal rhetoric and its profuse programmatics to see its political role. Although the establishment of the commission had some value for the Johnson administration in the way of "crisis management" (as one staff official put it), most of its original purposes are lost, unremembered, or unimportant. One major article—"Riot Commission Politics," by Michael Lipsky and David Olson, in the April 1968 *Trans-action* (from a longer academic study financed, in part, by Kerner Commission funds)—puts forth several useful political points. But no one has yet detailed the report's lasting effect in the set of signals it delivered to corporations, foundations, research companies, and government planners to assume management of urban affairs on the model of foreign aid and counterinsurgency programs of the early 1960's.

For the report does not exist outside of its political context. It can logically escape neither the conflicts which informed its operations, nor the uses to which it will be put. Strictures on thinking "unthinkable" thoughts about Vietnam (among other unthinkables) made impossible a realistic assessment of the nature of a riotous America. Total concern for the way resources of the society are allocated—rather than control of the allocation process—eliminated discussion of the possibilities of serious social change. Acceptance of pluralistic myths about the opera-

tion of American institutions limited the report to the exposition of a
narrow ideology. Failure to analyze in any way the "white racism" asserted by the commissioners in the report's summary transformed that
critical category into a cheap slogan. And overall, the report's mindless
attention to documenting conventional perceptions and drowning them
in conventional wisdom made meaningless the commissioners' demands
for social reconstruction.

The very acceptance—and acceptability—of the report is a clue to
its emptiness. It threatens no real, commanding interests. It demands,
by implication or explication, no real shifts in the way power and
wealth are apportioned among classes; it assumes that the political and
social elites now in control will (and should) remain in their positions.
By avoiding an approach to the riots as events of political insurrection,
or as part of a worldwide response to an overbearing American empire,
the report makes sure that social therapy will be applied only to surface
effects, not systemic faults. In the end, it asserts some truths—or
truisms—about America, but it does not dissect them. "We could have
tackled problems from any angle," one top commission official said recently; "from class, racism, the economic system. But we didn't follow
any of them through, because everyone knew exactly where dissection
would lead: to the power and the interests of the people sitting right
there on our commission."

President Johnson chose eleven members for his National Advisory
Commission on Civil Disorders, a collection remarkable chiefly for its
predictable moderation. There could, and would, be no surprises. The
list was comprised of men (and one woman) representing various aspects of economic and political elites in the United States: expansive
corporatism (Charles B. Thornton, the president, director, and chairman
of Litton Industries); bureaucratic labor (I. W. Abel, president of the
United Steel Workers); the pre-1965 civil rights establishment (Roy
Wilkins, executive director of the NAACP); Republicans (Rep. William M. McCulloch, of Ohio, and Sen. Edward W. Brooke, of Massachusetts); Democrats (Rep. James Corman, of California, and Sen. Fred
Harris, of Oklahoma); old-style machine politics (Chairman Otto Kerner, governor of Illinois); new-style urban politics (Vice-Chairman John
Lindsay, mayor of New York City); the police (Chief Herbert Jenkins,
of Atlanta); and women-in-politics (Katherine Graham Peden, then
commerce commissioner of the State of Kentucky).

Many of the commissioners brought more than one constituency with
them. Brooke added one body to the two-man Negro team as well as the

Republican side. Kerner was meant to contribute at least part of Mayor Richard Daley's famous Chicago "clout." Jenkins was a modern southerner as well as a good cop. Mrs. Peden was there to augment the conservative side of the internal balance of the commission. Then, too, the president was able to pay off friends and allies with commission appointments, or help some Democrats in their careers, or (if it came to that) implicate potential enemies in an administration production. Corman's appointment was a reward for loyalty to the administration in Congress at a time when other Democratic liberals were sharply critical of the president. Harris, who takes credit for first broaching the idea of a "riot commission," was a (rare) White House link with Senate liberals. Lindsay's appointment was the most intriguing: he would give the Republican cover to a Democratic instrument; but if things on the commission fell apart, he could be stigmatized with blame. In any event, he was forced into a Democratic game, and had to play on the terms set by his political opponents. To some extent, Johnson's gambit worked: Lindsay attributes his defeat in the 1969 Republican primary in New York in some part to his well-publicized "liberalism" on the commission.

The commissioners were chosen by the "White House in-group," as a staff official called it. The principal assembler of names was Presidential Assistant Joseph Califano. Others, such as Attorney General Ramsey Clark, also submitted names. Johnson himself picked Mrs. Peden; she hoped to run for higher office in Kentucky, and needed prominent political exposure. For Staff Director David Ginsburg, however, she was to represent the standard of conservatism against which the commission staff would test its liberal efforts. "If she could be convinced," Ginsburg said, "anyone could."

Like all presidential commissions, the Kerner panel was designed not to study questions but state them, not conduct investigations but accept them, not formulate policy but confirm it. That design begins to appear early in the commission's life: in late October, Police Chief Herbert Jenkins, one of the "liberal" commissioners, wrote a letter to David Ginsburg setting forth his views of the commission's concerns. For the most part, it was a list of well-intentioned but unexamined assumptions about American society ("I believe that if the commission could communicate the real feelings of desperation of the American Negro to the American white, half the problem would be solved."). But the treatment of the role of the police is a good illustration of the restrictions which liberal ideology put on the commission.

"Law and order must always be the first order of business," Jenkins wrote. "The highest value of the law is the keeping of the peace. I am convinced that the police powers of the local, state, and federal governments can quickly put down any act of civil disobedience. We should, of course, make it clear to those so-called 'militants' that the full force of the law will be brought to bear on any and all violators of the law."

Only by accepting all the values of American society as it is presently organized could such sentences be written. In a different view, with an approach that emphasized the dynamics of rebellion and conflict, "violators of the law" would have an entirely different meaning. Then, the police could be seen not necessarily as agents of law and instruments of "control," but as an opposing army: the enemy. "Those so-called militants" would be "leaders"; the "full force of law" would be the full force of oppression.

Of course, no government commission could have sanctioned such a view; but that is the important point. The rhetoric of the Kerner Commission's Report as a "revolutionary" document is absurd. The idea that its millions of dollars spent on "analysis" and "investigation" would produce anything but elaborations on a predetermined ideological framework was always an illusion.

Although the commission conducted hundreds of hours of official "hearings" and traveled in groups of two and three commissioners to riot cities, the information and impressions thus gathered were useful more in the way of therapy than analysis. Talks with militants and walks in ghettos had a "fantastic impact" on the commissioners' manners, Senator Harris thought. "You never heard people in polite company say 'racism' before," he said. And David Ginsburg believed that "every one of those commissioners had to see it with his own eyes, taste it, feel it, before you could get to the larger problems." But the basic work on those "larger problems" would be done by the staff—and, in the case of the Kerner Commission, by the scores of outside consultants, specialists, and experts who were directed into the really critical policy-making roles. Together, these "outsiders" constituted a significant company in the elite of professional "urbanists" which has become the effective command-group for the management of social crises in America.

The key consultants were not the "pure" social scientists (for whom many staff officials had considerable contempt) but rather representatives of the new breed of political technologists, responsible (and responsive) to the big foundations, the great multiversities, and the vast corporate conglomerates which give them cover, employment grants, and, in the end, professional legitimacy. Staff Director Ginsburg called the first group of them together in the hours after President Johnson called out the troops and appointed the commission (and declared a national day of prayer—the total of his reaction to the convulsive riots then in progress). "We got in touch with *everybody* in the country," Ginsburg reported: Jack Conway, director of the Industrial Union Department of the AFL-CIO, and long-time Kennedy family cadre; Herbert Gans, then of the Center for Urban Education in New York; Richard Boone, then director of the Citizens' Crusade Against Poverty; Richard Scammon, former census director; Mitchell Sviridoff, of the Ford Foundation; Paul Ylvisaker, a former Ford Foundation director, and then a "community affairs" adviser to Governor Richard Hughes of New Jersey. The only black "urbanist" mentioned by Ginsburg was Oliver Lofton, a Newark legal services director. Another black, Kenneth Clark, was avoided because he was thought "too cynical" about the possibilities for the commission. Several representatives of the "everybody" in the country met at Ginsburg's house in Washington's whitest section for a thirteen-hour session which was to set the terms of the commission's work.

President Johnson's television speech on July 27, 1967, set up the commission and gave it three official "purposes": to find out what happened in the riots; to determine why it happened; and to suggest remedies. Those three steps, however, do not reveal the context of concerns which formed the groundwork of the commission's studies. "You have to understand the ambiance of Washington of July and August that year," a commission official said not long ago. "There was more than the black revolt going on. The blacks were striking real fear, but the national confusion rose out of a combination of issues: peace, students, Vietnam—as well as blacks. Johnson was in terrible trouble with the academic community. You have to set up that environment; it conditioned the politics and technics of the commission and its report."

Ginsburg remembers a much more specific concern: "the idea that these riots were a result of a conspiracy, communist or otherwise. It was our objective first to determine whether it was true, and if it was false, to kill it. It turned out to be a myth, but one that was held by people at *all* levels of the White House, and the highest levels of congressional leadership. No one in the White House had tried to contradict it."

For the most part, Ginsburg said, "we never discussed objectives, because we lived it. The central thing was to relate causes to consequences, to bring a sense of conviction that causes had to be eliminated, not produce a list of things to do. We've had a list for years. It was not credible in July of 1967, or today, that the Congress of the United States could do—not even *would* do—the kinds of things quickly that had to be done."

Ginsburg's perception of the commission as "an exercise in communication, education, and pedagogy" does not conflict with his function as the chief political cadre for the administration. His job was to manipulate the internal and external operations of the commission so as to produce a forward-looking report and avoid the worst pitfalls of controversy, bickering, and career damage. The disastrous example of the Warren Commission Report (one of his aides remarked) was fresh in Ginsburg's mind; that couldn't be allowed to happen again. An image of responsibility, independence, and, above all, harmony, was to be projected. "It was always my goal," Ginsburg says, "to secure unanimity."

Ginsburg's justification for his "one tactical problem" of unanimity inside the commission was the impact on government policy it would have. He seemed to think a unanimous report would have the effect of a unanimous decision of the Supreme Court. But that turned out to be an unrealistic idea of the commission's function. It was not meant to force action (as the Supreme Court's school desegregation decision was, for example) but to avoid it. There was not much difference between Johnson's three responses to the riots: troops, prayer, and a commission—all were more important in themselves than in their theoretical consequences.

President Johnson himself appointed Ginsburg as the commission's director shortly after he announced the names of the commissioners. It was an unusual move, and a source of some suspicion afterward; commissions like to hire their own hands. But the job of political organizer was too important to be left to any old bureaucrat. The White House had to keep control of the commission, even indirectly—*preferably* indirectly. David Ginsburg filled the required role to perfection. A quiet, commanding West Virginia lawyer, he had first met Johnson in New Deal days, and became one of his pool of Jewish lawyers (c.f., Abe Fortas, Edwin Weisl) available for odd jobs, big deals, and general counsel (myths of ethnic attributes grow tall in Texas). Ginsburg was offered an assistant secretaryship of state (for political affairs) in 1966, but turned it down. Lately, he had been advising the president on a wide range of political and administrative problems, from post office reorganization to balance of payments. (One of his newer law partners,

Tyler Abell, was assistant postmaster general, and was married to Lady
Bird Johnson's social secretary.) Ginsburg had served on presidential
boards investigating airline and railroad strikes. In 1969, he was named
general counsel to the Democratic National Committee. He ran a lucrative and highly political Washington law firm, with offices overlooking
the White House and the Executive Office Building across Seventeenth
Street on Pennsylvania Avenue. With his partners (one of whom was
John Kennedy's special counsel), Ginsburg represented the usual array
of interested parties: Flying Tiger Airlines, Occidental Petroleum, U.S.
Truck Lines, and the governments of France, Israel, and South Korea.

As Ginsburg was the political manager and manipulator of the commission, his deputy, Victor Palmieri, was the administrator and theore-
tician. Palmieri was a young southern California lawyer, very much in
the hard-living, aggressive Kennedy style. By the time he was 35 he had
become president of the Janss Corporation, one of the West's biggest
land-holding and development corporations. He moved freely in and out
of liberal West Coast politics, between real estate dealings of enormous
proportions (Sun Valley, Southern Ventura County, Snowmass-at-As-
pen, Hawaii, etc.). But in the months before the commission was
formed, Palmieri had grown tired of the Janss job, and the fascination
of urban politics was strong. He had once turned down the position of
poverty program director for Los Angeles, and had helped in liberal
Democratic political campaigns in California; after the commission was
disbanded, he toyed with the idea of entering politics in southern California himself, then worked in Robert Kennedy's presidential campaign.
In 1970, he became a chief organizer of Jesse Unruh's California
gubernatorial campaign.

Palmieri came to the commission staff by one of the several routes of
recommendations in the national network of political elites—a diffuse but serviceable American equivalent to the British "old boys' net."
The American version does not begin at prep school or college
(although friendships formed in law school can be important) but
more customarily grows out of professional liaisons. The networks
then turn out to be more meritocratic than hereditary—but no less elitist. Palmieri was recommended by U.S. Deputy Attorney General Warren Christopher, an old ally in liberal Democratic circles in California,
and—more important—an old associate in Palmieri's prestigeful Los
Angeles law firm, O'Melveney and Meyers. Mayor Lindsay also cleared
Palmieri with Bayliss Manning, dean of the Stanford Law School (Palmieri's alma mater), who is himself a political swinger in the liberal re-

form network. The ironies of elitism do not escape Palmieri; "It's such a groove," he mused some time ago. "It's like a slalom trail. You hit the first gate and it's downhill from there."

Operationally, Palmieri was the link to urbanist America. He knew the professionals and the theorists across the range of reform and radical ideologies, from Paul Jacobs to David Packard. His special business interests in community development—through Janss—gave him a special leg up. But Palmieri also occupied a distinct ideological position, best seen from the outside in the work of Anthony Downs, one of the most important consultants to the commission. In their ideology, social change is tied to a static view of political conditions. Although the kinds of programs Palmieri favored are considered "ultraliberal" or "far out" by many people, they are all built on current political demands. The effect is that the importance of political movements is discounted and the stability of political institutions is assumed; maneuvers become more important than divisions; techniques replace conflict.

If Ginsburg had a broad rhetorical view of the commission's purposes, Palmieri had a much more specific notion of what it was supposed to do. "We thought we had a damn good chance of moving to a major racial conflagration in the country," he said a few months ago. "All the graphs were going upward. Watts had put an edge of ideology and expressive activity to the thing. With the Vietnam war and everything else, we thought this country might be heading toward a general racial conflagration. From my point of view, there was only one purpose. I saw no reason for the violence in the cities to abate except for the 'exhaustion syndrome.' I thought the most important thing was what the response would be in the white police forces around the country. There was a kind of 'armed camp' response building in the cities. So, from my standpoint, the objective was to affect the posture of local authorities in the next summer."

That was the time when the newspapers and magazines were full of reports of police arming themselves with tanks and heavy artillery for the next battles in the war with black America. Paramilitary squads of vigilantes were shown practicing on the rifle range; suburban women were learning karate at the local Y. If the Kerner Report was to defuse such bombs, it would have to be published well before the next summer.

The various notions of the commission's objectives were influenced strongly by the bureaucratic demands on its schedule. President Johnson had called for two separate products from the commission: an "interim" document in March 1968, and a final report by August 1. But early on,

Palmieri and Ginsburg came to believe that the schedule of separate reports would have to be discarded. Their reason was that the commission had to influence events in the summer of 1968. "We absolutely had to come out in March with the whole report," Palmieri said. "That premise developed in August and September and it grew and grew until it became inevitable that we *would* come out in March. It would have been silly to come out with a report on the summer of 1967 in the middle of the summer riots of 1968. But nobody, literally nobody, knew of our decision. It was never explicit between Ginsburg and me, or between either of us and any commissioner."

Why an interim report would not have served as well for an "impact" on current politics is not clear from Ginsburg's and Palmieri's stated reason. But there were other problems left unsaid that seem to have influenced the implicit decision to terminate the commission's work in the winter. For one thing, the summer of 1968 would also see the beginning of the presidential campaign, and the commission's report could well be used for unpleasant political effect by opponents of President Johnson, who was assumed to be certain of the Democratic party nomination. For another thing, it was dangerous for the commission itself to make a public statement, such as an interim report, and remain in operation. It would then be vulnerable to attack from all those offended by its first effort, and to pressure from all those who wanted to affect the contents or tone of the second. "Wait for the end of the commission's life to take strong positions," Ginsburg once told a group of young staff assistants. "Then," he added, "we'll all have our airplane tickets and we can get away fast."

It fell to Victor Palmieri to begin assembling a crew of social scientists to document and analyze the "causes" of the riots which, in the most important way, everyone had agreed on before the commission's work ever started. President Johnson's television speech to the nation on July 26—written in part and edited by Justice Abe Fortas—asserted that the riots then engulfing scores of cities were "caused" by "ignorance, discrimination, slums, poverty, disease, not enough jobs. We should attack them," the President said, "because there is simply no other way to achieve a decent and orderly society in America." (The commission thought so much of that Fortas/Johnson passage that it was included as the epigraph to the published report.) That predetermined assessment of the "causes" of the riots utterly defined the commission's work. Social scientists, lawyers, journalists, investigators, and researchers had to be found who believed in—or would accept—the perspective on the riots which those phrases represented. Alternative approaches were implicitly eliminated: There could be no place for documentation or analysis based on the nature of exploitative capitalism, on the system of class and caste oppression (as opposed to "discrimination"), or on the riots as a form of revolutionary attack on domestic "colonial" domination.

It was Palmieri's job to find social scientists who accepted the commission's premises. Until very recently, there has been no tradition of radical analysis in the social sciences. Most of the most important figures in academic and political social science in the United States came of age in the late 1940's and 1950's, when the "end of ideology" was proclaimed, when C. Wright Mills was alone and isolated for his radicalism, and when the purpose of social science was to abstract ideas from the way people lived, the history people made, or the goals people fought for. But Palmieri's and Ginsburg's job turned out to be very difficult indeed.

"The academics told us to fuck ourselves when we came to them for help," one staff official recalled. "They thought Johnson was trying to con the country into another commission. There was a disenchantment with the Warren Commission, the McCone Commission in Los Angeles, the National Crime Commission, the whole idea of commissions as a substitute for programmatic solutions. We wound up with a very second-rate bunch of individuals, and that had a tremendous impact on the quality of the operation."

David Ginsburg was only marginally more polite. "Our debt to the academic and intellectual community in this country is minimal," he said in a recent interview. "They were all falling over each other—for a fee—but for mundane reasons they couldn't work for us; they had jobs that started in the fall, their kids were in school, and so forth."

The directors tried to enlist such stellar figures as James Coleman, of Johns Hopkins, who wrote an important and controversial study of school integration for the Office of Education a few years before. But while many of the social science stars agreed to "consult" with the commission, none would undertake a full-time commitment. The staff finally had to settle for a National Institute of Mental Health psychologist named Robert Shellow, who was a commissioned officer in the Public Health Service. "A number of social scientists wouldn't touch the commission with a 10-foot pole," Shellow allowed in an interview this year. "They were concerned about their reputations. They thought the report would be something that would pervert social science."

There was also some question about the acceptability to the administration of those academics who agreed to work in any capacity on the
report. Herbert Gans, for instance, was "vetoed" by the White House as
a regular consultant because he had indulged in antiwar activities. Palmieri (who was personally very much against the war, too) succeeded in
sneaking Gans' name in on a "contract" basis—a formula, another staff
official said, which would have allowed the commission "to get Karl
Marx if we wanted to." Gans, who eventually was to write Chapter 9 of
the report, was not paid by the commission. The White House veto operation was run by Presidential Assistant Marvin Watson, the notorious
hatchet man of the late Johnson years, who kept names of antiwar activists in a computer-file in the basement of the executive offices. Gans'
name turned up as a member of a group of artists, writers, and academics who declared that they would refuse tax payments as a protest
against the war in Vietnam.

Even with a politically clean staff of academics, Palmieri could never
quite keep the "social science input" from shorting the delicate circuitry
of the commission system. His notion was to invent a category of operation, both separate from, and connected to, the commission, which
might remove some of the heavy loads. His plan was for quasi-independ-
ent "task forces"—much like the Walker Task Force which the National Commission on the Causes and Prevention of Violence set up in
1968—to deal with touchy issues that might cause political damage to
the full commission. The task forces could publish their reports without
acceptance or disavowal by the commission, and the public could draw
its own conclusions about the validity of the task forces' material.

For instance, the commission staff knew that studies done in Detroit
implicated the police in provoking the riot there. But the commission
would certainly shrink from placing the blame where it belonged. "You
couldn't expect eleven national commissioners with political careers at
stake to take the heat that the exposure of the Detroit police would have
caused," one official said. But Ginsburg refused to buy Palmieri's
scheme, and in the end, the toughest questions—such as the Detroit
police—were avoided, as Palmieri had predicted.

As it happened, there are a few tangential panels set up on the edges
of the commission. An advisory commission on insurance in the ghetto
—made up entirely of insurance executives—issued a conventional and
practically worthless report along with the full commission document.
Naturally, it did not begin to analyze the pattern of racism and class
discrimination permeating the insurance industry.

In early November, the commission sponsored a conference on the effects of the communications media on the riots. The weekend meetings were held at "The Homestead," the IBM estate near Poughkeepsie, New York, which was made available by Burke Marshall, IBM's general counsel, a former U.S. assistant attorney general, and a leading Kennedy family cadre. The "Media Task Force" was headed by Abe Chayes, a former Harvard law professor and State Department official, who was also a New Frontier functionary. A $221,000 contract for studying the media had been let by the commission to the Simulmatics Corporation, one of the leading new social science research companies, specializing in "simulating" patterns of human behavior so that politics, purchasing, and war can be scientifically planned. Many of the commission's consultants were tied to Simulmatics (or similar outfits) in some way; for example, James Coleman, who refused full-time work but did many consulting jobs for the Kerner Commission, had been a vice-president and director of Simulmatics. The company had long been engaged in secret counterinsurgency research for the U.S. war effort in Vietnam, and in 1967 had contracts worth about $700,000 with the Pentagon's Advanced Research Projects Agency, according to James Ridgeway in his book, *The Closed Corporation.*

Chayes and Marshall attracted the biggest shots in publishing, broadcasting, and editing to The Homestead: Tom Griffith, editor of *Life;* Richard Salant, president of CBS News (and stepfather of John Lindsay's chief assistant, Peter Goldmark); Ed Guthman of the *Los Angeles Times,* a former speechwriter and press agent for Robert Kennedy; Ben Gilbert of the *Washington Post;* and Nicholas Johnson, the Federal Communications Commissioner. As with the insurance executives' panel, nothing much came of the media task force. According to one of those present, the panelists spent much of the time "trying to exculpate themselves" from responsibility for causing or contributing to the riots. "No one was trying to talk of substance," the participant continued. "There were papers by various journalistic theorists and academics; but The Homestead had an intimidating effect, which seems to have been the purpose of the whole thing. At one point, Salant exploded and wouldn't answer questions because Nick Johnson was there."

Within the commission staff itself, Palmieri tried management devices designed to provide alternate circuits and prevent overloading. (The derivation of Palmieri's administrative theories from space and electronic technology is typical of the emerging tradition of political management; his speech is full of techno-language: "failsafe," "abort," "social science input," etc.) He laid out his system of "failsafes" in an attempt to treat conclusively the data received from field researchers. According to Palmieri's plan, the investigative and research material would be worked over in three ways: sociologically, by Robert Shellow; journalistically, by Robert Conot, author of a book on the Watts riots of 1965; and practical–politically, by staff lawyers, such as Ginsburg, Palmieri, and Deputy Director for Operations Stephen Kurzman.

What happened in the end, as Palmieri once said, was that the system had an "abort" in its critical center—the social scientific, "intellectual" effort. The failsafe failed. To Palmieri's way of thinking, that failure gutted the whole report. The journalistic accounts, the statistical tables, and the political suggestions were never bound in a coherent analytical structure. "It was," Palmieri said with a somber, self-critical, and almost desperate sense, "simply devastating."

It was more than a month after the commissioners were appointed that the "critical" social science staff began its work. Having failed to enlist the undivided attentions of the top men at the universities and research centers around the country, Director Robert Shellow called for their recommendations for bright young assistants to round out his department. In time, he was provided with a half-dozen full- and part-time men, three undergraduate "interns" from Antioch College, and scores of consultants who would fly into Washington at $100 or $150 per diem. The actual staff assistants were supposed to develop studies, or "profiles," of about 15 cities that had had riots that year; then, Shellow would direct the writing of an overall analysis, focusing on the riots within a more general context of urban problems and political conditions.

Shellow had been led to believe that the "social science input" his staff would provide could give the report its ideological basis. With that promise, he was able to attract many of the academic stars as consultants who would not ordinarily have worked full time. So while the social science establishment did not exactly stake its reputation on the commission, it did seek profitable roles to play. Consultancy was a useful game all around. The social scientists were able to enhance their prestige at no particular risk to their careers, and at the same time perhaps pick up a little useful "data" along with their fees. Except for a run through Marvin Watson's security file, they encountered few of the bureaucratic hassles to which regular employees were subjected.

Some of Shellow's full-time staff assistants, for instance, had serious FBI clearance problems. Although all of them were finally cleared, the

experience was intimidating enough, and in addition to the rigid definitions of staff jobs imposed by the bureaucracy, it helped limit their perceptions of the freedom they had in commission work. One of them had
worked with civil rights organizations and had been arrested in the deep
South during a march. Another was strongly committed to antiwar activism. "I was uneasy about the clearance," he recalled. "I began to
think back; what have I done? what did I do that they have a hold on?
what did I sign? I began to think of all the FBI agents at colleges who
attend the rallies. If I'd ever considered the possibility of a governmental job it would be the kind of thing that would have made me think
twice in college days about getting involved in politics."

Like many government agencies, bureaus, and departments with contracts to let in the new fields of "social technology"—education, urban
development, antipoverty, welfare, health, and civil rights—the commission drew to it every academic entrepreneur with a scheme to sell.
"There were more guys in and out of the commission office from universities and research outfits, with proposals, requests for money, projects and whatnot," one staff member said. "They ended up with Shellow for some reason; he may have been supposed to screen them. A
professor from Minnesota showed up one day looking for a piece of the
action; he had tapes of white 'ethnics' recorded during one of Father
Groppi's marches, talking about concentration camps for blacks. It was
supposed to fit into some scheme to explain the riots. He was trying to
sell it to the commission."

Some of the entrepreneurs were more successful than others. Washington is full of small research firms where returned VISTAs, Peace
Corpsmen, or Appalachian Volunteers can earn $12,000 or $15,000 a
year trading on their brief associations with the poor, black, and oppressed. Such operations are often run by the returnees' old bosses at
the various government agencies which funded the volunteer projects in
the first place. Naturally, the commission was an obvious source of income for many of these outfits, and they swarmed around when shop
was set up.

The commission signed a contract, quite early in the game, with the
TransCentury Corporation, a Washington-based research, training and
job-placement company run by Warren Wiggins, a former deputy director of the Peace Corps, and staffed in large measure by returned volunteers and their friends. B. J. Warren, a competent if somewhat hyperac-
tive young woman who achieved fleeting fame in the liberal press as an

"angel of mercy" during the 1965 U.S. invasion of the Dominican Republic, had been working for TransCentury before shifting over to full-time staff membership at the commission. (Later, she joined the staff of the Robert Kennedy presidential campaign—a not unusual route for several commission staffers.) Several other TransCenturions followed Miss Warren to the commission. The company itself won its $18,000 contract to recruit staff. A few months before, it had completed a $159,000 study for the President's Youth Opportunities Council (run by Vice-President Humphrey), which had somehow impressed Kerner staffers by its conclusions that black ghetto youths were both angry and apathetic.

Hundreds of thousands of dollars went into research contracts. The Bureau of Applied Social Science Research at Columbia was given $45,540 for a study of arrest records of rioters. A University of Michigan spinoff research department got $40,488 for a study of the life habits of rioters. The International Association of Chiefs of Police won a $38,000 contract for the study of police preparedness. Some well-known academics were able to get enormous private grants for research connected with one or another commission study; for instance Peter Rossi and James Coleman (the latter formerly of Simulmatics, the Kerner consultancy staff, the Office of Education, etc.) got money from the Ford Foundation for a massive investigation of racial "attitudes."

One of the most important commission research contracts was given to Systemetrics, a subsidiary of the Real Estate Research Corporation of Chicago. Systemetrics is run by Anthony G. Downs, an old friend of Palmieri's. Downs is on the "new breed" side of a family that is intimately connected with Mayor Richard Daley's Chicago. Downs' father, James, was Daley's first city planning "expert." He is also on the board of directors of National Homes, the biggest prefabricator of houses in the United States. Anthony Downs' sister is married to David Stahl, Daley's deputy mayor. Anthony Downs himself has been called the "Herman Kahn of the cities." He is a major ideologist of "downtownism" and "urban land reform."

Systemetrics was assigned two jobs: to design research and management programs for the commission, and to combine and summarize the field research reports on twenty-four riots in twenty-three cities. Both functions were important; but the way the Systemetrics researchers perceived the riots in the twenty-four summaries could profoundly affect the commissioners' understanding of the process of conflict. If the summaries portrayed ghetto blacks as pitiable victims, surrounded by rats and roaches, and put upon by evil and prejudiced predators, that would be how the commissioners ultimately would perceive the situation.

Systemetrics did use that approach, of course, and it was the theme of the final report. It was entirely predictable that the private researchers would see things that way—just as it was predictable that the social scientists on the staff and on the consultants' list would have similar perceptions. The emerging theme, accepted almost without examination by the staff, the commissioners, and the private researchers, grows out of the "middle position" between reactionary and revolutionary ideologies. It expresses the notion that since the conflicts of black and white America are nonideological, no real shifts of power are needed to correct them. The problems which were seen in American cities in the summer of 1967 did not represent contradictions within the whole political economy, but malfunctions of one or another institution, the failure to get food or money or jobs to the black poor, to open housing to black people and whites in the same income group, to establish lines of communication between "control authorities" and the people they "serve." Racial prejudice, practiced by individuals alone or in groups, compounds the problems. But there is no real answer to prejudice; the "solution" to racial and urban problems must always be put in technical terms. And although it may be extremely difficult, solutions can be produced by the existing political elites.

Much of the foundation for that "middle position" (the term itself implies that the other positions are "extreme," and hence unworthy, dangerous, or both) was laid in an early paper written for the commission by Howard Margolis, of the Institute for Defense Analyses, the secret war research corporation that acts as a kind of glue for the military–industrial–university complex, sticking academic study and Pentagon war-making together. Margolis did several odd jobs for the commission, but left before the final report was issued—paradoxically, because he feared that that document would be too conservative for his tastes. Margolis' early memorandum—never made public—reportedly laid out three possible perspectives for the commissioners to ponder: (1) the "right-wing" theory that a conspiracy lay behind the riots, and that program recommendations should emphasize the restoration of the "law and order"; (2) the "left-wing" theory that the riots represented a para-political rebellion of the black poor in America, and that only radical social change could integrate that rebellion into a new American "system"; and (3) the "middle position," focusing on the presumably "neutral" problems of migration, urban overpopulation, and historical Negro underprivilege. Programs designed to deal with those problems implied no threat to the current organization of corporate capitalism in America. Margolis admitted that the "left-wing" theory might correspond more closely to reality, but agreed that it would find no public acceptance, and would entail no programmatic consequences. In any case, the "middle position" was exactly what the commission wanted to hear.

The central contradiction of the entire commission's operation was embedded in the "middle position." As Margolis—and other staff assistants who read it in the first few months of the commission's autumn— understood, the position did not fit the realities of the black rebellions of the summer. The problem was not that it was "wrong," but that it did not represent the forces at work in the country. Its presentation was meant to serve a single political purpose.

For that reason, its unquestioned reception created a constellation of problems for the commission staff, for the commissioners themselves, and for the final report. The contradiction between theory and reality hampered the work of the field investigators, who felt themselves pulled apart between the blacks they were interviewing and the commission they were serving. It created fatal tensions within the social science section, which was charged with intergrating research materials and historical perspectives in a framework which was abstracted from real conditions. It made the official "hearings" before the full commission quite irrelevant, for it gave values to the parameters of testimony before anyone ever was heard. And finally, it denied meaning to the report, for it based programs on unrealistic theories.

The field investigation teams were the first to feel the tensions. Teams of investigators were sent to each of twenty-three cities. In each city, "subteams" of two people would speak with officials, private citizens in positions of power, and ghetto residents and activists. The teams were organized on racial lines. According to a memorandum from David Ginsburg to the commission staff, it was to be assumed that "only Negroes would be able to obtain information from residents in the ghetto areas." Whites, Ginsburg added, would be sent to interview officials and private citizens. The members of the teams were recruited from other government agencies for the most part (although some were hired on contract from one or another private research company). For example, the Detroit investigative team included lawyers from the National Labor Relations Board, the Department of Labor, the Office of Economic Opportunity, and the Federal Trade Commission; a researcher from the

Department of Justice; and two "contracted" employees from the Trans-Century Corporation. Almost all the team investigators agreed, in interviews later, that their history of government service influenced to a considerable degree their work in the field.

It was not long, however, before the black investigators began to sense that they were being used for purposes of which they were at least partly suspicious; that they were, in Eldridge Cleaver's famous phrase, more a "part of the problem" than a "part of the solution." Specifically, they were worried that the reports of their interviews would be misrepresented or misinterpreted when shown to the higher levels of the commission staff—and to the commissioners. More than that, they feared that information on militants might ultimately be passed on to law-enforcement agencies—local police, the FBI, the Justice Department, or the Pentagon's domestic counterinsurgency office—despite official assurances that it would go only as far as the National Archives. A particular object of suspicion was Milan C. ("Mike") Miskovsky, the former CIA agent who headed the investigations division of the commission staff. Miskovsky was charged with determining the facts of the "conspiracy" theory of the riots. "A lot of people misinterpreted his motives," one black lawyer on the staff said. "People thought he'd pass information on to the Pentagon or the FBI. If he had a choice, he wouldn't; but did he have a choice? We all thought that it would be likely that the material would ultimately be passed on."

The black investigators considered a plan to "sabotage Miskovsky's people in the cities," the lawyer said, by warning blacks not to talk to them, and by withholding information from the commission directors. But the idea was never carried through in a concerted way. "We didn't get much that we had to worry about letting out," he continued. What the blacks did, however, was assemble a meeting of all black staff members, to discuss the interview material and its presentation. Later, a group of five of the highest-ranking black officials on the staff arranged a meeting with Commissioner James Corman to protest what they thought was a "racist" avoidance of real issues by the commission and staff. "Nothing came of it," one of those present said later. "It was not worth the risk we took as junior staff members meeting with a commissioner."

Many black staffers, however, remained convinced that "the whole thing was a racist operation," as one of the field investigators put it, and many did withhold information on ghetto militancy. All the top policy-making jobs were held by whites, except for the post of general counsel, which had been given to a black man, Merle McCurdy. But although he was generally liked by the staff, he did not inspire much "black pride" among members of his race. "Merle was heralded as a black policy-maker," another black staff aide said, "but he thought whiter than white." There were only a few "token" black consultants in the long list appended to the report; the commission simply assumed and accepted the racist nature of the American academic establishment. There had been some attempt made to get a black man on the staff as deputy director; but the person chosen at first (an official of a state government) was found to have marks against him on some old score, and he conveniently "declined" the job.

Overall, the report was always thought of as a white document written by white writers and aimed at a white audience—*about* black people. It was primarily a response to the *white* response to the riots. It was supposed to prescribe policy for black people, not for whites. Although it named "white racism," it did not describe white racist society. It simply gave descriptions of black people and black communities. For to do otherwise would have given a different ideological sense to the effort. To describe and analyze white society would have exposed the conflicts of the ghettos as a product of the normal operations of American capitalist institutions.

The unease of the black staff members was never resolved. Most of them left with the feeling that they had been used by just one more racist institution, however "liberal" its sentiments. Most were already set in career patterns which they are not likely to break. They could go from the commission into law firms, business executive positions, or other government jobs. "We learned a lot on the commission," one black staff man said not long ago; "but what we really learned is that the commission was just as racist as the things they were looking into."

The central contradiction of the commission—between what was politic and what was real—was felt most strongly by the social science section, under Research Director Robert Shellow. It was expressed primarily in the drafting of the document, "The Harvest of American Racism," and "Harvest's" eventual rejection by Palmieri; and by the firing of Shellow and his entire staff in late December 1967. Although perceptions of the reasons for the firings differ widely, the context of contradictions is hardly arguable: the report was intended to serve particular political ends, and "Harvest" and the social scientists interfered.

Shellow had three assistants—David Boesel, Louis Goldberg, and Gary T. Marx—working on a series of case studies of riots; they were to be joined by a fourth, David Sears, in writing "The Harvest," a summary analysis that was to draw general conclusions from the case studies. All of them were young social scientists with liberal or radical tendencies. Boesel had the strongest Marxist orientation; Goldberg had been active in civil rights work with CORE. Other staff consultants, such as Derek Roemer of the National Institute of Mental Health; Nathan Caplan and Jeffery Paige of the University of Michigan; Elliott Liebow of the National Institute of Mental Health; Ralph Turner of UCLA, last year's president of the American Sociological Association; and Neil Smelser of the University of California at Berkeley, also helped in the effort. The method in writing the case studies was to assign staff people to read the research and investigative material on a selected list of riot cities. Boesel and Goldberg, for instance, did the major study of the riot in Cambridge, Maryland, and (with Marx) Plainfield, New Jersey. "We got excited about what we found," Boesel said. What excited them was the finding that the police (rather than Rap Brown of SNCC) primarily caused the disturbance in Cambridge; that the rioting blacks in Plainfield were *political* actors; and that the riot there had to be considered a political event, not simply an expressive spasm in response to bad slum conditions. The implications of those analyses ran counter to the "middle position" framing the commission's outlook: to the young social scientists, the riots were not incoherent freakouts, but rather specific responses (even if they were not planned) to oppression. They could not be understood without a conception of black struggle against white domination; and the "causes" were not to be found in the obviously bad living conditions, but in the system of distribution of power in the total society. In other words, the riots were rebellions.

It was never clear to the young staffers that Shellow understood the point they were making, but he did support his aides' work, and took their studies to the full commission. Boesel described the meeting with the commissioners:

Shellow gave a resumé of our papers while we sat there; most of the commissioners had not read them through, although Roy Wilkins said he had read the Plainfield analysis all the way through. Shellow and the commission and its top staff were at the large table. Second-echelon staff were at the table, too. Lou Goldberg and I were on chairs along the wall with about 30 others. Before going in, Shellow told Goldberg—who had a shaggy beard and tended to express his ideas aggressively—not to say anything. Shellow presented Cambridge in a neutral way, as a "disaster narrowly averted," or "a bloodbath narrowly avoided" by the good sense of a State Police captain.

The commissioners didn't seem to respond one way or another; I was struck mainly by their *lack* of response, as if they didn't seem to get into it.

Still, Shellow and his crew (their work was, in the hierarchical custom, now referred to as the "Shellow analysis") were encouraged by the absence of harsh criticism, and work on other cities accelerated. Derek Roemer began to write his analyses of Phoenix and Tucson, but they never did come before the commission; they were thought to be too "diffuse" and "sloppy," as one staff member said.

By early November, the Shellow section began to feel the critical press of time. No underlings had yet been told that there would be only one report, instead of the March interim document and the August final version. The researchers thought that a draft of the summary analysis of the riots would have to be finished by the end of November to meet the interim deadline. And in *preparation* for the summary document, which was to deal with the whole summer of riots, Shellow wanted his staff to finish the city case studies (about thirty pages each) on an average of one every three days.

"We were scrambling desperately to finish the city case studies by the beginning of November," one staff member recalled, "then by the middle of November. By that time, we had to give up on them and start the summary analysis, which we were supposed to complete by the end of the month. We wrote 'Harvest' in two weeks as a preliminary draft, expecting to have till June to revise, expand, and rewrite, though we thought a draft would appear in the interim report. But, unknown to us, there was a March first publication date for the final report, which meant that all material would have to be in close to final form by late December or early January. It was in the middle of that bureaucratic mess that the shit started hitting the fan."

David Boesel remembered the frantic pace:

I started to work on Milwaukee. Lou Goldberg started on Dayton and Cincinnati. Gary Marx was working on Cincinnati, too. Then I started working on New Haven and Atlanta. We didn't go into the field ourselves, of course; labor was very much divided. The core of the material we used came from the field interviews. It was compiled by Systemetrics. First, they called the summaries they did "scenarios," but later someone came into the office and with a pair of scissors cut off the front pages of each one and changed the name to "Field Research Reports"—FRRs. That may have had something to do with classifying them as internal agency memos and thus exempting them from the Freedom of Information Act.

In late October, Assistant General Counsel David E. Birenbaum had memorandized top staff to the effect that "interagency or intraagency memorandums" were exempt from the Freedom of Information Act, at which point most commission business was so classified, and removed from public scrutiny.

Boesel continued:

We were unhappy with the FRRs. It seemed to us they were hack jobs, pasteups of the interviews and related stuff. We finally abandoned them to work with the interviews themselves. We also had FBI reports from the cities, but they struck us as rather pedestrian efforts. At first, I had the feeling that I was looking at something important and secret in the FBI reports, but that soon waned. They turned out not to make much difference.

We also had at our disposal the resources of the research section: statistics, demographic information, census reports. We talked to field team members who had gone into the cities. Then, we occasionally looked at "testimony" of witnesses who came before the commission, but that was of very little value.

With all that, we were working around the clock. We often slept in our offices—they brought in cots—and wouldn't see daylight for several days at a time. It was crazy. We'd be found in our underwear shuffling across the hall in the mornings, just before people came to work. But we were really excited. We thought our original doubts about how the commission would operate were proving unfounded, and that we'd be able to say what we wanted.

What they wanted to say was contained in the 176-page summary, a document of forceful impressions if somewhat limited analysis. "The Harvest of American Racism" was hardly the kind of work that a government agency would be happy to endorse. It did not couch its ideology in the conventions of "neutrality," but stated its positions boldly. It also was confused and inconsistent even in its own terms, and mixed traditional liberal assumptions which even the commission would find perfectly acceptable with radical notions about the nature of oppression and the development of rebellion. The most extraordinary part was the last chapter: "America on the Brink: White Racism and Black Rebellion." Written in rather heated language, it went further than most top staff officials thought prudent in charging that racism infused all American institutions, and characterized the riots as a first step in a developing black revolution, in which Negroes will

feel it is legitimate and necessary to use violence against the social order. A truly revolutionary spirit has begun to take hold . . . an unwillingness to compromise or wait any longer, to risk death rather than have their people continue in a subordinate status.

As young French-educated Algerians fought a war of attrition against the French, so we might expect to see young militant American-educated Negroes refusing to accept the military occupation of Negro areas. Preferring to die on their feet than live on their knees, they will, *a la* guerrilla movements in other developing areas, go underground, surfacing periodically to engage in terrorist activities.

Both Palmieri and Ginsburg admit that they were appalled when they read "Harvest." Ginsburg, who was thought to be the soul of genteel manners and quiet control, spoke of the document in four-letter words. Palmieri said he fairly threw it across the room at Shellow after reading it. The problem was not that it was poorly done (it was no worse a job than much of the finished report) but that it defied the categories that top officials had established for the "social science input." Shellow was supposed to produce material that minded its manners; instead, he gave the commission a paper which challenged their major assumption. The fact that all the criteria of "quality" were attached to the conventional ideology made it all the more difficult for "Harvest" to be swallowed. Perhaps Goldberg, Boesel, and the others might have been more successful in selling "Harvest" if they had been able to use Palmieri's terms to describe their ideas. But that takes rare skill and a great deal of time—if, indeed, it is possible at all, or worth the effort—and the authors could not manipulate their data and arguments skillfully enough.

Not knowing quite what to do, Palmieri sent "Harvest" off to several experts and consultants of his acquaintance for their judgments. Nathan Caplan, who was listed as a consultant for the document itself, read it over and reported, "I'm sick to my stomach." Herbert Gans, while much kinder, thought that the "typology" was entirely wrong, and urged that different categories of study be used.

Palmieri "fired" Shellow on the spot, although the actual process of separation was much more ambiguous and drawn out over a period of time. But from that point on, Shellow was excluded from all important commission activities.

Lou Goldberg described the events around the reception of "Harvest" in a letter he never sent to Commissioner John Lindsay:

On Thursday, November 30, Dr. Shellow, Boesel, and I appeared at a meeting at which all the section heads and key personnel were present. I remember Palmieri beginning the meeting with a description of the reaction he had been receiving about our report: "fascinating, powerful, and compelling." On the other hand, it was clear as the meeting went along that there were serious questions in certain people's minds about how politically acceptable it was. Would the commission accept it? Would the city administrations accept it? Would the police accept it? I remember Ginsburg using the term "politically explosive." There were concerns about documentation, attribution of motives, the inclusion of events that might have legal implications. At some point Ginsburg announced that he was convinced that the commissioners would not go for this report at the present time, that they had not been sufficiently immersed in the factual material of the riots to accept the conclusions of the report. What was to be done? "Trust" Ginsburg to know what was best (that's what he said), while we busy ourselves working up more case studies for the commissioners.

The next day, two more meetings were held at which Dr. Shellow, Dave, and I appeared. One concerned plans for research in the second phase, after the interim report. The other was concerned with the responses of the field teams to our work. There were minor criticisms from them on certain sections, but overall it was clear that they gave us a high degree of support.

On Monday, the first bomb dropped. Bob Conot had completed his first draft of a narrative historical account of what happened during the disorders in various cities. Palmieri told Shellow that our material was being used as "back-up." It was clear that Conot's work had served Ginsburg and Palmieri with an escape hatch away from our analysis.

On Wednesday, the second bomb dropped. We received new instructions from Palmieri as to our mission. We were supposed to write answers to the fourteen questions which President Johnson had assigned to the commission. We were supposed to provide a respectable and solid social science input, and having operated for more than two months under that assumption, we could not understand how answering the fourteen questions—in one week —could legitimately fall within our scope. So Shellow called Palmieri and a meeting was quickly arranged to try to work out the differences.

The meeting that followed was both stormy and revelatory to us. According to Palmieri, "life is tough," and there was no reason why we couldn't work up a whole new report in one week's time. For the report we had already written was "politically unacceptable" on the one hand, and too academic on the other. We held our ground. With this began a little dance in which for about fifteen minutes Palmieri kept making gestures toward leaving the room, but then coming back in again. He said that if I wouldn't write the section on the riot process, he would do it himself, or get some other people who would. We said that he was free to go ahead and do either. Finally, a compromise of sorts was worked out which did allow Palmieri to leave the room. Boesel suggested that we write a document that would be a much shorter version of the original, and that focused on only a few key points. Palmieri said he thought this suggestion was at least "negotiable."

As it turned out, the proposal we made was not negotiated at all. On Thursday, December 7, Dr. Shellow was invited to a luncheon at which it was announced to him that all that was wanted from his group was a paper dealing with Negro youth, and a paper on the aftermath of the riots. In the third week of December, our papers were presented and apparently rejected.

Meanwhile, Palmieri had called in a Chicago academic named Hans Mattick to do a substitute for the Shellow document. But Mattick produced nothing but a complicated series of wall charts and graphs. "I repeated the whole mistake with Mattick," Palmieri said later. "It was just devastating." Finally, Palmieri gave up entirely on "social science input," a notion in which he once placed so much confidence, and gave the analysis section of the report to Stephen Kurzman, a lawyer who was a deputy director of the commission, to complete. Kurzman turned out a quick lawyer-like job, incorporating those portions of the "Harvest" thesis which were acceptable from the start, but removing the more threatening ideas.

Many of the 120 investigators and social scientists "released" from the commission staff in December 1967 will always believe that the firings were ordered by the Johnson administration on the basis of rumors that the report would be too liberal, or insulting to the president, or belittling of Great Society programs. But there is no real evidence for such conclusions, and instead there is every reason to believe that the action was undertaken by Palmieri (with Ginsburg concurring and approving) because of the failure of Shellow's group to produce an "acceptable" analytical section, and the redundancy of the field investigators after the decision was made to issue a single report in the winter. It was important, of course, to keep the internal operation of the commission staff running smoothly. The removal of those people most likely to be critical of the last months of work, and the final report, was a necessity in sound bureaucratic management.

(One "official" explanation for the firings was the lack of funds. Although the commission cost several millions of dollars—"You'll never know how much," Ginsburg said—the appropriations procedure was circuitous and inefficient. Ginsburg was constantly running around to different agencies of the government looking for a few hundred thousand dollars more for his commission. But while it's true that the money ran out in midyear, that fact provided more of a rationalization for ending the research program than it was a basic cause for such action.)

The commissioners themselves knew little of the firings or of the controversy surrounding them, until the few speculative reports in the press were seen. On December 8, Ginsburg gave the commission its first news that there might be only one report, to be published around the first of March. Although he and Palmieri had assumed as much for several months, the commission was kept in the dark. One staff member who was at the December 8 meeting reported later, "It was simply flabbergasting. Ginsburg said that the publication of the report in March wouldn't really mean the end of the commission, that there would be supplemental reports and such. And the commissioners allowed themselves to be deluded. 'Oh, well,' Kerner said, 'if it's not *really* going to be the end of the commission, then I guess it's all right.' He fell right in line, then Harris behind him, then Brooke. The rest of them sort of looked at one another. The decision was made in just fifteen minutes." Corman objected to the peremptory firings just before Christmas, and Lindsay put up a small argument against terminating the commission, but neither followed through.

It may have been that the commissioners were too concerned with internal problems then to worry about the future. Ginsburg was determined to have his unanimous report, but there were indications from both the "liberal" and "conservative" sides that the final document, as it was then emerging, might be unacceptable.

From the beginning, it was clear that John Lindsay was the chief political spokesman for the liberal position, and that Tex Thornton was the heavy for the conservatives. Lindsay's closest allies were Senator Harris, Chief Jenkins, and Roy Wilkins. Thornton had only Mrs. Peden as a full-time cohort. The others roamed around the middle, or, like Brooke, who had the worst attendance record, roamed elsewhere.

What the "liberal" side meant first of all was a full acceptance of the "middle position" as laid out long before in the Margolis memo. Beyond that, it entailed a rhetorical emphasis on the horrors of life for ghetto blacks, and a sense—as Hubert Humphrey once expressed it—that things were bad enough to explain (but not excuse) rioting. There was no agreement, however, that the riots were a positive or beneficial political act (as "Harvest" had proposed); nor, of course, was there any idea that the failure of black Americans to achieve equality with whites was a structural failure of the American political and economic system.

The "conservative" side grudgingly accepted that same "middle position" thesis, but emphasized the bad character of the criminal element in the ghettos rather than the conditions of life there. Thornton, for instance, was obsessed with the problem of Negro fertility; he saw the breakdown of the welfare system as a function of the rate of illegitimacy in the black community. Palmieri, who placed himself in the far

reaches of the liberal side, tried vainly to prove to Thornton that the illegitimacy rate was a function of class, education, and income levels, not
race. But Thornton was uncomprehending. Secret minutes of a commission meeting of November 10, 1967, taken by a staff member, illustrate
Thornton's firmness; in this instance, he was responding to a discussion
on "what causes riots":

In re "bitterness and despair": we're playing right into the hands of militants who will use it as justification for violence. Maybe bitterness and an
element of despair; but only 2 or 3 percent actually start the riots. It's also
the rewards, the benefit from free burglary. Put in . . . "an increasing lack
of respect for the law": that's what it is, and the report has to bring this out
loud and clear.
There's little restraint to participation in disorders. . . . Improve police
departments: the military should train soldiers about to come out of the
service in law-enforcement work. Help solve big recruitment problem. There
are up to 60,000 coming out per year. . . . No question that show of restraining force, quickly applied, actually has restraining effect. Show of military force (even with no bullets or bayonets fixed) quickly stopped militants.
We should provide maybe that federal troops be made available on standby
basis as a precautionary measure, and not have to wait until conditions get
beyond local capacity.
Let's not mention about the slave background and the poor Negro. Sins
of forefathers idea will fall on deaf ears. Only 10 to 15 percent of whites
had slave-owning forefathers.
No law and no courts will change the attitude of the whites. Labor unions
have this very bad attitude, as does the so-called establishment. . . . Open
housing helps force Negroes onto whites and releases bad and hostile attitudes. . . . If we voice poverty, etc., as a cause of riots, 30 million poor
people will use it as an excuse to riot. We've got to be realistic.

De facto alliances had been formed within the commission that effectively preset the discussion (which, most staff officials agree, never became very elevated in any case). For instance, labor's Abel and industry's Thornton canceled out each other's criticisms of the discriminatory
practices of their respective institutions; a tacit "agreement" was
reached in which neither labor nor industry would be analyzed for the
racist practices. Chairman Kerner did very little substantively, except to
steer a course between the political "sides." After Thornton disquisi-
tions in the November 10 meeting, for instance, he said, "Well, we all
agree very much, and disagree only in minutiae"—despite heated disagreement by Lindsay. On another occasion, before a commission vote
on housing, he looked at Mrs. Peden and said, "I voted with you guys
the last time; I'll vote with the others now." Staff members present said

he then voted with Lindsay, but for no obvious reason except arbitrary "balance."

Lindsay thought that the report, even in its finished form, was "wishy-washy." He was particularly angry that no mention was made of the war in Vietnam as a contributing factor to the riot process. But in a meeting of the commission to debate the point of "mentioning" the war, Lindsay was voted down—by what his aides called "a clear majority." Ginsburg had already made it clear that there could be no direct notice taken of Vietnam in the report.

"Lindsay said that Vietnam was right at the heart of everything," a staff officer said. "He was the only one who said so. But he never went farther than that. Lindsay tried to make that a theme of debate, but no one else even considered it." Palmieri, too, was personally opposed to the war, but could not push his point within the staff without crippling his relationship with Ginsburg.

Although there is no reason to think that President Johnson directed Ginsburg to avoid mention of the war, it is clear that Ginsburg was doing Johnson's bidding: that, indeed, was his function, and the reason he was picked to head the commission staff—by the president himself. Early fears that Lindsay entertained about Ginsburg's "daily" contact with Johnson were irrelevant. Ginsburg didn't have to see Johnson. In fact, there was very little contact at all. Meetings with the White House were all with Joseph Califano ("Joe Califano *ran* the domestic side of the administration in those days," one top staffer said); Johnson never saw the commissioners after the investiture—not even when the report was to be presented.

There was, however, one exception. Late in 1967, Thornton grew anxious about the final report's "liberalism." He was particularly worried that it would suggest legislation for enormous federal expenditures; and, more than that, that it would generate "expectations" in the black community which could never be fulfilled, and which would lead to more rioting. Thornton went to George Mahon, the Texas Democrat who heads the House Appropriations Committee, and asked him to intercede with the White House on behalf of the "conservative" side of the commission. Mahon, Thornton, and the president were, of course, all Texans. Mahon and Thornton were also allied through Litton Industries' intense interest in government appropriations. Mahon and Thornton did get to see the president, but apparently the visit had little direct effect on the report. It did, however, serve to intimidate Ginsburg and Palmieri, who knew about Thornton's move; those other commissioners, who had no entree to the White House, were similarly angered and frightened by Thornton's show of influence.

Thornton's end-run to the White House conditioned President Johnson's eventual response—or nonresponse—to the report. Califano was so worried at one point that he called Ginsburg and asked for a special summary for the president ("What in hell's in that report?" he demanded). Johnson never rid himself of the negative impression left by Mahon and Thornton.

On the "liberal" side, Lindsay was also readying a gambit to direct the politics of the report and assert his own importance as vice-chairman of the commission. In the last days before the report had to be approved, Lindsay and his staff assistants thought that he would be unable to sign the kind of document that was likely to be presented. Furthermore, Ginsburg's management of commission meetings on the basis of "consensus" made it impossible for any one member to stage a walkout. In Ginsburg's method, commissioners were led to debate each minor point and agree on a formulation that would seriously offend no one. Then a vote would be called before the commissioners knew exactly what was happening. So having agreed to vote in the first place, no one could claim exclusion from the common commitment. The debate and the argument were used not to alter the product, but to legitimize it.

On the night before the final meeting, Lindsay and his personal staff put together what he describes as an "end game." The plan was that Lindsay would "assume" at the next day's meeting that a summary would precede the full report. He would then read just such a summary —written in an all-night session by his two aides, Jay Kriegel and Peter Goldmark. In promoting the summary, Lindsay would tell how deeply he felt about the issues it raised. The implication was that he would not sign the report if the summary were not included. The move had three objectives. First, Lindsay's "support" of the report (with summary) would put the burden of "dissent" on the conservative side. Second, Lindsay got his own summary into the hopper before any others. Finally, the gambit would lay the emotional and intellectual basis for Lindsay's personal dissent, should his summary be defeated, or if the conservatives won their points.

But the game worked smoothly. At first, Thornton and Corman argued against Lindsay's summary, but Thornton's attempt to put together a majority against it (and, by implication, against the report as it stood) came to nothing.

Could the report have gone either way? Palmieri, for instance, thought there was a real danger that it could turn into an obviously il-liberal document. But the structure of the commission and the context in which it operated suggest that its tone could hardly have been other than "liberal." The finished product almost exactly reproduced the ideo-logical sense given it by President Johnson more than half a year ear-lier. The choice of commissioners, staff, consultants and contractors led in the same direction. The political constituency foremost in the direc-tors' minds—the audience to which the report was played—had been conditioned to expect and accept a catalogue of ills and a list of re-forms.

That's what it got. The long report began with a competent journalis-tic description of the riots of the summer. No attempt was made to find a politics to anchor them down. "We have been unable to identify con-stant patterns in all aspects of civil disorders," the report declared weakly. "We have found that they are unusual, irregular, complex, and, in the present state of knowledge, unpredictable social processes." The report then proceeded to what Gary Marx called an "analysis by de-scription," which was no analysis at all. Although complex patterns of intergroup relationships were presented, they floated free of any politi-cal net. And if there were no real politics in the theory of the riots, there could hardly be any political implications in the report itself.

"White racism"—the most celebrated contribution of the report to common parlance—was mentioned briefly in the summary and never again. It was not explained, analyzed, or put in context. Specific analy-sis of structural racism in American institutions was entirely avoided. The implied understanding of racism was that of individual prejudice: "Because it accuses everyone," Gary Marx wrote, "it accuses no one."

According to the directors, there was practically no argument within the commission on the chapters dealing with the riots themselves. The real fights, they said, came over the introduction to the "Recommenda-tions for National Action" section. That seventy-page chapter was sup-posed to outline the scope of a national program of social reforms, in employment, education, welfare, and housing, with no "price tag" at-tached.

The chapter was based on a thorough memorandum of program rec-ommendations drawn up for the commission by Anthony Downs, of Sys-temetrics. That company's work includes (according to its current catalogue) "development of master economic plans for major corpora-tions," "development of alternative strategies for eliminating substand-ard housing in metropolitan areas," "development of optimal location strategies for a major metropolitan police department," and "formulation of a land development strategy to be employed by the Corporation Venezolana de Guyana in creating a new city." Downs' work for the commission was exactly of that kind. His studies and recommendations were based on the methods of systems analysis developed by the Defense Department a decade ago, and transferred to "social" agencies after that (usually by the very men who had formulated the ideas at the Pentagon).

Downs' paper was designed to be "far out," and was perceived as such by most commissioners. But no matter; it was taken over in large part as the substance of the national action chapter, which was the idea in the first place. Its champion on the staff was Palmieri; on the commission, it was Lindsay.

The importance of the Downs' approach is not in the specifics of its programs, which in many cases are considered desirable by most right-thinking people, but in the nature of its political demands. Continuing, reinforcing, and to some degree setting the ideology of the commission, it assumes the dominance of the same elites now in power, minus the old fogeys and plus the new technocrats. While its theory of programming may be dynamic, its theory of power is static.

Downs, Palmieri, and the supporters of their position—notably The Urban Coalition and Urban America, Inc.—found that strategy so attractive because it provided an alternative to New Deal and Great Society notions of reform by government bureaucracy. Downs all but stated his assumption that the federal legislature will be unwilling to provide the funds and direction for a national program of reform of social welfare. In the face of that assumption, there was a limited choice of strategies. One was a call for organizing social movements to change the basis of the distribution of power in America; one result of such changes would be the creation of new priorities for the use of financial resources. The other was a plan for corporate and private sectors of the existing "establishment" to enter the area of social reform. That, at least, would have the benefit of maintaining and strengthening the positions of power those sectors now have.

In the end—as in the beginning—the second approach found acceptance from both the "liberal" and "conservative" sides of the commission. Its rhetoric of reform encouraged John Lindsay in his losing battle to find a way to make New York City work. It mollified "fiscal conservatives" like Reps. Corman and McCulloch, who wanted to relieve the federal government of the strain of financing reform. And it pleased corporatists like Thornton, who stood to profit from the diversion of resources to corporations for welfare work (his Litton Industries runs Job Corps camps in the same way it builds war machines). And it charmed the industrialists of Urban America, Inc., who became the report's most ardent supporters.

In March 1969, Urban America, Inc., and The Urban Coalition published a report called "One Year Later," which found that the conditions described in 1968 in the Kerner Commission Report had not improved in the ensuing year, nor had much progress been made in setting out on the path of social reconstruction which the urbanists suggested.

Characteristically, the "One Year Later" document blamed the vague reactionary forces in American life for the failure. It did not recognize that the seeds of failure were incorporated into the commission itself. As Todd Gitlin has said, "liberal reform proposals lend themselves to panglossism." Managerial liberalism must assume the validity of present social relationships. Reform is meant to correct random distortions of those valid relationships. Hence, the tendency to "balance blame" between victims and executioners; hence, too, the proposals for improvement of police methods along with slum rebuilding. In every set of liberal reforms there are carrots and sticks; but in almost every instance, the carrot yields to the stick. At that point, liberalism is helpless.

The Kerner Commission and its report sent out signals to both government and "private" institutions to get working on carrots. Since government efforts had been tried during most of the decade and had been found wanting, private corporations and corporate satellites (universities, research foundations) were seen as the last best hope for accomplishing reform. Because of their independence from traditional political pressures—and because their resources were expanding so rapidly —corporate institutions could move rapidly to alleviate social problems. The methods were varied: construction companies could build low-income housing, universities could train unskilled workers, media corporations could technologize primary education, foundations could influence legislation, and so on.

Private institutions built on great corporate wealth have indeed picked up on the commission's signals, and on those sent by similar bodies. They seem to be in motion now, particularly in companion to the "benign neglect" which (though it be specific policy or merely mentality) the Republican administration imposes on social injustice. But "two years later," the conditions of black urban life seem not much improved, even if the expressions of discontent are less explosive than they were in the summer the Kerner Commission studied.

What is wrong with Kerner reformism is not that it is "impossible" (which it very well may be in present-day America), but that the programs it proposes must always fail to meet people's needs. For instance, administered "participation" in community decision making negates the very basis of participation in the first place; it reduces the honest struggle of people to control their lives to a technocratic misstatement of that need.

The Kerner Commission and others like it are institutional analogues to the "national day of prayer" which President Johnson declared at the time of the 1967 urban riots. Like prayer, the commission report is a declaration of faith in the present, and a vain hope for improvement. Piety, after all, is as much a refuge for the politician as for the priest.

12. OFFICIAL INTERPRETATIONS OF RACIAL RIOTS
Allan Silver

AMERICA has had an affinity for collective violence—the violence of vigilante groups, lynch mobs, strikers, strike-breakers, and private police. Unlike the violence of daily life, unorganized crime or juvenile delinquency, collective violence expresses the values and interests of groups which must be taken into account by reason of their power, size, or strategic location. To describe America as prone to collective violence is to say that significant conflicts among groups contending for political, economic, and social goals have often been expressed in joint acts of attack on life and property.

Nevertheless, there is a special sense in which America can be said not to have developed a *tradition*—as distinct from a *history*—of collective violence. As Daniel Bell has observed about labor violence, the great bulk of it took place far removed from political centers—

Reprinted with permission from "Urban Riots: Violence and Social Change," *Proceedings of The Academy of Political Science* 29, no. 1 (July 1968): 146–158.

indeed, it might be added, often remote from relatively cosmopolitan cities. Minefields in Pennsylvania and Colorado, steel towns along the Monongahela River, lumbering centers in the Far West, mill towns in New England, factory districts in Detroit—these, rather than New York, Chicago, Washington, Philadelphia, and Boston were the characteristic sites of large-scale labor violence, especially after the tense decade of the 1870's triggered the building of armories in urban locales. There were few American counterparts to Paris, Berlin, St. Petersburg, and Moscow—cities where large numbers of political, social, and intellectual elites resided, and also where class violence recurred. Regional traditions of popular violence—such as southern lynching and western vigilantism—were also typically found in smaller cities and rural settings. Large-scale racial violence in American cities characteristically took the predominant form of white attacks on Negroes in circumstances aggravated by dislocations stemming from war—New York in 1863, East St. Louis in 1917, Chicago and Washington in 1919, and Los Angeles and Detroit in 1943. Morris Janowitz has suggested the term "communal riots" for these outbursts. They featured white invasion of Negro areas, centered on the struggle to dominate areas whose social character was put in question by rapid demographic and social change, and involved extensive struggles between the races.

In part for such reasons, America has never developed a tradition of collective violence in urban settings by an "underclass" expressing discontent and demanding change, the forms and content of which are jointly understood by rioters and their targets alike. A group of social historians—George Rudé, Eric Hobsbawm, Charles Tilly, Joseph Hamburger—has helped to document the requirements for a tradition of riot: a variety of formats for disorder, demonstration, or violence occasioned by recurrent difficulties such as the price of bread, grain, or labor. As Hobsbawm in *Primitive Rebels* has summed up the character of these riots: "There was the claim to be considered. The classical mob did not merely riot as a protest, but because it expected to achieve something by its riot. It assumed that the authorities would be sensitive to its movements, and probably also that they would make some immediate concession; for the 'mob' was not simply a casual collection of people united for some ad hoc purpose, but . . . a permanent entity, even though rarely permanently organized as such." [1]

Both for preindustrial and early industrial societies, many of these writers document that these rioting crowds were composed, not of drifting, unattached, semicriminal rabble—the "dangerous classes," or the "lumpenproletariat," as they were variously called in the nineteenth century—but of residentially stable artisans, shopkeepers, and workers solidly integrated into their societies. Indeed, they expressed that integration in terms of the tradition of riot itself. Local and national elites, the targets and audiences of these riots, faced them at different points and in different circumstances with dread and fear or with confidence and calm, but usually in no doubt about the causes of the riotous behavior and the policies, typically lying well within the repertoire of the times, which would placate popular unruliness. It was a feature of "traditional" political society that "it often provided the unorganized poor with a language by which, in the absence of representative institutions or the ability to participate in them, they might articulately address the propertied classes through riot and disorder. . . . However richly endowed with representative and responsive institutions, [America] has not provided such a language for those in its cities who have long been outside their compass—a language whose grammar is shared by speaker and listener, rioter and pillaged, violent and frightened." [2]

The point is beautifully caught in a comment by a Boston notable in 1837. Reacting to local riots, and aware of contemporary riots in Europe, he declared: "Whatever may be the case in other countries, it is manifestly impossible that any sufficient or justifying cause for popular violence exists in this, where republican institutions secure to every individual his just share of the government of the whole." [3] The early and pervasive development of representative institutions in America thus helped to do away with the classical popular riot as a mode of relationship between governors and the governed.

Collective disorder among urban Negroes appears to be shaping itself into modern equivalents of the traditional forms of riotous protest: a self-conscious drama that substitutes shops, consumer goods, police, and white passers-by for granaries and grain-carts, tax officials, local notables, and townhouses. The burst of rioting that followed Martin Luther King's assassination was the first time that Negro collective disorder was set off in response to a single, politically significant national event. Potentials for disorder heretofore activated by local incidents of a routine character may increasingly be catalyzed by the course of distinctively political affairs.

Of immediate concern, however, is the character of white responses to urban riot. The focus is not on the responses of groups unremittingly or overtly hostile to Negro aspirations, but rather on those responses that have taken concerned, remedial, and egalitarian forms. Thus, less will be said about the substance of policy proposals than about the ideologies and methods of the people who formulate these latter, "liberal" responses to the events they seek to interpret.

Obvious places to start are the reports of commissions occasioned by one or another riot, the latest and most comprehensive of which—the *Report of the National Advisory Commission on Civil Disorders* (Kerner Commission)—has recently been published. Such reports date back to 1921, when the Chicago Commission on Race Relations made its report on the 1919 riot in that city. The 1935 Harlem riot led to a commission appointed by Mayor LaGuardia. State-sponsored reports on the riots in Watts in 1956 and Newark in 1967 have also appeared. In all these reports, with the exception of the McCone Commission's on Watts, the "liberal" mentality dominated among commission members, and free use was made not only of legal expertise but of social scientists. Indeed, the Chicago report is dominated by the tone and approach of the University of Chicago's Robert Park, a founder of American urban sociology; its most influential research director was a graduate student of Park, as were many of the research staff. The research director of the Harlem Report in 1936 was E. Franklin Frazier, at the time professor of sociology at Howard University. This style of officially interpreting collective violence in America did not begin in 1921, nor was it restricted to the theme of race. In 1915, a Presidential Commission on Industrial Relations included John R. Commons, and the reports of its staff, many of whom were his students, widely reflected the perspectives of institutional economics. It is of special interest, as we shall see, that the social science view of things did not prevail in the case of the commission on labor violence. With the Kerner Commission, the utilization of social science as an interpretive tool proceeded on a very large scale, and could no longer be identified with a dominant personality. All these commissions, whether dealing with labor or racial violence, attempted in some part to analyze outbursts of collective violence in terms of causal doctrines prevailing in American social science at the time.

This is surely not surprising, and that social science has much to contribute in these matters one has no doubt. But the perspective of "diagnostic sociology," to speak in a broad, not a specialized and professional sense, is not without its ideological assumptions, functions, and consequences. It is, to begin with, a way of coping with a dilemma. The American notables who made up these commissions—like those middle- and upper-class liberals and professionals who form a sympathetic audience for their reports—have tended broadly to support some or many key aspirations of Negroes. At the same time, they are perhaps among those most likely to accord high priority to the vision of a pervasively pacific society. Certainly their commitment to what Sorel called the "doctrine of social peace" is greater by far than is the case for the unruly poor, for radical ideologues, or those committed to the continued subordination or segregation of Negroes. To adopt the methods of diagnostic sociology is to objectify the causes of violence, to show their roots in environment and social structure, to depersonalize the connection between particular violent groups and the specific content of violent acts.

Apart from the Kerner report's national scope, more urgent tone, and explicit indictment of "white racism," there is hardly an interpretive diagnosis, as the report conspicuously admits, that has not been fully anticipated in the earlier statements. Migration patterns, police brutality and disrespect, unemployment, exclusion from key labor unions, poor and segregated housing, inferior education, inadequate garbage collections—all made their appearance in the reports as causal factors long before Kerner. Indeed, even in 1936, the Harlem riot of the previous year was ascribed, in part, to "smoldering resentments . . . against poverty in the midst of plenty." That report also described looting in ways that adumbrate current interpretations of looting in terms of exclusion from the "consumer society":

People seized property when there was no possible use it could serve. They acted as if there were a chance to seize what rightfully belonged to them but had long been withheld. . . . Some of the destruction was carried on in a playful spirit. Even the looting, which has furnished many an amusing tale, was sometimes done in the spirit of children taking preserves from a closet to which they have accidentally found the key.

Just as the group of social historians of riot mentioned earlier is concerned to document the meaningful and patterned character of earlier riotous protest in Europe, so the American commission reports from the beginning stress the socially caused, uncollusive character of collective violence in twentieth-century America. As early as 1915, the majority report of the Commission on Industrial Relations described "the origin of industrial violence" in these terms:

Violence is seldom, if ever, spontaneous, but arises from a conviction that fundamental rights are being denied and that peaceful methods of adjustment cannot be used. . . . The arbitrary suppression of violence by force produces only resentment which will rekindle into greater violence when opportunity affords. Violence can be prevented only by removing the causes of violence; industrial peace can rest only on industrial justice.

The Chicago report, after a lengthy analysis of the 1919 riot, begins its summary of its extensive investigation into "the conditions that made possible so serious and sudden an outbreak" with a more perfunctory statement of the diagnostic perspective: "The riot was merely a symptom of serious and profound disorders lying beneath the surface of race relations in Chicago." The language of the 1936 report on Harlem is similar:

> The explosion on March 19 would never have been set off by [a] trifling incident . . . had not existing economic and social forces created a state of emotional tension which sought release on the slightest provocation. As long as the economic and social forces which were responsible for that condition operate, a state of tension will exist in Harlem and recurrent outbursts may occur.

The Kerner report is but an elaborated version of the same imagery.

It is the lack of an indigenous tradition of collective violence by the urban poor—a tradition which would have involved the kind of people that have dominated the commissions—that gives special point to the use of social science techniques and imagery. They supply at once a basis for understanding and an acceptable definition of the situation. What social science perspectives do for liberals is to make it possible for them to maintain broad political sympathy for the urban Negro "underclass" and simultaneously come to terms with popular unruliness, riot, and violence even though these things are especially disturbing to them. This function of social science perspectives also testifies to the remoteness of the relationship between the rioting classes and those officially designated to interpret this behavior.

In the classical tradition of riot, the targets and audience were not insulated by social position, professional police, residential separation, or anonymity from the riots themselves. Their very homes, clubs, and persons were the primary objects of attack by a population that dwelt in close proximity, and could discriminate shrewdly among potential targets. Analogously, in the classical tradition of riot, rioters and their audiences shared a set of understandings about the role, content, and purposes of popular violence in terms of which conflicts of interest were expressed. But over the last two centuries there has been a profound rise in standards of public order in civil society, and no group has been more unconditionally committed to this development, its maintenance, and its enhancement, than the professional, upper, and middle classes concerned with liberal democracy and social meliorism. Diagnostic sociology, in a sense, supplements general notions of social justice in aiding liberals to come to terms with riotous and violent behavior about which they especially are likely to feel squeamish.

But the stance of diagnostic sociology is subject to erosion as a means of ideologically coping with riot and collective violence that may increase in frequency, scale, and spatial dispersion in the cities—that is, make its appearance on a more organized basis in residential and business areas heretofore largely immune. The demand for law and order as part of the constitutional fabric may well strain the ideological resilience of diagnostic sociology. This is likely to happen before it strains egalitarian commitments, because the perspectives of social science are, after all, commitments of a secular rather than a sacred kind. In any case, using sociology as a diagnostic tool may explain and depersonalize collective violence but does not serve—as the Kerner report makes utterly clear at its outset—to legitimate it: "Those few who would destroy civil order and the rule of law strike at the freedom of every citizen. They must know that the community cannot and will not tolerate coercion and mob action." It is instructive to contrast this statement with the majority report of the Commission on Industrial Relations in 1915, which was largely carried by labor union representatives: "Through history where a people or group have been arbitrarily denied rights which they conceived to be theirs, reaction has been inevitable. Violence is a natural form of protest against injustice." In such a formulation, diagnostic sociology has scant function: it is a matter of natural law, of elemental and self-evident justice. Diagnostic sociology is not required because collective violence as a response to injustice is rooted in the innate order of things.

Interestingly enough, this formulation was rejected not only by the representatives of industrial capitalism on the commission but also, in a separate report, by John R. Commons and the upper-class reformer, Mrs. Florence J. Harriman. Their recommendations stressed the costs of the "civil war" over industrial questions since 1877 and of military solutions, warned of extremist potentials if the causes of industrial violence were unremedied, and endorsed a program of research, applied expertise, and class reconciliation through remedial legislation and nonpartisan industrial commissions. Commons was acting in the spirit of the "Wisconsin Idea," that early and seminal instance of the institutionalized relationship between social science expertise and public policy in the service of social reform, then in flower at the University of Wisconsin. Frank Walsh, the commission's chairman—a Progressive radical and leader of the labor union majority—successfully prevented this style from dominating the commission's work.[4] But the affinity of diagnostic sociology and liberal reformism was thus palpable before the emergence of racial violence as an officially acknowledged problem. That affinity is all the stronger, one might suggest, for being tied not to the theme of race as such but to the whole question of popular disorder and collective violence.

This sort of ideological response to riot and disorder is potentially fragile not only because of possible strains between a diagnostic stance and a profound commitment to civil order. Its case for responding positively to riot in terms of remedy and justice rests, implicitly but crucially, upon a view of collective violence as remorselessly caused rather than as an active choice by oppressed people. Obviously one cannot here enter into the bearing of doctrines of social causation on the possibilities of initiative and choice. It is sufficient to suggest that in the world of riot commission reports, it is legitimate for political authority and the general society to respond positively and remedially to acts of collective violence that, in terms of democratic doctrines, cannot enjoy intrinsic legitimacy, to the extent that violence is causally inevitable. The medical metaphor is worn but unavoidable, since the reports themselves constantly invoke it. The sick body cannot but produce symptoms like fever and pain that it finds distressing; a society afflicted by gross injustice cannot but produce violence—in ways, however, amenable to diagnosis, intervention, and cure.

But Negro urban violence has already produced spokesmen—not only visible ideologues but anonymous rioters briefly quoted in the Kerner report itself—whose definitions of Negro rioting affirm it as a positive and voluntary act. It is not only that such affirmations are likely to outrage the great white public that shares the commission's perspectives partially if at all and, in the end, also to offend the commission's sympathetic audience. Also, much would be lost—humanly, politically, and from the viewpoint of social science—if official interpretive ideology functions to elide or ignore Negro definitions of riot as purposeful, affirmative, and actively chosen. Men who engage in dangerous and desperate behavior—indeed, any behavior—have a certain claim to have taken seriously the meanings which they see in their own acts, and wish others to see in them.

But even if such voluntaristic definitions of riot do not become current, we are likely to face, in the seeable future, a period in which some sort of remedial action, at an unknown level of scope and investment, is likely to coexist with continuing and perhaps mounting levels of collective violence among Negroes.[5] The Kerner Commission itself predicts that not only the continuation of present national policy, but also the "enrichment" option and even that program which represents the most radical restructuring of American society in its repertoire, the "integration" option, are likely to result in roughly equal levels of urban riot and violence in the short run. It does so, wisely, on the grounds that even strong integration policies are unable to deflect the massive momentum of the present situation quickly and thoroughly, and that the enhanced contrast between current reality and elevated expectations— already a cause of collective violence under present conditions—would almost certainly not result in a rapid diminution of the disposition to riot and might even increase it.

This exercise in the social causation of riot may satisfy the commission and part, at least, of its sympathetic audience, but it implies political and ideological strains of a considerable order. One could not do better than take one's text from Sorel's discussion in *Reflections on Violence* of a comparable state of affairs six decades ago, as social reformism and the parliamentary state sought to incorporate the industrial working classes:

> To repay with *black ingratitude* the benevolence of those who would protect the workers, to meet with insults the homilies of the defenders of human fraternity, and to reply by blows to the advances of the propagators of social peace . . . is a very practical way of indicating to the middle class that they must mind their own business and only that. . . . It may be useful to thrash the orators of democracy and the representatives of the government, for in this way you insure that none shall retain any illusions about the character of acts of violence. But these acts can have historical value only if they are the *clear and brutal expression of the class war.* . . . The middle classes must not be allowed to imagine that, aided by cleverness, social science or high-flown sentiments, they might find a better welcome at the hands of the proletariat. (Italics in the original.)

Fittingly enough, among the objects of Sorel's scorn was "Professor Durkheim," who, in his classic analysis of modern society's potential for social integration, had analyzed the "class war" as an "abnormal form" of social organization.

Certainly, diagnostic sociology will do its best to interpret, and thus to soften, the ideological strains of continued civic disorder in the face of massive "enrichment" or "integrationist" policies. But one may wonder whether explanations of, say, the role of frustrated rising expectations in promoting riots will suffice to alter the Sorelian scenario. Even the optimal American short run will thus be a most perilous time.

The great white public remains, on the whole, unconvinced of the premises and conclusions of such reports as that of the Kerner Commission. More will be learned about the perspectives on these matters of the general public, white and Negro, when an opinion survey of residents in fifteen cities sponsored by the commission is published. Meanwhile, one must make do with data from less satisfactory, scattered surveys based on less sharply focused samples—not of key cities but of the national population. These preliminary indications are not encouraging. Louis Harris reports that at most a third of whites, usually less, agree with the Kerner Commission that "white racism" brought on the riots, that riot arrestees should get better legal counsel and fairer trials, that the rioting is not organized, and that the level of welfare payments should be raised. Only slightly more agree that lack of progress in extending equality to Negroes and too few jobs are major causes of riots. Forty-five percent see lack of decent housing as a cause of riot, but only 23 percent are willing to pay higher taxes to remedy this. Only one in ten thinks police brutality has conduced to riot. On the positive side, however, relatively few whites see urban Negroes as actively preferring riot—a quarter or less agree that among the causes are Negroes' desires for violence and wish to loot stores.

The picture afforded by surveys taken before Kerner is generally also dreary. Just under half of whites in national samples, a heavy plurality, think that high among the major causes of riots is "outside agitation" (45 percent) and that Communist involvement was major (48 percent). Asked to perform an extraordinary act of empathy, to imagine how they would react to discrimination if they were Negroes, only a quarter produced such responses as being "mad, resentful, and fighting back." Two-thirds endorse the shooting of looters and firebombers. To prevent riots, 41 percent of whites suggest stronger repressive measures, the punishment of outside agitators, and increasing police forces; a comparable number propose a variety of remedial actions, including some that echo the spirit of the Kerner report, but no one of these attracts the proportions that prefer repression. Between June 1963 and October 1966, the percentage of whites believing that "demonstrations by Negroes have helped . . . the advancement of Negro rights" fell from 36 to 15; the percentage believing that they have "hurt" rose from 45 to 85. In proportions that range in recent years from 45 to 59, whites report that they have increased fears for their personal safety in daily life. Echoing the belief that most Negroes are peaceful, however, more than eight in ten believe that "only a minority of Negroes" support riots, as do three-quarters of Negroes interviewed. Relatively few whites see Negroes as actively preferring riots and a quarter or less agree that major causes of riots are that Negroes desire violence and wish to loot stores. Whites in lower-income groups, however, are much less likely than those with higher incomes to agree that most Negroes believe in nonviolence.[6]

These responses must be placed in the broad setting that verbal standards of racial tolerance and egalitarianism, as measured by opinion polls over the last few decades, show an uninterrupted rise.[7] It is too soon to tell whether Paul Sheatsley, who has helped document this trend, is correct in predicting that sustained rioting "will [not] halt the massive attitudinal changes we have demonstrated over the last generation." [8] If the American dilemma was severe before a new and unprecedentedly large population of urban Negroes began to question basic assumptions about public order, it is surely premature to expect its favorable resolution under these transformed conditions. The most one can say is that the dilemma's terms have both shifted and sharpened.

Perspectives on race alone do not exhaust these matters. Pluralities or majorities of whites surely do not share the perspective toward disorder and violence that characterizes the social and professional groupings from which the commissions are drawn, and which attend sympathetically to their analyses. The long-range rise in standards of public order, and in the extent to which legitimate violence has tended increasingly to become in America a monopoly of government, has been accompanied—indeed, has required—a kind of "psychic disarming" of a large number of Americans. That "softening of manners" which is a theme of the older social historians, the rise in standards of peacefulness in family life and occupational experience that Sorel saw as critical to the bourgeois doctrine of "social peace"—perhaps all have operated psychologically to disarm the middle and professional classes, especially liberals, more than any comparable group. Indeed, the loss of the capacity or will for voluntary self-defense among the new commercial and urban middle classes would appear to be among the conditions that promoted the creation of professional policing. But one's impression of southern life, of the volume of gun sales in many cities, and of the few —so far controlled—instances of incipient "communal riot" of the older type (Chicago, Milwaukee, and East New York), all suggest strongly that the "physic disarming" of very many white Americans is far from complete or advanced. Combined with the widely shared demand for historically unprecedented levels of civil order, and with continuing racial hostility, these are ominous convergences. So far, the ecology of segregation, police tactics, and the disposition dominant among rioting populations have forestalled the fulfillment of these potentials.

The American dilemma persists, and the reports of the commissions on racial disorders are essentially elitist in assumption, tone, and values —more so than was the case of the majority report of the Commission on Industrial Relations with respect to labor violence more than fifty years ago. But the elite that has produced them is significantly different in social composition in one critical respect; formerly dominated by interest group representatives and civic and philanthropic notables, the Kerner Commission was dominated by the most significant of modern elites, professional politicians. The relationship among professional politicians, popular democracy, egalitarianism, and elitist functions is one of the most charged themes in American society. Historically, elites in America—in Karl Mannheim's classic definition as special groups responsible for the maintenance of standards—have not easily been drawn from professional politicians.

Under present conditions, however, the critical burden of response can fall on no other group. To sponsor hard decisions in the political economy, to mobilize sufficient assent for these decisions, and to win elective office while doing these things—all present a trial without precedent for American professional politicians. Above all, the attempt to define as legitimate remedial responses to illegitimate violence creates extraordinary strains on the ideological resources of egalitariansim, diagnostic sociology, and the capacities of professional politicians to respond, manage, and lead. Never have professional politicians in this greatest of popular democracies been summoned to a role at once more profoundly democratic and more distinctively elitist.

NOTES

1. Eric Hobsbawm, *Primitive Rebels* (New York: Praeger, 1963), p. 111.

2. Allan Silver, "The Demand for Order in Civil Society," in David Bordua, ed., *The Police* (New York: John Wiley, 1967), pp. 23–24.

3. Samuel A. Eliot, quoted in Roger Lane, *Policing the City* (Cambridge, Mass.: Harvard University Press, 1967), pp. 30–31.

4. Graham Adams, Jr., *Age of Industrial Violence* (New York: Columbia University Press, 1966), pp. 204–214.

5. This and other matters connected with what I have called the "diagnostic sociology" of collective violence are acutely considered in Aaron Wildavsky's "Black Rebellion and White Reaction," *The Public Interest* (Spring 1968): 3–16.

6. All these results are drawn from Hazel Erskine's compilation, "The Polls: Demonstrations and Race Riots," *Public Opinion Quarterly* (Winter 1967–1968): 655–677.

7. See Herbert H. Hyman and Paul Sheatsley, "Attitudes towards Desegregation," *Scientific American* 211 (July 1964): 16–23; Paul Sheatsley, "White Attitudes towards the Negro," *Dædalus,* 95 (Winter 1966): 217–238; and Mildred A. Schwartz, *Trends in White Attitudes toward Negroes,* National Opinion Research Center, University of Chicago, Report no. 119 (1967).

8. Sheatsley, *op. cit.,* p. 236.

III

Social and Historical Perspectives

The ghetto riots have been the most important of a series of events which have engendered a deep national concern about violence. The absence of widespread domestic violence between World War II and the 1960's led to a definition of this period as normal, and in this frame of reference the current violence appeared to many as little short of cataclysmic. Yet a longer view makes it clear that domestic violence has ebbed and flowed, though not in a regular pattern, and has been as much a part of American history as domestic tranquility. Violence, both official and popular, has crested in the 1960's, in the early and middle 1930's during the depression, around the time of World War I, around the turn of the century, and so on back. Indeed, insurgent and repressive violence has been so much a part of the American scene that it must be considered integral to the political system. The intriguing thing about that system is not that its formal-legal structure has proved unusually accessible and responsive to underdog groups (for it has not) but rather that it has had the capacity to absorb the popular and official violence that has so often attended the efforts of these groups to break into history.

The essays by Henry Wade and Meier and Rudwick examine America's violent past, with particular attention to racial conflict, and relate it to the recent ghetto riots. Those in the section titled "Institutional Crisis

275

and the Growth of Revolt" look more closely at the contemporary background to the outbreaks, with particular emphasis on white institutions.

The two studies of black attitudes by Nathan Caplan and David Sears show how closely the riots are related to the consolidation of black consciousness. In the ten years before the riots the most dramatic change in the ghettos was the rapid growth of race consciousness and race pride, of which the riots were an expression. The causes of this change were complex, but key factors were the 1954 Supreme Court decision and the subsequent (televised) civil rights movement, the achievement of African independence after an anticolonial struggle, and the emergence of a generation of black youths whose entire experience was northern and urban. The rise of black militancy, particularly among the youths, within the context of obsolescent urban social controls, provided the impetus for the ghetto revolts. As Caplan indicates, those who rioted were likely to be younger, more militant, and more politically aware than those who did not. The riots not only gave expression to black militancy, they greatly reinforced it. Caplan and Sears both see a consolidation of black consciousness in the aftermath of the riots.

In arguing against an "underclass" interpretation of the riots, Caplan's study is to some extent at odds with the introduction to this book. While the differences between the two analyses are real, they are not as great as they first appear to be. In the introduction the underclass is defined more broadly than in Caplan's essay as including all those who are on the margins of America's corporate economy, rather than only the very poor. Hence the characteristics seen as belonging to the underclass are different in each case, as would be the meaning of violence attributed to it. In arguing that the riots are not underclass violence, Caplan means that they are not anomic outbursts of the abject poor. In arguing that they are a form of underclass violence, the introduction refers to a militant revolt against white control by the economically marginal, spearheaded by teenagers and young men.

The last section of the book looks at some of the implications of the riots for the larger society. Bettye Eidson uses public opinion polls as the basis for an interpretation of "white backlash," and Peter Rossi assesses the future of American cities in the light of the ghetto revolts.

The Riots in History

13. VIOLENCE IN THE CITIES:
A HISTORICAL OVERVIEW
Richard C. Wade

VIOLENCE is no stranger to American cities. Almost from the very beginning, cities have been the scenes of sporadic violence, of rioting and disorders, and occasionally virtual rebellion against established authority. Many of these events resulted in only modest property damage and a handful of arrests. Others were larger in scale with deaths running into the scores and damages into the millions. This essay attempts to survey briefly some of these outbreaks and to analyze their origins and consequences. We confine ourselves, however, to the larger ones, and omit any discussion of individual acts of violence or the general level of crime. In addition, to keep these remarks relevant to the present crisis, we have confined our analysis to disorders in urban areas.

There has been, in fact, a good deal more violence and disorder in the American tradition than even historians have been willing to recognize. The violence on the frontier is, of course, well known, and in writing, movies, and television it has been a persistent theme in our culture. Indeed, one of America's favorite novelists, James Fenimore Cooper, transformed the slaughter and mayhem of Indians into heroic, almost patriotic, action. As the literary historian David Brion Davis has observed: "Critics who interpret violence in contemporary literature as a symptom of a sick society may be reassured to know that American writers have always been preoccupied with murder, rape, and deadly combat." To be sure, violence is not "as American as cherry pie," but it is no newcomer to the national scene.

Though serious scholarship on this dimension of the American past is shamefully thin, it is already quite clear that disorder and violence in our cities were not simply occasional aberrations, but rather a signifi-

From the University of Chicago Center for Policy Study, *Urban Violence*, pp. 7–25. Copyright © University of Chicago, 1969.

cant part of urban development and growth. From the Stamp Act riots of the prerevolutionary age, to the assaults on immigrants and Catholics in the decades before the Civil War, to the grim confrontation of labor and management at the end of the nineteenth century and its sporadic reappearance after World War I and during the Depression, through the long series of racial conflicts for two centuries, American cities have known the physical clash of groups, widescale breakdown of established authority, and bloody disorder.

Nor is it hard to see why this early history had more than its share of chaos. American cities in the eighteenth and nineteenth centuries were very young. They had not yet the time to develop a system of orderly government; there was no tradition of habitual consent to local authority; there was no established police system. In addition, these cities grew at a spectacular rate. In the twentieth century, we have used the term "exploding metropolis" to convey the rapid pace of urbanization. It is not often remembered that the first "urban explosion" took place more than a century ago. Indeed, between 1820 and 1860 cities grew proportionately faster than they had before or ever would again. The very speed of this urban development was unsettling and made the maintenance of internal tranquillity more difficult.

The problem was further compounded by the fact that nearly every American city was born of commerce. This meant that there was always a large transient population—seamen engaged in overseas trade, rivermen plying the inland waters, teamsters and wagonmen using the overland routes, and a constant stream of merchants and salesmen seeking customers. At any moment the number of newcomers was large and their attachments to the community slight. Hence when they hit town, there was always some liveliness. After exhausting the cities' museums and libraries, sailors and teamsters would find other things to do. In the eighteenth and nineteenth century, transients comprised a significant portion of those who engaged in rioting and civil disorders.

In addition to being young, rapidly growing, and basically commercial, American cities also had very loose social structures. Unlike the Old World, they had no traditional ruling group, class lines were constantly shifting, and new blood was persistently pumped into these urban societies. One could say that up until the last part of the nineteenth century, mercantile leaders dominated municipal government; but even that commercial leadership changed continually. Later, immigrant groups shared high offices in municipal affairs, thus underlining the shifting nature of the social structure of most cities. Within this looseness there was always a great deal of mobility, with people rising and falling in status not only from generation to generation but within a single lifetime.

This fluid social system contrasted sharply with other, older societies, yet it contained a high incidence of disorder. For it depended on the constant acceptance of new people and new groups to places of influence and importance, and their incorporation into the system on a basis of equality with others. This acceptance was only grudgingly conceded, and often only after some abrasive episodes. The American social structure thus had a large capacity to absorb revolutionary tensions and avoid convulsive upheavals. But it also bred minor social skirmishes which were not always orderly. It is significant that in the pre-Civil War South, where slavery created a more traditional social structure, there was less rioting and civil disorder than in the North (though one ought not underestimate the individual violence against the slave built into institutional bondage).

The American social structure was also unique because it was composed not only of conventional classes, but also of different ethnic, religious, and racial groups. They had at once an internal cohesion that came from a common background and a shared American experience and also a sense of sharp differences with other groups, especially with the country's older stock. These groups, the Negro excepted, were initially both part of the system and yet outside of it. The resultant friction, with the newcomers pressing for acceptance and older groups striving for continued supremacy, was a fruitful source of disorder and often violence. Since it was in the city that these groups were thrown together, became aware of their differences, and struggled for survival and advancement, it would be on the streets rather than on the countryside that the social guerrilla warfare would take place.

If the internal controls in the American social structure were loose, the external controls were weak. The cities inherited no system of police control adequate to the numbers or to the rapid increase of the urban centers. The modern police force is the creation of the twentieth century; the establishment of a genuinely professional system is historically a very recent thing. Throughout the eighteenth and nineteenth centuries, the force was small, untrained, poorly paid, and part of the political system. In case of any sizable disorder, it was hopelessly inadequate; and rioters sometimes routed the constabulary in the first confrontation. Josiah Quincy, for example, in Boston in the 1820's had to organize and arm the teamsters to reestablish the authority of the city in the streets. Many prudent officials simply kept out of the way until the worst was over. In New York's draft riots, to use another instance, the mayor wandered down to see what the disturbance was all about and nearly got trampled in the melee.

Moreover, since some of the rioting was political, the partisanship of the police led official force to be applied against one group, or protection to be withheld from another. And with every turnover in the mayor's office, a substantial and often a complete change occurred in the police. In Atlanta, for instance, even where there was only one party, each faction had its own men in blue ready to take over with the changes in political fortunes. In some places where the state played a role in local police appointments, the mayor might even be deprived of any control at all for the peace of the city. In New York in the 1850's there was an awkward moment when there were two police forces—the Municipals and the Metropolitans—each the instrument of opposing parties. At the point of the most massive confusion, one group tried to arrest the mayor and an armed struggle took place between the two competing forces.

The evolution toward more effective and professional forces was painfully slow. Separating the police from patronage proved difficult, the introduction of civil service qualifications and protection came only in this century, and the development of modern professional departments came even later. To be sure, after a crisis—rioting, widescale looting, or a crime wave—there would be a demand for reform, but the enthusiasm was seldom sustained and conditions returned quickly to normal. The ultimate safety of the city thus resided with outside forces that could be brought in when local police could not handle the mob.

These general considerations account in large part for the high level of disorder and violence in American cities over the past three centuries. The larger disorders, however, often stemmed from particular problems and specific conditions and resulted in widescale bloodshed and destruction. Though these situations varied from place to place and time to time, it is perhaps useful to divide them into a few categories. Some rioting was clearly political, surrounding party struggles and often occasioned by legislation or an election. Some sprang from group conflict, especially the resistance to the rising influence of immigrant groups. Still others stemmed from labor disputes. And the largest, then as now, came out of race conflict. A few examples of each will convey some of their intensity and scale.

Politics has always been a fruitful source of disorders. Indeed, one of the most significant groups of riots surrounded the colonial break with Great Britain. In Boston, Samuel Adams and other radical leaders led the otherwise directionless brawling and gang warfare around the docks and wharfs into a political roughhouse against British policy. The Stamp Tax Riots, the Townshend Duty Riots and, of course, the Boston Massacre were all part of an organized and concerted campaign by colonial leaders. The urban middle classes initially tolerated the disorders because they too opposed certain aspects of British policy; they later pulled back when they felt that radical leadership was carrying resistance beyond their own limited objectives. Yet for nearly a decade, rioting and organized physical force were a part of the politics of the colonies.

This use of violence in politics was not as jarring to the eighteenth century as it would be today. Rioting had been a common occurrence, and not always among the underclasses. As early as 1721, Cotton Mather, one of Boston's most prominent citizens, could bewail in his diary the exploits of his "miserable, miserable, miserable son Increase. The wretch has brought himself under public infamy and trouble by bearing a part in a Night-riot, with some detestable rakes in town." Two decades later, Philadelphia witnessed widespread disorder during its "Bloody Election" in 1742. The widening of the franchise greatly reduced the resort to violence in politics, for the ballot provided an alternative to rock-throwing and physical force on important public questions. Yet historically the stakes of political victory have always been high enough to induce some to employ force and mob action.

Attacks against immigrants comprise another theme in the story. Often the assault by older, more established groups was against individuals or small groups. But in other cases it would be more general. The string of riots against Catholic churches and convents in the nineteenth century, for example, represented an attack on the symbols of the rise of the new groups. In the summer of 1834, for instance, a Charlestown (Mass.) convent was sacked and burned to the ground; scuffles against the Irish occurred in various parts of nearby Boston; some Irish houses were set afire. At the outset, the episode was carefully managed; then it got out of hand as teen-age toughs got into action. Nor was this an isolated incident.

Characteristic of this period too was the resistance to the incorporation of immigrants into the public life of the city. "Bloody Monday" in Louisville in 1855 will perhaps serve as an illustration. Local politicians had become worried about the increase of the immigrant (German and Irish) vote. The Know-Nothings (a party built in part on anti-immigrant attitudes) determined to keep foreign-born residents away from the polls on election day. There was only a single voting place for every ward, thus numbering only eight in the entire city. Know-Nothing followers rose at dawn and occupied the booths early in the morning. They admitted their own reliables, but physically barred their opponents. The preelection campaign had been tense and bitter with threats of force flying across party lines. By this time some on each side had armed themselves. Someone fired a shot, and the rioting commenced. When it was all through, "Quinn's Row," an Irish section, had been gutted, stores looted, and Catholic churches damaged. A newspaper which was accused of stirring up feeling only barely escaped destruction. The atrocities against the Irish were especially brutal with many being beaten and shot. Indeed, some of the wounded were thrown back into the flames of ignited buildings. Estimates of the dead range from fourteen to one hundred, though historians have generally accepted (albeit with slim evidence) twenty-two as the number killed.

Labor disputes have also often spawned widescale disorder. Indeed, at the turn of the century, Winston Churchill, already a keen student of American affairs, observed that the United States had the most violent industrial relations of any western country. Most of this rioting started with a confrontation of labor and management over the right to organize, or wages and hours, or working conditions. A large portion of these strikes found the workers in a vulnerable if not helpless position, a fact which has led most historians to come down on the side of labor in these early disputes. Moreover, unlike the disorders we have previously discussed, these were nationwide in scope—occurring at widely scattered points. There was no question of their being directed since a union was usually involved and it had some control over local action throughout the country. Yet the violence was seldom uniform or confined to strikers. It might flare up in Chicago and Pittsburgh, while St. Louis, where the issues would be the same, might remain quiescent. Often, as in the case of the railroad strike of 1877, the damage to life and property was large. In the Homestead lockout alone, 35 were killed and the damage (in 1892 dollars) ran to $2,500,000. In the 1930's the organizing steel, auto, and rubber unions brought a recrudescence of this earlier grisly process.

The "Great Strike of 1877" conveys most of the elements of this kind of violent labor dispute. One historian of the episode observes that "frequently, law and order broke down in major rail centers across the land;

what was regarded as 'domestic insurrection' and 'rebellion' took over."
He calculated that "millions of dollars worth of property were destroyed, hundreds of persons were injured, and scores killed in rioting
in pitched battles with law enforcement officials." The cities affected
stretched across the country, including Baltimore, Pittsburgh, Philadelphia, Buffalo, Cleveland, Toledo, Columbus, Cincinnati, Louisville, In-
dianapolis, Chicago, St. Louis, Kansas City, Omaha, and San Francisco.

The strike began on July 16, 1877, in the midst of hard times when
railroads tried to adapt to the depression by cutting wages 10 percent.
The workers' resistance began in Martinsburg, West Virginia, where the
militia called to the strike scene soon fraternized with the workers.
President Rutherford Hayes then dispatched troops to the town and no
bloodshed occurred. But in Baltimore, the situation turned ugly and
spilled over into violence on July 20. It is hard to know how many genuine strikers were involved and how much of the fighting and damage
was done by others. At any rate, eleven people were killed and twenty
wounded and the president again dispatched troops to the troubled area.
After these eruptions, the riots spread elsewhere. One historian describes the subsequent disorders as "undirected, unplanned, and unman-
aged save by impromptu leaders." "Everywhere," he continued, "but especially in Baltimore, Pittsburgh, and Chicago, the striking trainmen
were promptly joined by throngs of excitement-seeking adolescents, by
the idle, the unemployed, the merely curious and the malicious."

Pittsburgh suffered the worst. As trouble first threatened, the governor called up the local militia whose members very quickly began to
fraternize with the strikers as the latter took over the trains. The governor then called for troops from Philadelphia. In the furious clash that
resulted, sixteen soldiers and fifty rioters were killed. "For two days
Pittsburgh was ruled by mobs," one account asserts, "which burned,
looted, and pillaged to their heart's content, and attacked savagely all
who resisted them. Finally the riot died out into harmlessness. The city
was left in ruins." In the last stages, however, the same historian observed that "the rioting had little or no connection with the strike, and
few strikers were included in the mobs." In addition to the lives lost,
property destroyed included 500 freight cars, 104 locomotives, and 39
buildings.

The strike reached Chicago on July 23. Men left the job and large
crowds began to collect. By nightfall, the city was paralyzed. Police
were dispatched to disperse the throng and in the first clash they fired
into the crowd, killing seven and wounding twenty. The militia arrived

and citizens' groups began to arm. The superintendent of police estimated that there were 20,000 armed men in Chicago by the second day.
On the 26th the United States Army arrived. At 16th Street, 350 police
faced a mob of about 6,000 and after an hour's battle at least twelve
died and two score or more were seriously wounded. Like most riots,
the point of origin and the purpose of the strike were soon forgotten.
Indeed, an astute student of the event asserts that "practically none of
the rioting may be fairly ascribed to the strikers." Rather, he asserts,
"the disturbances were mainly caused by roughs, idlers, unemployed
persons, and the criminal element. A surprisingly large percentage of
the mobs was composed of women and young boys, and these elements
were at the same time the most destructive and the hardest for the police to disperse." He adds, however, that the blame was not one-sided:
"It seems also that a good deal of the disturbance was precipitated by
the rough tactics of the police."

The Pullman strike in Chicago almost twenty years later also contained most of the familiar elements of a riot growing out of a labor
dispute. It, too, stemmed from a wage reduction in the middle of a depression. On May 11, 1894, the strike began in a quiet and orderly
fashion. As the gap between the workers and the Pullman Company
deepened, the American Railway Union called for a general boycott of
sleeping cars. A federal court, however, issued an injunction against the
boycott to ensure the movement of mail. On July 4 federal troops arrived in Chicago. Until that time a labor historian observed that "there
had been little violence in Chicago proper. Some acts of sabotage had
occurred and there had been occasional demonstrations but the police
had effectively controlled the latter."

Now the temper of the episode changed. Crowds roamed over the
tracks "pushing over freight cars, setting a few of them on fire, and otherwise blocking the movement of trains. Switches were thrown, signal
lights changed, and trains stoned—much of the trouble caused by half-
grown boys who seemed to welcome the opportunity for excitement and
deviltry." Furthermore, "a large proportion of women and children"
mingled in a crowd that reached 10,000. Adding to the incendiary possibilities was an "abnormally large group of hoodlums, tramps, and
semicriminals, some of whom had been attracted to Chicago by the Co-
lumbian Exposition and left stranded by the depression." "In the movement of the mobs," the same historian continues, "there was seldom any
purpose or leadership. Most of the destruction was done wantonly and
without premeditation."

July 6 was the day of the greatest property destruction. A reporter from the *Inter Ocean* described the scene at the height of the frenzy. "From this moving mass of shouting rioters squads of a dozen or two departed, running towards the yards with fire brands in their hands. They looked in the gloaming like specters, their lighted torches bobbing about like will-o'-the-wisps. Soon from all parts of the yard flames shot up and billows of fire rolled over the cars, covering them with the red glow of destruction. The spectacle was a grand one. . . . Before the cars were fired those filled with any cargoes were looted. . . . The people were bold, shameless, and eager in their robbery. . . . It was pandemonium let loose, the fire leaping along for miles, and the men and women became drunk on their excess." By nightfall 700 cars had been destroyed. The next day clashes between the crowd and a hastily organized militia left four more dead and twenty wounded. In all, in three chaotic days, thirteen people had been killed, fifty-three seriously wounded, several hundred more hurt, and incalculable property damage done, not to mention money lost in wages and railroad earnings. One estimate fixes the total at $80,000,000.

Of all the sources of civil disorder, however, none has been more persistent than race. Whether in the North or South, whether before or after the Civil War, whether nineteenth or twentieth century, this question has been at the root of more physical violence than any other. There had been some sporadic slave uprisings before emancipation, the largest being the Nat Turner rebellion in 1831. But most which moved from plot to action occurred on the countryside rather than in the cities. Yet even the fear of a slave insurrection took its toll; in 1822, for instance, Charleston, South Carolina, officials, acting on tips and rumors, hanged thirty-seven Negroes and deported many more for an alleged plot to capture and burn the city. Seven years later, in a free state, whites invaded Cincinnati's "Little Africa" and burned and killed and ultimately drove half the colored residents from town. In the same period mobs also assaulted abolitionists, sometimes killing, otherwise sacking buildings and destroying printing presses.

Even the New York City riot against the draft in 1863 took an ugly racial twist before it had run its course. The events themselves arose out of the unpopularity of the draft and the federal government's call for more men as Lee headed into Pennsylvania. The situation was further complicated by a crisis in the police department as a result of the conflicting claims of command by a Republican mayor and a Democratic governor. The rioting broke out July 13 and the first target was the provost marshal's office. Within a short time 700 people ransacked the building and then set it afire. The crowd would not let the firemen into the area and soon the whole block lay gutted. Later the mob began to spill over into the Negro area where many blacks were attacked and some killed.

The police were helpless as the riot spread. The few clashes with the mob saw the police retreat; the crowd wandered about almost at will. Political leaders did not want to take the consequences for action against the mob, and soon it started to head toward the business district. Slowly the police reorganized, by Tuesday they began to win engagements with the rioters, and in a little while they were able to confine the action to the original area. The mobs were, however, better armed and organized and gave a good account of themselves in pitched battle. On the third day federal troops arrived and the control swung over to the authorities and quiet was restored. But in three days the casualties ran to at least seventy-four dead and many times that number wounded. The property damage was never accurately added up, but claims against the county exceeded $1,500,000 by 1865.

Emancipation freed the Negro from bondage, but it did not grant him either equality or immunity from white aggression. From the New Orleans riot of 1866, through the long list of racial disorders to the end of World War II, with datelines running through Atlanta, Springfield, East St. Louis, Washington, Chicago, Mobile, Beaumont, Detroit, and Harlem, something of the depth of the crisis and the vulnerability of American cities to racial disorders is revealed. These riots were on a large scale, involved many deaths, millions of dollars of property damage, and left behind deep scars which have never been fully erased. Most of these riots involved the resort to outside military help for containment; all exposed the thinness of the internal and external controls within our urban society.

In fact, the war had scarcely ended before racial violence erupted in New Orleans. The occasion of the outbreak was a Negro procession to an assembly hall where a debate over enfranchising the blacks was to take place. There was some jostling during the march and a shot fired; but it was only after the arrival at the convention that police and special troops charged the black crowd. In the ensuing struggle Negroes were finally routed, but guns, bricks, and stones were generously used. Many Negroes fell on the spot; others were pursued and killed on the streets trying to escape. Later General Sheridan reported that "at least ninetenths of the casualties were perpetrated by the police and citizens by stabbing and smashing in the heads of many who had already been wounded or killed by policemen." Moreover, he added that it was not just a riot but "an absolute massacre by the police . . . a murder which the mayor and police . . . perpetrated without the shadow of necessity." Federal troops arrived in the afternoon, took possession of the city, and restored order. But thirty-four Negroes and four whites were already dead and over 200 injured.

Smaller places, even in the North, were also affected with racial disorder. In August 1908, for instance, a three-day riot took its toll in Springfield, Illinois. The Negro population in the capital had grown significantly in the years after the turn of the century, and some whites sensed a political and economic threat. On August 13 a white woman claimed she had been violated by a Negro. An arrest was made and the newspapers carried an inflammatory account of the episode. Crowds gathered around the jail demanding the imprisoned black, but the sheriff quickly transferred the accused and another Negro to a prison in a nearby town without letting the public know. "The crowd outside was in an ugly mood," writes a historian of the riot, "the sun had raised tempers; many of the crowd had missed their dinners, which added to their irritation; and the authorities seemed to be taking no heed of their presence. By sundown the crowd had become an ugly mob."

The first target of the rioters was a restaurant whose proprietor presumably had driven the prisoners from jail. Within a few minutes his place was a shambles. They then headed for the Negro section. Here they hit homes and businesses either owned by or catering to Negroes. White owners quickly put white handkerchiefs in their windows to show their race; their stores were left untouched. A Negro was found in his shop and was summarily lynched. Others were dragged from streetcars and beaten. On the 15th the first of 5,000 National Guardsmen reached Springfield; very quickly the mob broke up and the town returned to normal. The death toll reached six (four whites and two blacks); the property damage was significant. As a result of the attack, Springfield's Negro population left the city in large numbers hoping to find better conditions elsewhere, especially in Chicago.

A decade later the depredations in East St. Louis were much larger, with the riot claiming the lives of thirty-nine Negroes and nine whites. The best student of this episode points out that the 1917 riot was not a sudden explosion but resulted from "threats to the security of whites brought on by the Negroes' gains in economic, political, and social status; Negro resentment of the attempts to 'kick him back in his place';

and the weakness of the external forces of constraint—the city government, especially the police department." Tensions were raised when the Aluminum Ore Company replaced white strikers with Negro workers. In addition to these factors, race had become a political issue in the previous year when the Democrats accused Republicans of "colonizing" Negroes to swing the election in East St. Louis. The kindling seemed only to lack the match.

On May 28 came the fire. A Central Trades and Labor Union delegation formally requested the mayor to stop the immigration of Negroes to East St. Louis. As the men were leaving City Hall they heard a story that a Negro robber had accidentally shot a white man during a holdup. In a few minutes the word spread; rumor replaced fact. Now it was said the shooting was intentional; that a white woman was insulted; that two white girls were shot. By this time 3,000 people had congregated and the cry for vengeance went up. Mobs ran downtown beating every Negro in sight. Some were dragged off the streetcars, others chased down. The police refused to act except to take the injured to hospitals and to disarm Negroes. The next day the National Guard arrived to restore order.

Two days later the governor withdrew troops although tension remained high. Scattered episodes broke the peace, but no sustained violence developed. The press, however, continued to emphasize Negro crimes and a skirmish broke out between white pickets and black workers at the Aluminum Company. Then on July 1 some whites drove through the main Negro neighborhood firing into homes. The colored residents armed themselves, and when a similar car, this time carrying a plainclothesman and reporter, went down the street the blacks riddled the passing auto with gunshot.

The next day was the worst. At about 10:00 A.M. a Negro was shot on the main street and a new riot was underway. A historian of the event asserted that the area along Collinsville Avenue between Broadway and Illinois Avenue became a "bloody half mile" for three or four hours. "Streetcars were stopped: Negroes, without regard to age or sex, were pulled off and stoned, clubbed and kicked. . . . By the early afternoon, when several Negroes were beaten and lay bloodied in the street, mob leaders calmly shot and killed them. After victims were placed in an ambulance, there was cheering and handclapping." Others headed for the Negro section and set fire to homes on the edge of the neighborhood. By midnight the South End was in flames and black residents began to flee the city. In addition to the dead, the injured were counted in the hundreds and over 300 buildings were destroyed.

Two summers later the racial virus felled Chicago. Once again, mounting tension had accompanied the migration of blacks to the city. The numbers jumped from 44,000 in 1910 to 109,000 ten years later. Though the job market remained good, housing was tight. Black neighborhoods could expand only at the expense of white ones, and everywhere the transition areas were filled with trouble. Between July 1, 1917, and March 1921, there had been fifty-eight bombings of Negro houses. Recreational areas also witnessed continual racial conflict.

The riot itself began on Sunday, July 27, on the 29th Street Beach. There had been some stone-throwing and sporadic fighting. Then a Negro boy, who had been swimming in the Negro section, drifted into the white area and drowned. What happened is not certain, but the young blacks charged he had been hit by stones and demanded the arrest of a white. The police refused, but then arrested a Negro at a white request. When the Negroes attacked the police, the riot was on. News of the events on the beach spread to the rest of the city. Sunday's casualties were two dead and fifty wounded. On Monday, attacks were made on Negroes coming from work; in the evening cars drove through black neighborhoods with whites shooting from the windows. Negroes retaliated by sniping at any white who entered the Black Belt. Monday's accounting found twenty killed and hundreds wounded. Tuesday's list was shorter, a handful dead, 139 injured. Wednesday saw a further waning and a reduction in losses in life and property. Rain began to fall; the mayor finally called in the state militia. After nearly a week, a city which witnessed lawlessness and warfare quieted down and began to assess the implications of the grisly week.

The Detroit riot of 1943 perhaps illustrates the range of racial disorders that broke out sporadically during World War II. There had been earlier conflicts in Mobile, Los Angeles, and Beaumont, Texas, and there would be some others later in the year. No doubt the war with its built-in anxieties and accelerated residential mobility accounted for the timing of these outbreaks. In Detroit, the wider problem was compounded by serious local questions. The Negro population in the city had risen sharply, with over 50,000 arriving in the fifteen months before the riot; this followed a historical increase of substantial proportions which saw black residents increase from 40,000 to 120,000 in the single decade between 1920 and 1930. These newcomers put immense pressures on the housing market, and neighborhood turnover at the edge of the ghetto bred bitterness and sometimes violence; importantly, too, recreational areas became centers of racial abrasiveness.

On June 20 the riot broke out on Belle Isle, a recreational spot used by both races, but predominantly by Negroes. Fistfighting on a modest basis soon escalated, and quickly a rising level of violence spread across the city. The Negro ghetto—ironically called Paradise Valley—saw the first wave of looting and bloodshed. The area was, as its historians have described it, "spattered with blood and littered with broken glass and ruined merchandise. The black mob had spared a few shops owned by Negroes who had chalked COLORED on their windows. But almost every store in the ghetto owned by a white had been smashed open and ransacked." Other observers noted that "crudely organized gangs of Negro hoodlums began to operate more openly. Some looters destroyed property as if they had gone berserk."

The next morning saw the violence widen. The police declared the situation out of control and the mayor asked for state troops. Even this force was ineffective, and finally the governor asked for federal help. Peace returned under the protection of 6,000 men; and the troops remained for more than a week. The dead numbered thirty-four, twenty-five Negroes and nine whites; property damage exceeded $2,000,000. And almost as costly was the bitterness, fear, and hate that became part of the city's legacy.

This survey covers only some of the larger and more important disorders. Others reached significant proportions but do not fall into convenient categories. For example, in the eighteenth century a protest against inoculation led to widespread rioting; mobs hit the streets to punish men who snatched bodies for medical training. In times of economic hardship, "bread riots" resulted in ransacking stores; crowds often physically drove away officials seeking to evict tenants who could not pay rent.

Two disorders perhaps best suggest the miscellaneous and unpredictable character of this process. One is so bizarre that only its bloody climax has kept it from being among the most amusing episodes of American history. It revolved around the rivalry between two prominent actors, the American Edwin Forrest, and William Macready, an Englishman. Both were appearing in *Macbeth* on the same night, May 7, 1849, in New York City. Some rowdies, mostly Irish, decided to break up the Macready performance, and when he appeared on the stage they set up such a din that he had to retire. After apologies and assurances, the English visitor agreed to try again on May 9. This time, the police extracted the troublemakers and Macready finished the play. But a mob gathered outside after the final curtain and refused to disperse on police orders. Finally, the edgy guard fired into the crowd, killing twenty-five persons.

Another dimension is revealed in the events of March 1884, in Cincinnati. They came in the midst of what the city's best historian has dubbed "the decade of disorder." Two men were tried for the murder of a white livery man. Though one was Negro and the other German, race does not seem to be at issue. When the German was found guilty of only manslaughter, a public campaign developed to avenge the decision. A meeting at Music Hall, called by some leading citizens, attracted 10,000 people, mostly from the middle class, who were worried about a general breakdown of law and order and thought the light sentence would encourage criminals. The speakers attacked the jury and the administration of justice in the city. Afterward a crowd headed for the jail. In the first encounter with the police, casualties were light. But the next day the militia moved in and hostility climbed. Finally, a pitched battle ensued in which fifty-four died and over 200 were wounded. Thus, a meeting called to bring about law and order wound up ironically in disorder and violence.

This survey, which is only suggestive and not exhaustive, indicates that widescale violence and disorder have been man's companion in the American city from the outset. Some generalizations out of this experience might be useful in the light of the present crisis.

First, most of the rioting has usually been either limited in objective or essentially sporadic. This, of course, is not true of racial conflict, but it is characteristic of a large number of the others. In those, the event was discreet; there was no immediate violent sequel. After a labor dispute, especially if it involved union recognition, bitterness and hate persisted, but there was no annual recurrence of the violence. Attacks on immigrants seldom produced an encore, though they might have an analogue in some other city in the same month or year. In short, though there was enough disorder and mob action to create a persistent anxiety, the incidence of overt conflict was irregular enough to preclude predictions of the next "long hot summer."

Second, this sporadic quality meant that the postmortems were usually short and shallow. It was characteristic to note the large number of teenagers who got involved; to attribute the disruption to outsiders (especially anarchists and communists); to place a large responsibility on the newspapers for carrying inflammatory information and spreading unfounded rumors; to blame the local police for incompetence, for prejudice, for intervening too soon or too late, or at all. After any episode, the urge to fix blame led to all kinds of analyses. The historian of the 1877 railroad violence, for example, observes that "the riots were variously ascribed to avarice, the expulsion of the Bible from the schools, the protective tariff, the demonetization of silver, the absence of General Grant, the circulation of the *Chicago Times* and original sin." Others saw in it a labor conspiracy or a communist plot. And the *New York Times* could assert after the Chicago riot in 1919 that: "The outbreak of race riots in Chicago, following so closely on those reported from Washington, shows clearly enough that the thing is not sporadic (but has) . . . intelligent direction and management . . . (It seems probable) that the Bolshevist agitation has been extended among the Negroes."

There were a few exceptions. After the Chicago race riot, for example, an Illinois commission studied the event in some detail and also examined the deteriorating relations between the races which lay at the bottom. Others occasionally probed beneath the surface at the deeper causes of unrest. But most cities preferred to forget as soon as possible and hoped for an end to any further disorder. Indeed, even the trials that followed most riots show how rapidly popular interest faded. The number of people brought to trial was small and the number of convictions extremely small; and, most significantly, there was little clamor for sterner measures.

Third, if the analyses of the riots were shallow, the response of cities and legislatures was not very effective. After quiet was restored, there would almost certainly be a discussion of police reform. Customarily little came of it, though in Louisville the utter ineptness and obvious partisanship of the police in 1855 prompted a change from an elective to an appointive force. Legislation usually emphasized control. As early as 1721, Massachusetts responded to growing disorders with an antiriot act. And Chicago's Commercial Club made land available for Fort Sheridan after the events of 1877 in order to have troops nearby for the protection of the city. But most cities rocked back to normal as soon as the tremors died down.

Fourth, there was a general tendency to rely increasingly on outside forces for containing riots. Partly, this resulted from the fact that in labor disorders local police and even state militia fraternized with strikers and could not be counted on to discipline the workers. Partly, it was due to inadequate numbers in the face of the magnitude of the problem. Partly, too, it stemmed from the fact that sometimes the police were involved in the fighting at the outset and seemed a part of the riot. The first resort was usually to state troops; but they were often unsatisfactory, and the call for federal assistance became more frequent.

Fifth, while it is hard to assess, it seems that the bitterness engendered by riots and disorders was not necessarily irreparable. Though the immigrants suffered a good deal at the hands of nativists, it did not slow down for long the process of their incorporation into American life. Ten years after Louisville's "Bloody Monday" the city had a German mayor. The trade unions survived the assaults of the nineteenth century and a reduction of tension characterized the period between 1900 and the depression (with the notable exception of the postwar flare-ups). And after the violence of the 1930's, labor and management learned to conduct their differences, indeed their strikes, with reduced bloodshed and violence. It is not susceptible of proof, but it seems that the fury of the defeated in these battles exacted a price on the victors that ultimately not only protected the group but won respect, however grudgingly, from the public.

At any rate the old sources of major disorders, race excepted, no longer physically agitate American society. It has been many years since violence has been a significant factor in city elections and no widespread disorders have even accompanied campaigning. Immigrant groups have now become so incorporated in American life that they are not easily visible and their election to high offices, indeed the highest, signals a muting of old hostilities. Even when people organized on a large scale against minority groups—such as the Americans' Protective Association in the 1890's or the Ku Klux Klan in the 1920's—they have seldom been able to create major riots or disorders. And though sporadic violence occasionally breaks out in a labor dispute, what is most remarkable is the continuance of the strike as a weapon of industrial relations with so little resort to force. Even the destruction of property during a conflict has ceased to be an expectation.

Sixth, race riots were almost always different from other kinds of disorders. Their roots went deeper; they broke out with increasing frequency; and their intensity mounted rather than declined. And between major disorders the incidence of small-scale violence was always high. Until recently, the Negro has largely been the object of the riot. This was true not only in northern cities where changing residential patterns bred violence, but also in the South where this question was less pervasive. In these riots the lines were sharply drawn against the Negroes, the force was applied heavily against them, and the casualties were always highest among blacks.

Finally, in historical perspective, if racial discord be removed, the level of large-scale disorder and violence is less ominous today than it has been during much of the past. As we have seen, those problems which have produced serious eruptions in the past no longer do so. In fact, if one were to plot a graph, omitting the racial dimension, violence and disorder over a long period have been reduced. Indeed, what makes the recent rioting so alarming is that it breaks so much with this historical trend and upsets common expectations.

Yet to leave out race is to omit the most important dimension of the present crisis. For it is race that is at the heart of the present discord. Some analysts, of course, have argued that the problem is class and they emphasize the numbers caught in widening poverty, and the frustration and envy of poor people in a society of growing affluence. Yet it is important to observe that though 68 percent of the poor people in this country are white, the disorders stem almost wholly from black ghettos. The marginal participation of a few whites in Detroit and elsewhere scarcely dilutes the racial foundations of these disorders.

In fact, a historical survey of disorders only highlights the unique character of the present problem. For the experience of the Negro in American cities has been quite different from any other group. And it is in just this difference that the crisis lies. Because the black ghetto is unlike any ghettos that our cities have known before. Of course, other groups knew the ghetto experience too. As newcomers to the city they huddled in the downtown areas where they met unspeakably congested conditions, occupied the worst housing, got the poorest education, toiled, if fortunate enough to have a job, at the most menial tasks, endured high crime rates, and knew every facet of deprivation.

The urban slum had never been a very pleasant place, and it was tolerable only if the residents, or most of them, thought there was a way out. To American immigrants generally the ghetto was a temporary stage in their incorporation into American society. Even some of the first generation escaped, and the second and third generation moved out of the slums in very large numbers. Soon they were dispersed around the metropolitan area, in the suburbs as well as the pleasant residential city wards. Those who remained behind in the old neighborhoods did so because they chose to, not because they had to. By this process, millions of people from numberless countries, of different national and religious backgrounds made their way into the main current of American life.

It was expected that Negroes would undergo the same process when they came to the city. Thus, there was little surprise in the first generation when black newcomers did indeed find their way into the central city, the historic staging grounds for the last and poorest arrivals. But the ghetto proved to be not temporary. Instead of colored residents dispersing in the second generation, the ghetto simply expanded. Block by block it oozed out into the nearby white neighborhoods. Far from breaking up, the ghetto grew. In fact, housing became more segregated every year; and the walls around it appeared higher all the time. What had been temporary for other groups seemed permanent to Negroes.

The growth of the Negro ghetto created conditions which had not existed before and which generated the explosiveness of our present situation. In the first place, the middle-class Negroes became embittered at their exclusion from the decent white neighborhoods of the city and suburbs. These people, after all, had done what society expected of them; they got their education, training, jobs, and income. Yet even so they were deprived of that essential symbol of American success—the home in a neighborhood of their own choosing where conditions would be more pleasant and schools better for their children. For this group, now about a third of all urban Negroes, the exclusion seemed especially cruel and harsh.

As a result they comprise now a growingly alienated and embittered group. The middle-class blacks are now beginning to turn their attention to organizing among the poor in the worst parts of the ghetto. Their children make up the cadres of black militants in the colleges. And when the riots come, they tolerate the activity even though they usually do not themselves participate. In short, the fact of the ghetto forces them to identify with race, not class. When the riots break, they feel a bond with the rioters, not white society. This had not been true of the emerging middle class of any immigrant group before.

If the ghetto has new consequences for the middle class, it also creates a new situation among the poorer residents of the ghetto, especially for the young people. They feel increasingly that there is no hope for the future. For other groups growing up in the ghetto there had always been visible evidence that it was possible to escape. Many before had done it; and everyone knew it. This produced the expectation that hard work, proper behavior, some schooling, and a touch of luck would make it possible to get ahead. But the young Negro grows up in increasing despair. He asks himself—"What if I do all they say I should—stay in school, get my training, find a job, accumulate some money—I'll still be living here, still excluded from the outside world and its rewards." He asks himself, "What's the use?" Thus, the hopelessness, despair, and frustration mount and the temperature of the ghetto rises. Nearly all our poverty programs are stumbling on the problem of motivation. To climb out of the slum has always required more-than-average incentive. Yet this is precisely what is lacking in the ghetto youth.

The present riots stem from the peculiar problems of the ghetto. By confining Negroes to the ghetto we have deprived them of the chance to enter American society on the same terms as other groups before them. And they know increasingly that this exclusion is not a function of education, training, or income. Rather, it springs from the color of their skin. This is what makes race the explosive question of our time; this is what endangers the tranquillity of our cities. In the historian's perspective, until the ghetto begins to break, until the Negro middle class can move over this demeaning barrier, until the young people can see Negroes living where their resources will carry them and hence get credible evidence of equality, the summers will remain long and hot.

14. BLACK VIOLENCE IN THE TWENTIETH CENTURY: A STUDY IN RHETORIC AND RETALIATION
August Meier/Elliott Rudwick

F O R most Americans, the increasingly overt talk of retaliatory violence among Negro militants and the outbreaks in the urban ghettos over recent summers signify something new and different in the history of Negro protest. Actually, retaliatory violence has never been entirely absent from Negro thinking. Moreover, advocacy of retaliatory violence and actual instances of it have tended to increase during periods of heightened Negro protest activity.

Thus the past decade of rising Negro militance has been no stranger to the advocacy of retaliatory violence. For example, as far back as

From Ted Robert Gurr and Hugh Davis Graham, eds., *The History of Violence in America* (New York: Bantam Books, 1969), pp. 399–411.

1959, Robert F. Williams, at the time president of the Monroe, North Carolina, branch of the NAACP, came to public attention when the Union County Superior Court acquitted two white men of brutal assaults on two Negro women, but sentenced a mentally retarded Negro to imprisonment as a result of an argument he had with a white woman. Williams angrily told a reporter, "We cannot take these people who do us injustice to the court, and it becomes necessary to punish them ourselves. If it's necessary to stop lynching with lynching, then we must be willing to resort to that method." The NAACP dismissed Williams as branch president, but he remained a leader of Monroe's working-class Negroes, who for several years had been using guns to protect their homes from white Klansmen. In 1961, falsely charged with kidnaping a white couple, he fled from the country. Williams became the most famous of that group of militants existing at the fringe of the civil rights movement, who in their complete alienation from American society articulated a revolutionary synthesis of nationalism and Marxism.[1] From his place of exile in Havana, Cuba, Williams undertook the publication of a monthly newsletter, *The Crusader*. In a typical issue, he declared:

Our only logical and successful answer is to meet organized and massive violence with massive and organized violence. . . . The weapons of defense employed by Afro–American freedom fighters must consist of a poor man's arsenal. . . . Molotov cocktails, lye, or acid bombs [made by injecting lye or acid in the metal end of light bulbs] can be used extensively. During the night hours such weapons, thrown from roof tops, will make the streets impossible for racist cops to patrol. . . . Yes, a minority war of self-defense can succeed.[2]

Subsequently Williams was named chairman in exile of an organization known as the Revolutionary Action Movement (RAM),[3] a tiny group of college-educated people in a few major northern cities, some of whose members have been recently charged with plotting the murder of Roy Wilkins and Whitney Young.

Williams, RAM, and the better known Black Muslims [4] were on the fringes of the Negro protest of the early 1960's. More recently violence and the propaganda for violence have moved closer to the center of the race relations stage. Well over 200 riots have occurred since the summer of 1964. The incendiary statements of the Rap Browns and the Stokely Carmichaels became familiar TV and newspaper fare for millions of white Americans. The Oakland, California, Black Panthers and other local groups espousing a nationalist and revolutionary rhetoric thrived and received national publicity. As has been often pointed out, there is no evidence that the race riots of the 1960's have any direct relations to the preachings of Williams, of these various groups, even of the SNCC advocates of armed rebellion and guerrilla warfare. Yet both the statements of these ideologists and the spontaneous actions of the masses have much in common. For both are the product of the frustrations resulting from the growing disparity between the Negroes' status in American society and the rapidly rising expectations induced by the civil rights revolution and its earlier successes.

Historically, this doctrine of retaliatory violence has taken various forms. Some have advocated self-defense against a specific attack. Others have called for revolutionary violence. There are also those who hopefully predicted a general race war in which Negroes would emerge victorious. Though seldom articulated for white ears, and only rarely appearing in print, thoughts of violent retaliation against whites have been quite common. For example, Ralph Bunche, in preparing a memorandum for Gunnar Myrdal's *American Dilemma* in 1940, noted that "there are Negroes, too, who, fed up with frustration of their life here, see no hope and express an angry desire 'to shoot their way out of it.' I have on many occasions heard Negroes exclaim, 'Just give us machine guns and we'll blow the lid off the whole damn business.' " [5]

In surveying the history of race relations during the twentieth century, it is evident that there have been two major periods of upsurge both in overt discussion by Negro intellectuals concerning the desirability of violent retaliation against white oppressors, and also in dramatic incidents of actual social violence committed by ordinary Negro citizens. One was the period during and immediately after World War I. The second has been the period of the current civil rights revolution.

W. E. B. Du Bois, the noted protest leader and a founder of the NAACP, occasionally advocated retaliatory violence, and somewhat more often predicted intense racial warfare in which Negroes would be the victors. In 1916, inspired by the Irish Rebellion, in an editorial in the NAACP's official organ, *The Crisis,* he admonished Negro youth to stop spouting platitudes of accommodation and remember that no people ever achieved their liberation without an armed struggle. He said that "war is hell, but there are things worse than hell, as every Negro knows." [6] Amid the violence and repression that Negroes experienced in the postwar world, Du Bois declared that the holocaust of World War I was "nothing to compare with that fight for freedom which black and brown and yellow men must and will make unless their oppression and humiliation and insult at the hands of the White World cease." [7]

Other intellectuals reflected this restless mood. The postwar years were the era of the militant, race-conscious New Negro of the urban North, an intellectual type who rejected the gradualism and conciliation of his ancestors. The tone of the New Negro was recorded by Claude McKay, who in 1921 wrote his well-known poem, "If We Must Die": "If we must die/let it not be like hogs; hunted and penned in an accursed spot!/. . . . If we must die, oh, let us nobly die/dying but fighting back." A. Philip Randolph, editor of the militant socialist monthly, *The Messenger,* organizer of the Brotherhood of Sleeping Car Porters, and later leader of the March on Washington Movements of 1941 and 1963, also advocated physical resistance to white mobs. He observed that

Anglo-Saxon jurisprudence recognizes the law of self-defense. . . . The black man has no rights which will be respected unless the black man forces that respect. . . . We are consequently urging Negroes and other oppressed groups concerned with lynching or mob violence to act upon the recognized and accepted law of self-defense. [8]

The legality of retaliatory violent self-defense was asserted not only by A. Philip Randolph, but also by the NAACP, which Randolph regarded as a moderate, if not futile organization, wedded to the interest of the Negro middle class. In 1925, half a dozen years after *The Messenger* article, the NAACP secured the acquittal of Dr. Ossian Sweet and his family. The Sweets were Detroit Negroes who had moved into a white neighborhood, and fired on a stone-throwing mob in front of their home, killing one white man and wounding another. [9] More than a quarter of a century later, at the time of the Robert Williams episode, the NAACP, in clarifying its position, reiterated the stand that "the NAACP has never condoned mob violence but it firmly supports the right of Negroes individually and collectively to defend their person, their homes, and their property from attack. This position has always been the policy of the NAACP." [10] The views of intellectuals like Du Bois, McKay, and Randolph during World War I and the early postwar years paralleled instances of Negro retaliatory violence which actually triggered some of the major riots of the period.

The East St. Louis riot of 1917, the bloodiest in the twentieth century, was precipitated in July when Negroes, having been waylaid and beaten repeatedly by white gangs, shot into a police car and killed two white detectives. On the darkened street a Negro mob of 50 to 100 evidently mistook the Ford squad car for the Ford automobile containing white "joyriders" who had shot up Negro homes earlier in the evening. The following morning the riot began.[11]

In Houston, several weeks later, about 100 Negro soldiers broke into an Army ammunition storage room and marched on the city's police station. The troops, mostly northerners, were avenging an incident which occurred earlier in the day, when a white policeman used force in arresting a Negro woman and then beat up a Negro soldier attempting to intervene. A Negro provost guard was pistol whipped and shot at for asking the policeman about the wounded soldier. Even before these events, the Negro soldiers nursed a hatred for Houston policemen, who had attempted to enforce streetcar segregation, frequently used the term "nigger," and officiously patrolled the Negro ghetto. The Houston riot was not only unusual because it involved Negro soldiers, but also because white persons constituted most of the fatalities.[12]

By 1919 there was evidence that the Negro masses were prepared to fight back in many parts of the country, even in the Deep South. In an unpublished report to the NAACP board of directors, a staff member, traveling in Tennessee and Mississippi during early 1919, noted that "bloody conflicts impended in a number of southern cities." Perry Howard, the leading colored attorney in Jackson, and R. R. Church, the wealthy Memphis politician, both reported that Negroes were armed and prepared to defend themselves from mob violence. Howard detailed an incident in which armed Negroes had prevented a white policeman from arresting a Negro who had become involved in a fight with two white soldiers after they had slapped a colored girl. In Memphis, R. R. Church, fearing armed conflict, privately advised the city's mayor that "the Negroes would not make trouble unless they were attacked, but in that event they were prepared to defend themselves." [13]

The Chicago race riot of 1919 grew out of Negro resentment of exclusion from a bathing beach dominated by whites. One Sunday, while Negroes and whites scuffled on the beach, a colored teen-ager drowned after being attacked in the swimming area. That attack was the most recent of a long series of assaults against Negroes. A white policeman not only refused to arrest a white man allegedly involved in the drowning, but actually attempted to arrest one of the two complaining Negroes. The officer was mobbed and soon the rioting was underway.[14]

The Elaine, Arkansas, riot of 1919 was precipitated when two white law officers shot into a Negro church, and the Negroes returned the fire, causing one death. The white planters in the area, already angered because Negro cotton pickers were seeking to unionize and obtain an increase in their share-cropping wages, embarked upon a massive Negro hunt to put the black peons "in their place." [15]

The Tulsa riot of 1921 originated when a crowd of armed Negroes assembled before the courthouse to protest the possible lynching of a Negro who had just been arrested for allegedly attacking a white girl. The Negroes shot at white police and civilians who attempted to disperse them.[16]

In each of these conflagrations, the typical pattern was initial Negro retaliation to white acts of persecution and violence, and white perception of this resistance as an organized, premeditated conspiracy to "take over," thus unleashing the massive armed power of white mobs and police. In the southern communities, Negro resistance tended to collapse early in the riots. After the church incident in the rural Elaine area, most Negroes passively accepted the planters' armed attacks on their homes. At Tulsa, Negroes retreated from the courthouse to the ghetto, and throughout the night held off by gunfire the assaults of white mobs. But after daybreak, many Negroes fled or surrendered before the white onslaught burned down much of the ghetto.[17] One exception to this pattern was the Washington riot of 1919, where it appears that Negroes did not retaliate until the third and last day of the riot.[18]

Negro resistance generally lasted longer in northern riots than in southern ones, but even in East St. Louis and Chicago the death toll told the story: in East St. Louis, nine whites and at least thirty-nine Negroes were killed. In Chicago, fifteen whites and twenty-three Negroes lost their lives. Negroes attacked a small number of whites found in the ghetto or on its fringes. Negro fatalities mainly occurred when victims were trapped in white-dominated downtown areas or residential sections. Negroes were also attacked on the edges of their neighborhood in a boundary zone separating a colored residential district from a lower-class white area.[19] In the face of overwhelming white numerical superiority, many armed Negroes fled from their homes, leaving guns and ammunition behind. In East St. Louis, for example, there was a constant rattle of small explosions when fire enveloped a small colored residential district. Perhaps psychological factors contributed to the terrified inactivity of some Negroes. Despite the wish to meet fire with fire, over the years they had become so demoralized by white supremacy and race discrimination that effective armed defense could exist only in the realm of psychological fantasy.

During World War II, the most important race riot erupted in 1943 in Detroit, where nine whites and twenty-five Negroes were killed. In many respects the riot exhibited a pattern similar to East St. Louis and Chicago. The precipitating incident involved an attack on whites at the Belle Isle Amusement Park by several Negro teenagers who, a few days earlier, had been ejected from the white-controlled Eastwood Park. In the mounting tension at Belle Isle, many fights between Negroes and whites broke out, and the violence spread to the Negro ghetto where patrons at a night club were urged to "take care of a bunch of whites who killed a colored woman and her baby at Belle Isle." Although there had been no fatalities at the park, the night club emptied and revengeful Negroes stoned passing cars driven by whites. They began smashing windows on the ghetto's main business street, where the mob's major attention was directed to destroying and looting white-owned businesses.[20]

It was this symbolic destruction of "whitey" through his property that gave the Detroit holocaust the characteristic of what we may call the "new-style" race riot. It may be noted that in all the riots discussed above, there were direct clashes between Negroes and whites, and the major part of the violence was perpetrated by the white mobs. The riot pattern since the summer of 1964, however, has involved Negro aggression mainly against white-owned property, not white people. This "new-style" riot first appeared in Harlem in 1935 and 1943.[21] The modern riot does not involve white mobs at all, and policemen or guardsmen constitute most of the relatively small number of white casualties.

One can identify perhaps two major factors responsible for this contrast between the old-style and the new-style riot. One is the relatively marked shift in the climate of race relations in this country over the past generation. On the one hand, whites have become, on the whole, more sensitive to the Negro's plight, more receptive toward Negro demands, and less punitive in their response to Negro aggression. The black masses, on the other hand, have raised their expectations markedly and, disillusioned by the relatively slow pace of social change which has left the underprivileged urban Negro of the North scarcely, if at all, better off than he was ten or fifteen years ago, have become more restless and militant than before.

In the second place, there is an ecological factor. From South to North, the migration of the World War I period was a mere drop in the bucket compared to what it later became. The migration to the North in each of the decades since 1940 has been equal to or greater than the migration of the whole thirty-year period, 1910 to 1940. At the same time, owing to the Supreme Court's outlawing of the restrictive covenant in 1948, and the tearing down of the older slums through urban renewal, the Negro population has been dispersed over a wider area, thus accentuating the trend toward the development of vast ghettos. Indeed, compared to the enormous ghettos of today, the Negro residential areas of the World War I period were mere enclaves. Today, of course, Negroes are close to becoming a majority in several of the major American cities.

The character of American race riots has been markedly affected by these demographic changes. Even if white mobs were to form, they would be unable to attack and burn down the Negro residential areas; even in the nineteenth- and early-twentieth-century riots, white mobs did not usually dare to invade the larger Negro sections, and destroyed only the smaller areas of Negro concentration. Nor, since the Negroes are such a large share of the population of the central city areas, would white mobs today be in a position to chase, beat, and kill isolated Negroes on downtown streets. More important, from the Negroes' point of view, the large-scale ghettos provide a relatively safe place for the destruction and looting of white-owned property; it is impossible for local police forces to guard business property in the far-flung ghettos; even State Police and federal troops find themselves in hostile territory where it is difficult to chase down rioters beyond the principal thoroughfares.

It is notable that during the twentieth century, both the overt discussion of the advisability of violent retaliation on the part of Negroes and also actual incidents of violence were prominent in the years during and after World War I, and again during the 1960's. While there have been significant differences between the outbreaks characteristic of each era, there have been also important similarities. In both periods retaliatory violence accompanied a heightened militancy among American Negroes —a militancy described as the "New Negro" in the years after World War I, and described in the 1960's with the phrase, "the Negro Revolt." In neither case was retaliatory violence the major tactic, or the central thrust, but in both periods it was a significant subordinate theme. However, in both periods a major factor leading Negroes to advocate or adopt such a tactic was the gap between Negro aspiration and objective status. The rapid escalation of the aspirations of the Negro masses who shared Martin Luther King's "dream" and identify vicariously with the success of the civil rights revolution, while their own economic, housing, and educational opportunities have not improved, is a phenomenon of such frequent comment that it requires no elaboration here.

A comparable situation occurred during and shortly after World War I. The agitation of the recently founded NAACP, whose membership doubled in 1918–1919, the propaganda of fighting a war to make the world safe for democracy, and especially the great Negro migration to the northern cities which southern peasants and workers viewed as a promised land, all created new hopes for the fulfillment of age-old dreams, while Negro soldiers who had served in France returned with new expectations. But the Negro's new hopes collided with increasing white hostility. Northern Negroes assigned to southern army camps met indignities unknown at home. They rioted at Houston and came so close to rioting in Spartanburg, South Carolina, that the army hastily shipped them overseas. In the northern cities like East St. Louis and Chicago, Negroes found not a promised land, but overcrowded ghettos and hostile white workers who feared Negro competition for their jobs. The Ku Klux Klan was revived beginning in 1915, and grew rapidly in the North and South after the war ended. By 1919 economic opportunities plummeted as factories converted to peacetime operations. For a while Negroes resisted, protested, fought back, in the South as well as the North; but the superior might of the whites proved overpowering and the southern Negroes retreated into old paths of accommodation where they generally remained until the momentous events of the past decade.

There has been no systematic research on Negro advocacy of violence prior to World War I, but the available evidence supports the thesis that increased overt expression of this tendency accompanies peaks in other kinds of protest activity. For example, it appears likely that Negro resistance to white rioters was minimal in the riots at the turn of the century—at Wilmington, North Carolina, in 1898, and at New Orleans, Akron, and New York in 1900 [22]—which took place in a period when the sentiment of accommodation to white supremacy, epitomized by Booker T. Washington, was in the ascendency.

Again, during the antebellum period, one can cite two noted cases of incendiary statements urging Negroes to revolt—*David Walker's Appeal* of 1829, and Rev. Henry Highland Garnet's suppressed *Address to the Slaves of the United States of America,* delivered at the national Negro convention of 1843.[23] Both coincided with periods of rising militant protest activity on the part of the northern free Negroes. *Walker's Appeal* appeared on the eve of the beginning of the Negro convention movement, and at the time of intensified Negro opposition to the expatriation plans of the American Colonization Society.[24] Garnet's speech was made at a time when free Negro leaders were disturbed at the prejudiced attitudes of white abolitionists who refused to concern themselves with obtaining rights for the free people of color, or to allow Negroes to participate in the inner circles of the leadership of the antislavery societies. Consequently they had revived the Negro national convention movement which had been inactive since 1836. (Garnet's speech was also in part a product of disillusionment with the lack of actual progress being made by the antislavery societies toward achieving abolition.)

We lack any careful analysis of race riots during the nineteenth century. Some certainly were pogrom-like affairs, in which the Negroes were so thoroughly terrorized from the beginning that they failed to fight back. (Perhaps the Draft Riots and some of the Reconstruction riots as in Mississippi in 1876 were of this sort.) Yet other riots were characterized by some degree of Negro retaliatory violence, such as the Snow Hill riot in Providence, in 1831, and the Cincinnati riots of 1841. Both appear to have been, like the Chicago and East St. Louis riots, the climaxes to a series of interracial altercations. In the Providence riot, a mob of about 100 white sailors and citizens advanced on a small Negro section; a Negro shot a sailor dead, and within a half hour a large mob descended upon the neighborhood, damaging many houses.[25] In the Cincinnati riot, a pitched battle was fought on the streets; the blacks had enough guns and ammunition to fire into the mob such a volley that it was twice repulsed. Only when the mob secured an iron six-pounder and hauled it to the place of combat and fired on the Negroes were the latter forced to retreat, permitting the rioters to hold sway for two days without interference from the authorities.[26] A careful study of interracial violence during Reconstruction will undoubtedly produce evidence of comparable situations. These riots occurred at a time of high Negro expectations and self-assertiveness, and seem to have been characterized by a significant amount of fighting back on the part of Negroes.

One period of marked and rising Negro militance, however, was not accompanied by a significant increase in manifestations of Negro retaliatory violence. This was the one following World War II. Indeed, World War II itself witnessed far less Negro violence than did World War I. The reason for this would appear to be that the 1940's and early 1950's were years of gradually improving Negro status, and a period in which the expectations of the masses did not greatly outrun the actual improvements being made. In fact, from 1941 until the mid-1950's the relative position of the Negro workers, as compared to the white wage earners, was generally improving and it was not until the recession of 1954–1955, for example, that the Black Muslims, with their rhetoric of race hatred and retaliatory violence, began to expand rapidly.

It would appear that both in the World War I period and today—and indeed during the antebellum era and at other times when manifestations of violence came to the fore—there has been a strong element of fantasy in Negro discussion and efforts concerning violent retaliation. Robert Williams talked of Molotov cocktails and snarling up traffic as devices for a largely poverty-stricken ethnic minority to engineer a revolution. The Black Muslims talk of violence, but the talk seems to function as a psychological safety valve; by preaching separation, they in effect accommodate to the American social order and place racial warfare off in the future when Allah in his time will destroy the whites and usher in an era of black domination. Similarly, in view of population statistics and power distribution in American society, Du Bois and others who have spoken of the inevitability of racial warfare and Negro victory in such a struggle were engaging in wishful prophecies. And Negroes have been nothing if not realistic. The patterns of Negro behavior in riots demonstrate this. In earlier times, as already indicated, those who bought guns in anticipation of the day when self-defense would be necessary usually did not retaliate. And Negro attacks on whites occurred mainly in the early stages of the riots before the full extent of anger and power and sadism of the white mobs became evident.

Negroes of the World War I era resisted white insults and attacks only as long as they had hopes of being successful in the resistance. It should be emphasized that one of the remarkable things about the riots since 1964, in spite of their having been marked by particular resentment at police brutality, is the fact that Negro destruction was aimed at white-owned property, not white lives, even after National Guardsmen and policemen killed scores of Negroes. And in those cases where retaliatory violence has been attempted, Negroes have retreated in the face of massive white armed force. Economically impoverished Negroes press as far as they realistically can; and one reason for the explosions of recent years has been the awareness that whites are to some degree in retreat, that white mobs in the North no longer organize to attack, and that to a large degree the frustrated Negroes in slums like Watts, Detroit, Washington, or Newark, can get away with acts of destruction.

It is impossible, of course, to make any foolproof predictions for the future. Yet, judging by past experience and present conditions, it is our view that, despite all the rhetoric of engineering a social revolution through armed rebellion and guerrilla warfare, of planned invasions of downtown business districts and white suburbs, the kind of violence we are likely to witness will, at most, continue to be the sort of outbreaks against the property of white businessmen such as those we have witnessed in recent years. The advocacy and use of violence as a deliberate program for solving the problems of racial discrimination remain thus far, at least, in the realm of fantasy; and there they are likely to remain.

NOTES

1. For accounts, see Julian Mayfield, "Challenge to Negro Leadership," *Commentary* 31 (April 1961): 197–305; "The Robert Williams Case," *Crisis* 66, (June–July–August–September 1959): 325–329, 409–410: Robert F. Williams, *Negroes with Guns* (New York: Marzani & Munsell, 1962).

2. *Crusader* 5 (May–June 1964): 5–6.

3. See the RAM publication *Black America* (Summer–Fall 1965); *Crusader* (March 1965).

4. C. Eric Lincoln, *The Black Muslims in America* (Boston: Beacon Press, 1961), p. 205.

5. Ralph Bunche, "Conceptions and Ideologies of the Negro Problem," Memorandum prepared for the Carnegie–Myrdal Study of the Negro in America (1940), p. 161.

6. *Crisis* 12 (August 1916): 166–167; *Crisis* 13 (December 1916): 63.

7. W. E. B. Du Bois, *Darkwater* (New York, 1920), p. 49.

8. A. Philip Randolph, "How to Stop Lynching," *Messenger* 3 (April 1919): 8–9.

9. Walter White, "The Sweet Trial," *Crisis* 31 (January 1926): 125–129.

10. "The Robert Williams Case," *Crisis* 66 (June–July 1959): 327.

11. Elliott M. Rudwick, *Race Riot at East St. Louis* (Cleveland and New York: Meridian Books, 1968), pp. 38–39.

12. Edgar A. Schuler, "The Houston Race Riot, 1917," *Journal of Negro History* 29 (October 1944): 300–338.

13. *NAACP Board Minutes,* Secretary's Report for June 1919.

14. *The Negro in Chicago* (Chicago, 1922), pp. 4–5.

15. *Crisis* 19 (December 1919): 56–62.

16. Allen Grimshaw, *A Study in Social Violence: Urban Race Riots in the U.S.* Ph. D. diss. (University of Pennsylvania, 1959): 42–47.

17. *Ibid.*

18. Constance M. Green, *Washington, Capital City, 1879–1950* (Princeton, N.J.: Princeton University Press, 1962), pp. 266–267; John Hope Franklin, *From Slavery to Freedom* (New York: Knopf, 1947), p. 473; *New York Times,* 20–22 July 1919.

19. Rudwick, *op. cit.,* pp. 226–227; *Negro in Chicago, op. cit.,* pp. 5–10.

20. Alfred McClung Lee and Norman D. Humphrey, *Race Riot* (New York, 1943), pp. 26–30.

21. Roi Ottley, *New World A-Coming* (Boston: Beacon Press, 1943), pp. 151–152; Harold Orlansky, *The Harlem Riot: A Study in Mass Frustration* (New York, 1943), pp. 56, 14–15; *New York Age,* 30 March 1935 and 7 August 1943.

22. In the New York riot, however, the precipitating incident was a physical

altercation between a white policeman and a Negro; see Gilbert Osofsky, *Harlem: The Making of a Ghetto* (New York: Harper & Row, 1966), pp. 46–52.

23. Herbert Aptheker, *A Documentary History of the Negro People in the United States* (New York: Citadel, 1951), pp. 93–97, 226–233.

24. Founded in 1817 by a group of prominent white Americans, the American Colonization Society officially encouraged colonization as a means of furthering the cause of antislavery. Most Negroes, even most of those who themselves at one time or another advocated emigration to Africa or the Caribbean as the only solution for the Negro's hopeless situation in the United States, denounced the society as a cloak for those attempting to protest slavery by deporting free Negroes.

25. Irving H. Bartlett, "The Free Negro in Providence, Rhode Island," *Negro History Bulletin* 14 (December 1950): 54.

26. Carter G. Woodson, "The Negroes of Cincinnati Prior to the Civil War," *Journal of Negro History* 1 (January 1916): 13–15.

Institutional Crisis and the Growth of Conflict

📓 15. WHITE INSTITUTIONS
AND BLACK RAGE
David Boesel/Richard Berk/Eugene Groves/
Bettye K. Eidson/Peter H. Rossi

FIVE summers of black rebellion have made it clear that the
United States is facing a crisis of proportions not seen since the Great
Depression. And one of the root causes of this crisis, it has also become
clear, is the performance of white institutions, especially those in the
ghetto. Some of these institutions—police and retail stores, for example
—have done much to antagonize Negroes; others, such as welfare departments and black political organizations, have tried to help and have
failed.

Why have these white institutions helped engender black rage? One
way to find out might be to study the attitudes of the men working for
them—to discover what their personnel think about the racial crisis itself, about their own responsibilities, about the work they are doing.
Therefore, at the request of the National Advisory Commission on
Civil Disorders (the riot commission), we at Johns Hopkins University
visited fifteen northern cities and questioned men and women working
for six different institutional groups: major employers, retail merchants,
teachers, welfare workers, political workers (all Negro), and policemen.
All of the people we questioned, except the employers, work in the
ghetto, and are rank-and-file employees—the cop on the beat, the social
caseworker, and so on.

From *Trans-action* 6, no. 5 (March 1969): 24–31.

Employers' Social Responsibility

The "employers" we questioned were the managers or personnel officers of the ten institutions in each city that employed the most people, as well as an additional twenty managers or personnel officers of the next 100 institutions. As such, they represented the most economically progressive institutions in America. And in their employment policies we could see how some of America's dominant corporate institutions impinge on the everyday lives of urban Negroes.

Businessmen are in business to make a profit. Seldom do they run their enterprises for social objectives. But since it is fashionable these days, most of the managers and personnel officers we interviewed (86 percent, in fact) accepted the proposition that they "have a social responsibility to make strong efforts to provide employment for Negroes and other minority groups." This assertion, however, is contradicted by unemployment in the Negro community today, as well as by the hiring policies of the firms themselves.

Businessmen, as a whole, do not exhibit openly racist attitudes. Their position might best be described as one of "optimistic denial"—the gentlemanly white racism evident in a tacit, but often unwitting, acceptance of institutional practices that subordinate or exclude Negroes. One aspect of this optimistic denial is a nonrecognition of the seriousness of the problems that face black people. Only 21 percent of our sample thought that unemployment was a very serious problem in the nation's cities, yet 26 percent considered air pollution very serious and 31 percent considered traffic very serious. The employers' perspective is based upon their limited experience with blacks, and that experience does not give them a realistic picture of the condition of Negroes in this country. Employers don't even think that racial discrimination has much to do with the Negroes' plight; a majority (57 percent) felt that Negroes are treated at least as well as other people of the same income, and an additional 6 percent felt that Negroes are treated *better* than any other part of the population.

This optimistic denial on the part of employers ("things really aren't that bad for Negroes") is often combined with a negative image of Negroes as employees. Half of those employers interviewed (51 percent) said that Negroes are likely to have higher rates of absenteeism than whites, so that hiring many of them would probably upset production schedules. Almost a third thought that, because Negro crime rates are generally higher than white crime rates, hiring many Negroes could lead to increased theft and vandalism in their companies. About a fifth (22 percent) thought that hiring Negroes might bring "agitators and trouble-makers" into their companies, and another one-fifth feared that production costs might rise because Negroes supposedly do not take orders well.

The employer's views may reflect not only traditional white prejudices, but also some occasional experience he himself has had with Negroes. Such experiences, however, may stem as much from the employer's own practices and misconceptions as from imputed cultural habits of Negroes. As Elliott Liebow observed in his study of Negro street-corner men (*Talley's Corner*), blacks have learned to cope with life by treating menial, low-status, degrading jobs in the same way that the jobs treat them—with benign nonconcern.

Most of the employers believe that Negroes lack the preparation for anything but menial jobs. A full 83 percent said that few Negroes are qualified for professional jobs, and 69 percent thought that few are qualified for skilled positions. When it comes to unskilled jobs, of course, only 23 percent of the employers held this view. The employers seem to share a widespread assumption—one frequently used as a cover for racism—that for historical and environmental reasons Negroes have been disabled to such an extent as to make them uncompetitive in a highly competitive society. And while it is certainly true that black people have suffered from a lack of educational and other opportunities, this line of thinking—especially among whites—has a tendency to blame the past and the ghetto environment for what is perceived as Negro incompetence, thus diverting attention from *present* institutional practices. So, many employers have developed a rhetoric of concern about upgrading the so-called "hard-core unemployed" in lieu of changing their employment policies.

To a considerable extent our respondents' assessment of Negro job qualifications reflects company policy, for the criteria used in hiring skilled and professional workers tend to exclude Negroes. The criteria are (1) previous experience and (2) recommendations. It is evident that because Negroes are unlikely to have *had* previous experience in positions from which they have long been excluded, and because they are unlikely to have had much contact with people in the best position to recommend them, the criteria for "qualification" make it probable that employers will consider most Negroes unqualified.

NEGROES GET THE WORST JOBS

In short, the employers' aversion to taking risks (at least with people), reinforced by the pressure of labor unions and more general discriminatory patterns in society, means that Negroes usually get the worst jobs.

Thus, although Negroes make up 20 percent of the unskilled workers in these large corporations, they fill only a median of 1 percent of the professional positions and only 2 percent of the skilled positions. Moreover, the few Negroes in the higher positions are unevenly distributed among the corporations. Thirty-two percent of the companies don't report Negroes in professional positions, and 24 percent do not report any in skilled positions. If these companies are set aside, in the remaining companies the median percentage of Negroes in the two positions rises to 3 percent and 6 percent, respectively. Further, in these remaining companies an even-larger percentage (8 percent in both cases) of *current* positions are being filled by Negroes—which indicates, among other things, that a breakthrough has been accomplished in some companies, while in others Negro employment in the upper levels remains minimal or nonexistent.

Even among those companies that hire blacks for skilled jobs, a Negro applicant's chances of getting the job are only one-fourth as good as those of his white counterpart. For professional positions, the chances are more nearly equal: Negro applicants are about three-fourths as likely to get these jobs as are white applicants. It seems that Negroes have come closest to breaking in at the top (though across all firms only about 4 percent of the applicants for professional positions are Negro). The real stumbling-block to equal employment opportunities seems to be at the skilled level, and here it may be that union policies—and especially those of the craft unions—augment the employers' resistance to hiring Negroes for, and promoting Negroes to, skilled positions.

What do urban Negroes themselves think of employers' hiring practices? A survey of the same fifteen cities by Angus Campbell and Howard Schuman, for the riot commission, indicates that one-third (34 percent) of the Negro men interviewed reported having been refused jobs because of racial discrimination, and 72 percent believed that some or many other black applicants are turned down for the same reason. Almost as many (68 percent) think that some or many black people miss out on promotions because of prejudice. And even when companies do hire Negroes (presumably in professional positions), this is interpreted as tokenism: 77 percent of the black respondents thought that Negroes are hired by big companies for show purposes.

The companies we studied, which have little contact with the ghetto, are very different from the other institutions in our survey, whose contact with the ghetto is direct and immediate. The corporations are also up to date, well financed, and innovative, while the white institutions inside the ghetto are outdated, underfinanced, and overloaded. In historical terms, the institutions in the ghetto represent another era of thought and organization.

Ghetto Merchants

The slum merchants illustrate the tendency of ghetto institutions to hark back to earlier forms. While large corporations cooperate with one another and with the government to exert substantial control over their market, the ghetto merchant still functions in the realm of traditional laissez-faire. He is likely to be a small operator, economically marginal and with almost no ability to control his market. His main advantage over the more efficient, modern retailer is his restricted competition, for the ghetto provides a captive market. The difficulty that many blacks have in getting transportation out of the ghetto, combined with a lack of experience in comparative shopping, seems to give the local merchant a competitive aid he sorely needs to survive against the lower prices and better goods sold in other areas of the city.

The merchants in our study also illustrate the free-enterprise character of ghetto merchandising. They run very small operations—grocery stores, restaurants, clothing and liquor stores, and so on, averaging a little over three employees per business. Almost half of them (45 percent) find it difficult to "keep up with their competition" (competition mainly *within* the ghetto). Since there are almost no requirements for becoming a merchant, this group is the most heterogeneous of all those studied. They have the widest age range (from 17 through 80), the highest percentage of immigrants (15 percent), and the lowest educational levels (only 16 percent finished college).

Again in contrast to the large corporations, the ghetto merchant must live with the harsh day-to-day realities of violence and poverty. His attitudes toward Negroes, different in degree from those of the employers, are at least partly a function of his objective evaluations of his customers.

Running a business in a ghetto means facing special kinds of "overhead." Theft is an especially worrisome problem for the merchants; respondents mentioned it more frequently than any other problem. There is, of course, some basis in fact for their concern. According to the riot commission, inventory losses—ordinarily under 2 percent of sales—may be twice as great in high-crime areas (most of which are in ghettos). And for these small businesses such losses may cut substantially into a slender margin of profit.

Thus it is not surprising that, of all the occupational groups interviewed in this study, the retail merchants were among the most likely to consider Negroes violent and criminal. For example, 61 percent said that Negroes are more likely to steal than whites, and 50 percent believed that Negroes are more likely to pass bad checks. No wonder, then, that black customers may encounter unusual surveillance and suspicion when they shop.

Less understandable is the ghetto merchant's apparent ignorance of the plight of ghetto blacks. Thus, 75 percent believe that blacks get medical treatment that is equal to or better than what whites get. A majority think that Negroes are not discriminated against with regard to treatment by the police, recreation facilities, and so forth. Logically enough, 51 percent of the merchants feel that Negroes are making too many demands. This percentage is the second-highest measured (the police were the least sympathetic). So the merchants (like all other groups in the survey except the black politicians) are inclined to emphasize perceived defects in the black community as a major problem in their dealings with Negroes.

The shaky economic position of the merchants, their suspicion of their Negro customers, and the high "overhead" of doing business in the ghetto (because of theft, vandalism, bad credit risks) lead many merchants to sell inferior merchandise at higher prices—and to resort to other stratagems for getting money out of their customers. To elicit responses from the merchants on such delicate matters, we drew up a series of very indirect questions. The responses we obtained, though they no doubt understate the extent to which ghetto merchants provide a poor dollar value per unit of goods, are nevertheless revealing. For example, we asked the merchants to recommend various ways of "keeping up with business competition." Some 44 percent said that you should offer extra services; over a third (36 percent) said you should raise prices to cover unusually high overhead; and the same number (36 percent) said that you should buy "bargain" goods at lower prices, then sell them at regular prices. (To a small merchant, "bargain goods" ordinarily means "seconds," or slightly spoiled merchandise, because he doesn't do enough volume to gain real discounts from a wholesaler.) A smaller but still significant segment (12 percent) said that one should "bargain the selling price with each customer and take whatever breaks you can get."

The Campbell–Schuman study indicates that 56 percent of the Negroes interviewed felt that they had been overcharged in neighborhood stores (24 percent said often); 42 percent felt that they had been sold spoiled or inferior goods (13 percent said often). Given the number of ghetto stores a customer may visit every week, these data are entirely compatible with ours. Since one-third of the merchants indicated that they were not averse to buying "bargain" goods for sale in their stores, it is understandable that 42 percent of the Negroes in these areas should say that at one time or another they have been sold inferior merchandise.

It is also understandable that during the recent civil disorders many Negroes, unable to affect merchants by routine methods, struck directly at the stores, looting and burning them.

Teachers in the Ghetto

Just as ghetto merchants are in a backwater of the economy, ghetto schools are in a backwater of the educational system, experimental efforts in some cities notwithstanding.

Negroes, of course, are most likely to be served by outmoded and inadequate schools, a fact that the Coleman Report has documented in considerable detail. In metropolitan regions of the Northeast, for example, 40 percent of the Negro pupils at the secondary level attended schools in buildings over forty years old, but only 15 percent of the whites did; the average number of pupils per room was thirty-five for Negros but twenty-eight for whites.

The teachers covered in our survey (half of whom were Negro) taught in ghetto schools at all levels. Surprisingly, 88 percent said that they were satisfied with their jobs. Their rate of leaving, however, was not consistent with this. Half of the teachers had been in their present schools for no more than four years. Breaking the figures down year by year, we find that the largest percentage (17 percent) had been there only one year. In addition, the teachers' rate of leaving increased dramatically after they had taught for five years.

While the teachers thought that education was a major problem for the cities and especially for the ghettos, they did not think that ghetto schools were a source of the difficulty. A solid majority, comparing their own schools with others in the city, thought that theirs were average, above average, or superior in seven out of eight categories. The high quality of the teaching staff, so rated by 84 percent of the respondents, was rivaled only by the high quality of the textbooks (again 84 percent). The one doubtful area, according to the teachers, was the physical plant, which seemed to them to be just barely competitive; in this respect, 44 percent considered their own schools below average or inferior.

The teachers have less confidence in their students than in themselves or their schools. On the one hand, they strongly reject the view that in ghetto schools education is sacrificed to the sheer need for order: 85 percent said it was not true that pupils in their schools were uneducable, and that teachers could do little more than maintain discipline. On the other hand, the teachers as a group could not agree that their students were as educable as they might be. There was little consensus on whether their pupils were "about average" in interest and ability: 28 percent thought that their pupils were; 41 percent thought it was partially true that they were; and 31 percent thought it was not true. But the teachers had less difficulty agreeing that their students were *not* "above average in ability and . . . generally cooperative with teachers." Agreeing on this were 59 percent of the teachers, with another 33 percent in the middle.

The real problem with education in the ghetto, as the teachers see it, is the ghetto itself. The teachers have their own version of the "Negro disability" thesis: the "cultural deprivation" theory holds that the reason for bad education in the ghetto is the student's environment rather than the schools. (See "How Teachers Learn to Help Children Fail," by Estelle Fuchs, *Trans-action,* September 1968.) Asked to name the major problems facing their schools, the teachers most frequently mentioned community apathy; the second most-mentioned problem, a derivation of the first, was an alleged lack of preparation and motivation in the students. Fifty-nine percent of the teachers agreed to some extent that "many communities provide such a terrible environment for the pupils that education doesn't do much good in the end."

Such views are no doubt detrimental to education in the ghetto, for they imply a decided fatalism as far as teaching is concerned. If the students are deficient—improperly motivated, distracted, and so on—and if the cause of this deficiency lies in the ghetto rather than in the schools themselves, then there is little reason for a teacher to exert herself to set high standards for her students.

There is considerable question, however, whether the students in ghetto schools are as distracted as the teachers think. Events in the last few years indicate that the schools, especially the high schools and the junior high schools, are one of the strongest focuses of the current black rebellion. The student strike at Detroit's Northern High School in 1966, for example, was cohesive and well organized. A boycott by some 2,300 students, directed against a repressive school administration, lasted over two weeks and resulted in the dismissal of the principal and the formation of a committee, including students, to investigate school conditions. The ferment in the ghetto schools across the country is also leading to the formation of permanent and independent black students' groups, such as the Modern Strivers in Washington, D.C.'s Eastern High, intent on promoting black solidarity and bringing about changes in the educational system. In light of such developments, there is reason to think that the teachers in the survey have overestimated the corrosive effects of the ghetto environment on students—and underestimated the schools' responsibility for the state of education in the ghetto.

Social Workers and the Welfare Establishment

Public welfare is another area in which old ideas have been perpetuated beyond their time. The roots of the present welfare structure lie in the New Deal legislation of the 1930's. The public assistance provisions of the Social Security Act were designed to give aid to the helpless and the noncompetitive: the aged, the blind, the "permanently and totally" disabled, and dependent children. The assumption was that the recipient, because of personal disabilities or inadequacies, could not make his way in life without outside help.

The New Deal also provided work (e.g., the W.P.A.) for the able-bodied who were assumed to be unemployed only temporarily. But as the Depression gave way to the war years and to the return of prosperity, the massive work programs for the able-bodied poor were discontinued, leaving only those programs that were premised on the notion of personal disability. To a considerable extent today's Negro poor have had to rely on the latter. Chief among these programs, of course, is Aid for Dependent Children, which has become a mainstay of welfare. And because of racial discrimination, especially in education and employment, a large part of the Negro population also experiences poverty as a permanent state.

While most of the social workers in our survey showed considerable sympathy with the Negro cause, they too felt that the root of the problem lay in weaknesses in the Negro community; and they saw their primary task as making up the supposed deficiency. A hefty majority of the respondents (78 percent) thought that a large part of their responsibility was to "teach the poor how to live"—rather than to provide the means for them to live as they like. Assuming disability, welfare has fostered dependency.

The social workers, however, are unique among the groups surveyed in that they are quite critical of their own institution. The average welfare worker is not entirely at one with the establishment for which she works. She is likely to be a college graduate who regards her job as transitional. And her lack of expertise has its advantages as well as its disadvantages, for it means that she can take a more straightforward view of the situations she is confronted with. She is not committed to bureaucracy as a way of life.

The disparity between the welfare establishment and the average welfare worker is evident in the latter's complaints about her job. The complaints she voices the most deal *not* with her clients, but with the welfare department itself and the problems of working within its present structure—the difficulty of getting things done, the red tape, the lack of adequate funds, and so on. Of the five most-mentioned difficulties of welfare work, three dealt with such intra-agency problems; the other two dealt with the living conditions of the poor.

There is a good deal of evidence to support the social worker's complaints. She complains, for example, that welfare agencies are understaffed. The survey indicates that an average caseload is 117 people, each client being visited about once a month for about fifty minutes. Even the most conscientious of caseworkers must be overwhelmed by such client-to-worker ratios.

As in the case of the schools, welfare has engendered a countervailing force among the very people it is supposed to serve. Welfare clients have become increasingly hostile to the traditional structure and philosophy of welfare departments and have formed themselves into an outspoken movement. The welfare rights movement at this stage has a dual purpose: to obtain a more nearly adequate living base for the clients, and to overload the system with demands, thus either forcing significant changes or clearing the way for new and more appropriate institutions.

Black Political Party Workers

Usually when segments of major social institutions become incapable of functioning adequately, the people whom the institutions are supposed to serve have recourse to politics. In the ghetto, however, the political machinery is no better off than the other institutions. Around the turn of the century Negroes began to carve out small niches for themselves in the politics of such cities as Chicago and New York. Had Negro political organizations developed along the same lines as those of white ethnic groups, they might today provide valuable leverage for the ghetto population. But this has not happened. For one thing, the decline of the big-city machine, and its replacement in many cities by "nonpolitical" reform governments supported by a growing middle class, began to close off a route traditionally open to minority groups. Second, black politicians have never been regarded as fullfledged political brokers by racist whites, and consequently the possibility of a Negro's becoming a powerful politician in a predominantly white city has been foreclosed (the recent election of Carl Stokes as mayor of Cleveland and Richard D. Hatcher, mayor of Gary, Indiana, would be exceptions). Whites have tended to put aside their differences when confronting Negro political efforts; to regard Negro demands, no matter how routine, as racial issues; and hence to severely limit the concessions made to black people.

Today the sphere of Negro politics is cramped and closely circumscribed. As Kenneth B. Clark has observed, most of the Negroes who have reached high public office have done so *not* within the context of Negro politics, but through competition in the larger society. In most cities Negro political organizations are outmoded and inadequate. Even if, as seems probable, more and more Negro mayors are elected, they will have to work within the antiquated structure of urban government, with sharply limited resources. Unless things change, the first Negro mayor of Newark, for example, will preside over a bankrupt city.

Our survey of Negro political workers in the fifteen cities documents the inadequacy of Negro politics—and the inadequacy of the larger system of urban politics. The political workers, understandably, strongly sympathize with the aspirations of other black people. As ghetto politicians, they deal with the demands and frustrations of other blacks day after day. Of all the groups surveyed, they were the most closely in touch with life in the ghetto. Most of them work in the middle and lower levels of municipal politics; they talk with about 75 voters each week. These political workers are, of course, acutely aware of the precipitous rise in the demands made by the black community. Most (93 percent) agreed that in the last few years people in their districts have become more determined to get what they want. The strongest impetus of this new determination comes from the younger blacks: 92 percent of the political workers agreed that "young people have become more militant." Only a slight majority, however (56 percent), said the same of middle-aged people.

Against the pressure of rising Negro demands, urban political organizations formed in other times and on other assumptions, attentive to other interests, and constrained by severely limited resources, find themselves unable to respond satisfactorily. A majority of the political workers, in evaluating a variety of services available to people in their districts, thought that all except two—telephone service and the fire department—were either poor or fair. Worst of the lot, according to the political workers, were recreation, police protection, and building inspection.

In the view of these respondents, the black community has no illusions about the ability of routine politics to meet its needs. While only 38 percent of the political workers thought that the people in their districts regarded their councilmen as friends fighting for them, 51 percent said that the people considered their councilmen "part of the city government which must be asked continually and repeatedly in order to get things done." (Since the political workers were probably talking about their fellow party members, their responses may have been more favorable than frank. A relatively high percentage of "don't know" responses supports this point.)

Almost all the Negro politicians said that they received various requests from the voters for help. Asked whether they could respond to these requests "almost always, usually, or just sometimes," the largest percentage (36 percent) chose "sometimes"—which, in context, is a way of saying "seldom." Another 31 percent said they "usually" could respond to such requests, and 19 percent said "almost always." Logically enough, 60 percent of the political workers agreed that in the last few years "people have become more fed up with the system, and are becoming unwilling to work with politicians." In effect, this is an admission that they as political workers, and the system of urban politics to which they devote themselves, are failing.

Police and the
Black Community

When economic and social institutions fail to provide the life-chances that a substantial part of a population wants, and when political institutions fail to provide a remedy, the aspirations of the people begin to spill over into forms of activity that the dominant society regards either as unacceptable or illegitimate—crime, vandalism, noncooperation, and various forms of political protest.

Robert M. Fogelson and Robert B. Hill, in the *Supplemental Studies* for the riot commission, have reported that 50 percent to 90 percent of the Negro males in ten cities studied had arrest records. Clearly, when the majority of men in a given population are defined as criminals—at least by the police—something more than "deviant" behavior is involved. In effect, ghetto residents—and especially the youth—and the police are in a state of subdued warfare. On the one hand, the cities are experiencing a massive and as yet inchoate social rising of the Negro population. On the other hand, the police—devoted to the racial status quo and inclined to overlook the niceties of mere law in their quest for law and order—have found a variety of means, both conventional and otherwise, for countering the aims of Negroes. In doing so, they are not only adhering to the norms of their institution, but also furthering their personal goals as well. The average policeman, recruited from a lower- or middle-class white background, frequently of "ethnic" origins, comes from a group whose social position is marginal and who feel most threatened by Negro advances.

The high arrest rate in the Negro community thus mirrors both the push of Negroes and the determined resistance of the police. As the conflict intensifies, the police are more and more losing authority in the eyes of black people; the young Negroes are especially defiant. Any type of contact between police and black people can quickly lead to a situation in which the policeman gives an order and the Negro either defies it or fails to show sufficient respect in obeying it. This in turn can lead to the Negro's arrest on a disorderly conduct charge or on a variety of other charges. (Disorderly conduct accounted for about 17 percent of the arrests in the Fogelson–Hill study.)

HARASSMENT TECHNIQUES

The police often resort to harassment as a means of keeping the Negro community off-balance. The riot commission noted that

because youths commit a large and increasing proportion of crime, police are under growing pressure from their supervisors—and from the community—to deal with them forcefully. "Harassment of youths" may therefore be viewed by some police departments—and members even of the Negro community—as a proper crime-prevention technique.

The commission added that "many departments have adopted patrol practices which, in the words of one commentator, have 'replaced harassment by individual patrolmen with harassment by entire departments.' "

Among the most common of the cops' harassment techniques are breaking up street-corner groups and stop-and-frisk tactics. Our study found that 63 percent of the ghetto police reported that they "frequently" were called upon to disperse loitering groups. About a third say they "frequently" stop and frisk people. Obviously, then, the law enforcer sometimes interferes with individuals and groups who consider their activities quite legitimate and necessary. Black people in the ghetto—in the absence of adequate parks, playgrounds, jobs, and recreation facilities, and unwilling to sit in sweltering and overcrowded houses with rats and bugs—are likely to make the streets their front yards. But this territory is often made uninhabitable by the police.

Nearly a third of the white policemen in our study thought that most of the residents of their precinct (largely Negro) were not industrious. Even more striking about the attitudes of the white police working in these neighborhoods is that many of them deny the fact of Negro inequality: 20 percent say the Negro is treated better than any other part of the population, and 14 percent say he is treated equally. As for their own perception of police treatment of Negroes, the Campbell–Schuman survey reported that 43 percent of the black men, who are on the streets more than the women, thought that police use insulting language in their neighborhoods. Only 17 percent of the white males held this belief. Of the Negro men, 20 percent reported that the police insulted them personally and 28 percent said they knew someone to whom this had happened; only 9 percent and 12 percent, respectively, of the whites reported the same. Similarly, many more blacks than whites thought that the police frisked and searched people without good reason (42 percent compared to 12 percent); and that the police roughed up people unnecessarily (37 percent as compared to 10 percent). Such reports of police misconduct were most frequent among the younger Negroes, who, after all, are on the receiving end most often.

The policeman's isolation in the ghetto is evident in a number of findings. We asked the police how many people—of various types—they knew well enough in the ghetto to greet when they saw them. Eighty-nine percent of the police said they knew six or more shopowners, managers, and clerks well enough to speak with, but only 38 percent said they knew this many teenage or youth leaders. At the same time, 39 percent said that most young adults, and 51 percent said that most adolescents, regard the police as enemies. And only 16 percent of the white policemen (37 percent of the blacks) either "often" or "sometimes" attended meetings in the neighborhood.

The police have wound up face to face with the social consequences of the problems in the ghetto created by the failure of other white institutions—though, as has been observed, they themselves have contributed to those problems in no small degree. The distant and gentlemanly white racism of employers, the discrimination of white parents who object to having their children go to school with Negroes, the disgruntlement of white taxpayers who deride the present welfare system as a sinkhole of public funds but are unwilling to see it replaced by anything more effective—the consequences of these and other forms of white racism have confronted the police with a massive control problem of the kind most evident in the riots.

In our survey, we found that the police were inclined to see the riots as the long-range result of faults in the Negro community—disrespect for law, crime, broken families, etc.—rather than as responses to the stance of the white community. Indeed, nearly one-third of the white police saw the riots as the result of what they considered the basic violence and disrespect of Negroes in general, while only one-fourth attributed the riots to the failure of white institutions. More than three-fourths also regarded the riots as the immediate result of agitators and criminals—a suggestion contradicted by all the evidence accumulated by the riot commission. The police, then, share with the other groups —excepting the black politicians—a tendency to emphasize perceived defects in the black community as an explanation for the difficulties that they encounter in the ghetto.

The state of siege thinking evident in many police departments is but an exaggerated version of a trend in the larger white society. It is the understandable, but unfortunate, response of people who are angry and confused about the wide-spread disruption of traditional racial patterns and who feel threatened by these changes. There is, of course, some basis for this feeling, because the Negro movement poses challenges of power and interest to many groups. To the extent that the movement is successful, the merchants, for example, will either have to reform their practices or go out of business—and for many it may be too late for reform. White suburbanites will have to cough up funds for the city, which provides most of them with employment. Police departments will have to be thoroughly restructured.

The broad social rising of Negroes is beginning to have a substantial effect upon all white institutions in the ghetto, as the situation of the merchants, the schools, and the welfare establishment illustrates. Ten years ago, these institutions (and the police, who have been affected differently) could operate pretty much unchecked by any countervailing power in the ghetto. Today, both their excesses and their inadequacies have run up against an increasingly militant black population, many of whom support violence as a means of redress. The evidence suggests that unless these institutions are transformed, the black community will make it increasingly difficult for them to function at all.

16. AN ANALYSIS OF THE GHETTO RIOTS
David Boesel

A National Revolt

The current black revolt is generally thought to have started in the South and, after a flourishing "classic" phase, to have spread to the northern cities. There, according to the argument, the civil rights movement faltered in the face of more complex and radical problems and

NOTE: This essay was presented at the April, 1969 meeting of The Southern Sociological Society in New Orleans.

began to break apart, to be followed for the next five years by ghetto riots.[1]

If one's attention is confined to organized civil rights activities, this pattern is fairly self-evident. The Supreme Court decision of 1954 opened the door to revolt the following year in Montgomery, Alabama, where leadership of a prolonged bus boycott brought Martin Luther King to national prominence. After several years of activity, there followed a more militant phase of the southern movement, beginning with the sit-ins in 1960. It was not until 1963, in the wake of Birmingham, that organized black protest became very pronounced in northern cities, and even then the civil rights activists were not able to evoke the commitment of the ghetto masses or to force significant social change. In 1964 the outbreak in Harlem signaled the start of rioting that has involved ordinary black people as the civil rights movement never did. One could conclude from this that a movement begun in the South failed to adapt itself to conditions in the North, and that consequent upon this failure, angry and dissatisfied blacks spilled out into the streets to riot.[2] This line of argument is not dead wrong; but, as I hope to show, in focusing primarily on organized protest activity, it fails to take into account developments in the northern cities which put the revolt in a very different light.

Rather than talking about a two-stage revolt, starting in the South and spreading to the North, I think that it accords better with the facts to view the black revolt as a single event which emerged on a nationwide scale in the years 1955–1960, but which took different forms in different social contexts.

In the South it took the form of organized nonviolent direct action. To a considerable extent the organization and character of power in the South determined the lines along which the civil rights movement evolved. Jim Crow was a highly visible formal-legal system whose coherence and structure facilitated disciplined counteraction. Since the system of oppression was clearly outlined, the revolt against it could be correspondingly clear and deliberate. Moreover, Jim Crow was an archaic system under attack by the federal government, which for its part enjoyed the growing support of indignant public opinion in the North. To a considerable extent, civil rights strategy was aimed at bringing forth more federal intervention in the South and at turning northern indignation to advantage. Finally, Jim Crow was a violently repressive system; blacks in the South had long been conditioned by terror and intimidation to fear whites. From time to time they used arms to defend themselves against white attacks,[3] but rarely if ever did they initiate any assault on white persons, property, or authority. Nonviolent direct action, then, was an appropriate tactic not only because it decreased the possibility of an overwhelmingly violent white response, but also because it better suited the temperament of the rank-and-file protesters.

Conditions in the North favored the emergence and evolution of a different form of revolt. The northern system of racial subordination, rooted in *de facto* discrimination, never achieved the clarity and visibility that characterized Jim Crow. Working indirectly and veiled by a liberal ideology, the northern system made disciplined and foresightful mass action extremely difficult. The sources of power seemed remote and diffuse, though the effects of power were immediate and tangible. Targets were hard to find, visible demands hard to generate. Such a context favored the development of spontaneous and undisciplined counteraction. Further, the fear of whites inculcated in the South gradually lost its force for black people living in the northern ghettos. The number and concentration of blacks, their physical control of the streets, and the less repressive policies of white authorities all contributed to a growing sense of power among blacks.[4] The anonymity of the cities afforded protection to those ready to challenge white authority directly. Under the circumstances, a violent revolt against the system of white hegemony was to be expected and had, in fact, been a theme of black literature for some time.

The roots of black revolt in the North are not to be found in the civil rights movement, nor in the riots strictly speaking. Spontaneous direct action against white authority began to take shape in northern cities several years before the first full-scale riots in 1964. It took the form of a sharply increasingly number of clashes between black mobs and the police. The conflict usually centered around the arrest of a black man; often he would resist; within minutes a crowd would assemble and try to free the prisoner or assault the police. In 1967 Detroit Police Commissioner Ray Girardin told the Kerner Commission:

> It is more difficult to make an arrest now than it was ten years ago, or eight years ago, or whenever. Often there is more interference from the crowd, the people on the street. Many of our men complain that they are called names and they are pushed and slugged, and I know that we have . . . rather a large number injured every year.[5]

By 1961 overt antagonism to the police in New York had reached proportions which alarmed authorities. In July 1960, 200 police officers

were assaulted; in July of the following year the figure was 292. Police
Commissioner Michael J. Murphy told the press,

> The police cannot fight crime and the public at the same time. . . . Un-
> less the public cooperates by aiding the police instead of hindering them,
> crime will go unchecked.[6]

In addition to resistance and assaults by street crowds, police in Harlem
were subject to rooftop barrages of bricks, bottles, garbage, and just
about anything else that would drop.

In Newark, Philadelphia, San Francisco, and other cities the number
of injuries to police patrolling the ghettos increased. A confrontation in
Los Angeles in the spring of 1961, though larger than most, illustrates
the dynamics of these skirmishes. On Memorial Day a 17-year-old
black youth boarded a carousel in Griffith Park without paying. Having
tried without success to remove the youth, the operator of the concession called the police. After a brief scuffle, they arrested the boy, but a
crowd of some 200 blacks blocked their way to the patrol car. One of
the officers said later, "The crowd took our prisoner from us, and he escaped in the disturbance that followed." When a white person tried to
help the policemen, he was beaten by members of the crowd. Seventy-
five officers were rushed to the scene as the crowd continued to grow.
Police cars were stoned when they entered the park; one was overturned. Four policemen were injured before order was restored, and
twenty-two persons were arrested, fifteen of them juveniles.[7]

Gradually, from the early to the middle 1960's the number and size
of confrontations between police and black mobs grew. Still, these encounters did not become ghetto riots, as we understand the term, until
the Harlem outbreak in the summer of 1964. The earlier clashes were
primarily the province of black youth, they usually consisted of only
one "incident," and there was only one target—the police. With the
Harlem riot, however, a new dimension was added. There the battle between youth and the police broke the balance of the situation, and masses
of ordinary people burst onto the scene; they rioted for several days
in Harlem and Bedford–Stuyvesant; their antagonism was directed not
only at the police, but also at white merchants and occasionally at other
targets. Both the number of actors and the scope of the action had expanded significantly.

The development of individual riots after 1964 tended to recapitulate
the development of the riots as a whole. Typically a disorder would
begin with a confrontation of the sort that became widespread in the

early 1960's. Then the initial clash with the police would break down the restraints on the larger crowd, and a sizable segment of the ghetto masses would join the action, transforming a "racial incident" into a riot.

It would be pointless to try to locate a definite "starting date" for the revolt in the North. If there is a northern equivalent to Mrs. Parks' refusal to leave her seat in that Montgomery bus, it has not been recorded. But we can safely say that by 1960 or 1961 the tendency to collective action against white authority was well developed. The southern and northern aspects of the black revolt probably did not begin at the same time, the southern movement getting started a few years earlier. But in light of the increasing number of clashes between police and ghetto street crowds—which had nothing to do with civil rights demonstrations—it is difficult to make the case that the revolt spread, or was carried, from the South to the North. It would be going beyond the evidence to say that the southern movement had no role in the beginnings of revolt in the North, but I think that its influence was slighter than is generally supposed.

The Context of Revolt in the North

The revolt in the South, we have seen, was able to achieve organizational coherence in large part because it developed within, and was directed against, a clearly defined system of oppression. The fact that the North had no Jim Crow system, however, has led some observers to conclude that systematic racial oppression did not play a major role there.[8] They have chosen, instead, to emphasize the *exclusion* of blacks from dominant institutions. Since it is agreed that revolt can take place only within an institutional context (for that is what defines oppressors and oppressed), they see the ghetto violence mainly as anomic behavior. Richard Cloward, for example, puts the case this way:

Blacks have become an urban people in just two or three decades, and this has set them loose from existing structures of social control. Although a repressive feudalistic system persists in the South, a great many Negroes have been liberated from it by just no longer being there. Nor have they been absorbed by the main institutions of the city, especially the economic system. Ghetto institutions, such as churches and political machines, have also not incorporated them. Furthermore, the press of numbers is disrupting

traditional accommodations [as in housing and schools] upon which social
peace depends. . . . When tensions rise as institutional controls weaken, the
eruption of violence should not be surprising.[9]

Ghetto violence, from this perspective, is something that "erupts" as
a consequence of tension and weak social controls. A product of displaced people, it is viewed more as directionless social pathology than
as meaningful collective action.

The opposite is true, I think. While there is unquestionably an anomic component in the ghetto violence, the riots should be viewed first
of all as a form of collective action. Black people are not simply "left
out"—on the whole they have a definite, and subordinate, position in
the social structure. To be sure, blacks are disproportionately out of
work, out of school, and so on. But most black men are regularly employed (in any case, employment seems to be no guarantee against participation in riots); and most black youths are in school (education
seems, if anything, to increase the predisposition to riot).[10]

More important, the ghetto itself provides the institutional context
for revolt. It is not simply a repository for an aggregate of uprooted
black people—unlike those sprawling shanty towns on the outskirts of
cities in the Third World. Rather the ghetto represents a system of control presided over by white people, the main function of which has been
to prevent the urban influx of blacks from disrupting established social,
economic, and political relations in white society. As the concrete expression of white racial hegemony in the cities, it is a social institution
of much the same magnitude as slavery and Jim Crow.

The ghetto as a system for the maintenance of racial hegemony (that
is, for the preservation of the dominant pattern of white power and interest) is composed of a series of functionally reciprocal institutions run
by whites, which provision and control the black residents. The corner-
stone, a segregated housing market tightly controlled by white realtors,
confines black people to a restricted area, providing a basis for—among
other things—largely segregated and decidedly inferior schools, again
run by whites. The schools for their part keep black youths off the
streets and turn out a large number of "graduates" prepared only for
menial jobs (whites will decide eligibility for employment and give the
orders on the job). Undereducated and underemployed blacks living in a
restricted area constitute a captive market for ghetto merchants—
mostly white—many of whom keep their customers strung out on
credit. Police protect the stores and over time arrest a solid majority of
all men in the ghetto for one reason or another. Though about only

one-third of those arrested are ever convicted, all those with police records are likely to have even more difficulty finding jobs than they ordinarily would.[11] A segment of the ghetto population also provides a ready supply of poor people to be serviced and maintained at a manageable subsistence level by white-controlled welfare agencies. And black politics has, for the most part, provided the illusion of power without the substance.

The mutual reciprocity of those institutions has caused them to fit together as parts of a control system through which the decisions of white people with power determine the major outlines of the lives of black people without power. Of course the ghetto understood in this way is not the product of some master plan for keeping blacks down. Rather, it is the product of innumerable discrete calculations of power and interest which use race as a criterion for decision-making. Over time such calculations among those who have had at least a modicum of power have tended to accommodate themselves to each other to form a pattern which fairly consistently subordinates and deprives blacks. From whatever angle one approaches the question, he will find that whites give most of the orders and blacks take them.

Unlike the Jim Crow system, the ghetto is by and large a product of urban liberalism. It is not reinforced by specifically racial laws (for racial distinctions are not supposed to have any legal standing), and it has not been as directly repressive as its southern counterpart. Rather, its controls are characteristically indirect and oblique. (Thus, blacks are not flatly denied managerial positions, but they are denied the education and social contacts that entry into this occupational stratum requires.) Further, as was noted earlier, the social boundaries of the ghetto are not clearly defined; both as a place and as an institution it is large and loosely structured. Housing, for example, is never completely and rigidly segregated, the schools even less so. Instead of looking for sharp lines of demarcation, analysis of the ghetto must proceed on the basis of aggregates and probabilities.

Enveloping and further obscuring the power relations in this system of hegemony is a liberal rhetoric which acknowledges the "unfortunate" plight of blacks, but fails to recognize the hard facts of power and interest that perpetuate it. A characteristic source of this rhetoric are those agencies euphemistically called "human relations commissions," the first of which was set up in Chicago after the 1919 race riot (though it was, in fact, called the Chicago Commission on Race Relations). The operating assumption of these agencies is that bad race relations are a consequence of imperfect communication between the races, that if only whites and blacks could get together and talk things over harmony would prevail. The difficulty with this assumption is that bad race relations are not some sort of aberration caused by a lack of mutual understanding. They are rather the normal state of a situation in which whites are on top and blacks are on the bottom. The only reason why this fact has not obtruded itself on whites until recently is that blacks have lacked the power and resources to make an open fight of it.

Thus while urban blacks are part of a comprehensive social institution developed specifically for them, they are nevertheless faced with great difficulty in moving against this system, the dimensions and outlines of which are not clear. The importance of a clear and close institutional context in structuring revolt has been emphasized in the preceding discussion of the southern movement. In the North its importance has been evident in the numerous strikes and riots in black high schools over the last five years, in the rapid growth of the welfare rights movement, and most recently in the organization of radical black unions in the auto industry. Collective action in these cases—some of it violent —has been quite coherent and well focused.

The Evolution of the Ghetto Revolt

Given the obliqueness of control in the broad and loosely structured ghetto, popular direct action against the system necessarily began with the most immediate, tangible, and direct agents of white control—the police. The clashes between police and black crowds in the years preceding the riots illustrate Camus' principle that revolt begins when someone says "No!" [12]—in this case, "No, you're not going to arrest that man!" Out of such spontaneous and unself-conscious protest there evolved a stage of mass participation—the ghetto riots—and an increasingly evident collective rationality. Diffuse and ill-focused though the riots have been, they have from the beginning shown inchoate political tendencies which are sorting themselves out year by year. At the root of these tendencies is the challenge to white authority implicit in the mob assaults upon the police.

A complex dialectic of ideas and events is rationalizing and politicizing black violence. On the one hand, the riots have had a substantial impact on the black community. First, as mythic events, in Sorel's sense, they have done a good deal to clarify the dimensions and outlines of white control of the ghetto; and they have engaged the energies and emotions of a considerable portion of the black population—especially among the young. In short, they have activated a significant segment of the black masses. Second, they have greatly augmented the ranks of the black radical elite. An increasingly large portion of lower middle-class and middle-class youth are breaking away from the pursuit of careers and turning to political activism, a process begun earlier in the civil rights movement. The working places of the new elite are the literally thousands of storefront action centers in ghettos across the country.

The other side of the dialectic is the development of a rhetoric which, in providing an interpretive framework for the black masses, is changing the course and character of black violence. With each succeeding year, the radical elite and others have been drawing out the implications of the riots, mixing in theory, exhortation, and a certain amount of fantasy. The result is not yet ideology—it is not strongly enough articulated nor comprehensive enough—but the beginnings of ideology are clearly visible in such documents as the Black Power manifesto and the program of the Black Panther Party. This broadening of perspectives is reflected in the changing character of events which have precipitated riots. The outbreak in Rochester in 1964, for example, grew directly out of a policeman's attempt to arrest a disorderly black youth at a dance. In April 1968 blacks in many cities rioted in response to a *national* event—the assassination of Martin Luther King. In April 1969 disturbances broke out in Chicago, Memphis, and other cities on the first *anniversary* of the assassination.

The riots have involved a great variety of motives and styles of behavior—opportunism, expressive gratification, individualism, collective solidarity, and so on. But there have been two political themes in these ghetto outbreaks from the beginning. The first I would call coercive protest, and the second, rebellion.[13] Both had their antecedents in earlier tendencies in the black movement; both were implicit in the first riots and since then have become more overt and instrumental; now both seem to be carrying over beyond the riots into another stage of the movement.

Tactically, black coercive protest may be seen as a logical extension of some of the principles of the civil rights demonstrations—creating a crisis and using it as a means of negotiating with authorities; and its goal—full participation in American society—may be seen as an extension of the more narrowly conceived integrationist tendency in the black movement. But while the civil rights demonstrations were by and large the disciplined action of a few, the riots have consisted of undisciplined action by many.

The riots as coercive protest may perhaps be best understood as a sort of wildcat strike.[14] From this perspective they appear to be, simultaneously, a revolt of the ghetto rank and file against an established black leadership which, because of cooptation and other reasons, has failed to deliver the goods, and a form of direct action intended to communicate grievances and apply pressure on the white "managers" of the ghetto. This sort of coercive protest is reformist rather than revolutionary. In a limited way, it breaks the rules of the game, but does not repudiate the game itself.

The second political theme in the riots is much more radical—even potentially revolutionary—and not as easily discerned as the first. The riot as rebellion—a current expression of the black nationalist tendency going back to Garvey and beyond—consists of an impulsive, large-scale effort to break the control of white authorities over the ghetto, to seize territory and property by force, and to replace white authority with indigenous control. Needless to say, it has proved much easier to disrupt white control temporarily than even to begin to establish black control, but an examination of some of the more recent riots reveals fitful efforts in that direction.

As they have shown themselves in the riots since 1964, these two themes have not been mutually exclusive, and though they are distinguishable, the relations between them have been extraordinarily complex. The temporary seizure of control, for example, has been used, as in Plainfield, New Jersey, to wring concessions from white authorities; and coercive protest with the threat of violence has been used, as in the Ocean Hill–Brownsville school fight, to promote community control. With these reservations in mind, I want to look more closely at the two themes in the context of the riots and the development of a mass movement.

The riot as coercive protest involves a number of different levels of articulation. The spontaneous airing of grievances by a crowd assembled around an incident at the beginning of a riot is perhaps the lowest common denominator of protest in the outbreaks. The main complaint to arise ordinarily concerns the incident which has caused the crowd to assemble—more often than not some action involving a policeman and a black citizen. If such is the case, indignation over the police action is expressed, together with statements of sympathy for the victim. Usually an investigation or indictment of the policeman is demanded. From there, the scope of the grievances will expand, often to a broader airing of hostility against the police, then to a whole range of injustices.

Once the first store window is broken, the "strike" is on, and established black leadership is rejected. An incident in the first riot of this series—Harlem, 1964—prefigured the experience of hundreds of black moderates in the outbreaks to come. As crowds of young people ranged up and down the streets breaking windows, an NAACP sound truck appeared on the scene: "Please. Don't stay on the streets. Go home before more people get hurt." The reply came back: "We are home, baby." Then the truck was attacked.[15]

The second level of protest, also pretty universal in the riots, is a desire on the part of rioters to command the attention of both white authorities and white society in general. One of the commonest experiences of reporters covering the riots, if they are in contact with people on the streets, is to be collared by angry blacks and given a "message" to white society to be printed in the paper or broadcast over television.

A third level of protest common to most of the riots is somewhat more concrete than the first two: it is a demand that the mayor or other public officials come to the area to hear grievances and, in the words of a rioter in Cleveland, "Look at the mess you've got us in." Whether the politicization of black collective action continues along the lines of coercive protest depends in part on whether public officials respond to such demands (or even initiate meetings themselves).

In the first two years of the rioting, 1964–1965, no mayor, to my knowledge, went to the ghetto or met with rioters or their representatives. In the midst of the Watts riot, Mayor Yorty apparently felt that it would be unconscionable to break a speaking engagement at the Commonwealth Club in San Francisco, and so left town, despite the fact that there was widespread resentment in Watts at his failure to visit the ghetto even once since his election. Police Chief William Parker turned down a demand for a meeting with some widely publicized racially tinged remarks about the rioters. (He compared them to monkeys in a zoo.)

In 1966, however, after public officials had had a chance to think about what their own responses to a riot ought to be, mayors in a number of cities did go to the ghettos in the midst of the rioting to meet directly with the people on the streets. On the whole, these efforts were not very successful, largely because the people were too angry, and grievances too ill-formulated, to enable any communication to take place. Barrages of angry words became a verbal substitute for bricks. In Atlanta, after some rather obtuse comments to the crowd, Mayor Allen was toppled off the car on which he had been standing. In San Francisco, according to the *Chronicle:*

[Mayor Shelley], surrounded by a wedge of detectives . . . climbed the stairs to the front door of the center [where the meeting was to take place] and tried to talk to the angry pressing mob through a bullhorn. His voice was lost in a thunder of jeers and bellowing. A group of youngsters shouted. "We want him (the policeman) charged with murder right now." [16]

After more futile attempts to start a dialogue with the people inside the hall, Shelley left in frustration. In Omaha, Mayor Sorenson was somewhat more successful; in his meeting with youthful rioters, one message came across clearly—the insistent demand for jobs for young people. Immediately after the riot an emergency employment center was set up in the ghetto; it seems to have operated more effectively than its counterparts in other cities, especially in providing stable, long-term employment.

In 1967, meetings between public officials and rioters or their militant spokesmen were fairly commonplace, and in some cases intensive, almost formal negotiations took place. The pattern of riot and negotiation which developed in New Brunswick, New Jersey, is almost a classic of coercive protest. In the aftermath of the Newark upheaval, black youth in New Brunswick deliberately staged a riot; after planning their moves, they ran down a business street breaking windows, and then, when all the preselected targets had been hit, retired for the evening. The following day there ensued negotiations between the youth and the liberal woman mayor. Shortly thereafter the mayor announced over the radio that she had gotten assurances of a sizable antipoverty grant, and a few of the youth went on the radio to urge their "brothers and sisters" to cool it. That ended the New Brunswick "riot."

The riot in Plainfield, New Jersey, spearheaded by militant youth (as most ghetto riots have been), also involved extensive negotiations between the youth and public officials. After the initial outbreak there developed a pattern of alternating violence and negotiation by the youth. Mayor George Hedley was quite willing to meet with the young rioters, but he proved to be consistently unable to get the point of their protests. They were demanding a swimming pool, yes, yes. But what was new about that? He'd heard it all before.

After two days of alternating force and bargaining, an assembly of some 200–400 youths met in a park to draw up a list of grievances and, in the most democratic tradition, to elect representatives to present their petition to the mayor. This effort might have ended well had it not been for the rigidity of the county police, who had jurisdiction over the park. The chief observed that the assembled youth did not have a park permit and, despite pleas by older black leaders, ordered the assembly dispersed. The young people, fiercely angry, returned to the ghetto to start a phase of the rioting that was to turn into an overt political rebellion. Coercive protest having failed, rebellion followed.

Turning to the riots as rebellion, one can see that the question of territorial control has played a part in many of the outbreaks. If a disturbance is quelled in its early stages—shortly after the first rocks have been thrown and the first windows broken—this tendency does not have a chance to assert itself. But if authorities fail to bring massive force to bear quickly, the situation is likely to develop into a contest between police and young blacks for control of the streets.

Viewed superficially and immediately, the movement of young blacks to take over the streets seems to be merely a tactical prerequisite to looting and other riot activity. But I think there is more involved. As Robert Penn Warren has suggested, the desire to have land of one's own has been a constant theme in black thought, going back to Reconstruction times. It is of course a prominent theme in black nationalist thought, and it seems to be amenable to any number of contemporary adaptations ("We are home, baby!").

During the riots, in the contest with police youthful rioters employ a variety of stratagems to break white control. The intent of their action is to harry, distract, and disrupt police efforts to the point where they can no longer exercise control of the streets. Police officers are thrown off balance by the taunts of young rioters and by other forms of harassment. The coordination of police forces is often disrupted by phony alarms called in to the station. One rioter in Chicago said:

> It was easy. We'd pick up the phone and say, "Hello, police? There's some dudes over here breaking into the supermarket. You'd better get over here." They'd come running and leave a big stretch of Roosevelt Road open.[17]

The same sort of tactics are employed to disrupt fire-control efforts. False alarms are called in, or real fires set, and ambushes laid for the trucks. As firemen in Watts were battling one blaze, a black man with an axe approached and cut the hose: "We didn't set this fire just to have you come along and put it out!" [18]

On the one hand, the breaking of police control produces a giddy euphoria—the often-noted carnival atmosphere that prevails when the streets are open and the stage of mass popular involvement in the riot begins. On the other hand, the successful disruption of police efforts is a prelude to the most dangerous phase of the rioting. For in disrupting the control of police over the streets, the rioters may also break the control of the police command over individual officers, and repressive measures are likely to assume the form of a retaliatory riot by policemen.

This was the course of events in the three largest riots—Watts, Newark, and Detroit. Watts stands out as a turning point in this respect, as in many others. In Watts for the first time the sheer weight of numbers overwhelmed white authorities and left rioters in de facto control of the streets. A wave of enthusiasm swept through the ghetto with the realization that the rioters had "beat the police" and that the National Guard had to be called in. Then the death toll began to mount. Despite the losses suffered by blacks, however, and despite the reimposition of white authority, the Watts upheaval was still widely regarded as a victory for black people, and the ghetto became the scene of an annual commemorative festival.

The first major theoretical statement of the black rebellion followed on the heels of the Watts riots when, in the winter of 1965–1966, members of SNCC drafted the Black Power manifesto and radical spokesmen such as Stokely Carmichael and Rap Brown began to popularize the idea. It was not an outright statement of rebellion, as it remained ambiguous on the question of violence and on the extent of community control contemplated. In its tamest aspect Black Power could be interpreted as the patient building of black economic and political power to the point where black people could command their due in a pluralist context. In its radical aspect it suggested breaking the white man's control over blacks by force and seizing territory and property. On the latter, here is Rap Brown speaking in Cambridge, Maryland, in July 1967:

You got to own some of them stores. I don't care if you have to burn them down and run him out. You got to take over them stores. The streets are yours. Take them. They gave you the streets a long time ago. Before they gave you houses, they gave you the streets. So we own the streets, take them. They won't give it to you. [19]

By 1967, the impulse to rebellion and seizure was beginning to manifest itself clearly in some places. In Newark, for example, looting in one instance took the form of collective expropriation:

On the corner of Springfield and Belmont Avenues, five teen-agers went inside Sampson's Liquor Store and passed out bottles to a line of twenty-five adults waiting outside. It was an assembly-line process. With the line stretching around the corner. It took them fifteen minutes to clean the store out. Expensive whiskeys and scotches went first, followed by champagnes. They left the cheap wine until the last, but that finally went, too.[20]

The Plainfield riot stands as the clearest case of outright rebellion to date. After the incident in the park, described earlier, the youths, together with other residents, renewed their rioting in the ghetto. A white police officer, pursuing a black youth apparently to arrest him, shot and wounded the youngster. At that point a furious mob of blacks fell upon him and stomped him to death. Young militants stole forty-six carbines from a nearby plant and distributed them in the ghetto. Public officials, fearful of the cost in lives of trying to reassert control over the area, cordoned it off but did not allow police to enter. Then, for a period of over twenty-four hours, state authority over the ghetto was in abeyance as militant youth exercised a loose de facto control. Finally the standoff was broken by negotiations between public officials and the representatives of the rioters.

Rap Brown quickly recognized the Plainfield rebellion as a practical example of the principles he had been espousing:

But look what the brothers did in Plainfield. The brothers got their stuff. They got forty-six automatic weapons. . . . Then they went back to their community . . . and they told that peckerwood cop, they said, "Don't you come in my community. We going to control our community." And the peckerwood cop says, "Well, we got to come down there and get them weapons." The brother told him. "Don't come in my community." He didn't come. And the only reason he didn't come was 'cause he didn't want to get killed. And the brothers had the material to do it. They had forty-six carbines down there. That's what he respects—power. He respects that kind of power.[21]

After the Riots

The riots represent a stage in the development of a black social movement, a phase in which large segments of the ghetto masses have been activated and in which a framework has been developed for a popular critique of white hegemony. This stage now seems to be coming to a close. Most cities have had only one large riot bracketed before and after by smaller disorders. On the one hand, the riots have brought about a public response which has tended to inhibit the emergence of further spontaneous outbreaks. This has been particularly true of police tactics, which, following the recommendations of the Kerner Commission, have stressed the overwhelming deployment of force to quell disturbances at the outset. On the other hand, the riots have had a traumatic effect on the ghettos, and over the past several years have brought about a determination not to tear up black territory, but to seek more pointedly rational and effective ways of pursuing black goals.

This determination seems to be leading in two direction. First, coercive protest seems to be evolving into a form of mass-political action covering a broad range of aims and tactics. The key to this type of action is the mobilization of large numbers of ghetto blacks in support of specific political goals. The tactics run the gamut from electoral politics through strikes and demonstrations to the threat, and occasionally the use, of violence. In Los Angeles and many other cities mass-political action has been evident in the packing of court trials and public hearings by angry blacks. In New York it was manifest in the mobilization of the black community, with the implicit threat of violence, to retain the Ocean Hill–Brownsville school decentralization program. In Washington it can be seen in the alliance formed between militant school board member Julius Hobson and black students ready to strike for better education. Presently in Detroit it is taking the form of intense demonstrations of support for Judge George Crockett, who brooked the police and county prosecutor to release black nationalists arrested after one officer was killed and another wounded, probably by a member of a nationalist paramilitary group.

For the first time the energy, numbers, and cohesion of black communities are beginning to provide a measure of parity with white political forces on specific issues in the cities. (It should be stressed that there is little probability of large-scale change emanating from this parity, for the resources of the cities are too meager to permit it.) The issues at stake have in many cases become highly volatile because whites, unaccustomed to seeing their power seriously challenged by blacks, have coalesced in countermovements permeated with racist sentiments. The school strike split New York along racial lines as no other issue in recent history has. The Crockett case in Detroit seems likely to do the same, as whites mobilize in support of their "first line of defense," the police. Mayor Carl Stokes' handling of the July 1968 riot in Cleveland provoked intense racial controversy; and in Gary, Indiana, a white section of the city is trying to "secede" in order to escape the authority of Mayor Richard Hatcher.

The second political tendency noted in the riots, black rebellion, also seems to be evolving into another stage. A rhetoric of guerrilla warfare to achieve territorial autonomy has been developing in the ghettos for some years. It has been clearly expressed by Eldridge Cleaver, the ideologist (gone underground) of the rapidly growing Black Panther Party. Arguing that blacks are a people colonized by American imperialism, he has compared them to Jews as an oppressed people in search of a land. The ultimate goal of uniting nation and territory must be achieved by armed struggle, for, according to Cleaver, Mao's dictum that power comes out of the barrel of a gun is essentially correct.

So now we are engaged openly in a war for the national liberation of Afro–America from colonial bondage to the white mother country. In our epoch, guerrilla warfare is the vehicle of national liberation all around the world.[22]

To date there have been no unequivocally clear cases of guerrilla attacks organized ahead of time and carried out by black militants. While there have been incidents that could plausibly be interpreted as such, too little is yet known about the actors or their motives to be able to draw firm conclusions. But there has been mounting evidence in that direction. In addition to a wide range of documented arson and sniper attacks which appear to have been racially motivated, there have been a number of cases in the past year which can best be interpreted as political action by black radicals, among them a machine-gun attack on a Jersey City police station (two days after seven Black Panthers had been arrested), and several attempts—one of them successful—to bomb police stations and patrol cars in black sections of New York.

There have been numerous arrests of radical nationalists on conspiracy charges, the most prominent of these involving the recent indictment in New York of twenty-one Panthers on charges of plotting to kill policemen and to dynamite city department stores, a police station, and a commuter railroad. But since public authorities in many cities have shown a determination to break the Panthers and similar organizations, one must be aware of the possibility of political motives behind such arrests.

The incidents that come closest to guerrilla warfare involve a brand of armed nationalism which has repeatedly pitted black radicals against police in a series of pitched gun battles. The shootouts have been most numerous on the West Coast, particularly in the San Francisco–Oakland area, where four separate clashes in just over a year have left one policeman and one Black Panther dead, with several wounded on each side. (As a result of the first battle, Panther leader Huey Newton has been convicted of murder; as a result of the second, Eldridge Cleaver has had his parole revoked and has gone into hiding.)

The largest gunfight to date occurred in Cleveland in July 1968, when Ahmed Evans and members of his Black Nationalists of New Libya shot it out with police for over an hour. Three policemen and one nationalist were killed in the battle, as were five black citizens in the riot which followed. Evans surrendered and is awaiting trial for murder. In Detroit recently one patrolman was killed and another wounded, apparently by an elite guard of the Republic of New Africa, a nationalist organization which was meeting in a west-side church. Police then shot up the church and arrested 142 persons. As mentioned earlier, a black judge's release of nearly all the prisoners has caused a furious racial controversy in the city.

In most of these cases, we have too little information about the beginnings of the battles to be clear about the motives on either side. So far the only pattern discernable has the police approaching armed nationalists, at which point shooting breaks out. But it is only a short step from here to a situation in which the antagonists on either side plan their moves ahead of time.

It would be surprising, then, if the black revolt in the cities did not take on some of the aspects of nationalist rebellions in other parts of the world, including the growth of an underground based on close-knit groups, the intensification of ideological commitment and hence of schismatic tendencies, organized attacks upon the police, and the use of terror as a political weapon. On the other side we may expect to see the growth of police techniques traditionally employed to counter organized rebellion: the development of a large intelligence apparatus, the deployment of spies and *agents provocateurs,* a reliance upon political arrests, and so on.

To say that these tendencies exist and are becoming more pronounced today is not to say that we are necessarily headed for a police state. On the one hand, the reaction of public authorities to the growth of black rebellion is forcing elements on this side of the movement underground, and there is reason to think that rebellion and police-state tactics will develop dialectically. On the other hand, the politics of black coercive protest, which takes place *in public,* is beginning to pay some minor dividends, and it is conceivable that some sort of alliance between blacks and dissident whites can bring about changes on the scale required.

NOTES

1. For an example of this line of argument, see Lewis M. Killian, *The Impossible Revolution?* (New York: Random House, 1968), p. 65, and Howard Hubbard, "Five Long Hot Summers and How They Grew," *The Public Interest* (Summer 1968), 3–24.

2. The failure of southern tactics in the North is stressed by Hubbard, *op. cit.*

3. For example, in Elaine, Arkansas (1919), Negroes used arms to defend themselves against attacking whites. See Arthur Waskow, *From Race Riot to Sit-in* (Garden City, N.Y.: Doubleday, 1966), pp. 121–142. In 1959 protesting Negroes in a makeshift "Tent City" in Fayette County, Tennessee, put an end to white night-riding by shooting back.

4. Reflecting this growing sense of power, Lou Harris found in 1963 that a majority of Negroes felt that in a showdown with whites they would not lose. Louis Harris and William Brink, *The Negro Revolution in America* (New York: Simon and Schuster, 1963), p. 74.

5. Testimony of Detroit Police Commissioner Ray Girardin before the National Advisory Commission on Civil Disorders.

6. *U.S. News and World Report,* 9 October 1961, p. 106.

7. The incident is described in Jerry Cohen and William S. Murphy, *Burn, Baby, Burn!* (New York: Dutton, 1966), pp. 295–296.

8. For example, see Paul Goodman, "The Psychology of Being Powerless," *The New York Review of Books,* 3 November 1966, pp. 14–17.

9. Richard Cloward and Frances Fox Piven, "What Chance for Black Power?" *The New Republic,* 30 March 1968, p. 20.

10. For effects of employment and education on riot participation, see the survey conducted by Nathan Caplan for the Kerner Commission: *Report of the National Advisory Commission on Civil Disorders* (New York: Bantam, 1968), pp. 174–175.

11. President's Commission on Law Enforcement, *The Challenge of Crime,* p. 75.

12. Albert Camus, *The Rebel* (New York: Vintage, 1958), p. 13.

13. Killian, *op. cit.,* discusses the concept of coercive public protest, pp. 77 ff.

14. Professor Smelser has suggested viewing the ghetto riots as a form of wildcat strike.

15. Fred C. Shapiro and James W. Sullivan, *Race Riot in New York* (New York: Crowell, 1964).

16. *San Francisco Chronicle.*

17. Personal interview, 20 January 1967.

18. Personal interview, 3 March 1967.

19. Transcript of a recording of Rap Brown's speech in Cambridge, Md., 24 July 1967.

20. *New York Post,* 16 July 1967.

21. Brown transcript, *op. cit.*

22. Eldridge Cleaver, "The Land Question," *Ramparts Magazine,* May 1968, p. 53.

The Consolidation of Black Consciousness

🖋 17. THE NEW GHETTO MAN: A REVIEW
OF RECENT EMPIRICAL STUDIES
Nathan Caplan

W H A T clearly emerges from the recent research findings on Negroes is a picture of a new ghetto man: a black militant who is committed to the removal of traditional racial restraints by open confrontation and, if necessary, by violence; a man who is very different in his
actions and sympathies from the Negro of the past and from the white
ghetto dwellers of an earlier period in this country's history. He is a
man whose characteristics are seldom recognized and understood by
most white Americans. It is our purpose here to describe him based on
existing empirical data—to determine what he is like as a person, how
large a segment of the Negro community he represents, what he wants,
and how he intends to get it.

Profile of the
Black Militant

Political authorities tend to categorize militants who advocate social
and economic change through open confrontations as "riffraff"—
irresponsible deviants, criminals, unassimilated migrants, emotionally
disturbed persons, or members of an underclass. The "riffraff theory"
sees these militants as being peripheral to organized society, with no
broad social or political concerns, and views the frustration that leads to

From *Journal of Social Issues,* 26, no. 1 (1970): 59–73. Adapted from a paper
presented at the Second International Congress of Social Psychiatry, London,
August 1969.

rioting or other forms of militant confrontation as simply part of a long history of personal failure.

It is not difficult to understand why protestors are generally labeled in these terms. By attributing the causes of riots to individual deficiencies, the "riffraff theory" relieves white institutions of most of the blame. It suggests that individual militants should be changed through psychotherapy, social work, or, if all else fails, prolonged confinement. If protesting militants can be publicly branded as unable to compete successfully because of personal reasons, then their demands for system changes can be declared illegitimate with impunity. Authorities would have the right to use punitive and coercive forms of control in place of working to ameliorate structural deficiencies and injustices.

The data show, however, that the militants are no more socially or personally deviant than their nonmilitant counterparts. In fact, there is good reason to believe that they are outstanding on some important measures of socio–economic achievement. Tomlinson concludes from his study that the militants are "the cream of urban Negro youth in particular and urban Negro citizens in general." [1]

The Extent of Militancy

The available data run counter to the commonly held belief that militancy is characteristic of only a small fraction of the Negro community. Militancy in pursuit of civil rights objectives represents a considerable force in the ghetto. Its support approaches normative proportions.

As shown in Table 17–1, in seven studies using related criterion variables about one-third to one-half of the ghetto residents surveyed express support for riots and militant civil rights positions. The proportion of persons reporting active participation in riots is less, but the data across studies are equally consistent if differences in methodology and data sources are taken into consideration. Based on random probability sampling of general population, survey data show the level of self-reported riot participation to be 15 percent for Watts,[2] and 11 percent for Detroit.[3] In Newark, where only males between the ages of fifteen and thirty-five were sampled, 45 percent of the respondents reported riot activity. The riot participation figure for males in the same age group from the general population sample surveyed in Detroit is practically identical with the Newark findings.[4]

Table 17–1 / **Attitudes Expressed by Negroes Relating to Riots**

Attitudes Expressed	Percent Study Sample	Locale and Source
A. RIOT SYMPATHY		
In sympathy with militant positions on civil rights	30	Watts[a]
Do not view riots as "essentially bad"	50	Nationwide[b]
Support militant positions	45	New York City, 1964[c]
In sympathy with militant attitudes and actions	40	Miami area[d]
In sympathy with rioters	54	Fifteen American cities [e]
Believe riots are helpful	30	Houston, 1967[f]
Believe riots are helpful	51	Oakland, 1967[f]
B. RIOT PARTICIPATION		
Active participation in Watts riot	15	Watts[g]
Active participation in Detroit riot	11	Detroit[h]
Active participation in Newark riot	45 (Males, age 15–35)	Newark[h]
Active participation in riots	20	Six major riot cities, 1967[i]
Willingness to participate in riots	15	Nationwide[j]
Advocated use of violence	15	Fifteen American cities [e]

[a] T. M. Tomlinson, "The Development of a Riot Ideology among Urban Negroes," *American Behavioral Scientist* 11, no. 4 (March–April 1968): 27–31.

[b] R. Beardwood, "The New Negro Mood," *Fortune* 77 (1968), 146–152.

[c] G. T. Marx, *Protest and Prejudice: A Study of Belief in the Black Community* (New York: Harper & Row, 1967).

[d] P. Meyer, "Negro Militancy and Martin Luther King: The Aftermath of Martyrdom," *Knight Newspapers* (Washington, D.C., 1968).

[e] A. Campbell and H. Schuman, "Racial Attitudes in Fifteen American Cities" (*Supplemental Studies for the National Advisory Commission on Civil Disorders,* Government Printing Office, 1968).

[f] W. McCord and J. Howard, "Negro Opinions in Three Riot Cities," *American Behavioral Scientist* 11, n. 4 (March–April 1968): 24–27.

[g] D. O. Sears and J. M. McConahay, "Riot Participation: Los Angeles Riot Study" (Unpublished, 1967).

[h] N. S. Caplan and J. M. Paige, in O. Kerner et al., *Report of The National Advisory Commission on Civil Disorders* (New York: Bantam, 1968): 127–137, footnotes 111–143, 171–178.

[i] R. M. Fogelson and R. B. Hill, "Who Riots? A Study of Participation in the 1967 Riots" (*Supplemental Studies for the National Advisory Commission on Civil Disorders,* Government Printing Office, 1968).

[j] W. Brink and L. Harris, *Black and White* (New York: Simon and Schuster, 1966).

Interpolating from arrest records, Fogelson and Hill estimated that
20 percent of ghetto residents participated in riots that occurred in their
cities.[5] Finally, two studies involving surveys in a number of different
cities report that 15 percent of the ghetto population advocate or express willingness to participate in riots.[6]

In most of these studies, riot sympathy and riot participation related
to age and sex. The militant, particularly the rioter, is usually young
and most likely male. Insofar as it is possible to determine from the
available literature, the differences between militants and nonmilitants
to be discussed here hold up after age and sex are controlled.

Income—Absolute

According to one variety of the riffraff theory, the rioter is a member
of a deprived underclass, part of the "hard core" unemployed—often
out of work for long periods of time or chronically unemployable because he lacks skill or education. Having lost contact with the job market and all hope of finding work, he is economically at the very bottom
of Negro society.

Data from the major research studies do not support this hypothesis.
There is no significant difference in income between rioters and nonrioters. In fact, income and militancy are related only in the way Karl
Marx predicted: In the main, the black lumpenproletariate is quiescent,
not militant. The available data show that those in the lowest
socio–economic position are the least militant and the least likely to
riot.[7]

The poorest of the poor are also low on those variables which show
relationships with active protest. Caplan and Paige found that the low-
est-income group tends to score low on black pride and more readily
accepts the traditional deprecating Negro stereotypes.[8] Campbell and
Schuman reported a surprising degree of job satisfaction among those
who are the most economically disadvantaged.[9] Brink and Harris found
that approval of "Black Power" was lowest among those in the poorest
group.[10] Only 13 percent of their low-income respondents approved of
the term, compared with 31 percent in the lower-middle-income group
and 26 percent in the middle- and upper-income groups. Apparently,
continued injustice and the severe withdrawal of resources increase a
deprived group's dependency behavior and approval of those who control scarce resources. These findings argue strongly against an "under-

class" or strictly economic interpretation of militancy and violent protest in the ghetto.

Income—Relative

Objective poverty in the sense of destitution is not the only issue associated with economic standing which has drawn research attention. The subjective meaning of one's wealth, or the absence of it, in relation to what others have, may also be important in producing the frustration that leads to unrest and rioting.

The widening gap between income levels of whites and blacks often has been cited as a possible cause for the present social unrest. The assumption is that members of the black community are concerned not so much with what they have as with what they feel they deserve compared with the whites. Attention to the discrepancy arouses a sense of social injustice that generates the frustration leading to rioting.

In order to examine the relation of the racial economic gap to riot participation, Caplan and Paige asked respondents whether they thought the income gap between Negroes and whites was increasing, remaining the same, or decreasing.[11] They found that 45 percent of the rioters but 55 percent of the nonrioters said the gap was *increasing*. Although the difference between these groups is small, it is opposite in direction to what one would predict on the basis of a relative deprivation hypotheses. More important, when these respondents were questioned about the income gap between the wealthier and poorer Negroes, these percentages were reversed. Fifty-five percent of the rioters and 45 percent of the nonrioters said the gap between the very poor and the higher-income-level Negroes was increasing.

Thus the rioters are particularly sensitive to where they stand in relation to other Negroes, not to whites. If the "black capitalism" idea, as presently formulated, is carried out seriously as a remedial step to prevent further rioting, it is likely to increase this income gap among Negroes and thereby produce disturbing consequences.

Education

McCord and Howard found that educational attainment had no linear relationship to participation in civil rights activity although college-educated respondents in their study were the *least opposed* to the use of violence.[12] Campbell and Schuman reported no relationship between education and expressed favorability toward riots.[13] Conversely, Tomlinson found that militants in Watts had attained a higher level of formal education than their more conservative neighbors.[14] Marx reported a linear relationship between education and militancy—the higher the respondent's education, the greater the likelihood that he would score high on militancy measures. Forty-two percent of the militants in his study had attended college.[15]

There was a slight tendency for the Watts riot participants to be better educated than the nonparticipants, but the difference is too small to be statistically reliable.[16] Finally, Caplan and Paige reported that rioters in Detroit and Newark were significantly higher on an educational achievement scale than the nonrioters.[17]

Thus, while the average rioter was likely to be a high school dropout, data show that the average nonrioter was more likely to be an elementary school dropout. There is a significant relationship between schooling, militancy, and riot activity, but it is the militants and rioters who are better educated.

Employment

A major difficulty arises in interpreting the relationships between employment and militancy because researchers use varying definitions of unemployment and different criteria for ranking occupational skill levels. It is clear from the available evidence, however, that the militants are not the hard-core unemployed. Rather, the militants, particularly the rioters, have greater job dissatisfaction since they are continually on the margin of the job market, often employed but never for long.

Murphy and Watson found a tendency for unemployment to be higher among those who were active during the Watts riot although there was no relationship between riot sympathy and employment.[18] Fogelson and Hill reported a 25 percent unemployment rate among riot arrestees and pointed out that this is about the same level of unemployment as in comparable samples in the open community.[19]

In Detroit, Caplan and Paige found that the unemployment rate for rioters and nonrioters was practically identical, about 31 percent. But in Newark where the respondents were all young males, unemployment was higher among rioters: 31 percent as compared to 19 percent. Further, in Newark the rioters held higher job aspirations than nonrioters and were also more likely to blame their employment failures on racial barriers rather than on personal deficiencies. The same study showed that the rioters were not chronically but only temporarily unemployed and were marginally related to the labor force, i.e., persons who tended to move in and out of the labor force several times throughout the year.[20]

Social Integration and Values

Political theories often emphasize that the militant is isolated or cut off from the rest of the community. More parochial views speculate that the militant is a social deviant who is alienated from the more responsible elements and forces in the social environment. The data from these studies, however, do not support such views. At least two of the major studies show that the Negro who is militant in the pursuit of civil rights objectives is more likely to be the person best integrated into the black community.

Marx found a positive relationship between militancy and the number of organizational memberships held.[21] In Detroit and Newark, Caplan and Paige reported a similar relationship and, in addition, found that rioters socialized with their neighbors and others in the community more frequently than nonrioters.[22] Finally, Marx and Caplan and Paige demonstrated that the militants were more strongly identified with Negro cultural values and civil rights objectives than those in the black community who neither support nor participate in militant activities.[23]

Neither Murphy and Watson nor Caplan and Paige found any relationship between church attendance and riot participation.[24] Marx, however, found that militancy and church attendance related negatively.[25]

Several of the studies included questions intended to show whether or not militancy and rioting are related to differences in support for an important American value: belief in work and the Protestant ethic. Rioters and nonrioters were virtually identical in their responses to most of these questions.[26] About 75 percent of both groups in this study expressed the belief that hard work rather than luck or dependence upon help from others was important for achieving a successful life. Similarly, about 65 percent of the sample studied by Marx agreed that Negroes could get ahead through hard work.[27]

Fogelson and Hill found that the crime rate for the riot arrestees was similar to that of the community as a whole. They did, however, report a difference with respect to the types of past offenses. Rioters tended to have committed less serious crimes.[28]

Socialization

Several of the studies include information about some important elements of adjustment. The possibility that the frustrations of the militant may be caused by inadequate socialization because of family disorganization or migration has been investigated. Data on family background are available only in the study by Caplan and Paige which found that there was essentially no difference between rioters and nonrioters in the presence of an adult male in the home during formative years.[29]

Region of socialization has also been related to militancy in a number of different studies but the direction of the relationship is opposite to the riffraff hypothesis that rioters are most likely to be found among recent migrants to the urban area. On the contrary: The militant is no parvenu to the city. Rather, he is the long-term resident who knows urban life best.

Watts respondents born in California were more favorable to the riot [30] and more likely to participate in it [31] than those who migrated to the area. Rioters in Detroit and Newark were more likely than nonrioters to have been born and raised in the North. In Detroit, six out of ten of the rioters, in contrast to three out of ten of the nonrioters, were born in that city. The distinction between region and socialization and riot participation is even more clearly drawn in the Newark data from the same study. There almost half of the nonrioters but only a quarter of the rioters had been born and raised in the South.[32]

The readiness of the long-term, northern-born ghetto resident to participate in riot activity is even more clearly defined in Fogelson and Hill.[33] In addition to finding that the arrestees were more likely to be northern born, they also discovered that the highest proportion of northern-born rioters and the lowest proportion of southern-born rioters were arrested on the first day of rioting. The arrestees on and after the third day represented the highest proportion of southern born and lowest proportion of northern born. Fogelson and Hill also noted a tendency for the southern born to be involved in less flagrant aspects of the riot. They were least likely to have been charged with "assault" and most likely to have been arrested for looting.

Finally, in their study of the meaning of "Black Power" carried out in Detroit, Aberbach and Walker found that northern-born Negroes more frequently define this concept in militant, political terms. Southern-born Negroes were less likely to view the slogans favorably and to interpret it in a militant context.[34]

Black Consciousness

Possibly the characteristic of the new ghetto man which has the most etiological significance for understanding the rise of militancy is his black consciousness. Both the Detroit and the Newark studies indicate that rioters have strong feelings of racial pride and even racial superiority.[35] They not only have rejected the traditional stereotype of the Negro but also have created a positive stereotype.

In both cities, rioters were more likely to view their race more positively than nonrioters on racial comparison items involving dependability, smartness, courage, "niceness," etc. For example, about one-half of rioters but less than one-quarter of nonrioters felt Negroes were "more dependable" than whites. Responses in these studies reflect a higher level of black pride among rioters; those who attempted to quell the disturbance and control the level of destruction deviate in the opposite direction. When the sample was divided into rioters, the uninvolved, and counterrioters, the rioters were highest and counterrioters were lowest on several measures of racial pride. Furthermore, half of the rioters and only a third of the nonrioters preferred to be called "black" rather than "colored," "Negro," or "Afro—American." Similarly, Caplan and Paige found a tendency for rioters to be stronger in the belief that all Negroes should study Negro history and African languages in the high schools.[36]

Marx reported that militants prefer Negro newspapers and magazines, are better able to identify Negro writers and civil rights leaders, and have a more positive appreciation of Negro culture than nonmilitants.[37] Darrow and Lowinger also encountered feelings of a new, positive Negro self-image among the rioters they studied. Consequently, these authors argue against the psychoanalytic interpretations of rioting which hold that participants release aggression associated with self-hatred.[38]

This positive affirmation of racial identity is found not only among the militants but is widespread throughout the Negro community. Ninety-six percent of the sample in this study agreed that "Negroes should take more pride in Negro history." Also, four out of ten of the respondents thought that "Negro school children should study an *African* language" (italics mine).[39]

Thucydides said long ago that social revolution occurs when old terms take on new meanings. The wisdom of this statement is apparent in the dramatic, recent change of meaning for the term "black"—a word that has become a badge of intense pride which borders on racial superiority: "Black is Beautiful."

Attitudes toward Whites

The fact that racial pride is so high in the black community and the suspicion that it may play a causal role in the rise of militancy raises questions about Negro attitudes toward whites. Do black pride and the desire for black self-development go hand in hand with white hatred? What is the overall attitude of the ghetto toward whites?

Although there are some slight inconsistencies in the findings, in general, militancy does not appear associated with increased hostility toward whites; the black community as a whole is not markedly antiwhite nor preoccupied by social cross-comparison with whites.

Marx found that militancy and antiwhite attitudes were inversely related. The variables which were most closely related to militancy—intellectual sophistication, high morale, and a positive self-image—correlated negatively with antiwhite sentiment. Marx concluded that ". . . they don't hate (whites), but they don't like them either."[40] In an earlier study, Noel also found that those lowest in antiwhite feelings were the most militant proponents of civil rights actions.[41] Although he presents no supporting data, Tomlinson also reported that the militants in the UCLA study are not notably antiwhite.[42]

Murphy and Watson reported a slight tendency for the economically better-off riot participants to be more hostile toward whites.[43] Caplan and Paige similarly found the rioters to be slightly more antiwhite but equally hostile to more-affluent Negroes.[44] Also, it should be pointed out that several attempts to test whether or not rioters are more likely to use whites as social comparative referents have found no support.

When considered in the aggregate, the Negro community is probably far less antiwhite than most whites are prepared to believe. Campbell and Schuman found little evidence of antiwhite hostility in their study.

Only 13 percent of their respondents wanted to live in an all-black or mostly black neighborhood; only 6 percent believed that American Negroes should establish a separate black nation; and only 9 percent felt that Negroes should have as little as possible to do with whites. Furthermore, only 6 percent wanted Negro children to go to only Negro schools and 5 percent preferred to have only Negro friends. On the basis of responses to these and a number of similar items, Campbell and Schuman concluded: "Negroes hold strongly, perhaps more strongly than any other element in the American population, to a belief in nondiscrimination and racial harmony." [45]

In general, these findings are not different from the results of earlier studies. Noel and Pinkney found that 41 percent of Negroes sampled in four cities expressed no particular antipathy toward whites. [46] Among the respondents in the nationwide survey by Brink and Harris, 80 percent reported that they preferred to work with a racially mixed group; 68 percent preferred to live in an integrated neighborhood; 70 percent preferred to have their children attend school with white children, and only 5 percent supported black nationalism. [47] Only about 4 percent of Marx's total sample supported pronationalistic statements. [48]

In the Murphy and Watson and Caplan and Paige studies, antiwhite sentiment was most intense among riot participants when associated with perceived discrimination practices which restricted social and economic mobility for Negroes. Neither social envy of whites nor material greed motivates men to riot, but rather anger over the conditions that produce—and the practices that sustain—barriers denying Negroes the same freedoms and opportunities available to whites. [49]

Political Attitudes

Almost all recent studies of Negro communities have included political items in their interview schedules and, without exception, the data show that militants are politically more sensitive and better informed than nonmilitants: they are not, however, politically alienated. What they want is what is already guaranteed by law, not a new political system.

Tomlinson reported that compared with nonmilitants, militants in Watts were politically more active, more likely to refer to the riot in "revolutionary" terms, and less trustful of elected officials. [50] Marx found that almost twice as many militants as nonmilitants voted during the 1960 presidential election (31 percent v. 17 percent). [51] Sears and

Sears and McConahay reported that Watts arrestees and riot participants expressed greater political discontent and were more cynical of
the responsiveness of local political powers to Negro grievances than
nonrioter samples.[52]

Caplan and Paige found that rioters were more familiar with the
identification of political personalities, more distrustful of politicians,
and more likely to cite anger at politicians as a cause of the riot. In
Newark, 44 percent of the rioters and 34 percent of the nonrioters reported "almost never" when asked if local government could be trusted
"to do what is right." In Detroit, 42 percent of the rioters but only 20
percent of the nonrioters cited "anger with politicians" as a major cause
of the riot.[53]

The kinds of discontents that are felt most intensely by the militants
reflect feelings that are widespread throughout the Negro community.
Sears reported that 45 percent of the random sample of Watts residents
said that "elected officials cannot generally be trusted"; this figure compares with 17 percent of a comparable white sample.[54] Despite these
discontents with political representation and the domination of the political system by whites, there is no evidence of broad rejection of the
political system itself. Brink and Harris found that 74 percent of the
Negroes in their sample expressed the desire to attain civil rights objectives through existing political channels.[55] Also, Campbell and Schuman
found no evidence indicating that Negroes want a new form of political
functioning.[56]

Fate Control

The final characteristic of the militant that must be given special emphasis can be called fate control or the power to maintain control over
those environmental forces that affect one's destiny. Although none of
the researchers conceptualize this variable as such, several findings
imply its distinct character as well as its significance to the emergence
of militancy in the ghetto.

For example, Marx identifies "intellectual sophistication" as one of
the three variables most strongly related to militancy. He describes intellectual sophistication as greater knowledge of the world and a way of
looking at the world. Two important related factors that make up this
variable are a broad, liberated world-outlook and great sensitivity to the

way social factors shape human behavior. In essence, Marx stresses that the militant is more likely to be cognitively correct about the external forces that influence his behavior and how they impede his ability to effectuate personal goals.[57]

Meyer concluded that Miami-area Negroes who scored high on militancy possess ". . . a strong feeling that they can and should shape their destinies." He based his interpretation on the association between the respondents' scores on militancy and their sense of personal and political efficacy.[58] In a survey study of Los Angeles Negroes, Ransford found that "powerlessness," which he defines as ". . . a low expectancy of control over events," was strongly related to the respondent's willingness to use violence. Those with the highest scores on powerlessness held the highest commitment to violence.[59]

Crawford and Naditch reexamined Ransford's data along with data from two other survey studies. By combining powerlessness with Rotter's internal–external schema, they found that the more militant respondents were characterized by a high sense of personal efficacy and low control over external forces that affect the probability of achieving personal goals.[60] Employing a similar analytical framework, Gurin et al. found a marked tendency for militancy among Negro students to be associated with the belief that they could not reach personal goals because of external or social systemic constraints.[61] Finally, the "blocked-opportunity theory which emphasized environmental rather than personal factors as the cause of riots is supported by the survey data from the Caplan-Paige study which found that rioters desire increased mastery over the distribution of resources rather than the mere acquisition of resources.[62]

Conclusions

There is a surprising degree of empirical regularity and basic coherence to the findings discussed here, even though they come from studies carried out in several parts of the country by different investigators employing various methodological approaches. This agreement allows us to draw some important conclusions with reasonable comfort and confidence in their validity, conclusions which should help achieve a better understanding of the militant and a safer evaluation of his behavior.

1. Militancy in the pursuit of civil rights objectives represents a considerable force within the ghetto. Its support approaches normative pro-

portions and is by no means limited to a deviant and irresponsible minority.

2. The militant is a man in search of practical responses to arbitrary institutional constraints and preemptions which deny him the same freedom and conventional opportunities as the white majority. He is the better educated but underemployed, politically disaffected but not the politically alienated. He is willing to break laws for rights already guaranteed by law, but under ordinary circumstances he is no more likely to engage in crime than his nonmilitant neighbor. He is intensely proud of being black, but neither desires revenge from whites nor is socially envious of them. He has little freedom of resources to effectuate his personal goals, but strongly desires freedom and ownership of his own life. Indeed, this new man of the ghetto is also a man of paradox.

3. The characteristics of the militants together with the large proportion of ghetto blacks who share their views certainly indicate that the fight for civil rights will not end with the recent riots. Even though the time and place of their occurrence may not be predictable and their instrumental value not always clear, the riots are neither random events nor marginal, temporary phenomena. The militants must be taken seriously and not simply treated as troublemakers.

4. With candor and a few frills, the Kerner Commission cited white racism as the major cause of ghetto riots. Undoubtedly, white racism is a root issue, but it has been present for over 300 years and, therefore, is insufficient as a sole explanation of riots of such magnitude and intensity as occur at this point in time. The logic of scientific proof would require that we look for causal factors whose relationships are more contemporaneous.

The findings reviewed here suggest that Negroes who riot do so because their conception of their lives and their potential has changed without commensurate improvement in their chances for a better life. In the midst of squalor and despair, Negroes have abandoned the traditional stereotypes that made nonachievement and passive adaptation seem so natural. Rather, they have developed a sense of black consciousness and a desire for a way of life with which they can feel the same pride and sense of potency they now derive from being black. Without these changes in self-perception, the demands to be regarded and treated as an individual with the same liberties as white Americans would never have reached the intensity that they have today. If this interpretation of the research is correct, it could be argued that the riots and other forms of civil rights protest are caused by the self-discovery of the American Negro and his attempt to re-create himself socially in ways that are commensurate with this new image. This battle for greater personal rights can be expected to continue as long as the Negro's political, social, and economic efficacy is not aligned with his new and increasing sense of personal potency.

5. The limited data available at this time do not permit us to make fine-grain projections about the maturation pattern of riot activity, the future forms of other protest activity, or their outcome. Possibly the most that one can say at this time about the meaning of these outbreaks is: first, they are more similar to the early slaveship uprisings than they are to the white-initiated interracial riots that occurred after World Wars I and II. Ghetto-locked blacks are claiming ownership of their behavior and are demanding the freedom and opportunity necessary to control their destiny. They are interested in bettering their position in American society; they are not interested in "white blood" or the glorification of violence. Second, it seems safe to conclude that the riots represent an elementary form of political activity. But, it must be emphasized that the political objectives are conservative. The militants are not rebelling against the system itself but against the inequities and contradictions of the system.

If this nation is serious about the application of democratic principles to human affairs, then it must increase the power of the black man to improve his position beyond anything now possible in American society. The stereotype of the Negro—which for seven generations has been used to destroy his initiative, motivation, and hope—is a reality apart from what these studies show him to be. He emerges in these studies as more American than those who built the ghetto and those who now maintain it. Unless this nation acts now to redress the balance in social and economic distance between the races, we will probably have lost forever the ideal of the democratic prospect and, like other nations in the past, will resort to what C. P. Snow calls "hideous crimes in the name of obedience." It is clear that the Negro will not give up the struggle for a better life. Unlike Negroes in the past, the present ghetto dwellers have neither the psychological defenses nor the social supports that permit passive adaptation to barriers that prevent implementation of their potential capabilities. In a sense, they are the hearing children of deaf parents.

NOTES

1. T. M. Tomlinson, "The Development of a Riot Ideology among Urban Negroes," *American Behavioral Scientist* 11, no. 4 (March–April 1968): 28.

2. D. O. Sears and J. M. McConahay, "Riot Participation: Los Angeles Riot Study" (unpublished, 1967).

3. N. S. Caplan and J. M. Paige, in O. Kerner et al., *Report of The National Advisory Commission on Civil Disorders* (New York: Bantam, 1968), pp. 127–137, footnotes 111–143, 171–178.

4. *Ibid.*

5. R. M. Fogelson and R. B. Hill, "Who Riots? A Study of Participation in the 1967 Riots (*Supplemental Studies for the National Advisory Commission on Civil Disorders,* Government Printing Office, 1968).

6. W. Brink and L. Harris, *Black and White* (New York: Simon and Schuster, 1966); A. Campbell and H. Schuman, "Racial Attitudes in Fifteen American Cities" (*Supplemental Studies for the National Advisory Commission on Civil Disorders,* Government Printing Office, 1968).

7. R. J. Murphy and J. M. Watson, *The Structure of Discontent: The Relationship between Social Structure, Grievance, and Support for the Los Angeles Riot* (Los Angeles: Institute of Government and Public Affairs, University of California, 1967); Caplan and Paige, *Commission on Civil Disorders;* C. Darrow and P. Lowinger, "The Detroit Uprising: A Psychosocial Study" (presented at the Meeting of the American Academy of Psychoanalysis, New York, 1967); J. Shulman, "Ghetto Residence, Political Alienation and Riot Orientation" (unpublished, Cornell University, 1967).

8. Caplan and Paige, *Commission on Civil Disorders.*

9. Campbell and Schuman, *op. cit.*

10. Brink and Harris, *op. cit.*

11. N. S. Caplan and J. M. Paige, "A Study of Ghetto Rioters," *Scientific American* 219, no. 2 (August 1968): 15–21.

12. W. McCord and J. Howard, "Negro Opinions in Three Riot Cities," *American Behavioral Scientist* 11, no. 4 (March–April 1968): 24–27.

13. Campbell and Schuman, *op. cit.*

14. Tomlinson, *op. cit.*

15. G. T. Marx, *Protest and Prejudice: A Study of Belief in the Black Community* (New York: Harper & Row, 1967).

16. Murphy and Watson, *op. cit.*

17. Caplan and Paige, *Commission on Civil Disorders.*

18. Murphy and Watson, *op. cit.*

19. Fogelson and Hill, *op. cit.*

20. Caplan and Paige, *Commission on Civil Disorders.*

21. Marx, *op. cit.*

22. Caplan and Paige, *Commission on Civil Disorders.*

23. Marx, *op. cit.;* Caplan and Paige, *Commission on Civil Disorders.*

24. Murphy and Watson, *op. cit.;* Caplan and Paige, *Commission on Civil Disorders.*

25. Marx, *op. cit.*

26. Caplan and Paige, *Commission on Civil Disorders.*

27. Marx, *op. cit.*

28. Fogelson and Hill, *op. cit.*

29. Caplan and Paige, *Commission on Civil Disorders.*

30. Murphy and Watson, *op. cit.*

31. Sears and McConahay, *Riot Participation.*

32. Caplan and Paige, *Commission on Civil Disorders.*

33. Fogelson and Hill, *op. cit.*

34. D. Aberbach and L. Walker, "The Meanings of Black Power: A Comparison of White and Black Interpretations of a Political Slogan" (presented at the Annual Meetings of the American Political Science Association, Washington, D.C., 1968).

35. Caplan and Paige, *Commission on Civil Disorder* and "Study of Ghetto Rioters."

36. *Ibid.*

37. Marx, *op. cit.*

38. Darrow and Lowinger, *op. cit.*

39. Campbell and Schuman, *op. cit.*

40. Marx, *op. cit.,* p. 179.

41. D. L. Noel, "Group Identification among Negroes: An Empirical Analysis," *Journal of Social Issues* 20 (May 1964): 21–84.

42. Tomlinson, *op. cit.*

43. Murphy and Watson, *op. cit.*

44. Caplan and Paige, *Commission on Civil Disorders.*

45. Campbell and Schuman, *op. cit.,* p. 17.

46. D. L. Noel and A. Pinkney, "Correlate of Prejudice: Some Racial Differences and Similarities," *American Journal of Sociology* 69, no. 6 (1964): 609–622.

47. Brink and Harris, *op. cit.*

48. Marx, *op. cit.*

49. Murphy and Watson, *op. cit;* Caplan and Paige, "Study of Ghetto Rioters."

50. Tomlinson, *op. cit.*

51. Marx, *op. cit.*

52. D. O. Sears, "Political Attitudes of Los Angeles Negroes" (Los Angeles: Institute of Government and Public Affairs, University of California, 1967); D. O. Sears and J. M. McConahay, "The Politics of Discontent: Los Angeles Riot Study" (unpublished, 1967).

53. Caplan and Paige, *Commission on Civil Disorders.*

54. Sears, *op. cit.,* p. 21.

55. Brink and Harris, *op. cit.*

56. Campbell and Schuman, *op. cit.*

57. Marx, *op. cit.*

58. P. Meyer, "Negro Militancy and Martin Luther King: The Aftermath of Martyrdom," *Knight Newspapers* (Washington, D.C., 1968), p. 22.

59. H. E. Ransford, "Isolation, Powerlessness, and Violence: A Study of Attitudes and Participation in the Watts Riot," *American Journal of Sociology* 73 (1968): 581–591.

60. T. J. Crawford and M. Naditch, "Unattained and Unattainable Goals: Relative Deprivation, Powerlessness, and Racial Militancy" (presented at the American Psychological Association Convention, San Francisco, 1968).

61. P. Gurin, G. Gurin, R. Lao, and M. Beattie, "Internal–External Control in the Motivational Dynamics of Negro Youth," *Journal of Social Issues* 25, no. 3 (1969).

62. Caplan and Paige, "Study of Ghetto Rioters."

18. BLACK ATTITUDES TOWARD THE POLITICAL SYSTEM IN THE AFTERMATH OF THE WATTS INSURRECTION
David O. Sears

UNTIL recently Negroes have been a "silent minority" in the American political system. Their direct political impact has been relatively slight, except for their rather special influence on southern politics, which has not generally involved much overt political action on their part. This low level of political activity has, of course, coexisted with severe mistreatment at the hands of institutions and individual citizens alike. To mention only the most obvious case, the level of physical violence to which blacks have been subjected is only paralleled by that administered to the Indians, from whom the territory was originally wrested.

This essay is addressed to the contemporary black man's political response to this situation.[1] Unequal and vicious treatment might be expected to produce antagonistic attitudes toward the American political system. It would be understandable if blacks felt the system was not working in their behalf, and sought radical changes in it. Indeed widespread revolutionary sentiment would not be surprising. On the other hand, many observers have felt that Negroes were, in Myrdal's phrase, "exaggerated Americans who believed in the American creed more passionately than whites."[2]

The purpose of this essay is to determine which of these more closely characterized the feelings of the black community under a unique political circumstance: as it looked back and attempted to interpret the gigantic upheaval that was the Watts insurrection. Three different dimensions of black citizens' relationship to politics will be dealt with: (1) attachment to the American political system and to its institutions; (2)

From the *Midwest Journal of Political Science* 13, no. 4 (November 1969): 515–544. Reprinted by permission of Wayne State University Press and the author. Copyright © Wayne State University Press.

satisfaction with its current operation; and (3) the ability to contribute to changes in the system and its operation, in terms of mobilization for effective political action. This last may, in turn, be confidence in one's own political effectiveness and current level of political activity.

There is particular reason today to be concerned about blacks' attachment to the American system and to its institutions. For one thing, it has been coming under increasing attack from black militants. "I do not want to be a part of the American pride," said Stokely Carmichael. "I don't want to be part of that system." The militant critique varies between recommending greater black participation in political decisions and greater black control over the destiny of the black community, on the one hand, and, on the other, pressing for the destruction of existing institutions and their replacement with new forms. Indeed, the black movement is seen as a "revolution" by many militants. Historically, blacks have generally been thought to be as loyal to America as any other minority group, but today the wisdom of this attachment is being called into question.[3]

At the same time, recent race riots have been, at least prima facie, small revolutions. Constituted authority has repeatedly been completely overthrown, even if only for short periods of time. Whether organized or anarchistic, the riots obviously present the appearance of insurrection. And the black community has generally interpreted the riots as being revolutionary in nature. For example, 38 percent of our representative sample of blacks in Los Angeles described the Watts disturbance as a "revolt," "revolution," or "insurrection," and only 46 percent used the term applied universally by the media and authorities, "riot." Most blacks described the rioting as a purposeful protest. Similarly, most blacks attributed the riots to specific grievances such as discrimination, unfair treatment, or pent-up hostility.[4]

This might imply no more than the existence of a few rebels in the ghetto who get a riot going, rather than widespread disaffection from the system, except for two things. First, the size of the riots and the extent of participation indicate a broad community base for them. Second, the black communities in riot-torn cities have generally been sympathetic to the rioting. Though blacks, as well as whites, have deplored the killing and destruction, they have not generally joined in condemnations of the rioters, nor in viewing the riots as counterproductive. In both cases blacks have actually been rather sympathetic to the rioting, while whites have been strongly antagonistic. This sympathy with insurrection gives some reason for thinking that widespread revolutionary sentiment, rather than mere dissatisfaction with current incumbents and policies, may exist in America's black ghettos.[5]

Many observers now believe that this matter of attachment to the political system is settled in childhood by early political socialization. In this view, the individual's orientations toward the political system have become quite firmly entrenched by early adolescence, and do not change very much thereafter. However, little is known about the early political socialization of black children. Most published studies have dealt mainly with white, middle-class children, who express quite normative views about American institutions and rules. The extreme alienation that has been found in one sample of poor white children in Appalachia gives reason to think that Negro children may also be socialized rather differently, however, and with considerable cynicism about politics.[6] Hence it is quite possible that their attachment to the American system is rather flimsy, and leaves them susceptible to later militant appeals.

Alternatively, this positive response to the riots may not reflect lack of attachment to the American system so much as dissatisfaction with its current operation. Black children may be socialized into as firm acceptance of American norms as white children. But as they mature they may become more conscious and expressive of their dissatisfaction with their particular status in society. There certainly is ample evidence that Negroes are currently more dissatisfied with government actions than are comparable whites.[7] The question is whether or not more serious disaffection is common in the ghetto.

Given considerable dissatisfaction with current government policies, a further question concerns the degree of potential mobilization for political change within the black community. This raises two rather separate issues. First, collective action is required. The power of any relatively deprived minority group is partly dependent on its ability to act in concert. So the question is whether or not blacks can be mobilized along racial lines.

Here the most conventional model is that of ethnic politics. Members of ethnic groups have traditionally exercised political influence by producing leaders from their ranks and forming coalitions with other groups sharing similar interests.[8] For ethnic politics to be effective, group members must be prepared to support their own leaders. So here we wish to determine the extent to which "racial partisanship" characterizes the political attitudes of the black community.

Second, to what extent are blacks psychologically mobilized for confident political action? Several steps are involved here. Those of public officials may be a prerequisite to feeling they can be influenced by normal means. The citizen must feel that public officials are accessible, that he knows where to go to solve a problem, and that he can have a hearing. Further, he must feel that he can influence official behavior, that he will be listened to and his case judged fairly. Perhaps the best guarantee of competence in these areas is past experience; if he has done it before, he is more likely to feel he can do it in the future.

Previous studies have suggested that blacks have not, in the past, been especially effectively mobilized for political action. They clearly have been more discouraged about the reception they can expect: they have been lower than whites in the sense of political efficacy, more reluctant than whites to approach public officials, and they have not expected equal treatment from government officials or the police. Consequently their rate of political participation has been considerably below that of whites, even in the absence of legal barriers to it.[9]

The Watts riot may have marked a real watershed in black political orientations. It, and the riots that have followed, have approximated as closely as anything else in this century mass revolutionary uprisings against constituted authority. The major question we wish to pose in this essay is whether or not the dissatisfaction that Negroes have typically felt with government had, in the aftermath of insurrection, been converted into estrangement from the American political system. Second, what has been the riot's effect upon the degree of political mobilization in the black community? Is there evidence of increased racial partisanship and political effectiveness? We wish to determine whether estrangement or politically effective partisanship is now more common.

Of course much has happened since the Watts riot, in the black and white communities alike. The black community has apparently moved increasingly toward the militants, though the degree of change is a matter of controversy. If we cannot be entirely clear about where matters stand at the present time, at least we can gain clarity about where it began, in the community just then recovering from the most massive Negro rebellion the country had ever known. The picture that emerges from the Watts of late 1965 is one, we think, that renders explicable much of what has happened subsequently throughout the nation. The nature of racial partisanship that became clear then makes the subsequent "racism" more comprehensible.

The Data

The data on which this essay is based were obtained from interviews conducted with two samples of respondents in Los Angeles County in late 1965 and early 1966. The most important was a representative sample (n = 586) of Negroes living in the large area (46.5 square miles) of South-Central Los Angeles sealed off by a curfew imposed during the rioting. The curfew zone contains about three-fourths of the more than 450,000 Negroes living in Los Angeles County, and is over 80 percent Negro. Hence it represents the major concentration of Negroes in the Los Angeles area. Black interviewers living in the curfew zone did the interviewing. Though the interviews were long (averaging about two hours), interest was high and the refusal rate low. Checks were run on the possible biases introduced by the interviewers' own views and these do not give unusual reason for concern.

The sampling was done by randomly choosing names from the 1960 census lists, then oversampling poverty level census tracts by a cluster sampling procedure to compensate for the underrepresentation of low-income respondents due to residential transience. While sampling biases are common in surveys of black ghettos, we believe this sample is as close to being representative of the area as is normally achieved.

The other sample included 583 white respondents from six communities in Los Angeles County, half of which were racially integrated and half nonintegrated, with high, medium, and low socio–economic levels. This sample is thus not wholly representative of the county, overrepresenting high SES and racially integrated areas. Some, but not all, of the items on the Negro interview schedule were also used with white respondents. Our main emphasis in this paper is upon Negro opinion, so the white sample is not referred to except when explicitly indicated.[10]

Black Disaffection

TRUST OF GOVERNMENT

First let us make an overall assessment of the Negro community's attachment to conventional political mechanisms. Blacks clearly felt considerable ambivalence about the adequacy of their representation and whether or not they could trust their political representatives. Fifty percent felt that "elected officials can generally be trusted," while 45 percent felt that they could not be. In contrast, 79 percent of the whites trusted elected officials, and only 17 percent did not. Forty-two percent of the blacks responded positively to "how do you feel about the way you are represented?" and 42 percent responded negatively. Whites saw the Negro's situation much more favorable: when asked "do you think the Negro is fairly represented politically?" 55 percent said "yes," and 22 percent said "no." These measures, then, indicate substantial black disaffection.

NATIONAL PARTISAN POLITICS

The "Negro vote" has in recent years become of keen interest to the national political parties and their candidates. Most Negroes today have a basic loyalty to the Democratic party, though their votes often "swing" rather easily from one side to the other, as illustrated by the fact that only about 60 percent of Negro voters supported the Democratic presidential candidate in 1956, while almost all voted for Lyndon B. Johnson in 1964 and Hubert Humphrey in 1968.

Quite aside from the importance of these votes to the two parties, vigorous electoral partisanship reflects acceptance of and participation in the traditional mechanisms of the American political system. A rabid partisan also tends to be a loyal, democratic American.[11] Did the use of violence in rioting lead Negroes to reject the act of commitment to one of the conventional partisan alternatives, reflecting a more general loss of faith in the American system?

Los Angeles Negroes did not withdraw from the arena of national partisan politics after the riot. Almost all regarded themselves as Democrats, and held far more favorable attitudes toward the Democratic party and its leaders than toward the Republicans. When asked the standard Survey Research Center item on party identification, 84 percent of the Negroes sampled indicated they were Democrats, 6 percent Republicans, and 5 percent Independents. Their presidential votes in 1964 had been equally strongly pro-Democratic; 74 percent had voted for Johnson, 2 percent for Goldwater, and many of the remainder failed to vote only because they were not eligible to do so. In both cases their level of partisanship compared favorably with that of whites, 84 percent of whom claimed identification with one party or the other, and 73 percent of whom voted for president in 1964.

This preference for the Democrats was not simply a preference for

Table 18–1 / **Evaluations of Leaders and Groups
in National Partisan Politics**

Leaders and Groups	Evaluations			
	Favorable (1)	Unfavorable (2)	Net Effect (1–2)	No Opinion
DEMOCRATIC				
Lyndon B. Johnson, President	95%	3%	+92%	1%
Democratic Party	89	4	+85	7
Edmund G. ("Pat") Brown, Governor	81	12	+69	6
AFL–CIO	58	16	+42	26
Mean:	81%	9%	+72%	
REPUBLICAN				
George Murphy, U.S. Senator	15	33	−18	52
Republican Party	30	56	−26	15
Mean:	22%	44%	−22%	

NOTE: The items used were of a standard evaluation type: "How good a job is President Johnson doing? Is he doing well, doing fairly well (both favorable), doing nothing, or doing harm (both unfavorable)?" The proportions "doing well" were 63 percent, 64 percent, 34 percent, and 35 percent respectively, for the pro-Democratic set. The "no opinion" column includes those who "never heard of him," "don't know how he does," and those who failed to answer.

the "lesser of two evils." As shown in Table 18–1, attitudes toward the Democratic party and toward its two most visible leaders, President Johnson and then-Governor Brown, were highly favorable. The Republican party and conservative Senator George Murphy both were regarded highly unfavorably. Thus, Democratic party identification meant positive regard for the Democrats and active rejection of the Republicans. Most Los Angeles blacks seem to have maintained their pro-Democratic partisan commitments, even in the wake of the riot, and had not rejected their traditional white liberal allies.

LOCAL GOVERNMENT

An important consequence of the migration and urbanization of Negroes has been to throw much of the responsibility for meeting their needs upon local government in large northern cities. Some local public agencies, most notably the police force and welfare agencies, devote a disproportionate amount of their resources to the problems of the urban

Negro population. How satisfied was the black community with the efforts of local government in the aftermath of the riot?

White-dominated Politics / Most local political figures are white, in Los Angeles as elsewhere. Evaluations of them were extremely mixed, as shown in Table 18–2. Pointed hostility was directed at two: Mayor Sam Yorty and the late William Parker, then chief of the Los Angeles Police Department. Both were widely disliked and distrusted. Chief Parker's intransigence on the race issue was both long-standing and quite public, and Yorty had firmly supported him before, during, and after the riot. In other respects, as well, Yorty was thought to be unresponsive to the black community, though he had run moderately well there in the mayoralty campaign a few months earlier. Finally, there was relatively little antagonism toward the two local white politicians whose districts included part of the riot area, City Councilman Gibson and County Supervisor Hahn.

Table 18–2 / **Evaluations of Local White Politicians**

	Evaluations			
	Favorable (1)	Unfavorable (2)	Net Effect (1–2)	No Opinion
Sam Yorty, L.A. Mayor	25%	66%	−41%	9%
William Parker, Chief of L.A.P.D.	10	76	−66	8
John Gibson, L.A. City Council	27	5	+22	67
Kenneth Hahn, L.A. County Supervisor	58	3	+55	39
Mean:	40%	38%	+ 2%	

NOTE: Standard evaluation question used. (See Note to Table 18–1.)

Administrative Agencies / Some local administrative agencies received a great deal of criticism, while others did not. The Los Angeles Police Department was extremely negatively regarded. There was much antagonism toward the police chief, as noted above. Many expressed the feeling that the rioting represented a retaliation against the police force. Most obviously, blacks were vastly more concerned about the frequency of police misconduct than were whites. Ninety-two percent of the whites and only 41 percent of the blacks felt "you generally can trust the police," while 54 percent of the blacks and only 6 percent of the whites felt you could not. Both groups were asked whether the police lack respect or use insulting language in their dealings with Negroes, and 71 percent of the blacks, against 59 percent of the whites, felt they did. Similarly, 72 percent of the blacks and 64 percent of the whites felt Negroes were rousted, frisked, and searched without good reason. Indeed, the races polarized more over the issue of the police than any other single question.[12]

The evaluations of other service agencies are less unfavorable, but expressed considerable dissatisfaction, as shown in Table 18–3. Negative evaluations of the State Employment Agency, or even of the Bureau of Public Assistance and the Aid to Dependent Children program, were not uncommon. In no case was a majority unfavorable to an agency, but substantial minorities were.

Other evidence of discontent is provided by perceptions of racial discrimination in various public agencies. The most obvious case is the school system, a classic example of de facto segregation. Seventy-three

Table 18–3 / **Evaluations of Local Service Agencies**

Agency	Evaluation of Agency Performance			
	Favorable (1)	Unfavorable (2)	Net Effect (1–2)	No Opinion
State Employment Agency	50%	29%	+21%	21%
L.A. Human Relations Commission	32	10	+22	58
Bureau of Public Assistance	56	19	+37	24
Aid to Dependent Children	54	15	+39	31
Mean:	48%	18%	+30%	

Agency	Perception of Racial Discrimination in Agencies				
	None (1)	Experienced It (2)	Heard of It (3)	Net Effect (1–2, 3)	No Opinion
Schools	26%	16%	57%	−47%	1%
Fire Department	52	5	41	+ 6	3
Welfare Agencies	56	8	32	+16	4
Park Department	67	6	24	+37	3
Garbage Collection	67	10	19	+38	3
Mean:	54%	9%	35%	+10%	

NOTE: The item used for evaluation was "Do you think it does a good job (favorable), does nothing, or does harm (both unfavorable)?" The discrimination items read, "Have you heard of or experienced discrimination against Negroes in (e.g.) the schools?"

percent of the sample indicated they had heard of, or personally experienced, discrimination by the schools. Perceptions of discrimination were also widespread with regard to the fire department and welfare agencies.

Antipoverty Program / Another set of local service agencies with a particular interest in the black community were those in the antipoverty program. At the time of our survey, most Negroes were optimistic about the War on Poverty. Forty-two percent thought it would "help a lot," 45 percent thought it would "help a little," and only 7 percent thought it would "have no effect." Evaluations of a number of specific antipoverty agencies showed the same pattern of generally favorable attitude. The local omnibus agency, the Economic and Youth Opportunities Agency, was positively regarded by 48 percent and negatively by 11 percent; Head Start, by 41 percent and 8 percent, respectively. The mean net affect over six agencies was +31 percent, which compares favorably with the net affects toward local white politicians and toward agencies of local government shown in Tables 18–2 and 18–3.

Many of the area's residents were unfamiliar with the newly created agencies, each of which was unknown to at least 40 percent of our black respondents. However, those who had heard of them tended to be quite favorable. This was also true of the white sample, though there the level of ignorance was even higher: 71 percent for EYOA and 64 percent for Head Start, compared with 40 percent and 47 percent, respectively, in the black sample.

Federal and Local Government / This optimism about the poverty program was part of the generally greater trust invested in the federal government. Each respondent was asked which does the best "for your problems." Four percent said the city government was best, 6 percent said the state government, and 58 percent cited the federal government. Most of the rest (25 percent) said they were all about the same.

Evaluations of the several legislative bodies show the same pattern, as Table 18–4 indicates. First, blacks are generally less satisfied with their work than whites: the Congress "represented well" 47 percent of the blacks and 65 percent of the whites; the state legislature, 30 percent and 49 percent, respectively, and the County Board of Supervisors, 28 percent and 36 percent.

Second, the federal Congress is praised considerably more by blacks than are the local bodies. A comparison of Tables 18–1 and 18–2 quickly reveals the generality of the greater support for federal than for local officials; most notably, the net affect toward the president was

Table 18–4 / **Evaluations of Legislative Bodies**

	Evaluations			
	Favorable (1)	*Unfavorable* (2)	*Net Effect* (1–2)	*No Opinion*
U.S. Congress	82%	10%	+72%	8%
California state legislature	70	13	+57	17
L.A. County Board of Supervisors	70	16	+54	14
Los Angeles City Council	73	15	+58	12
Mean:	74%	14%	+60%	

NOTE: The item read, "Do you feel that the U.S. Congress speaks for you or represents you well, a little (both favorable), or doesn't represent you (unfavorable)?" The evaluation item cited in previous tables was very highly correlated with this item when both referred to the same attitude object. Thus "net affect" scores can be meaningfully compared across tables.

+92 percent, and toward the mayor, −41 percent. And negative attitudes toward the poverty program agencies were only about half as common as they were toward state and local service agencies.

This greater support for federal officials and agencies and the serious dissatisfaction with local government are one of the most striking findings of the study. As might be expected, it is most obvious as a general disposition, and with respect to the most visible individuals at each level of government, such as the president, governor, mayor, and police chief.

Local Communications Media / Other potential mechanisms for the expression and satisfaction of the black community's needs are the local communications media. Publicity is one way of getting grievances redressed. Did Negroes generally feel their problems were fairly communicated by local press, television, and radio, or did they feel communication was blocked?

Again there was marked ambivalence, as shown in Table 18–5. Television, radio, and the Hearst evening newspaper (the *Herald Examiner)* were evaluated positively. However, the dominant view was that the *Los Angeles Times* did not treat Negro problems fairly. The *Times* has traditionally expressed the viewpoint of upper middle-class conservatism, almost invariably supporting Republican candidates (such as Nixon, Goldwater, and Reagan) and conservative policies (such as the anti–fair housing referendum of 1964, proposition 14). Its editorial policies have become more moderate in recent years, and it opposed Mayor Yorty vigorously over several of the issues raised by the Watts

371   DAVID O. SEARS

Table 18–5 / **Evaluations of Communications Media**

	Evaluations			
	Favorable (1)	Unfavorable (2)	Net Effect (1–2)	No Opinion
Community-wide Media				
Los Angeles Times	38%	44%	− 6%	19%
Los Angeles Herald Examiner	54	31	+23	14
TV in general	63	29	+34	8
Radio in general	64	26	+38	11
Mean:	55%	32%	+23%	
Negro-originated Media				
Muhammed Speaks	24%	30%	− 6%	47%
Los Angeles Herald Dispatch	35	17	+18	48
Los Angeles Sentinel	48	6	+42	46
KGFJ	76	7	+69	17
Louis Lomax	69	16	+53	16
James Baldwin	56	4	+52	40
Mean:	51%	13%	+38%	

NOTE: The question used for the first eight rows reads, "How fairly or unfairly do the following cover the problems of the Negro community?" For Lomax and Baldwin, the standard evaluation question was used. (See note to Table 18–1.)

riot. However, Negroes continue to regard it with suspicion, based no doubt on its long history of political and economic conservatism.

BLACK LEADERSHIP

Much of the black community's political disaffection seems to be due to the preponderance of white faces in political office. Black leaders were preferred: 62 percent felt that "Negro elected officials" could be trusted, as opposed to the 50 percent who felt elected officials in general could be. The preference for black leadership also emerged in responses to the question, "Who do you think really represents the Negro?" Fifty-eight percent cited some Negro or Negro group (the most common, Martin Luther King, was cited by 24 percent), while 24 percent said "no one" or did not know. Only 9 percent cited white people or white leaders, and 3 percent some political office. Perhaps, then, the generalized disaffection cited earlier refers primarily to white leadership. It may reflect more dissatisfaction with current incumbents (who are mostly white) than estrangement from the system.

Yet a common hypothesis has been that Negro leaders receive no real respect from rank-and-file Negroes. Many Negroes supposedly distrust "Negro leaders" and are constantly in fear of a "sellout." In the aftermath of the riot, many Negro leaders reported feeling that they had no control over the rioters, and very little following even among nonparticipants.[13] The community's feelings about black leaders must therefore be considered in more detail.

Local Black Politicians / At the time of the rioting, a number of blacks had attained elective office in Los Angeles: a congressman, two state assemblymen, three city councilmen, and a member of the city Board of Education. As shown in Table 18–6, they were all regarded very favorably, with the exception of Assemblyman Farrell (who soon retired from politics). The black community's preference for black representation is vividly seen by comparing Tables 18–2 and 18–6; the mean net affect for local black politicians was +53 percent, and for local white politicians, −2 percent. A substantial number of respondents had no opinion about each of these black officials, ranging from 35 percent in the case of Councilman Mills to 55 percent in the case of Assemblyman Dymally. Yet the proportion who expressed unfavorable attitudes was very small except toward Assemblyman Farrell. In these data, then, there is little evidence of the cynicism, distrust, and deroga-

Table 18–6 / **Evaluations of Local Black Politicians**

	Evaluations			
	Favorable (1)	Unfavorable (2)	Net Effect (1–2)	No Opinion
Augustus H. Hawkins, U.S. Congress	67%	3%	+64%	30%
Billy Mills, L.A. City Council	59	5	+54	35
Thomas Bradley, L.A. City Council	54	3	+51	44
Gilbert Lindsay, L.A. City Council	54	6	+48	40
James E. Jones, L.A. Board of Education	45	1	+44	54
Mervyn Dymally, California State Assembly	44	2	+42	55
F. Douglass Farrell, California State Assembly	35	21	+14	44
Mean:	60%	7%	+53%	

NOTE: Standard evaluation question (see note to Table 18–1) was used in all cases. Proportion "doing well" was 43 percent, 32 percent, 30 percent, 21 percent, 23 percent, 22 percent, 14 percent, respectively.

tion often thought to be characteristic of Negro evaluations of Negro politicians.

Civil Rights and Racial Nationalism / The other major source of black leadership stems from more national individuals and groups, most originally centered around civil rights organizations. Two contradictory assertions were especially common in the aftermath of the riot about support for this leadership. Some said that the black community had become too militant for the moderates in the civil rights movement, and thus had rejected their leadership in favor of violence and anarchy. On the other hand, the mayor and the police chief, and many other white people, alleged that the violence was inspired by the preaching of civil rights' spokesmen and demonstrators.

The data suggest that both views were incorrect; that in fact racial partisanship, rather than militant radicalization or particular attraction to civil rights leadership, was the dominant pattern. In the first place, there is no evidence of broad public rejection of the civil rights movement as a whole, or even of any specific groups of leaders. All civil rights groups and leaders were evaluated positively, whether "assimilationist" or "protest" in orientation. These data are shown in Table 18–7.

Second, the main exceptions to this were the radical Muslims, the most visible black nationalists of the day. The sample as a whole consistently evaluated the Muslims negatively. The proportion of those who are positive is fairly stable across questions, ranging from 22 percent to 30 percent. The percent negative varies considerably across questions as shown in Table 18–7, but it is consistently higher than the percent positive. The stability of positive ratings and the variability of negative ratings across items suggest that Muslim support was fairly well informed and constant, whereas opposition was more common but less informed.

Aside from the Muslims, however, preferences among these several leaders and organizations seem to have been based more upon their relative visibility than their militancy. As Table 18–7 reveals, the proportion receiving negative evaluations is very small in every instance. Insofar as they were known at all, they were positively evaluated. The same point may be made by comparing the relative militancy of the most popular (e.g., Martin Luther King and the NAACP) and the least popular (Thurgood Marshall and the Reverend Brookins, the central individual in the local unified moderate civil rights effort). They scarcely represented polar opposites on a militancy dimension.

If anything, the most popular national groups and leaders were those

Table 18–7 / **Evaluation of Black Leaders and Organizations**

	Evaluations			
	Favorable (1)	Unfavorable (2)	Net Effect (1–2)	No Opinion
Assimilationists				
NAACP	91%	2%	+89%	7%
Urban League	83	4	+79	13
Ralph Bunche	70	5	+65	26
United Civil Rights Council	60	6	+54	34
Thurgood Marshall	50	3	+47	47
Reverend H. H. Brookins	42	9	+33	49
Mean:	66%	5%	+61%	
Protest				
Martin Luther King	92%	4%	+88%	4%
SCLC	83	2	+81	15
CORE	77	4	+73	18
SNCC	60	8	+52	32
Mean:	78%	4%	+74%	
Nationalism				
John Shabazz	22%	23%	− 1%	55%
Elijah Muhammed	22	33	−11	32
Black Muslims	29	54	−25	17
Mean:	24%	37%	−12%	

NOTE: For the Urban League, SCLC, and SNCC, the standard representation item was used (see note to Table 18–4). In all other cases, the standard evaluation question was used (see note to Table 18–1).

that represented a position of open collective protest rather than more passive or individualistic strategies. Racial partisanship, rather than individual assimilation or racial nationalism, was the most popular stance.[14]

Negro media / Finally, Negro-originated communications media were thought to treat Negro problems more fairly than city-wide media. This is shown in Table 18–5. The two local black newspapers are evaluated more favorably than the two white papers, a predominantly Negro radio station more favorably than radio in general, and two black entertainment figures evaluated extremely favorably. The sole exception is again nationalistic: the Muslim newspaper, *Muhammed Speaks,* is not so favorably regarded. Here again, then, the dominant view is that blacks are the only ones who are in a position to deal fairly with problems in the black community.

POLITICAL EFFECTIVENESS

Given the racial partisanship of the black community, what about the other necessary ingredient for political effectiveness, the level of political mobilization? Do blacks have political contacts, do they vote regularly, do they participate politically in other ways, and do they have confidence in their own ability to influence political decisions?

Negroes in Los Angeles were almost as likely as whites to know someone politically influential. Eighteen percent of the Negroes did, as did 22 percent of the whites. Similarly, blacks were about as politically active as whites. In 1964, 73 percent of our black sample voted for a presidential candidate, while 78 percent of the white sample did so. In 1964, 53 percent of the blacks reported they had voted on Proposition 14, a referendum repealing fair housing legislation, whereas 63 percent of the whites reported having voted. When asked, "Did you do anything besides voting in the 1964 election?" 24 percent of the blacks and 22 percent of the whites said they had. These several measures indicate that racial differences in participation were small, though whites were generally somewhat more active.

However, blacks had a great deal less confidence in their own political effectiveness, as measured by two items from the Survey Research Center's scale of "political efficacy." Sixty percent of the blacks and 27 percent of the whites agreed that "public officials don't care what people like me think." And 78 percent of the blacks and only 47 percent of the whites agreed that "voting is the only way people like me can have any say about how the government runs things." Thus, despite approximate equality in political contacts, in voting rates, and in other forms of political participation, blacks felt much less able to influence public policy.

Racial Partisanship v. Estrangement

The central question of this paper is whether or not the black community in a riot-torn city has become estranged from government and from conventional societal institutions. Indeed, blacks trusted elected officials considerably less than did whites, and felt quite unhappy about the way they were represented politically. However, the most likely interpretation is that this discontent reflects dissatisfaction with current political incumbents and their policies, rather than a more general loss of attachment to the American political system. There are several reasons for reaching this conclusion.

First, Negroes have in recent years consistently expressed firm support for American democracy. In a revolutionary era, historical precedent may not seem to count for much, but at least it does not indicate widespread black estrangement. A variety of indicators make the point. Wartime loyalty has appeared to be at a reasonably high level. Brink and Harris report that only 9 percent of the Negroes in 1966 felt the country was not worth fighting for, despite the lack of hospitality given blacks by other Americans and the growing opposition to the Vietnam War.[15] Negroes also have been at least as strong defenders of democratic ideology as whites. There are few differences on such issues of civil liberties as freedom of speech; Negroes have generally been somewhat less anti-Semitic than whites; they consistently favor living in racially mixed areas more than whites or do not care about the racial composition of their neighborhood; and are generally more egalitarian and more willing to mix racially on the job.[16]

Attachment to the American system is also suggested by the general rejection of violence and separatism as solutions to racial conflicts. Negroes were only slightly more willing to engage in rioting than whites in a major survey of urban areas conducted in 1968, and nonrioting Negroes typically have rejected the actions of the rioters despite expressing sympathy for the rioters and their motives. Similarly, separatist ideology has attracted very little broadbased support in the black community.[17]

Negroes also have consistently regarded the present conditions of their personal lives as improvements over previous years, and have expected continued improvement. When asked directly about the American system, substantial minorities do report dissatisfaction; for example, Beardwood found 43 percent of a 1967 Negro sample said they could not get what they want under the United States system, and Cantril reports a large minority of southern Negroes felt they would be treated no worse if the Nazis or Japanese conquered the United States.[18] Historically, then, Negroes have expressed discontent with their lot but have apparently supported the American democratic system as completely as have whites.

Second, the Los Angeles black community's discontent is focused upon local government and upon the white incumbents in it. It is greatest with respect to local government's most visible symbols, such as the mayor, the school system, the police chief and the police force, but it is discernible with respect to almost all local agencies, and even the local newspapers. However, local black politicians are most important exceptions to this. The highly favorable attitudes toward local black politicians indicate dissatisfaction not with local government per se but with white local government.

And the black community seems not to have rejected its liberal allies. There is little evidence of withdrawal from national partisan politics after the riot; they remain strong Democrats, and apparently feel that the Democratic party is an attractive partisan champion of their cause. Similarly, they are much more favorable to the federal government than to local government.[19] So it would appear that the rejection of white-dominated local government is not a rejection of the political system, but a complaint about inadequate attention and inadequate service.[20]

The pattern thus seems to be more one of racial partisanship and self-interest than of estrangement from the American political system. This resembles some elements of the notion of Black Power, especially (1) mistrust of whites and dissatisfaction with politics that are dominated by whites, (2) racial partisanship, and (3) active political participation.

From this one might think that Black Power ideology would attain some considerable popularity in the black community, particularly those versions of it that stress black political control over arms of government that most immediately affect the black community. It is a little surprising, then, that nationalist leaders have not generally enjoyed wide popularity among blacks. However, these same leaders have tended to advocate separatism as well as increased black political power, and separatism has been even less popular. Perhaps black nationalist leadership has been discredited, to some degree, by its advocacy of separatism. The greater approval given local black politicans may be due to their support of enhanced political power for the black community, without the implication of separatism.[21]

The New Generation

What can be expected about black political attitudes in the future? One indicator is the degree of disaffection in the new generation. The old, southern-born, rural semiliterates are swiftly being replaced by better-educated urban northerners. How do the political attitudes of the young and the better educated differ from those of older and less-educated persons? [22]

First, lack of trust in elected officials is substantially greater among the younger and better educated. Table 18–8 gives the data. The same holds for feelings of adequacy of representation. Of the college educated, 54 percent felt badly represented, whereas only 39 percent did so among the grade-school educated; among those under thirty, 47 percent felt badly represented, as did 37 percent of those 45 years of age and above. On a generalized scale of disaffection, including those two items and two others on trust and adequacy of representation, the young proved to be significantly more disaffected than the old ($F = 7.80$, 2/477 df, $p < .001$), and greater education was also associated with greater disaffection, though not significantly so ($F = 1.10$, 3/477 df, n. s.).[23]

Table 18–8 / **Percent Saying Elected Officials Can Be Trusted by Age, Education, and Race**

	Respondent's Race		
	White	Black	Racial Difference
Age			
15–29	76%	42%	+34%
30–44	79	49	+30
45+	81	60	+21
Education			
College	85	46	+39
High school graduate	76	47	+29
Some high school	71	47	+24
Grade school	63	64	− 1
Total	79%	50%	+29%

This greater disaffection of the young and better-educated blacks is an important and disturbing departure from the pattern that has been typical in America. Previous studies of whites have almost without exception found education to be strongly and positively related to democratic beliefs and attachment to the political system, and in most cases youth has been as well.[24] Table 18–8 also gives the data for our white sample, and confirms this general expectation. Greater education substantially decreased disaffection from the political system, and age made relatively little difference. The greater black disaffection was most vivid among precisely those groups rising in political importance in the black community: the young and the well educated.

Looking at more specific instances of discontent, there is a clear tendency for the young to be especially disenchanted with white leadership, whether national and liberal, or local and not so liberal. The young were less positive on a scale of attitudes toward white liberals (listed in Table 18–1; $F = 7.40$, 2/494 df, $p < .001$); they were more inclined to criticize the several legislative bodies ruling them (listed in Table 18–4; $F = 5.33$, 2/516 df, $p < .005$); and they were less favorable toward the several white officeholders asked about (the president, governor, mayor, and local white legislators) ($F = 12.74$, 2/521 df, $p < .001$). Education affected none of these significantly, though in each case the college educated were least favorable.

Dissatisfaction with local government is particularly common in the black community, as indicated above. Perhaps for this reason, there is nothing especially unique about the discontent of the young and better educated. The young were more negative ($F = 3.33$, 2/519 df, $p < .05$) on a scale of attitudes toward the local political structure; they were more inclined to believe in widespread police brutality ($F = 4.64$, 2/511 df, $p < .01$); and more likely to criticize the fairness of local white media's coverage of the black community, to criticize the performance of local service agencies, and to perceive racial discrimination in their operation (though not significantly so). There was also a nonsignificant tendency for the better educated to be more dissatisfied in each case.

Discontent with the local situation was sometimes more closely related to education (e.g., regarding the *Los Angeles Times,* which is read primarily by better-educated persons) and sometimes to age (e.g., with respect to the police, who are in more contact with the young than the old). But the striking thing is that on virtually every one of the dimensions tested for, the young and better educated are more dissatisfied than are the older and less educated.

The greater disaffection and dissatisfaction with the political system in general and with white leadership in particular, among the young and well educated, imply some greater realism in their views. More generally, they express more skepticism about people in general than do older blacks, or whites of any age, as shown in Table 18–9. They seem to have a more vivid impression of the selfishness or the self-interestedness of people's behavior. This too may contribute to increasing racial partisanship and political participation; if one cannot trust others' altruistic impulses, one needs to have power over their behavior. Black power advocates emphasize this very point.

Table 18–9 / **Percent of Blacks Trusting People by Age and Education**

Education	Age		
	15–29	30–44	45+
College	47%	70%	86%
High school graduate	57	65	69
Some high school	48	63	71
Grade school	29	74	73
Total	51%	66%	72%

NOTE: Over 80 percent of the whites in each category said they trusted people.

POLITICAL MOBILIZATION

However, it is not so clear that the new generation is moving toward effective political participation, by the several criteria advanced earlier.

First, the young are less likely to be strong Democrats. Of those under 30, 61 percent were strong Democrats, while of those over 44, 76 percent were. And the young tended to be less positive toward noted white liberals ($F = 7.40$, $2/492$ df, $p < .001$; education had no effect: $F < 1.0$). However, this does not mean they were more attracted to the Republican party. On a scale of attitudes toward the GOP, neither age ($F = 1.40$, $2/492$ df, n. s.) nor education ($F < 1$) had a significant effect. Thus the young are simply more indifferent partisans rather than being potential converts for the Republican party.[25]

Second, what about black leadership? The degree of positive feeling toward black leaders and black organizations actually *increased* with greater education, quite unlike the situation with white leadership. However, with respect to age the familiar pattern holds; the young tend to be the less enthusiastic about most traditional leaders. Specifically, the old and the well educated were more enthusiastic than the young and the poorly educated about assimilationist leaders (such as Martin Luther King, the NAACP, etc.), civil rights organizations (ranging from the Urban League and the NAACP to CORE and SNCC), and local black politicians.[26] Before too much is made of this, it should be noted that even among the young and the poorly educated negative evaluations were very rare. Thus these effects are due more to differential familiarity with the leaders than to differential antagonism toward them. Considering everything, therefore, no great disaffection from black leadership appears among the young and college-educated, quite unlike the situation with white leadership.

And in fact the reverse held with the nationalist Black Muslims, toward whom the young were actually more favorable ($F = 3.12$, $2/491$ df, $p < .05$). There were no significant education differences, but the college-educated tended to be the most favorable. It is apparent that while sympathy with racial nationalism is not universal in the black community, it is greatest among the young.

Third, the young and better educated seem to be more politicized than the older generation. By every standard, greater education is related to greater political mobilization. For example, the better educated vote more frequently, and have more political knowledge. They were higher on a general scale of familiarity with white politicians ($F = 7.60$, $3/461$ df, $p < .001$), and on a scale of familiarity with poverty agencies ($F = 5.18$, $3/499$ df, $p < .005$). Only 31 percent of the college educated, as against 57 percent of the grade school educated, did not know of Councilman Bradley; the percentages for then-Assemblyman Dymally were 34 percent and 73 percent, respectively; for CORE, 3 percent and 25 percent.

The young appear to be as politicized as the old, contrary to the pattern that normally holds for white Americans.[27] They voted at approximately the same rate as older blacks in 1964, and they were not universally less informed than their elders. They were less informed about white politicians ($F = 10.37$, $2/461$ df, $p < .001$), but the young and old alike were better informed than the middle-age group (30–44) about poverty agencies ($F = 4.32$, $2/499$ df, $p < .025$), and with respect to black leaders, age differences varied widely depending upon the individual in question. For example, 16 percent of the old and 10 percent of the young were unfamiliar with the Muslims, while 38 percent of the old and 49 percent of the young were unfamiliar with Councilman Bradley.

Two disturbing signs accompany this high level of politicization in the coming generation. One is a discouraging sense of political ineffectiveness. The sense of political efficacy does not increase with education among blacks. Of the several combinations of age and education afforded by our standard cut-off points, the greatest efficacy is among the middle-aged (30–44), college-educated whites, as might be expected. Eighty-two percent disagreed that "I don't think public officials care about people like me." However, the lowest were the young black (15–29) high school graduates, of whom only 30 percent disagreed.

This is, then, a troublesome combination among the young and better-educated blacks; relatively high levels of political activism, but little confidence that the system as it currently exists will be responsive to them.

The other is that local black political leadership appears to be out of touch with much of the black community. Among blacks it is primarily the old and well educated who are in contact with political influentials, as shown in Table 18–10. To a degree the same holds for whites, but with far less serious consequences, because those in contact are more numerous. Whites are more than twice as likely to have been to college, and young whites are not as numerous, not as politically significant, and not as removed from political influentials as young blacks.[28]

Table 18–10 / **Percent Knowing Someone Politically Influential by Age and Education**

	Respondent's Race		
	White	Black	Racial Difference
Age			
15–29	21%	13%	+8%
30–44	24	18	+6
45+	20	24	−4
Education			
College	32	29	+3
High school graduate	13	14	−1
Some high school	8	15	−7
Grade school	10	18	−8
Total	21%	18%	+3%

The dangers in this situation have been clear for some time to the moderate political leadership of the black community. Their lack of contact with the young and the lower class sometimes leaves them more conservative than the black community as a whole. Clearly the potential for racial solidarity exists, as witnessed by young blacks' readiness to endorse black leadership. However, the preconditions for truly effective leadership may be difficult to achieve; for example, leaders must maintain contact throughout the black community, and factionalizing must not reach bitterly competitive heights. In this sense the future depends to a large degree on the capabilities of leadership elements within the black community; the opportunities are there.

Summary and Conclusions

The purpose of this paper has been to investigate the attitudes of the black community in Los Angeles toward the political system after the devastating, though not unpopular, Watts rebellion of 1965. The most important findings are these:

1. Considerable political disaffection and lack of trust of elected officials existed. Dissatisfaction was especially great with local government, with complaints of poor service, indifference, lack of attention, and racial discrimination. There was much more satisfaction with the federal government. There seems to have been less estrangement from the political system than dissatisfaction with the way it was currently being run, and with the people running it.

2. Blacks remained highly partisan Democrats, and apparently enthusiastic ones. They were about as active in politics as whites. Nevertheless, they were much less likely to believe that government officials would be responsive to their efforts.

3. Strong racial partisanship characterized attitudes toward black leadership. Local black politicians and national civil rights leaders were strongly supported. Local Negro-originated media are praised. These positive feelings contrasted vividly with the dissatisfaction expressed with white leadership. The only exception to this praise for black leaders was the minority support accorded black nationalists.

4. Disaffection from white leadership was particularly acute in the "new generation." The young and well educated were more dissatisfied with white officeholders, and trusted elected officials less, than did older and less-educated blacks.

5. The "new generation" appears to be more racially partisan, and more politicized, than the old. The well educated approved of black leaders more than did the poorly educated. The young approved of nationalists more, and assimilationists less, than the old. Political participation is high in both groups. However, there is a tendency for sense of efficacy to be lower in the "new generation," and for political influentials to be in contact primarily with older and high-status blacks.

The principal conclusion of the study is that racial partisanship, rather than estrangement from the political system, was dominant in the black community after the riot, and appears likely to remain so.[29] To put it most bluntly, in the Watts of 1965 there was already widespread support for many of the tenets of black power. However, the riot apparently did not have the effect of amassing support in the black community for revolutionary change, though it clearly crystallized hostility against many aspects of the current social and political system. While there have been numerous subsequent disturbances in the area, none have approached its scale. A more political, and more pragmatic, approach has replaced the violence of that first explosion.

These data suggest that the future holds increasing racial polarization, with blacks increasingly placing confidence in blacks in the "ethnic politics" model, and being less willing to place their interests in the hands of the white Establishment.

Open opposition to white leadership seems likely to become increasingly vociferous. The rejection of white leadership is apparent already in these data, in the aftermath of the Watts riot. Even the most liberal whites seem unlikely to be able to sustain the support and the trust of the black community in the long run. At the same time, continued allegiance to the Democratic party suggests that alliances between Democrats and a solidary black community are not unrealistic. However, it is apparent that increased black control over government policies that most affect the black community is imperative. The white community must take account of this need, and provide the mechanisms by which blacks can exercise power over their own destinies within the normal political channels. And this appears to be particularly urgent at the local level of government, which affects the black community most directly.[30]

A more pessimistic note could be struck by a close look at the young, especially their greater attraction to the nationalists, their greater disaffection from white political leadership (even from the Democratic party), their lack of contact with conventional black political leadership, and their lack of any sense that they can influence government as matters now stand, to say nothing of their considerably greater participation in, and support for, the riot. The data do not indicate that they yet are estranged from the system, but that appears to remain an open possibility for the future. In the "ethnic politics" model, cooptation of leadership from emerging groups is essential. And, if the Los Angeles community is typical, continued paternalism, whether white or black, endangers these young blacks' commitment to the current political system. Their active participation in governmental decision-making, whether in the school system or in partisan politics, would seem to be an obvious, and essential, defense against violence and anarchy.

NOTES

1. This research was conducted under a contract between the Office of Economic Opportunity and the Institute of Government and Public Affairs at UCLA as part of the Los Angeles Riot Study, Nathan E. Cohen, Coordinator. Thanks are due to the many people who worked on this study, particularly to Paula Johnson, John B. McConahy, Diana TenHouten, T. M. Tomlinson, and Richard E. Whitney.

2. D. Marvick, "The Political Socialization of the American Negro," *The Annals of the American Academy of Political and Social Science* 361 (1965): 122.

3. See S. Carmichael, "Black Power," in J. Grant, ed., *Black Protest* (New York: Fawcett, 1968), p. 464; S. Carmichael and V. Hamilton, *Black Power* (New York: Vintage, 1967); E. Cleaver, *Soul on Ice* (New York: McGraw-Hill, 1967).

4. In contrast, only 13 percent of our sample of whites in Los Angeles used revolutionary terminology in describing the riot. Black attitudes toward the riots are described by W. Brink and L. Harris, *Black and White* (New York: Simon and Schuster, 1966); A. Campbell and H. Schuman, "Racial Attitudes in Fifteen American Cities," in *Supplemental Studies for the National Advisory Commission on Civil Disorders* (Washington, D.C.: Government Printing Office, 1968), pp. 1–67; Hazel Erskine, "The Polls: Negro Housing," *The Public Opinion Quarterly* 31 (1967): 482–498; and D. O. Sears and T. M. Tomlinson, "Riot Ideology in Los Angeles: A Study of Negro Attitudes," *Social Science Quarterly* 49 (1968): 485–503.

5. For the data on riot participation, see the *Report of the National Advisory Commission on Civil Disorders* (New York: Bantam, 1968); R. M. Fogelson and R. B. Hill, "Who Riots? A Study of Participation in the 1967 Riots," in *Supplemental Studies, op. cit.,* pp. 217–248; D. O. Sears and J. B. McConahay, "Riot Participation," *Los Angeles Riot Study* (Los Angeles: Institute of Government and Public Affairs, UCLA, 1967).

6. See especially D. Easton and R. D. Hess, "The Child's Political World," *Midwest Journal of Political Science* 6 (1962): 229–249; F. I. Greenstein, *Children and Politics* (New Haven: Yale University Press, 1965); R. D. Hess and Judith V. Torney, *The Development of Political Attitudes in Children* (Chicago: Aldine, 1967). Data from children in Appalachia are given by D. Jaros, H. Hirsch, and F. J. Fleron, Jr., "The Malevolent Leader: Political Socialization in an American Subculture," *American Political Science Review* 62 (1968): 564–575. For a recent summary of these findings, see D. O. Sears, "Political Behavior," in G. Lindzey and E. Aronson, eds., *Handbook of Social Psychology,* rev. ed., vol. 5 (Reading: Addison-Wesley, 1969).

7. Brink and Harris, *op. cit.;* Campbell and Schuman, *op. cit.;* Marvick, *op. cit.*

8. P. E. Converse and A. Campbell, "Political Standards in Secondary Groups," in D. Cartwright and A. Zander, eds., *Group Dynamics,* 2d ed. (Evanston: Row, Peterson, 1960), pp. 300–318; N. Glazer and D. P. Moynihan, *Beyond the Melting Pot* (Cambridge: M.I.T. Press, 1963); R. E. Wolfinger, "The Development and Persistence of Ethnic Voting," *American Political Science Review* 59 (1965): 896–908.

9. For example, see A. Campbell, G. Gurin, and W. E. Miller, *The Voter Decides* (Evanston: Row, Peterson, 1954); United States Commission on Civil Rights, *Political Participation* (Washington, D.C., 1968); Marvick, *op. cit.;* D. R. Matthews and J. W. Prothro, *Negroes and the New Southern Politics* (New York: Harcourt, Brace and World, 1966); and L. W. Milbrath, *Political Participation* (Chicago: Rand McNally, 1965).

10. For more complete accounts of the method, see T. M. Tomlinson and Diana TenHouten, "Method: Negro Reaction Survey," and R. T. Morris and V. Jeffries, "The White Reaction Study," *Los Angeles Riot Study, op. cit.*

11. See Hess and Torney, *op. cit.*; H. McClosky, "Consensus and Ideology in American Politics," *American Political Science Review* 58 (1964): 361–382.

12. See W. J. Raine, "The Perception of Police Brutality in South Central Los Angeles Following the Riot of 1965," *Los Angeles Riot Study, op. cit.*; Sears and Tomlinson, *op. cit.*; Campbell and Schuman, *op. cit.*; National Advisory Commission, *op. cit.* By 1969 there was no evidence that this racial polarization over the police had diminished; if anything it had become worse. See R. T. Riley, D. O. Sears, and T. Pettigrew, "Race Unrest, and the Old Angelino: The Bradley Defeat in Los Angeles" (unpublished manuscript, Harvard University, 1969).

13. See J. Q. Wilson, *Negro Politics: The Search for Leadership* (New York: Free Press, 1960); H. M. Scoble, "Negro Politics in Los Angeles: The Quest for Power," *Los Angeles Riot Study, op. cit.*

14. This general pattern, of consistent and strong support for moderate black leadership, and only minority support for militancy, has been obtained repeatedly in other surveys. See Campbell and Schuman *op. cit.*; Brink and Harris, *op. cit*; G. T. Marx, *Protest and Prejudice* (New York: Harper Torchbook, 1969). However, the power of militant organizations and leaders may not be indexed at all well by their general popularity throughout the black community. For example, since the rioting, all black leaders have moved toward more militant positions because of pressures from within the black community. For analyses of subgroups which were considerably more favorable to the militants than was the black community as a whole, see D. O. Sears and J. B. McConahay, "The Politics of Discontent: Blocked Mechanisms of Grievance Redress and the Psychology of the New Urban Black Man," and T. M. Tomlinson, "Ideological Foundations for Negro Action: A Comparative Analysis of Militant and Non-militant Views of the Los Angeles Riot," *Los Angeles Riot Study, op. cit.*

This overwhelming support for local black politicians was again demonstrated in the 1969 mayoralty race in Los Angeles, in which the moderate liberal black councilman, Thomas Bradley, received almost unanimous support from an unprecedentedly high turnout in black precincts. (See Riley et al., 1969, *op. cit.*)

15. Brink and Harris, *op. cit.*

16. S. A. Stouffer, *Communism, Conformity, and Civil Liberties* (New York: Doubleday, 1955). Hazel Erskine, "The Polls: Religious Prejudice, Part 2: Antisemitism," *Public Opinion Quarterly* 29 (1965): 649–664; "The Polls: Demonstrations and Race Riots," *Public Opinion Quarterly* 31 (1967): 655–677; "The Polls: Negro Employment," *Public Opinion Quarterly* 32 (1968): 134–153. This preference for racial integration among Negroes is obviously based on more than just adherence to democratic ideology. However, the point is that insofar as democratic ideology can be operationally defined Negroes have consistently been on the supportive side more often than the opposition side.

17. See footnote 14.

18. R. Beardwood, "The New Negro Mood," *Fortune* 78 (1968): 146ff.; Brink and Harris, *op. cit.*; Matthews and Prothro, *op. cit.*; H. Cantril, *Gauging Public Opinion* (Princeton: Princeton University Press, 1944), p. 116.

19. This preference for the federal government has been shared in recent years by most Americans (see Sears, 1969, *op. cit.*). It may in addition be a short-term consequence of the more sympathetic attention given to Negro problems by all branches of the federal system, whether executive, legislative, or judicial, than by local or state systems in the few years preceding the study.

One does sense, though, that much of the Negro's ultimate faith in the benevolence and attentiveness of the white community rests upon the reputation of the federal government. No doubt Negro attachment to the American political system is sturdy. One does wonder, nevertheless, about the consequences of a possible change in federal policy to a more punitive, less generous stance. It would certainly remove one currently important prop from that basic commitment to the American system, but how much actual change would occur is unclear.

20. The theme of concern about inadequate attention is a salient one in the black respondents' answers to open-ended questions throughout the interview schedule. To use just one objective index of white attention to the black community, the amount of coverage of blacks in local newspapers has consistently lagged far behind the proportion of the population that is black. See Paula B. Johnson, D. O. Sears, and J. B. McConahay, "Black Invisibility and the Los Angeles Riot" (paper presented at the 1969 meetings of the Western Psychological Association, Vancouver, British Columbia).

21. This is also unusual in that support for a charismatic leader often outstrips the support for his ideology. For examples, see the cases of Father Coughlin, Senator Joseph McCarthy, the John Birch Society, and numerous other domestic political movements (S. M. Lipset, "Three Decades of the Radical Right: Coughlinites, McCarthyites, and Birchers—1962," in D. Bell, ed., *The Radical Right* (Garden City, N.Y.: Doubleday, 1963), pp. 313–378; Sears, 1969, *op. cit.*). Yet with racial nationalism the situation seems to be reversed: relatively strong support for many of the basic ideological components of black power, but generally unfavorable attitudes toward its advocates. The issue of separatism is the one that most clearly divides the thinking of the militant leaders from that of conventional black politicians.

22. See K. E. Taeuber and A. F. Taeuber, "The Negro Population in the United States," in J. P. Davis, ed., *The American Negro Reference Book* (Englewood Cliffs, N.J.: Prentice-Hall, 1966), and D. O. Sears and J. B. McConahay, "Racial Socialization, Comparison Level, and the Watts Riot," *Journal of Social Issues,* in press, for discussions of demographic changes in the black community and some of their political consequences.

23. For details on the several scales discussed in this section, see Sears and McConahay, "Politics of Discontent," *op. cit.* The age effects in this section are tested with two degrees of freedom, since age was trichotomized, and the education effects are tested with three degrees of freedom, since four levels of education were used. For the general procedure, see B. J. Winer, *Statistical Principles in Experimental Design* (New York: McGraw-Hill, 1962).

24. For example, see J. W. Prothro and C. W. Grigg, "Fundamental Principles of Democracy; Bases of Agreement and Disagreement," *Journal of Politics* 22 (1960): 276–294; Stouffer, *op. cit.*; McClosky, *op. cit.*; J. Dennis, "Support for the Party System by the Mass Public," *American Political Science Review* (1966): 600–615; and S. M. Lipset, *Political Man* (Garden City, N.Y.: Doubleday, 1960), among others.

25. The lesser partisanship of the young has been also characteristic of whites. Whether this simply represents the immaturity of youth or genuine generational differences is not yet clear. See Sears, 1969, *op. cit.*

26. For age, $F = 16.85$, $2/508$ df, $p < .001$; $F = 3.80$, $2/515$ df, $p < .025$; $F = 4.67$, $2/517$ df, $p < .025$, respectively; and for education, $F = 13.15$, $3/508$ df, $p < .001$; $F = 11.65$, $3/515$ df, $p < .001$; and $F = 6.39$, $3/517$ df, $p < .001$, respectively.

27. See Milbrath, 1965, *op. cit.*; and Sears, 1969, *op. cit.*

28. For one thing, the rioting was mainly done by young blacks. See Sears and McConahay, "Riot Participation," *op. cit.*; National Advisory Commission, *op. cit.* Even so, one can speculate about the remoteness of the young and less-educated whites from the white political Establishment; some have ascribed the popularity of Eugene McCarthy and Ronald Reagan, respectively, to their appeals to those left-out groups.

29. This is a striking contrast with Wilson's (*op. cit.*) description of the Los Angeles black community in the 1950's as being partisan neither politically nor racially. While his data were impressionistic, it does seem likely that the riot was a politicizing event in the black community.

Also, this is not to deny that both estrangement and partisanship may coexist in the same individual as well as in the community as a whole. It would be a gross oversimplification to ignore the ambivalence that must exist in most black citizens about the symbols of the American creed. Black attitudes toward the riot expressed this ambivalence eloquently; many took great pleasure in getting back at the white man, while equally genuinely abhorring the burning and killing (Sears and Tomlinson, *op. cit.*). Similarly ambivalent attitudes no doubt exist toward success as it is defined in conventional white, middle-class American terms, and about integration itself. It is doubtful that most lower-class blacks take as seriously as do most middle-class whites the objectives of success as defined in white, middle-class terms. However, the important issue is not whether or not the American creed has been completely internalized, but that there is so little commitment to the militants' ideology, along with a good deal of behavioral conformity to mainstream norms.

30. Districting for elective office is a good case in point. Unlike many eastern cities, the "core city" of Los Angeles includes many of the "bedroom suburbs" that elsewhere are separate municipalities. Thus the white middle class is a considerable voting majority. The city council, the state assembly and senate, and Congress are all districted to provide seats directly representing South–Central Los Angeles, but the Board of Education is not (it has only at-large seats), nor is the County Board of Supervisors (its districts are too large to allow any control by blacks or Mexican–Americans). Reform here is a high-priority item.

The Riots and White America

⚑ 19. WHITE PUBLIC OPINION IN AN AGE OF DISORDER
Bettye K. Eidson

 SINCE the early days of the civil rights movement liberal supporters have repeatedly warned against new initiatives in militancy by raising the specter of white backlash. "If you [demonstrate, push too hard, demand too much, resort to violence] you will alienate people who are sympathetic to your cause and augment the forces of reaction." And since that time the modest (though courageous) sit-ins have been succeeded by large-scale peaceful demonstrations, by disorderly and disruptive demonstrations, by riots of various dimensions, and by the emergence of a revolutionary black political party. At the other end of the spectrum we have seen the career of George Wallace flourish, from the days when he stood in the schoolhouse door, through his first tentative forays into the North in 1964, to his third-party candidacy in the presidential election of 1968.

 On the surface it would seem that the liberal predictions have come to pass: as black militancy grew, so did the Wallace army. But we also know that the association of two events need not imply a direct causal relation; it is important to examine the connecting links. Have the black demonstrations and the ghetto riots alienated previously sympathetic whites? Has white antagonism toward black aims risen since blacks started "pushing"?

 In the first section of this essay we shall examine the public's opinions on riots and on earlier forms of black protest. Next we will look at the level of public support for the goal of an integrated society—in preriot and in riot periods. The index of support for an integrated society will be white attitudes toward the desegregation of public education. (While there is some evidence that blacks rank job opportunities

389

above integrated education as their most crucial goal, the most consistently collected white opinions on race relations refer to schools, not jobs.) The final part will consider the sources of white backlash in the light of the first two sections.

White Opinion on Forms of Black Protest

Table 19–1 shows the public's reactions (1961–1967) to organized civil rights actions, such as demonstrations, sit-ins, marches and picketing, as well as to the ghetto riots.

Clearly, the public disapproved of ghetto riots. Equally clearly, the public disapproved of alternate forms of black protest. A wide majority disapproved of the Freedom Rides in 1961, disapproved of the March on Washington in 1963, disapproved of picketing political conventions in 1964, disapproved of sit-ins, lie-ins, boycotts, and demonstrations— before Harlem and Watts.

Opposition to mass demonstrations continued as riots picked up in tempo. In 1963, 65 percent of whites in the North (73 percent in the South) were opposed to mass demonstrations. In 1964, the figure for whites nationwide was 73 percent. Though opposition dipped to 63 percent in 1966, by the next year, 1967, 82 percent of the white public were critical of mass demonstrations.

Little distinction seems to have been made in these years between legal and illegal direct actions. In 1964, the public was about as likely to disapprove of the picketing of political conventions (76 percent) as they were to believe that riots in New York, Rochester, and Jersey City were "hurting the black cause" (87 percent). In 1967 we find a similar pattern: 82 percent of the white public were opposed to black demonstrations in general; 88 percent thought that riots had hurt the cause of civil rights. (The possibility that most respondents who thought riots hurt the black cause also sympathized with black goals is considered later.)

In the 1963 Harris poll, civil disobedience ("go to jail to protest discrimination") was considered only slightly less objectionable (56 percent) than sitting-in at lunch counters (67 percent), even though the later was a breach of custom, not law. And nationwide opposition to the use of such tactics as lying in front of trucks was as widespread in 1963 (91 percent) as was opposition to rioting the following year (87 percent).

Table 19–1 / **Public Reaction to Demonstrations and Riots, 1961–1967**

Reference	Date and Source of Question	Public Reaction
Freedom Riders	June 1961 Gallup	Unfavorable, 64% (of 63% of public who knew of the activity)
Mass demonstrations by blacks	July 1963 Gallup	Unfavorable, whites only South, 73% North, 65%
March on Washington	August 1963 Gallup	Unfavorable, 63% (of 69% of public who knew of the activity)
Black tactics, specific:	October 1963 Harris	Unfavorable, whites only

	Nationwide	South
Lie down in front of trucks at construction sites	91%	94%
Sit-in at lunch counters	67	84
Go to jail to protest discrimination	56	75
Boycott products whose manufacturers do not hire enough blacks	55	66

Reference	Date and Source of Question	Public Reaction
Actions blacks have taken to obtain civil rights, general	December 1963 NORC	Unfavorable, whites only South, 78% North, 59%
Nature of black protest movement	December 1963 NORC	Percent white who say movement has been generally violent rather than peaceful: South, 63% North, 47%
Picketing of political conventions	July 1964 Harris	Unfavorable, 76%
Riots in New York, Rochester, and Jersey City	August 1964 Gallup	Unfavorable, 87%
Continued demonstrations	November 1964 Gallup	Unfavorable, whites only, 73%
Participation of clergymen in protest marches	April 1965 Gallup	Unfavorable, 56%
Extent of Communist involvement in civil rights demonstrations	November 1965 Gallup	Percent white who say: a lot 51% some 27%
Black demonstrations, general	1966 Harris	Unfavorable, whites only, 63%
	June 1967 Harris	Unfavorable, whites only, 82%
"Recent" riots	August 1967 Harris	Unfavorable, whites only, 88%
Riots as organized efforts vs. spontaneous eruptions	August 1967 Harris	Percent who see riots as organized, whites only, 71%

SOURCE: Compiled from Hazel Erskine, "The Polls: Demonstrations and Race Riots," *Public Opinion Quarterly*, Winter 1967–1968, pp. 655–677.

Judging from responses to the 1963 Harris poll, there does seem to be one criterion by which the public distinguishes among different forms of black collective action. In general, the more passive and unobtrusive the effort, the less the white public is inclined to object to it. At one end of the scale, the public strongly opposed blocking of construction activities, a dramatic and disruptive protest likely to receive wide newspaper and television coverage. Sit-ins were considered the next most objectionable, followed by going to jail as protest. Least objectionable, though still disapproved by a majority, was the boycott which, while potentially disruptive of economic routine, is essentially passive in that it calls upon blacks not to patronize certain stores.

This reading of the data is strengthened by results of a 1968 survey conducted by CBS news, in cooperation with the Opinion Research Corporation. One question on black protest activities included a series of tactics similar to those in the 1963 Harris poll (Table 19–2).

As in the earlier Harris poll, the more overt and dramatic the protest, the more the public objects to it. On two points blacks and whites are in close agreement: demonstrations that might lead to violence are "not good ways for people to use to get what they want" and "holding meetings" are. But at the prospect of more vigorous displays of protest, black and white respondents part ways. Sixty-eight percent of blacks, as contrasted with 32 percent of whites, approve of "peaceful demonstra-

Table 19–2

"Now let's turn to some of the things that have been going on in this country lately. There have been many types of action aimed at the problem of equal rights for Negroes (blacks)—both whites and Negroes (blacks) have participated in these actions. As I read some of these actions to you, tell me if you think they are good ways or not good ways for people to use to get what they want."

	Good Way		Not Good Way		No Opinion	
	Black	White	Black	White	Black	White
Holding meetings	89%	88%	4%	10%	7%	2%
Peaceful demonstrations	68	32	22	64	10	4
Boycotting stores	71	29	19	66	10	5
Picketing stores and businesses	59	17	30	78	11	5
Demonstrations that might lead to violence	6	2	86	97	8	1

SOURCE: CBS News Public Opinion Survey, "White and Negro Attitudes towards Race Related Issues and Activities" (Princeton, N.J.: Opinion Research Corporation, 9 July 1968, p. 12.

tions." Seventy-one percent of blacks and 29 percent of whites condone boycotts of stores. The gap between blacks and whites is equally wide in their evaluations of the usefulness of "picketing stores and businesses."

While neither blacks nor whites approve of violence, the critical difference between the races on this question is the intransigence with which the majority group withheld approval of alternative forms of collective action. The message of white America seems to be, "Talk as much as you like, but don't rock the boat."

White respondents in the CBS survey felt they themselves would not rock the boat either. Asked whether they would use the tactics mentioned above for a cause *they* thought was very important, most whites replied they would hold discussions but not otherwise resort to collective action (Table 19–3).

One can plausibly argue that the whites' greater numbers and resources produce a heightened sense of personal efficacy and make it more difficult for them to imagine circumstances under which they would turn to collective behavior. Substantial numbers of the white public have assumed that blacks have no more reason to be disruptive of routine than they themselves. A 1968 Gallup poll found that 70 percent of whites nationally believed that blacks in their communities were treated as well as whites. Asked whether local businesses discriminated in hiring blacks, 68 percent said "No," while 52 percent denied that local labor unions discriminated against blacks in their

Table 19–3

"I am going to read the list again. This time tell me if you would or would not do each of these things for a cause that you thought was very important."

	Would Do		Would Not Do		No Opinion	
	Black	White	Black	White	Black	White
Going to meetings	86%	78%	9%	21%	5%	1%
Peaceful demonstrations	63	22	27	76	10	2
Boycotting stores	65	23	27	74	9	2
Picketing stores or businesses	48	8	42	89	9	2
Demonstrations that might lead to violence	3	1	88	98	8	1

SOURCE: CBS News Public Opinion Survey, "White and Negro Attitudes towards Race Related Issues and Activities" (Princeton, N.J.: Opinion Research Corporation, 9 July 1968, p. 13.

membership practices. A majority of whites (58 percent) thought blacks more to blame for their condition than were white people.[1]

Sustained protest and confrontations appear not to have changed the white public's mind about the difficulties faced by the black community. The perception whites had in 1968 of barriers against black mobility is consistent with their responses to an open-ended question in a Gallup survey three years earlier. Here we find them admonishing blacks to get an education, stay in line, work hard, and be quiet (Table 19–4).

Table 19–4

"Blacks are interested in getting better jobs and gaining respect in their communities. What advice would you give them as a race to achieve these goals?"

September, 1965 (whites only)	
Get more education	44%
Work harder, try harder, don't expect something for nothing	19
Improve themselves, be good law-abiding citizens, earn respect	15
Be less aggressive, more cooperative, take it slower	14
Stop riots, demonstrations, civil rights activities	12
Cultivate self-respect	3
Work together, become united	2
All other responses	5

SOURCE: Gallup Opinion Index, Report no. 4.

Since whites tended to deny that blacks suffered injustice, they also were inclined to deny that the blacks' situation was *in itself* sufficient to give rise to protest. According to a 1965 Gallup poll, 51 percent of whites nationwide considered Communist involvement in civil rights demonstrations to have been extensive. An additional 27 percent of the white public saw at least "some" Communist involvement in these activities (Table 19–1). If direct-action techniques were seen by the public as unnecessary challenges to the "bootstrap and ballot" assumptions of upward mobility in America, it is not incomprehensible that 78 percent of the white public saw in these actions the work of agents hostile to our economic and political forms. From Table 19–1, again, we learn that two years later, in 1967, a Harris poll recorded that 71 percent of whites nationwide considered riots to be "organized efforts" as opposed to "spontaneous eruptions." Erroneous, perhaps—as the National Advisory Commission on Civil Disorders would maintain the following year—but a public perception perfectly consistent with their earlier assessment of the conditions of collective black protest.

There is some evidence that white evaluation of black collective action is not divorced from assessment of the desirability of black goals. In 1963, for example, the National Opinion Research Center found the following relationship between evaluation of black collective actions (marches, demonstrations) and the respondents' own attitudes toward an integrated society (Table 19–5).

Table 19–5 / **White Attitude toward Integration by Evaluation of Black Collective Actions**

Whites, by attitude toward integration	Percent in each category who think black actions, on the whole, have hurt their cause
Highly in favor of integration	24%
Moderately in favor of integration	45
Moderately opposed to integration	52
Highly opposed to integration	71

SOURCE: Compiled from Hazel Erskine, "The Polls: Demonstrations and Race Riots," *Public Opinion Quarterly,* Winter 1967–1968, p. 656.

What Table 19–5 says is that approval of means is positively associated with approval of ends. There is a clear tendency for those who disapprove of black actions to oppose integration. At the same time, there is some slack in this relationship: one-fourth of whites highly in favor of integration did fear that direct-action techniques would impede changes in racial patterns, and about one-fourth of those highly opposed to integration suspected that direct-action techniques would be effective.

Thus far we have seen that the public disapproved rather steadily of any active display of black protest. They disapproved of riots, of course, but they also disapproved of alternate forms of collective protest. In some respects, this aversion to black collective action appears to be racially neutral. That is, whites had difficulty in the early and middle

1960's imagining a situation where they themselves would take to the streets. Hence, their disapproval of organized black actions was not entirely prejudicial but, in part, derivative from standards they also would apply to themselves. Most whites seem to be opposed to any disruption of what they regard as social peace.

Since protests, riots, and other disruptions continue, many whites have come to feel that public authorities are failing in one of their primary responsibilities—the maintenance of law and order. A Harris poll in 1966 revealed that 69 percent of the public thought citizens would be more likely to vote for a candidate who favored making participation in riots a federal offense. In August 1967, 68 percent of whites felt that people who throw firebombs in riot situations should be shot; similar numbers of whites (62 percent) agreed in 1967 that looters also should receive "summary justice." (Blacks, interestingly, distinguished more clearly between firebombers and looters; 47 percent thought that firebombers should be shot, while 27 percent thought that looters should be shot.) [2]

By the summer of 1968, CBS found that 70 percent of whites were critical of their local police—thinking that "police should have been tougher in their handling of riots." A combined 85 percent of whites felt police in general had been either "soft" (27 percent) or "fair" (58 percent) in their treatment of blacks. But the sense of breakdown of public authority is evident among members of both races when the subject of *crime* is combined with that of violence. Fifty-two percent of the whites and even more blacks (65 percent) felt in 1968 that they personally would have to be prepared to "defend their homes against crime and violence" instead of relying upon protection of local police. [3]

The demand on those in authority for protection and for order *is and has been throughout the 1960's* partially independent of the individual respondent's race. Near the end of the decade, a majority of both blacks and whites were denying the efficacy of the local law enforcement official's claims to a monopoly of force.

In the next section we ask: How much did blacks *as a group* come to be perceived as responsible for the cumulative erosion of public authority? Quite specifically, did blacks become so perceptually linked with this type of erosion that white sympathy for legitimate black goals and aspirations also began to decay?

White Attitudes toward the Desegregation of Public Education

The most consistent work on attitudes toward school desegregation has been that of the National Opinion Research Center. In 1956 and in a 1964 sequel, NORC reported a steady movement toward acceptance of the principle of racial integration—not only in public schools but in neighborhoods and in public accommodations.[4] In the 1964 article, the authors asked whether the long-term trend toward the acceptance of racial integration had been halted or reversed by the pace and scope of the black protest movement. They found that whereas fewer than 40 percent of northern whites and 2 percent of southern whites endorsed integrated schools in 1942, by 1956 three out of five northerners and one out of seven southerners approved of school integration. In the period from 1956 to 1963, the proportion of the white North approving school integration rose to 73 percent, and the proportion of white southerners approving climbed even more dramatically from 14 to 34 percent. The responses reported by NORC refer to the question, "Do you think white students and black students should go to the same or separate schools?" By December 1963, 62 percent of whites nationwide said, "same schools."

By mid-1965, NORC found that the proportion of southern whites who favored integrated schools had almost doubled in 18 months, moving from 30 percent in December 1963 to 55 percent in June 1965.[5]

The trend toward acceptance of the principle of an integrated society was not reversed by the growth and spread of direct-action techniques. With this trend in mind, we turn to a consideration of acceptance of actual changes in the racial structure. Mildred Schwartz, in *Trends in White Attitudes toward Negroes,* reviews white reaction to the possibility of implementing the Supreme Court decision on school desegregation.[6] While cautioning that comparison of responses over time is limited by slight variation in the wording used in different surveys, she was able to compile measures of the public's preference for "immediate" as contrasted with "gradual" integration of schools. Reporting the proportions in favor of "immediate" school integration best approximates the similarity in responses to differently worded questions (Table 19–6).

Though these data suggest a slight increase in the national proportion favoring immediate school integration, the remarkable contrast here is between the amount for support for "immediate" implementation of the law and the proportion who favored—in principle—school integration. In 1956, for example, 49 percent of whites nationwide approved of the principle of desegregation of public education, as compared with the 10 percent that same year who favored the "immediate" integration of schools.

Beginning in 1962, the Gallup organization asked the public whether the federal executive branch was "pushing integration too fast, or not fast enough." Table 19–7 shows responses for the years of the Kennedy and Johnson administrations.

There appears to be an upward trend, judging from Table 19–7, in the perception that the federal executive branch is pushing "too fast." Though a "hard-core" one-third of the nation consistently felt the pace

Table 19–6 / **Percent in Favor of Immediate School Integration**

Date	Source	Percent
May 1956	AIPO release May 9, 1956	18%
September 1956	Roper Survey 64	10
September 1957	AIPO study 589-K	27
September 1958	AIPO study 604-K	27
June 1961	AIPO release June 28, 1961	23

to be too swift, the change in administrations in 1963 was accompanied by a reduction in the level of criticism of federal actions. It was not until two years after President Johnson took office that some of the peaks of criticism in the Kennedy era were approached. By November 1966, the public was as critical of President Johnson as they had been of his predecessor in 1963.

How much school desegregation had occurred, in fact, by 1966? In that year, the United States Office of Education, in its national survey entitled *Equality of Educational Opportunity,* reported that twelve years after the Supreme Court decision on school desegregation, 65 percent of all first-grade black pupils surveyed attended schools that had an enroll-ment 90 percent or more black, while almost 80 percent of all first-

Table 19–7

"Do you think the (Kennedy) (Johnson) administration is pushing integration too fast, or not fast enough?"

Percent Saying "Too Fast"

Date		Source
Kennedy administration		Gallup Opinion Index; Report 18
May 1962	32%	(May 1962–November 1966)
October	42	
May 1963	36	
June	41	
July	48	
September	50	
October	46	
Johnson administration		
February 1964	30%	
April 1965	34	
August	40	
July 1966	46	
September	52	
November	53	
August 1967	44	Gallup Opinion Index; Report 35
April 1968	39	Gallup Opinion Index; Report 35
June 1968	45	Gallup Opinion Index; Report 37
October 1968	54	Gallup Opinion Index; Report 40

grade white students surveyed attended schools that were 90 percent or more white. A substantially greater proportion of black students attended schools that were 50 percent or more black. Approximately 87 percent of all black first-graders were in such schools—72 percent in the urban North, 97 percent in the urban South.[7]

In 1967, the United States Commission on Civil Rights reported that the proportion of black children in majority black schools was due in part to an *increase* in the segregation of northern school systems. For southern and border state school systems, the *proportion* of blacks in totally black schools had decreased since the 1954 Supreme Court decision but—because of rising black enrollment—the *number* of black children attending all-black or nearly all-black schools actually rose sharply between 1954 and 1965.[8]

In that same report, the United States Commission on Civil Rights recommended to the president and the Congress that any school more than 50 percent black be declared racially segregated and that federal funds be withheld from such districts—North and South.[9] By the spring of 1970, the Nixon administration reported that 40 percent of black children in the South were attending schools held to be in compliance with the law. The stated expectation was that by the following year twice that many black children in the South would be attending schools in districts held to be in compliance.

"Held to be in compliance" would not imply that classrooms were equal to or less than 50 percent black, according to a statement from President Nixon to the nation on March 24, 1970. The president distinguished carefully between de facto and de jure segregation and left little doubt that his own interpretation of the 1954 Supreme Court ruling would require elimination of the latter but not the former. To appreciate the political sensitivity of this position, we refer to Table 19–8, which shows 1969 responses to the Gallup question: "What is your opinion—do you think the racial integration of schools in the United States is going too fast, or not fast enough?" While the question was asked during the first year of the Nixon administration, no direct reference is made to the actions of the executive branch. The breakdown for whites, by region, is presented in Table 19–8.

Table 19–8 / **Perceived Speed of School Integration, by Region, August 1969**

Region	Too Fast	Percent Saying: Not Fast Enough	About Right	No Opinion
Northern whites	44%	24%	24%	10%
Southern whites	58	10	25	7

SOURCE: AIPO release, 17 August 1969.

On March 24, 1970, President Nixon addressed a South and a North that had converged in their estimates of the pace of school integration: 44 percent of northern whites and 58 percent of southern whites had thought the pace of school integration to be "too fast" by August 1969.

Regional convergence is shown even more dramatically in the responses of parents to a series of questions Gallup has asked since 1963. These questions are:

Would you, yourself, have any objection to sending your children to a school where

more than half of the children are blacks?
half of the children are blacks?
a few of the children are blacks?

Table 19–9 shows how white parents, North and South, have defined the tolerable limits of school integration.

In 1963, the strong contrast between northern and southern white parents was with respect to their acceptance of symbolic, or token, integration. Whereas 87 percent of northern parents in 1963 accepted the idea of a "few" black children sharing educational facilities with their own, 49 percent fewer southern white parents would have done so without objection. During the height of the civil rights movement's disruption of southern routine—from 1963 to 1966—the proportion of southern white parents accepting symbolic integration doubled. By 1969, a difference of 15 percent distinguished levels of regional acceptance of token integration. Over three-fourths of white parents in both regions found the notion of a few black children tolerable.

Almost as dramatic is the change in southern white acceptance of the idea of equal proportions of black children—an increase from 17 percent to 47 percent in six years. Though in 1969 still below the 1963 level of northern acceptance, approval among southern parents rose by 30 percentage points in six years while their northern counterparts showed a 13 percent gain in the same time period.

Where the South has moved some and the North hardly at all is in regard to the idea of a majority black classroom. Still, in 1969, the idea that blacks should constitute a majority was objectionable to the "natural" majority—both North and South. In these years, changes in attitude in the North toward the idea of a black majority were of considerably smaller magnitude than changes within the South. The net result of

Table 19–9 / **Limits of School Integration, by Region**

	Percent of Northern and Southern White Parents Who Would Not Object to Sending Their Children to a School Where					
	More than half are blacks		*Half are blacks*		*A few of the children are blacks*	
	Northern	*Southern*	*Northern*	*Southern*	*Northern*	*Southern*
1963	31%	6%	56%	17%	87%	38%
1965	37	16	65	27	91	62
1966	32	27	64	44	93	74
1969	39	26	69	47	93	78
Difference 1963–1969	+ 8%	+20%	+13%	+30%	+ 6%	+40%

SOURCE: AIPO release, 17 August 1969.

these changes—incremental in the North, swift in the South—was that by the end of the decade the regions had approached consensus upon the tolerable limits of school integration.

Backlash Reexamined

The opposition of whites in the South to the *principle* of integration in the years after the Supreme Court's 1954 decision made it possible for the rest of the country to define the growing racial crisis as a predominantly southern problem. Opposition to black gains could be regarded as coming from a dwindling bloc of reactionary southerners—an outnumbered and declining minority in an essentially egalitarian and well-intentioned nation. Potential support for an overtly racist politics on a national scale could be deflected into liberal politics by branding racism as a southern phenomenon. Thus the existence of what was perceived as a Klannish South helped ease strains that were developing within the northern liberal coalition—especially those between blue-collar workers, on the one hand, and blacks, upper-middle-class intellectuals, students, and church groups, on the other. At the same time the federal government could be viewed as reflecting the will of a progressive people in moving against obstinate and retrograde regional institutions in the South.

But as the South began to abandon its rigid commitment to de jure segregation and to exhibit more of the northern de facto pattern, the differences between the regions became less pronounced and obvious. By the early 1960's many black leaders realized that after the southern resistance subsided, Negroes were going to have the much more difficult task of moving against the national consensus on the tolerable limits of integration. And the focus of black action was going to be not reactionary southern institutions but the liberal establishment which maintained patterns of de facto segregation.

The growth of the black movement in the North challenged the control of liberal elites, including those in the federal government. Their response in the middle and late 1960's was to make a series of concessions to blacks in hopes of buying off discontent. But often these concessions were made at the expense of working- and lower-middle-class whites. It was their schools that were primarily affected by busing, their jobs that were threatened by nondiscriminatory or preferential hiring policies, and occasionally their neighborhoods that were "integrated" with primarily black housing developments. Of course such measures were not very extensive and did not directly affect many whites. But the more important point is that white workers saw that they were expected to take on a disproportionate share of the "cost" of these liberal policies. Moreover, they regarded expanded welfare roles and the poverty program (both of which had a more substantial impact on the black community) as instances of the government's tendency to give *their* tax dollars to people whose only qualification was an ability to shout and make trouble.

Not only was the government failing to maintain order, but it seemed to be rewarding the disorderly at the expense of patient, law-abiding whites. This lies at the root of what is usually called "backlash." George Wallace's winning 7 percent of the presidential vote outside the South in 1968 does not reflect a rising tide of antiblack sentiment (that seems to be declining slowly), nor does it reflect increasing disapproval of demonstrations and disorder (which has always been strong). Racism and the law-and-order mentality are of course crucial to the Wallace movement, but they are not new elements in the formula.

What is new is the loss of faith in the liberal establishment among many working- and lower-middle-class whites—the growing conviction that it does not represent their interests, is misusing them to serve its own ends, and at the same time is losing its ability to govern. Their defection followed logically from liberal efforts to buy off the black movement in the North. Both the movement and the response, in turn, followed from the South's growing acceptance of the principal of integration. With the North as the new arena of conflict, the movement attacked liberal institutions of de facto segregation, and liberal elites could no longer sidestep the issue by pointing an accusing finger at the South.

A loss of confidence in the liberal establishment and the availability of a third-party candidate who could no longer be dismissed as a carpetbagging southerner catalyzed antiblack and law-and-order sentiments, converting them into a political force. In the 1968 presidential election, the Democratic coalition won 56 percent of the labor vote, the smallest proportion since the beginning of the New Deal.

The term "backlash" and the rhetoric surrounding it have proved useful to liberal elites intent on containing the black movement and maintaining their own position. They have responded to black demands by making "concessions" which affect the interests of lower-income whites more than their own. And when these low-income whites have cried out in anger, the cries have been termed "backlash" and used to admonish the blacks against demanding too much. There is, of course, a reactionary movement in the United States; but to interpret it as evidence of backlash is to miss the point. The same people who gave us the term gave us the fact.

THE CASE OF LAMAR

In the spring of 1970, the specter of violent "white blacklash" materialized in Lamar, South Carolina, in a form that could not have been predicted from knowledge only of local white opinions of blacks. Its focus was not riots, nor the New Left, nor crime, but state and local police and two school buses delivering Negro children to the high school in Lamar. According to charges filed by the State Police, members of the Darlington County Freedom of Choice Association "congregated and armed themselves with axe handles, chains, bricks, stones, rocks, pieces of cement blocks, clubs, dirks, bottles, jars, pistols, metal bolts and other dangerous weapons." [10]

Since February 18, 1970, when the county's school board adopted a new midyear integration plan ordered by the federal court, the freechoice people had been trying to undo it. Lamar has two high schools, each with adjoining elementary schools, as legacies of the era of lawful segregation. Under the new integration plan, an attendance boundary divides the town of 1,200 in two, each part including some of the surrounding rural area.

About 130 white children—many of whose parents were following the leadership of Jeryl Best, head of the Freedom of Choice Association—were included in the zone for the black schools, where they would be' in the minority among the 600 students. About 500 black children were to enter the predominantly white high school where the enrollment is 400.

Mrs. Best, wife of the Freedom of Choice Association leader, explained the source of their bitter outburst. They deplore violence, she insisted, but, "We feel betrayed by our leaders. There are no lawyers, no doctors, no city councilmen, and no school board members who were placed in the zone where their children would have to attend the Negro school. I think our local school board along with what might be considered the more prominent citizens got together to draw this jagged school zone."

The accusation was denied by school officials. Ben Greer, the school board attorney, said the plan was drawn by civil rights officers of the U.S. Department of Health, Education, and Welfare, not by the local school board, and it followed the principle of sending children to the school building nearest their homes. Mr. Greer blamed the midyear court order and the hasty change in school attendance for the trouble.

But Mrs. Best's complaint that the white elites were sacrificing the interests of the poor white minority was echoed in conversations on the courthouse square. "There's a conspiracy in Darlington all right," said J. C. Odum, a 36-year-old factory worker. "It's a conspiracy among the politicians. Jeryl Best is the only one speaking up for white people."

Bert Smith, a tobacco farmer, added: "They said HEW drew that line but there ain't nobody in HEW can follow a creek and a pine tree the way that line does. These doctors and lawyers took care of themselves."

NOTES

1. Hazel Erskine, "The Polls: Recent Opinion on Racial Problems," *Public Opinion Quarterly,* Winter 1968, pp. 697–703.

2. Hazel Erskine, "The Polls: Demonstrations and Race Riots," *Public Opinion Quarterly,* Winter 1967–1968, pp. 655–677.

3. CBS News Public Opinion Survey, "White and Negro Attitudes towards Race Related Issues and Activities" (Princeton, N.J.: Opinion Research Corporation, 9 July 1968), p. 15.

4. Herbert H. Hyman and Paul B. Sheatsley, "Attitudes toward Desegregation," *Scientific American* 211 (July 1964): 16–23.

5. Paul B. Sheatsley, "White Attitudes toward the Negro," *Dædalus* 95 (Winter 1966): p. 235.

6. Mildred A. Schwartz, *Trends in White Attitudes toward Negroes* (The University of Chicago: National Opinion Research Center, 1967), p. 30.

7. James S. Coleman et. al., *Equality of Educational Opportunity* 3 (1966).

8. U.S. Commission on Civil Rights, *Racial Isolation in the Public Schools,* vol. 1 (Washington, D.C.: U.S. Government Printing Office), pp. 8–10.

9. *Ibid.,* pp. 209–210.

10. This account of the Lamar, South Carolina, episode is taken from *The Washington Post,* 6 March 1970.

20. URBAN REVOLTS AND THE FUTURE OF AMERICAN CITIES
Peter H. Rossi

G U N N A R Myrdal's analysis of America's racial inequality as a crisis in collective moral conscience was published at the end of the

New Deal era. *An American Dilemma* was published when the major push of New Deal liberalism had begun to slow down after accomplishing the first major steps toward transforming the United States into a liberal welfare-oriented state. Perhaps it was the contrast between the democratic egalitarian ethos espoused in the liberal rhetoric of the Roosevelt regime and the position of American blacks as a semicaste which led Myrdal to his diagnosis of the "race problem." In any event, Myrdal expected that the United States would resolve over time the contradiction by removing barriers of segregation and discrimination gradually.

The New Deal did not do very much for blacks as such, although welfare-oriented national policies could not help but make some improvement in the position of blacks at least in the economic sphere. Unemployed blacks could get on the WPA up North; some of the low-rent public housing was set aside for blacks, and the Civilian Conservation Corps had black units. Eleanor Roosevelt was seen by blacks as an influential friend and by racially conservative whites as a national disgrace, but Franklin D. Roosevelt was remarkably silent on the race issue. He moved only weakly in the direction of breaking down barriers of discrimination after black "militants" led by A. Philip Randolph threatened a march on Washington in 1941.

World War II accentuated even more the contradiction between racial segregation and discrimination, on the one hand, and, on the other hand, the liberal democratic ideology in the name of which the United States entered the war. The war against fascism was fought with a segregated armed forces and the "arsenal for democracy" was staffed through discriminatory employment policies. Of course the war against the Japanese was fought with racial overtones and Japanese–Americans were herded into concentration camps, some for the duration of the conflict. Yet the predominant ideological tone of World War II was anti-racist and liberal democratic.

The years immediately following the war saw some important changes in the direction of reducing the American dissonance in conscience. Harry Truman desegregated the armed forces. The Supreme Court ruled against segregation in interstate transportation, against racially restrictive covenants in real estate deeds, and, finally, in 1954 ordered the desegregation of public schools throughout the land. The 1954 school desegregation decision was the most important blow struck at the southern caste system. It was easy to put up with sitting next to blacks in airplanes and interstate buses, but the thought of white and black children sitting next to each other in elementary and high schools was anathema.

Public opinion polls during the postwar period recorded a steady decline in public support for the principle of racial separation. The principle of equal treatment for blacks each year gained more and more adherents in the general population: America was getting better all the time. Of course, civil rights legislation could not pass the Senate; blacks were being piled into the northern urban ghettos and black–white income and occupational differences still persisted. In the period from World War II to the end of the Eisenhower administration, the climate of official and popular opinion shifted toward a balance in favor of racial equality although changes in institutional practices were slower in coming about.

The changes that took place in the 1940's and 1950's were engineered and pushed through by the *Establishment,* black and white. A liberal Supreme Court under Chief Justice Warren, which heard favorably suits pressed by the NAACP, made most of the fundamental changes in the law regarding the position of blacks. The court's decisions were applauded by a liberal audience and implemented slowly by middle-of-the-road national administrations. In that period the NAACP and the Urban League were the best-known organizations of blacks, with the former regarded as the most militant then on the scene. The masses of blacks in the northern cities and in the South favored the new changes, but the driving force pushing for desegregation was a coalition of elite blacks and liberal Establishment whites. Nor was there much foot-dragging by the masses of whites; eventual desegregation gradually accomplished was accepted as in the cards for the future. The action was taking place on the floors of legislatures, in the courts, in public agencies, in the White House, but, with rare exceptions,[1] was *not* taking place in the streets.

The scene of the action shifted from the halls of the Establishment to the bus stations, lunch counters, and then to the streets in the period between 1956 and 1963. In the last Eisenhowever administration, young blacks and whites began to challenge segregation and discrimination in bus stations and lunch counters. New organizations appeared on the scene, CORE, SNCC, and the Southern Christian Leadership Conference being the most notable. Besides the national organizations, local communities formed their own, some transitory and others more permanent.

The civil rights movement began in this period. It was a movement in the sense of involving large numbers of people. Furthermore, a general unity of purpose was shared by the many local groups. Even more important there developed a strong sense of solidarity. What was going on in Montgomery, Alabama, was sympathetically followed by those who were working in Knoxville, Tennessee, and toward the end of the great southern drive, an impending action like the march across the bridge in Selma would attract hundreds of people from all over the country to participate. In addition, thousands participated vicariously through the extensive television coverage afforded by the major networks.

The civil rights movement started out as a coalition of white liberals and militant blacks. It was a mixture of many ideological strains ranging from militant revolutionary socialism to fundamentalist Christianity all united around a common goal, the removal of barriers to full political and economic participation of blacks in American society, particularly in the Deep South where the barriers were higher and more visible.

Although the movement did not achieve its aims entirely, the Deep South is changed. At the same time the movement itself has been transformed: It is no longer interracial, but predominantly black. It is no longer mainly a southern movement but has penetrated into all parts of the country. Its ideology has moved more to the left and contains strong strains of ethnocentrism. A newly self-conscious American ethnic group has been created, the Afro–American.

In the early part of the 1960's the focus of attention on race relations began to shift in a northerly direction. In 1963 and 1964 "civil disorders" began to occur in northern ghettos. Rochester, New York, Chicago, and New York City experienced riots in which blacks took to the streets, wrested control over their neighborhoods from the police, and destroyed some commercial properties. In each case, the riots appeared to be spontaneous reactions to particular incidents which triggered them. The national press paid some attention to these events but they were not seen as particularly serious. Nor were they seen initially as expressing much more than reactions to local conditions. They were certainly not part of the movement although "movement people" often moved to positions of spokesmen within local communities.

With the assassination of President Kennedy in November 1963, the country dropped from the peak of postwar liberalism, at least in terms of its political mood. To be sure, the significant liberal legislation of the period was accomplished during the spring of 1964 by Kennedy's successor, Lyndon Johnson, but the pervasive mood of optimism concerning the fate of the country's domestic affairs began to dissipate.

Nineteen-sixty-four saw the enactment of two extremely important pieces of national legislation. The Civil Rights Act of 1964 marked the beginnings of a strong commitment on the part of the executive branch of the government to racial equality. The Economic Opportunities Act of 1964 signaled the beginning of the War on Poverty and started up a set of programs designed to increase the economic capabilities of the poor, black and white. This legislation plus the Elementary and Secondary School Education Act passed later was the finest flowering of post–World War II liberalism.

The War on Poverty had scarcely begun when a new phase in race relations in America started with the Watts riot in August 1965. Smaller riots had occurred in the previous two summers, but had mainly local impact. The significance of Watts was both its size and its timing. It was easy to understand why there were riots in Harlem: after all Harlem is widely thought to be the worst of urban ghettos, partially because Harlem has about the worst and most overcrowded housing in the country. But Los Angeles is the urban paradise to which so many Americans had migrated since World War II. Furthermore, the stucco bungalows of Watts hardly look like a slum to a nation accustomed to envisaging slums as five-story tenements.

The amount of propery damage sustained in Watts was presented in an exaggerated form in the national press, but even in more accurate later estimates amounted to $35 million. The battle raged for days while the smoke of pillaged stores hung over Los Angeles and was shown on every living room's television screen. Viewing National Guardsmen occupying one of our home territories was a shock to America.

Furthermore, the riots in Watts occurred after the poverty program had been underway for a year. Things were getting better, America felt, and a major rebellion was upsetting to a popular conception of continuing linear progress in the status of blacks in this country.

From August 1965 to the spring of 1968, city after city in the urban North experienced more or less extensive revolts in one or more of its black ghettos. None of the major metropolitan areas in the North escaped some form of ghetto revolt. In some cities—Detroit and Newark are the best examples—the battles between ghetto blacks and the police went so badly against the latter that the military establishment had to be called in to reestablish order. In other cities—for example, Boston and

Minneapolis—the riots were brief and easy for local authorities to bring under control. In all major northern cities, however, some form of civil disorder took place and even some southern cities, notably Atlanta, Tampa, and Miami, had their versions of what looked at first to be a peculiarly northern phenomenon.

In all cities the scars of the civil disorders of the 1960's are still evident; in some places in the still-standing gutted buildings and boarded-up stores; in others, in a residual atmosphere of nervous apprehension. The remains of the major civil disorders are still visible: the main commercial strip in Watts has yet to be rebuilt and Washington, D.C.'s 14th Street is dotted with empty lots paved with rubble and stores blackened by fires and now boarded up.

The Watts revolt was a great shock to white America. Among the first responses were attempts to understand what had caused the riot. The search for an explanation remained fixed on the specific conditions in Watts, looking for the incident which triggered the events, for the special circumstances of Watts which helped to sustain the riot for so long a time. Investigators, including some social scientists, swarmed over the area to determine what happened. They found that an incident involving the police had triggered the riot. They also found that those who participated in the riot were not particularly different from other residents of Watts except for being younger and more likely to be male: the riot was not started and sustained by criminal elements.

Surveys of social conditions in the Watts area documented that Watts was a deprived area, high on all the indicators of depressed social conditions—unemployment, poor housing, inadequate transportation, poor medical and social services, and so forth. These disclosures were hardly any news to the few social scientists who had been keeping track of black progress (or lack of it) since World War II. However, the disclosures were somewhat of a shock to those who felt that things were getting better all the time. The response of public officials was to apply more of the usual liberal remedies. The Office of Economic Opportunity took on Watts as a special project and programs began to appear on the scene (manpower retraining, a neighborhood health center, and so on) that had until then passed over the area. The problems of Watts were local ones which could be assuaged by locally applied remedies.

Nineteen-sixty-six saw additional ghetto riots. A small flareup, again in Watts, was followed by more serious eruptions in Chicago and in the Hough area of Cleveland. The Kerner Commission's report counted forty-three disorders and riots for that year, mostly on a fairly small scale.

The longest hot summer was that of 1967. Tampa, Florida, had a riot in June to be followed within a few days by Cincinnati and Atlanta. But these disorders were to be quickly overshadowed by the prolonged riots in Newark and Detroit. Each was to engage the attention of the nation for more than a week and to present television watchers with views of billowing smoke, looters, gutted stores, and destroyed dwellings. Following Newark, a serious riot developed in Plainfield, New Jersey, and outbreaks were narrowly averted in a number of northern New Jersey cities. Similar events occurred in Michigan, with riots breaking out in the black ghettos of a half a dozen smaller cities.

When the summer of 1967 came to an end, the nation was in shock. The Kerner Commission counted 164 "disturbances" that summer, of which eight were serious enough to involve calling out the military. Of course, Newark and Detroit were at the center of national attention because of the size of the riots in those two cities and the extensiveness of the damages to property and lives. In the total tally for the summer every section of the country was represented, although the East and Midwest experienced seven out of the eight serious disorders.

Shortly after Detroit had been restored to some semblance of normality President Johnson appointed Illinois Governor Otto Kerner to head up a National Advisory Commission on Civil Disorders. After a frenzy of activity (described in detail in the article by Kopkind in this volume) the Kerner Commission issued its famous report in March 1968. Indicative of the popular interest in understanding the disorders was the extraordinary sale of the commercial paperback edition of the report—1.5 million copies were sold within the first year. The report has become a standard reference on the state of American blacks at the end of the decade of the 1960's.

It was only six weeks after the report was issued that the last round of major riots occurred. Sparked by the assassination of Martin Luther King, Jr., major riots broke out in the few major northern cities which had not experienced riots earlier—Baltimore, Washington, D.C., and Pittsburgh—plus a major disorder in Chicago and "minor" ones in more than a score of other places. By the end of 1968 every major northern city had experienced a civil disorder and a few places, like Chicago, had experienced several.

All cities nervously awaited the summer of 1969.

Nineteen-sixty-nine, contrary to anxious expectations, turned out to be relatively peaceful. A score of minor incidents occurred in the major cities, and a few of the smaller cities, notably York, Pennsylvania, had serious riots. The nation began to breathe a sigh of relief with the thought that the decade of urban riots was over. Civil disorders of the sort that marked the 1960's may or may not occur during the 1970's, but the nation has still to assimilate the experiences of the 1960's and to probe their political and social meaning. The civil disorders are still with us in this last sense along with the physical traces on the urban landscapes. America is still working over the meaning of the civil disorders and their connections with the status of black people in our society.

At first glance the northern urban civil disorders appear to have only coincidental connections with the civil rights movement. The movement was organized: the disorders were not. The movement was nonviolent: the disorders' most salient feature was the amount of damage inflicted upon property and individuals. The movement had at least the beginnings of an ideology: the disorders appeared to bring out the most self-interested actions on the part of rioters in the form of property looting. The movement had political aims: the civil disorders appeared to have no aims.

Yet these differences are primarily superficial. The northern disorders reflected the same underlying conditions as the movement in the South. They differed in that northern urban ghettos had neither existing strong institutions around which protest could be organized—the segregated black churches in the South could and did perform that function —nor were the targets of protest as clearly defined in the North. Black institutions in the South benefited from patterns of segregation by being forced to be black. Thus segregated schools meant that there were black teachers, black principals, and black university presidents. Segregated churches meant that there were black ministers; the refusal of the major life insurance companies to issue policies to blacks fostered the establishment of black-run insurance companies and on a local level mutual aid societies. A black middle class was fostered in the South to a greater extent than in the North.

E. Franklin Frazier's characterization of the black middle class as the black bourgeoisie missed an important point. Although the presidents of black insurance firms and black universities were not out in front in the southern civil rights movement, the children of the black bourgeoisie provided the leadership cadres for CORE and SNCC just like the children of the white upper-middle class in the North provided the cadres for student radicals.

In any event, blacks in the South had leaders and identifiable targets, and southern white society had instruments of repression which were considerably more difficult to buck than the police departments of northern cities. Hence the civil rights movement in the South was an organized movement relying heavily on middle-class leadership and unlikely to break out into spontaneous revolts in which control over black areas would be wrested away from the police.

The northern manifestations of the movement took the form of civil disorders because the essential ingredients for organized movements were absent. Black institutions were weak and fragmented. Black middle-class leadership could and did find places within the white establishment. The instruments of social control, particularly the police, were not as firmly in command of the streets of the northern ghetto as their southern counterparts were. Nor were white local officials and public opinion in general totally behind the police. The civil disorders in the North were spontaneous, unorganized, somewhat disorderly manifestations of the same sense of deprivation and alienation that characterized the southern civil rights movement. They have to be viewed as primordial political acts challenging the hegemony of local institutions of social control and disputing conventional property rights definitions. They were the manifestations of a movement without leadership, a movement which spread from city to city throughout the urban North as ghetto blacks saw in the mass media that their brothers in other cities were able to succeed in taking over the streets and become the focus of political attention.

The political character of the northern urban disorders, obscured as it was by the inarticulateness of the participating masses, was not immediately apparent to most commentators or to most public officials. Searching through their experiences to find explanations, commentators, public officials, and the general public alike hit upon the analogy of race riots. After all, race riots had occurred before in northern cities and even though such riots had involved quite different actions, the previous race riots had struck as much terror and fear in the hearts of urban residents. Thus the disorders were called "race riots," even though the confrontations were mainly between blacks and police. The disorders were also termed "violent" although the "violence" of the 1960's was of an entirely different order than the street fighting that broke out between roving crowds of whites and blacks that characterized the Detroit race riot of 1943 or the Chicago race riot of 1919.

The rhetoric initially employed to describe the urban disorders of the 1960's projected an imagery of mass confrontations between whites and blacks, just as had occurred in the past. Of course, for some whites—

particularly those who owned property in the ghetto or ran ghetto businesses—direct experiences confirmed the impressions of confrontation. And for many whites living far from the inner city the disorders were seen as only preludes to the next stages when blacks would venture out of their ghettos into white residential areas and "take over." As a consequence, gun and rifle sales rocketed throughout urban areas as fearful householders prepared to defend themselves in the street fighting to come.

Because they were lacking in definite form and organization, the urban disorders functioned like the ink blots of projective tests into which individuals can project their fears and desires. Thus Jewish defense organizations like the American Jewish Committee and the Anti-Defamation League worried that the disorders showed signs of black anti-Semitism. White householders began to fear guerrilla warfare. The police saw evidences of national conspiracies of "outside agitators." Revolutionaries saw signs that the revolution was beginning. Public officials like then-Governor Agnew could scold middle-class black leaders for not disowning the irresponsible radicals who obviously had fomented the disorders.

Nor was it clear that the southern civil rights movement and the northern civil disorders were alternative manifestations of the same underlying conditions, moulded into different patterns by the differences in the characters of the northern and southern conditions. The same northern liberals who applauded the black demonstrations in Selma, Alabama, deplored the "violence" in their own cities. Indeed, when Dr. Martin Luther King, Jr., shifted his attention from the Deep South to Chicago in 1966 there was hope expressed that northern blacks would turn away from "violence" to acceptable "nonviolence." [2] Dr. King's failure in Chicago has never been thoroughly analyzed, although it does seem likely that in the northern setting, public officials can easily absorb the noise of a southern-style movement because on the formal intellectual level, the values of racial equality are already publicly held and widely espoused official values. Northern officials and civil leaders do not espouse de jure segregation, although they may not acknowledge the existence of de facto segregation and discrimination. The central problem of northern ghetto blacks was how to achieve equality of treatment in an environment in which the right to such treatment is acknowledged as legitimate but in which institutional practices contradict those values. Civil rights victories on the level of official values and civil rights legislation had already been won. The appropriate struggle had to take place on another level entirely.

As city after city experienced civil disorders it became increasingly difficult to hold to an interpretation which saw them as race riots. There were no mass confrontations between blacks and whites: indeed, blacks showed little interest in moving out of their ghetto areas into other parts of the city.

Nor was it possible to hold to interpretations of the disorders which rested upon idiosyncratic local factors. Disorders occurred in liberal cities as well as conservative ones, in cities with small ghettos and those with very large ones, in cities with a highly segregated residential pattern of black settlement and in cities with dispersed patterns of settlement, and in relatively prosperous as well as economically depressed cities. Civil disorders occurred all over the northern and western parts of the country. The final blow to the localistic interpretation of civil disorders came with the April 1968 series in which ghetto disorders occurred in response to a national event, the assassination of Dr. Martin Luther King, Jr.

This ambiguity in meaning forms part of the background of the Kerner Commission's activities. From the administration's point of view, the civil disorders were especially puzzling, for more had been done for blacks in the early years of the Johnson administration than had been accomplished in the two decades of New Deal and Fair Deal administrations. Just at the point when significant programs were going into effect, blacks were risking the death of those programs by their behavior.

As Kopkind relates in this chapter in this volume, the Kerner Commission's staff went through several working theories about the disorders before finally adopting the rather eclectic stance that appears in the report. Although few, if any, of the staff believed that the disorders were part of a national conspiracy, almost the first moves undertaken by the staff were to look for evidence bearing on the "outside agitator" interpretation. Investigators sifted through police and FBI reports. Teams of investigators interviewed local officials, civil leaders, black leaders and participants in more than a dozen cities which had experienced disorders in 1967. Although there were many reports of "outside agitators," especially from police officials, the evidence tended to be quite vague and unsubstantiated by other persons interviewed. The "outside agitator" theory was one of the first explanations to be abandoned.

A more ambitious line of analysis was the attempt to link the appearance of disorders to local conditions. Under this interpretation, disorders were essentially a product of the failures of local officials to consider and take action on the grievances felt by their local ghettos. This line of explanation was also undermined by the findings of the research staff and their consultants. It became increasingly obvious that everywhere in the country levels of grievances held by blacks were high. Nor could it be said that some city officials who were especially responsive to blacks were by those actions alone likely to prevent their cities from having a civil disorder.[3]

Attempts to develop a "natural history" of civil disorders also came to naught as investigators brought back from each city narrative accounts of the disorders which showed a wide variation from place to place in how the disorders took place and how the ghettos were finally brought under control. The one attempt to construct a general model of civil disorders was so devastatingly criticized by the staff and its consultants that attempts in this direction were soon abandoned.

An early staff memorandum entitled "The Harvest of Racism," which put forth a line of analysis essentially blaming the disorders on the racism which permeated American society, was also rejected, especially by the higher-ranking members of the staff.[4]

In the end, the commission fell back to an eclectic position. It held that the disorders were the outcome of "centuries of neglect" and currently widespread "racism" which prevented blacks from achieving a position of equality of opportunity in our society. The disorders themselves, although fed by black resentment, were triggered by essentially local events usually involving local police.[5] Much of the report contains data documenting the extent to which blacks are socially and economically depressed. A few case histories of disorders are presented in the early part of the volume, essentially documenting how specific disorders got started and then escalated from minor incidents to widespread participation. The case histories emphasize that the action centered mainly around the actions of the police both in the triggering incidents and in the handling of the disorders as they unfolded.[6]

The commission's report is interesting not only for what it contains but for what is not touched upon. For example, the report almost totally ignores the southern civil rights movement and, by that token, is also unconcerned with the relationships between the disorders and the movement. Nor does the commission consider the disorders as a form of communication in which a political message is being delivered. Rather, the report is more concerned with the background of the disorders.

"White racism" stands out in the minds of most Americans as the major message of the Kerner Commission concerning the long-range causes of the civil disorders. The popularity of this interpretation of the report is especially puzzling because in terms of the actual emphases displayed in the report, white racism cannot be considered a major theme. It is mentioned in the body of the report in only one place (p. 91) and once in the summary (written, as Kopkind reports, almost at the last minute before publication).[7] Nowhere is the term defined in any detail: it appears in the text as a concept blanketing white attitudes, segregation and discrimination, and black poverty. White racism is presented as the basic cause of the disorders almost as if it is obvious what white racism is. It is true that racism is a word which appears frequently enough in everyday conversation and political discussion that everyone can have some notion of what is meant. Yet, for the purposes of precise political analysis and diagnosis more precision is needed than can be afforded by a term which is defined mainly by its connotations.

As a causal factor in the civil disorders, white racism is at best a truism and at worst a concept which may lead the society down many fruitless paths. It is true that a large part of the blame for the conditions under which blacks are living must be allocated to the fact that white Americans and the institutions which they control have systematically and thoroughly discriminated against blacks in almost every area of national and local life. In this sense, calling white racism the base cause of the civil disorders is a truism. Without further specification of what white racism is, it is not clear what follows in the way of social policy from the statement that white racism lies at the base of the civil disorders. By white racism, does one mean the distribution of attitudes toward blacks among whites? Does the term mean the customary practices concerning employment, the housing market, educational institutions serving blacks? Does white racism mean that amelioration of the position of blacks in American society will have to wait until the demise of white racism? How does the diagnosis of white racism square with the findings presented in Eidson's chapter in this volume that the more blatant statements of antiblack prejudice have been rejected by more and more whites each year during the period after World War II?

How did such a blanket phrase as "white racism" achieve such currency? Like the civil disorders themselves, the term "white racism" has enough ambiguity to enable a wide spectrum of political beliefs to use the term to their own profit. For black militants the term is quite useful both as an accusation to hurl at whites of every political persuasion and as a rallying cry for their black constituents. For conservative whites, white racism becomes a reason why changes cannot be expected to occur easily. To liberal whites, the term could be useful as well, for by purging themselves as individuals they can make a personal contribution to the solution of the plight of blacks.

It should also be noted that American social philosophy historically has tended toward explanatory theories in terms of individual characteristics and away from institutional explanations. The emphasis of American Protestantism has been on the importance of conscience and individual willful conformity to the will of God. A strain toward Social Darwinism has emphasized the importance of individual characteristics and processes in the evolution of American society. White racism fits in with the notion that only by mass conversion can the society be changed in its ways.

As an explanation for the civil disorders, white racism is inadequate in two important respects: first of all, the vagueness of the term makes possible adoption to a wide variety of uses. One can use the term to excuse the condition of blacks as being beyond hope, since one can never expect to extirpate white racism. Or the term can be used to excuse specific institutions because they are merely reflecting the value positions of the persons who are in charge of the institutions. And so on.

The second—and more important—inadequacy of the term lies in its almost total lack of connection with reasonable social policy. The use of the term suggests that we will have to wait for the demise of white racism for the amelioration of the condition of blacks. How does one go about getting rid of white racism? Is there any point in trying to change the practices of American institutions and official positions if the general endemic condition of white racism will merely make it impossible for such changes to take place?

It should be kept in mind that these criticisms of the term "white racism" are not directed at the Kerner Commission so much as they are directed at the way in which the term has been used in the popular discussion that has arisen since the report was issued. The Kerner Commission made a number of very specific recommendations about public policy all aimed at improving the conditions of blacks in urban ghettos and constituting a proposal involving heavy commitments of resources over a period of decades. These proposals have not been very much at the focus of attention.

Popular discussions over the issue of white racism has drawn attention away from the more fundamental question of what were the meanings of the civil disorders. It is difficult, in any event, to understand what are the implicit goals of instances of collective behavior like the civil disorders. Confronted with the phenomenon in which thousands of individuals apparently suddenly behave in ways which have little continuity with past behavior of the same people is to be confronted with a baffling puzzle. Collective behavior phenomena call into question the working assumptions we all hold concerning the predictability of day-to-day human behavior. Civil disorders also reveal a seeming fragility to the orderliness of everyday existence and give rise to fears that the complex fabric that is an industrial society has faults that could easily yield and give rise to chaos.

While the "causes" of the civil disorders may be properly sought in the history of the treatment of blacks in our society, the meaning of the civil disorders has to be sought in the disorders themselves. That is to say, that the behavior of the ghetto residents in the disorders themselves contains a message expressing substrata of attitudes and values which are exposed in the suspension of everyday behavior that took place. The central aspects of the behavior of participants in the civil disorders were the rejection of authority of law-enforcement officials and the usual rules governing the use of property. The disorders were collective expressions which challenged the legitimacy of existing authority and property institutions. Defying the police and looting commercial establishments, ghetto blacks suddenly expressed attitudes which they held all along to the effect that local institutions were not of their making, were inimicable to their interests, and had legitimacy only by virtue of definitions in which they did not share.

Under other circumstances, the civil disorders would have been considered revolutionary actions. Had the civil disorders either started through the actions of organized leadership or had such leadership emerged in the process of the disorders, their similarity to the revolutionary actions would have been quite complete. Of course, as the Kerner Commission investigators found, there was no evidence either of prior revolutionary organizations at work or of the emergence of such organizations in the course of the disorders. Perhaps it would be sensible to term the disorders "revolts," signifying something short of revolutionary actions but more fundamentally rejecting of everyday legitimacy than, say, the traditional holiday riots of college students at Fort Lauderdale.

The civil disorders were therefore revolts which bore the message that the masses of urban blacks were alienated from their local com-

munities and from the larger society. It was a message which was repeated from place to place and passed on from ghetto to ghetto. Only
those cities in which blacks could anticipate massive reprisals had no revolts by the time the 1960's were over.[8]

It is not clear whether the message has been solidly received by
American society. In part, the message is obscured both by the existence of triggering events and by the fact that the revolts appear to be
local in character. The triggering events—usually involving the police
or some ghetto merchant—lead to considering which policies might be
put into effect locally which would significantly reduce the probability
of the occurrence of such events. Indeed, suggestions along these lines
were made in the Kerner Commission Report and have affected police
practices in many cities. But triggering events are just that and diverse
phenomena can serve as triggers, as the April 1968 riots following the
assassination of Dr. Martin Luther King, Jr. indicate.

The seemingly local character of the revolts has led many local public officials to become thoroughly puzzled by the outbreak of a revolt in
their city. Mayors and police chiefs have sought to find *the* set of black
leaders with whom they could negotiate some sort of rapprochement, for
it was difficult for many to accept the idea that the revolts were without
leadership. It was even more difficult to accept the idea that there were
few local remedies which could be applied which would significantly reduce the chances that revolts would occur in their community. In many
cases the major results of such searches for the leaders of the black
community have been to produce a set of leaders where none have existed before. They have also led to the establishment of more civic committees than almost any other set of events over the past decade. Countless lunches have been consumed in the elusive search for local solutions
to essentially national problems.

The consequences of the urban revolts of the 1960's are still being
shaped. The immediate reactions of federal and local officials were to
push forward their efforts to ameliorate the conditions of the blacks.
The War on Poverty was intensified until in 1969 the war in Vietnam
began to eat into the funds for all domestic programs. Local city administrations attempted somehow to make contact with their ghettos, giving
rise in some places to a frenzied scramble among putative black leaders
for the newly created vacancies in the rosters of recognized black leaders.

Although it is too early to judge how well the War on Poverty was
waged, it is entirely too clear that no dramatic improvements in the po-

sition of blacks was achieved. Perhaps it was too much to ask that in the space of a few years, the accumulated deficits of the past would be made up, but it was certainly not asking too much to expect some closing of the gaps between whites and blacks in unemployment rates and in the lower levels of the occupational structure. It is clear that there has been some improvement in the position of blacks, but the improvement has not been large enough to be detected without the aid of sensitive statistical analysis.

Perhaps the most important consequences of the revolts have been to accelerate important changes within the black community. Blacks are transforming themselves into an ethnic collectivity with a new and different sense of positive attachment to their identity as blacks. Changes in dress and hair styling, away from down-playing toward emphasizing black characteristics, indicate a change from values which accepted white negative evaluations of black racial characteristics to ones which asserted at least equivalence in worth for such racial features. A new interest in their African heritage, including in some cases learning how to read and speak Swahili, is another indicator.

All signs point to the development of a new ethnic collectivity on the American scene. Blacks are becoming Black in the same way that locality-oriented peasants become Italian, Czech, or German as a consequence of the experience of being immigrants. Of course it is more difficult for blacks to make the transition because their ties to Africa have been cut so long that there are only a few traces left in existing folk cultures of blacks. The heritage has to be self-consciously built anew today from materials imported and selected over long distances in time and space.

Most significant are the political transformations taking place within the black ghettos. Black communities over the country are becoming better organized. The revolts showed what manifestations of solidarity could accomplish and demonstrated that power could be massed if individual blacks were more solidary. At the same time the new poverty and related agencies provided positions for black leaders. In the urban ghettos of the North, the quasi-public offices of Community Action Programs, Model Cities Agencies, Urban Coalition Committees, and the like provided positions with sufficient visibility that black leaders could become better known to their own communities and to the city officials. Just as the political machine provided opportunities for the previous newly arrived ethnic groups on their way up, so the health, welfare, and education industries are providing similar opportunities for blacks. New types of urban "machines" are being constructed, built upon bases different from the old-fashioned machines of the past, but perhaps just as efficacious in providing the organizational strength for the attainment of political power on the local scene.

There are many bitter ironies in the recent history of blacks in America, but among the bitterest of all may be the disappointment that may set in after achieving political hegemony in northern cities. The first black mayors of major cities were elected in 1967 and 1968 when Richard Hatcher took over the mayor's office in Gary, Indiana, and Carl Stokes became mayor of Cleveland, Ohio. Close mayoralty elections in Los Angeles and Detroit, where black candidates were defeated, indicate that it may not be long before those cities will have elected a black as mayor. After a bitter electoral struggle, Kenneth Gibson was very recently elected mayor of notorious Newark. In short, throughout the country in cities where there are sizable ghettos, black candidates are running for local offices and winning often enough to ensure that over the next decade a good proportion of big city mayors will be black.

Local political victories in this historical period will not lead easily to improvement in the objective positions of ghetto blacks. This is the irony of political victories. Even with the best of intentions and the most astute advice and competent staffs, there is very little that a mayor can do in this historical period. The degrees of freedom that are left to a mayor and the amount of new resources at his command are both so slight that the achievement of local electoral success can only lead to disappointment. The time to have been mayor was in the nineteenth century when local political systems were much more important for the lives of urban residents than at present. Today, when mayors and city councils are least able to command significant amounts of resources, it appears that winning the mayoralty is not going to have much more than a symbolic significance.[9] This is not to underplay the importance of symbolic victories, but merely to state that in the long run something more substantial than symbolic satisfactions will be necessary.

Although we cannot anticipate that substantial improvements will be made for the vast majority of blacks in the ghettos through the achievement of some degree of political power on the local scene, it is clear that some blacks will benefit. Despite the decline in patronage with the growth of civil service, there are still staff positions to which appointments can be made, service and materials procurement contracts which can be let, and improvements which can be made in the amount and distribution of municipal services to the ghettos. The rise to political power of blacks will be a decided benefit to some middle-class blacks and provide an employment base for the development of stable black leadership. In other words, what segregation accomplished in the South, political power can accomplish even more effectively in the northern cities.

Of course, the political organization of ghetto blacks along the lines of traditional city politics is only one of the directions in which one can anticipate that the politicization of blacks will go. The alienation from American society expressed in the urban revolts can also be expected to foster the growth of revolutionary movements. Indeed, the beginnings of such movements are already under way in such organizations, for example, as the Black Panther Party. So far it cannot be said that revolutionary movements have made much of an impact upon the rank and file of the ghetto, although there are signs, particularly among the young, that groups like the Black Panthers have enjoyed at least a sympathetic hearing from some blacks.

The future of black revolutionary movements is highly problematic. A revolutionary uprising of blacks alone would be sheer adventurism, bound to lead to a harsh repression and risking the chance of provoking a movement toward apartheid policies on the part of whites. Because blacks are so small a minority in the United States as a whole—14 percent—a black revolution is obviously doomed to failure except in coalition with some substantial portion of the white population. At the moment it is not clear with what groups revolutionary blacks can align themselves for maximizing their chances of success. White revolutionaries remain also an isolated and very small minority. The vast majority of white Americans have been untouched by revolutionary doctrines and at least at this point in time are hostile to such movements. For the foreseeable future, black revolutionary movements are bound to remain sectarian groups, capable at best of mounting a few terrorist attacks on the surrounding society and its institutions, but not capable of welding together a substantial proportion of blacks, let alone forming viable alliances with whites.

The future of the urban ghettos is problematic. The lasting results of the urban revolts have been to produce the beginnings of political solidarity among blacks, to make black ethnicity a viable collectivity, and to focus local and national attention on the pressing problems faced by ghetto blacks. The resultant growing political power of blacks will assure that ghetto problems will remain on the political agenda of local, state, and national public officials and legislatures. How much improvement in objective conditions can be expected as a result of such continued attention is hard to estimate. If we believe recent federal statistics on employment and earnings, blacks have made some gains during the last few years of the 1960's, but the improvements are by no means massive.

We can anticipate that the northern ghetto revolts of the 1960's will not be repeated in the 1970's. The growing political organization of black communities will lead to more orderly and more articulate political messages in the form of mass meetings, protest demonstrations, and explicit political campaigns. There is some question of whether southern cities will experience ghetto revolts, as the recent disorders in Augusta, Georgia, would intimate. But it seems highly unlikely that places like Cleveland, New York, Detroit, and Newark will again experience the same sorts of revolts that characterized the 1960's.

The growing political strength of ghetto blacks will tend to alleviate some of the more visible signs of discrimination. Municipal services to black areas will improve. Police practices involving harassment and brutality can be expected to decline, especially in those cities where the police departments are directly under local government control. For many cities housing discrimination will be difficult to change since the amount of low-rent housing available is severely restricted, but in all cities better housing opportunities for middle-class blacks can be expected. National government policies designed to improve the employment situation of blacks most likely will continue to make some difference for the better.

Of course, these are predictions which are based on a number of assumptions, themselves of a problematic nature. One assumption is that the tension between whites and blacks will not erupt into communal riots. Another assumption is that federal policies will continue to be committed to the improvement of the position of blacks and that sufficient resources will be made available for the purpose. A final assumption is that no severe economic recession or depression will occur. The fragility of these assumptions is self-evident: already one communal riot has occurred in the summer of 1969 in York, Pennsylvania. The present Republican administration is more committed to the Vietnam conflict than it is to the alleviation of domestic social problems. Finally, the American economy at the moment does not look as strong as it did during the 1960's.

The future of our great cities and their urban ghettos is at least as unsettled as the future of American society. The problems are massive and obvious. They overwhelm both the resources we seem able to bring to bear and the imagination we can master to concoct solutions. We only know that the decade of the 1970's will be a critical period: at this moment the range of possible outcomes spans both disaster and improvement.

NOTES

1. The two major exceptions were the Harlem riot of 1943 in which blacks took over the streets and inflicted damage on commercial properties, and the Detroit riot of 1943 in which blacks and whites contested the expansion of the black ghetto into white residential areas. The Detroit riot was the last of the communal riots in which masses of blacks and whites faced each other in face-to-face combat.

2. Of course, when the tactics of the southern civil rights movement were employed as in Milwaukee or in the marches through Cicero, Illinois, they were not seen locally as more acceptable than urban disorders. The Milwaukee and Cicero city fathers were no more moved to respond positively than had local urban disorders broken out. Indeed, a case might be made that a civil disorder in Milwaukee would have been more effective than the Selma-style marches which took place in obtaining positive response from local public officials.

3. It was while this explanatory scheme had its greatest support among the commission staff that two of the major researches sponsored by the commission were started. The Survey Research Center of the University of Michigan undertook sample surveys of blacks and whites in 15 cities varying in their experiences with civil disorders, and the present author undertook to interview city officials and civic leaders as well as rank-and-file members of city agencies in the same cities. Some of the early findings of the Johns Hopkins group are summarized in the Boesel et. al. article in this volume.

4. Ironically, this memorandum is closer to the more common interpretation of the line of analysis in the report than the report itself reveals.

5. Note that the report was issued some months before the last round of major disorders were triggered by a national event, the assassination of Dr. Martin Luther King, Jr., in April 1968.

6. These case histories represent a very small part of the documentary materials and interviews assembled by staff investigators who were sent out to local communities. Unfortunately, the commission has not made these documents available, having consigned them to the National Archives to become available only after a considerable period of time.

7. Tom Wicker's introduction to the report as published in the Bantam Book edition does give more prominence to the term, although he too neglects to spell out what is meant by it.

8. For example, in Jersey City, the police chief was reputed to have passed the word to ghetto leaders that any outbreak of rioting would bring the police out shooting. Similarly, a revolt in Atlanta or Mississippi (or for that matter any city in Georgia other than Atlanta) would bring about reprisals so severe that revolts would have been close to suicidal. The recent 1970 events in Augusta, Georgia, bear out this point.

9. It will make a difference, however, in the way in which blacks may be treated at the hands of local government agencies. In particular, one can expect that police treatment of blacks will improve, except in those cities where the police departments are not directly under the authority of the mayor.

Index

Cincinnati, Ohio: disturbances, 1884, 291; disturbances, 1967, 142, 146, 149, 152, 153, 157; riots, 1841, 305; white invasion of "Little Africa," 285
Civilian Conservation Corps, 406
Civil Rights Act of 1964, 409; impact in Los Angeles, 87
Clark, Kenneth, 319; Kerner Commission and, 231
Clark, Ramsey, 229
Clay, Cassius, 78
Clayton, Colonel: East St. Louis riot, 1917, 163
Cleaver, Eldridge, 244, 340; revocation of parole and flight, 341
Cleveland, Ohio: riot, 1968, 340, 341
Closed Corporation, The (Ridgeway), 238
Cloward, Richard, 328–329
Coleman, James, 236, 238, 241, 315
Colombo, Robert J., 189
Columbia University, Bureau of Applied Social Science Research, 241
Commission on Civil Rights, 399; California Advisory Committee, 87, 90–91
Commission on Industrial Relations, 262, 263–264, 265, 270
commissions, riot, *see* names of specific commissions, e.g.: Kerner Commission
Commons, John R., 262, 265–266
communications media, *see* media
Congress of Industrial Organizations (CIO), 6
Congress of Racial Equality (CORE), 407; leadership, 412; Negro attitude toward, 374, 380, 381; Newark riot, 31, 32, 43
Connor, Henry W., 24
Conot, Robert, 239, 250
control behavior, 158–182 (*see also* police); coordination, lack of, 175–176; crowd dispersal, 170–171; force, level of, 174–175; negotiate, failure to, 171–172; sniping, control of, 174
Convissor, Samuel M., 25, 26
Conway, Jack 231
Cooper, James Fenimoore, 277
CORE, *see* Congress of Racial Equality
Corman, James: Kerner Commission, 228, 229, 244, 252, 255, 257
Corporation Venezolana de Guyana, 257
courts, *see* judicial administration

Crime Commission, 236
criminal justice, *see* judicial administration
Crisis, The, 298
Crockett, George W., Jr., 135, 189, 191, 192–193, 339–340
Crusader, The, 297
Curvin, Robert: Newark riot, 31, 36, 43–50 *passim,* 66

Dahlke, A., 161
Daley, Richard, 24, 229
Darlington County (S.C.) Freedom of Choice Association, 404
Darrow, C., 351–352
David Walker's Appeal, 304–305
Davis, David Brion, 277
Dayton, Ohio: disturbances, 1967, 145–146, 149, 153; riot, 1966, 143
Debevoise, Dickinson R., 63
Democratic Party: labor vote for, 403; National Convention, 1948, 7; Negro support of, 365; racism and, 4; welfare system and, 10
desegregation, school: white attitude toward, 397–402
DeSimone, John, 40–43 *passim,* 50
Detroit, Mich.: Algiers Motel incident, 178; disorder, 1968, 176; Neighborhood Legal Service (NLS) Bail Bond Project, 192; Northern High School Strike, 1966, 317; Poor People's March, 1968, 176; Republic of New Africa incident, 341; riot, 1943, 6, 160–165 *passim,* 289–290, 301–302, 425; riot, 1967, 138–152 *passim,* 157, 173–180 *passim,* 185–195, 237, 337, 344–354 *passim;* Sojourner Truth Homes incident, 160
Detroit News, 189
Dixiecrats, and Democratic National Convention, 1948, 7
Dixon, Bertha: testimony on Newark riot, 62
Donnelly, Inspector: Newark riot, 54
Downs, Anthony, 234, 241, 256–257
Downs, James, 241
Draesel, Herbert G.: testimony on Newark riot, 58
draft riot, N.Y., 1863, 166, 260, 280, 285–286
DuBois, W. E. B.: racial warfare, 298–299, 306; Washington, D.C. riot, 1919, 162
Dughi, Daniel, 56
Durkheim, Émile, 266
Dymally, Mervyn: Negro attitude to-